Art Market and Connoisseurship

A Closer Look at Paintings by Rembrandt, Rubens and their Contemporaries

Art Market and Connoisseurship

A Closer Look at Paintings by Rembrandt, Rubens and their Contemporaries

Edited by Anna Tummers and Koenraad Jonckheere

Amsterdam University Press

The publication of this book has been made possible by a grant from the Gravin van Bylandt Stichting, the Jurriaanse Stichting and the Stichting Charema

Cover image: Pieter Brueghel the Elder, The Painter and the Connoisseur, mid-1560s, Grafische Sammlung Albertina, Vienna
Design: Frederik de Wal, Schelluinen

ISBN 97 8908964 0321
NUR 640/658

Table of Contents

Introduction

Eric Jan Sluijter

Determining Value on the Art Market in the Golden Age: An Introduction

Introduction

An art historian who assesses the attributions of particular paintings in a scholarly publication knows that this will have consequences for the art market. The art historian in question, however, usually prefers to ignore this because he sees his work as a value-free analysis of certain qualities of the artwork in the service of constructing art historical categorisations. However, the owner of the work will have a different opinion. What a painting is valued at on the art market – especially paintings dating from the last five centuries – mainly depends on the fact whether or not it is considered an autograph work of a certain artist. A *communis opinio* among experts about authorship guarantees a basic market value. The process of canon formation establishes a relative value: X is on average more expensive than Y, but cheaper than Z. These values may vary hugely, depending on the position of the master in the 'ranking', while other factors such as subject matter, condition, rarity, provenance, place of an individual work within the oeuvre of a master and temporary phenomena like fashions and trends add to the many imponderables that make the prices of works of art vary tremendously. But when a work loses its aura of being by a certain artist's hand, it is robbed of its identity and becomes an outcast, even if none of the physical qualities and appearance of the work have changed; the value plummets and becomes even more difficult to assess than an 'authentic' work.

Outsiders find these kinds of fluctuations in monetary value on the art market incomprehensible. This is nicely expressed by the Dutch saying, often used in this context, that a work of art is worth '*wat de gek ervoor geeft*' (what the fool will bid for it). When it concerns the value of art – and it applies to the works of the old masters as well as for currently popular artists – the general opinion is that everything depends on what an individual, based on his own idiosyncratic evaluation, is willing to pay for it. Naturally, also the behaviour of this 'fool' who might pay a price that seems outrageous, is determined by his or her social and cultural environment, economic circumstances and attitude towards market mechanisms.

In his essay 'Pricing the Unpriced' Marten Jan Bok referred to a discussion between the Rotterdam economist Arjo Klamer and a group of contemporary artists about their economic behaviour, in which the artists all emphasise their uncertainty about market value.[1] The essence of their remarks is that there is no standard method for setting a price, but that the name and fame of the artist are decisive and determine the basic level of his or her prices –we are confronted here with a ranking process – and that prices are flexible, depending on the assets of the interested client. One of the artists remarked: 'It depends on what you can get. If I have a price of $3,000 in mind for a painting and someone comes in who seems to be able to pay $10,000 I'll ask $10,000.' But in the end, they all agree, it is a process of trial and error. Remarkably, none of them mentioned the amount of time he or she spent on a work of art, the cost of labour invested, which remains the most common way of earning an income in most other professions. Did something like the attitude towards the art market as described above exist in the seventeenth century, or was the amount of labour involved a determining factor?

Giulio Mancini's words, written between 1617 and 1621, are strikingly similar to the modern artists' views: 'a painting in itself cannot have a definite price' because its value in part 'is linked to the quality of the patron who owns it and the artist who makes it'. Thus, the price depends 'mainly on the taste and wealth of the buyer, and the need of the owner [which might be the artist] to dispose of the work'.[2] But these are the words of a Roman art lover. Were opinions regarding the assessing of the value of a work of art different in the Netherlands? What were the accepted seventeenth-century practices? Which roles were played by the artists themselves, by connoisseurs, art lovers or art dealers? How was value related to artistic qualities, name and authorship? Who was credited with the ability to appraise and attribute pictures in theory and practice? Did seventeenth-century connoisseurs find it important that a picture was painted entirely by the hand of the master under whose name it was sold? And how did early modern connoisseurship change as the market situation evolved and became increasingly complex? The aim of the essays in this volume, which were generated by a conference on the joint study of the art market and early modern connoisseurship, organised by Anna Tummers and Koenraad Jonckheere (University of Amsterdam, November 2005), is to answer some of those questions.

Over the past two decades, research on the seventeenth-century art market has expanded enormously. However, as De Marchi and Van Miegroet already noted in 1994, these studies 'tended to accentuate the view that art is a commodity like any other'.[3] Naturally, art was and is not a commodity like any other, because many immeasurable factors come into play, such as technical, but especially the artistic qualities of the product; such qualities, which are usually considered unique and often perceived quite differently by everyone involved, can, over time, make this peculiar type of commodity much more expensive, but also much less, depending on changes in taste and fashion. Koenraad Jonckheere demonstrated that, in the exchange of art objects, not only commodities changed hands, but also information, favours, reputations, expectations, etc.[4] How values, ideas and attitudes concerning art, as well as the individual players, are connected with market practices, which are primarily about supply and demand and the monetary value this engenders, is a question that still needs much more research where the insights of art historians and socio-economic historians must come together. The studies in this volume focus on the interaction between artists, connoisseurs and art dealers in matters of authorship, value and pricing in particular, so that the fairly recent interest in early modern connoisseurship can be integrated into the current research on the art market.

One of the first scholars to examine seventeenth-century views on connoisseurship and judgements about the authenticity of paintings was Jeffrey Muller in his article 'Measures of Authenticity: The Detection of Copies in the Early Literature on Connoisseurship' (1989), in which he primarily examines cases involving the work of Rubens.[5] More recently, Jaap van der Veen published a very important study in the latest volume of *A Corpus of Rembrandt Paintings* (IV, 2005), titled 'By his own hand. The valuation of autograph paintings in the 17th century'.[6] In the 1990s, the economist Neil De Marchi and the art historian Hans Van Miegroet approached related questions from the perspective of the art market in two important articles 'Art, Value and Market Practices in the Netherlands in the Seventeenth Century' (1994) and 'Pricing Invention: "Originals", "Copies", and their Relative Value in Seventeenth Century Netherlandish Art Markets' (1996), while Marten Jan Bok's aforementioned 'Pricing the Unpriced: How Dutch Seventeenth-Century Painters determined the Selling Price of their Works' (1998), examined the artist's side of assessing value.[7] Recently, Marion Boers-Goosen's 'Prices of Northern Netherlandish Paintings in the Seventeenth Century' focused on the question of whether public authorities or wealthy patrons paid inflated prices, as has often been assumed. Thought provoking arguments about the effect of developing standards of quality were proposed by Ed Romein in 'Knollen en citroenen op de Leidse kunstmarkt: over de rol van kwaliteit in de opkomst van de Leidse fijnschilderstijl' (Turnips and lemons on the Leiden art market: about the role of quality and the emergence of the Leiden style of fine painting, 2001), while Elizabeth Honig came up with fascinating insights into the new roles of Antwerp's connoisseurs and the cultural value of paintings (1995).[8] The role of the city elite as a factor in the Antwerp art market in the age of Rubens was assessed thoroughly only recently by Bert Timmermans in his Ph.D. dissertation *Een elite als actor binnen een kunstwereld. Patronen van patronage in het zeventiende-eeuwse Antwerpen* (Leuven 2006).

In the essays published in this volume, the authors introduce new material and ideas, but simultaneously build upon the older publications. These essays also inspired the following introductory notes, which are mainly concerned with the question of how the monetary value of paintings was assessed in continuous interaction between artists and clients/patrons (art lovers, connoisseurs and art dealers).

Valore di fatica

Let us first consider the market behaviour of some seventeenth-century masters. In his magisterial study on Guido Reni, Richard Spear demonstrates that two extremes existed in Italy simultaneously; this is exemplified by the most famous artists of that period – artists who were both trained in the same studio and were fierce competitors: Guido Reni and Guercino. The latter had a straightforward and businesslike attitude towards the market. He determined his price carefully on the basis of the value of labour expended, the *valore di fatica*, and attached fixed prices to the number of painted figures: approximately 100 ducats for each full-length, 50 per half-length, and 25 for heads. According to Malvasia, Guercino had said that his pricing was determined by 'what was common use and what others charged'.[9] Moreover Guercino, who ran an efficient studio, strictly differentiated between his own paintings and the studio's. He was very upset once when a copy of an altarpiece by one of his students was sold as an original.

Reni, on the contrary, did not want set prices for pictures and, according to Malvasia, abhorred 'the mention of price in a profession in which, he said, it should be obligatory to negotiate on the basis of an honorarium or gift'. Malvasia recounts that 'it was Guido's practice not to put a price on the works he painted for great personages and men of means but rather to give the paintings to them. In this way he received much more for them than was the custom or than he himself would have asked'.[10] Reni tried to rely on the *valore di stima*, on the estimation of value or worth, not determined by the artist but by the client, the patron or a connoisseur after the painting was completed.[11] Another significant contrast to Guercino was that Reni organised his studio in such a way that the distinctions between autograph works, retouched works and good copies were blurred.[12] Spear concludes that Guercino 'by sticking to such firm and old-fashioned notions of pricing, by being so relatively forthright in indicating what is and isn't his, and by not promoting himself through marketing techniques, the artist stifled any speculation that might have arisen around his work. ... By contrast, Reni's attitude foreshadows aspects of our contemporary art market, where demand can outpace supply and be manipulated by clever artists and their agents'.[13] Regrettably, in the Netherlands there was no equivalent to Malvasia who recorded such a wealth of information about the Bolognese masters, but on the basis of a variety of sources it is possible to inquire whether similar phenomena can be discerned in the Netherlands.

The 'craftsmanlike' way of calculating price, largely determined by labour, in other words, the time spent producing a work of art, must have been used by many artists. In a few cases – and these are all 'fine painters' – we are certain they operated in this manner. The best paid artists of the Dutch Golden Age, Gerrit Dou and Frans van Mieris, were among them. Joachim von Sandrart informs us that Dou daily noted the exact number of hours he devoted to a painting and charged '*ein Pfund Flemsch*' (a Flemish pound = 6 guilders) an hour, while Houbraken noted that Van Mieris calculated one gold ducat (5 guilders) per hour.[14] Considering the practice recorded in the surviving account books of Adriaen van der Werff, undoubtedly the best paid artist of the following generation, as well as his pupil Hendrick van Limborch, it is entirely plausible that Dou and Van Mieris indeed determined a minimum price in this way, although the figures reported seem exaggerated. That Dou and Van Mieris were able to pocket excessive sums, however, is revealed by the fact that Dou received 4000 guilders from the States of Holland for *The Young Mother*, as part of the Dutch Gift to Charles II, and that Van Mieris was paid 2500 guilders by Cosimo III the Medici for a *Family Concert.* [15] In these cases, it seems that the status and wealth of the client – which was also mentioned by modern artists, as we have already seen – figures into the equation to a considerable degree.

Adriaen van der Werff and Hendrick van Limborch's account books, show that they continued with this method, offering accurate information about how artist calculated the price based on hours worked on a painting. Van Limborch noted with great precision every half a day he spent on an artwork (for history paintings the total number of days could vary between 45 and 160 days; portraits took much less time); regrettably he neither mentions the price for which a painting ultimately sold, nor the sum he charged per day. Based on circumstantial evidence, Guido Jansen assumed that the latter must have been approximately 10 guilders per day.[16] However, we do know Van der Werff's rates. Marten Jan Bok demonstrated that, whatever his subject, Van der Werff would charge a basic rate of 25 guilders a day; the total number of days would determine the minimum asking price, which served more or less as a bottom line for price negotiations with his patrons. To this he would add additional costs, such as the frame, packing and transportation costs. 'Then he would take a good look at the painting and decide what the market would bear: '*maer segge* ...' (but I will ask ...). In this way, he would arrive at a target figure for his negotiations. Sometimes he settled for less, but there were occasions when he received more.[17] Moreover, Van der Werff made a distinction – not for the customer, but for his own calculations – between his own labour and that of his brother and close collaborator Pieter. He calculated Pieter's labour, who did the groundwork for most of his paintings, at 25 guilders a day as well, which means that Adriaen did not differentiate between the price of a picture he painted all by himself – which he rarely did – and a painting he did with Pieter, even if the latter did the largest portion of the work.[18] However, according to Johan van Gool, Adriaen paid his brother only one ducat (5 guilders) a day, which means that Adriaen made an extraordinary profit on Pieter's labour.[19] The above demonstrates that ultimately Adriaen van der Werff guaranteed the quality of all the works that left his studio, pricing them on the basis of his personal reputation, regardless of the contribution made by his brother Pieter. I will eventually come back to this issue.

Bok also tested the relationship between size and labour and it appeared that three-quarters of the difference in invested labour can be explained by the difference in size of the panels. This must have often been the case. For example, we find a landscape by Herman Saftleven in the inventory of baron Willem Vincent van Wyttenhorst for which, according to his own notes, Van Wyttenhorst paid 120 guilders; for a landscape '*halff soo groot als de bovenstaende*' (half the size of the one mentioned above), Saftleven was paid exactly half that sum: 60 guilders.[20] A painter like Cornelis van Poelenburch probably used a similar method. Van Wyttenhorst's inventory, which was drawn up between 1651 and 1659, contains a large number of paintings by Van Poelenburch (57), most of which were purchased directly from the artist. The prices Van Wyttenhorst recorded having paid vary greatly, from 36 to 464 guilders. The inexpensive ones are recorded as being small landscapes (to which Van Wyttenhorst added that the value had risen, which means that he must have bought them a considerable time earlier and that, in the meantime, the prices for Van Poelenburch's work had increased). The most expensive piece is indeed described as being 'large'. That the price varies more than the difference in size would warrant, is due to the fact that it was a history painting. All the costly works by Van Poelenburch in this inventory are history paintings with numerous figures, such as 'a piece representing the Passion' or 'the martyrdom of St. Lawrence', which took a great deal more time to paint than a landscape containing only a few small figures.

Concerning calculations of monetary value, we do not have information about painters who used a rapid technique, but it seems likely that an artist like Jan van Goyen calculated the price in the same 'craftsmanlike' manner. These painters used a method of working that was geared towards high levels of production while saving labour, which resulted in lower prices per painting and – at least initially – higher profit margins. As far as we can gather from various sources, the prices of a painting by Van Goyen – who, Van Hoogstraten recounts, could produce a painting in one day – would have been approximately 10 guilders for a small painting and 60 for a large one.[21]

His artistry and incredible virtuosity must have been greatly admired by connoisseurs; Huygens mentions Van Goyen in the same breath as Van Poelenburch, while Orlers pays even more attention to him as to Rembrandt and emphasises that his work was greatly valued.[22] Van Poelenburch and Van Goyen could probably charge more or less the same daily rate. It seems reasonable to assume that Van Poelenburch, whose paintings appear to be on average about ten times more costly than Van Goyen's, indeed worked about ten times as long on a painting. Guessing from the prices and the time they presumably spent on a painting, I estimate that both calculated approximately eight to 10 guilders a day. This is more or less the same amount that, according to Houbraken, Nicolaes Berchem earned at the time he worked in the service of a certain patron.[23]

But what does it mean that the daily rates varied considerably between different artists when using this method of calculating monetary value? With this obvious question we arrive at the cost of the reputation of an artist. How was this reputation determined and how was it translated into hard cash? Also in the seventeenth century it was a matter of 'trial and error', as we shall see. Whenever there was a conflict, appraisers could be appointed by the guild, which means there must have been a certain level of consensus among professionals about the ranking according to reputation and the reflection of this in the daily rates they could charge. Based on the rates mentioned above – Dou and Van Mieris 6 and 5 guilders per hour respectively, Van der Werff 25 guilders a day (while his brother was paid only five), Van Limborch probably around 10 guilders, Berchem 10 guilders – the 3 guilders per hour charged by Caesar van Everdingen when he executed the shutters of the organ of the Alkmaar St. Lawrence church in 1643, may come as a surprise.[24] This is similar to the rates charged by mediocre Antwerp painters like Justus Daneels (4 guilders) or Abraham Snellinck (3 guilders),[25] while the services of Jan Brueghel II could be had for a rate that was equivalent to 5 or 6 guilders per day.[26] Considering Van Everdingen, however, we should not only realise that the rates of Dou, Van Mieris and Van der Werff were excessively high, but also that this low figure undoubtedly has to do with the stage of his career: he was 26 years old and as yet only a local celebrity who executed those organ shutters after designs by Jacob van Campen.[27] Another daily rate that we are able to calculate more or less is that of Bartholomeus van der Helst. He received some 10 guilders a day during the period that he worked on two portraits of Van Wyttenhorst and his wife. He worked on the paintings for six weeks and was paid 350 guilders; but he also received bed and board, since he lodged with Van Wyttenhorst, during the weeks he was painting the portraits, as the baron meticulously noted.[28]

The rates that Dou, Van Mieris and Van der Werff charged seem outrageous, indeed, but, as Marten Jan Bok pointed out to me, it is a common phenomenon in these kind of rankings that it leads to extremes at the high end of the market. Such distributions are found everywhere and seem quite natural (this is certainly the case with present-day soccer players: the best one is paid twice as much as the second best, who is paid two thirds more that the third best, who is paid 50% more than the fourth best, and so on).

That a painter could miscalculate his reputation is evident from another case concerning Van der Helst. From the proceedings of a lawsuit that dates from 1665, we learn how his reputation was expressed in terms of money.[29] Van der Helst charged no less than 1000 guilders for a family portrait (representing husband, wife, child and greyhound) and this price was contested. The painting was subsequently valued by two independent appraisers, the painters Dirck Bleecker and Jacob Coolen. They estimated the portrait was worth 400 guilders. In fact, they appraised it at 300 guilders, but 'considering the good name and reputation of the painter' (*ten respecte van de meester syn name ende reputatie*) 100 guilders could be added to the estimate.[30] Hence, Van der Helst's reputation was evaluated at a premium of one third of what they considered the minimum price of such a portrait (in terms of Van Wyttenhorst's payment, this would have meant about five weeks of work). Obviously Van der Helst was of a different opinion, but in this case his 'trial' ended up as a total 'error'. He had hoped to be paid for the *valore di stima*, but had far overrated the value of his name and reputation, and was subsequently punished with a lawsuit and rebuked by the judgement of two respectable colleagues from Haarlem.

Painters often tried to see how high they could go, not unlike the twentieth-century artist who declared that he would put the price at $10,000 for a painting he valued at $3,000 if he thought he could sell it for that amount. Vroom's bizarre proposal of charging 6,000 guilders for a large painting of the *Battle of Gibraltar* is well known. It was to be a painting offered as a present by the Amsterdam admiralty to Prince Maurits; Vroom did not receive the commission.[31] Jacob Jordaens attempted to pocket 800 guilders for a painting in the town hall of Hulst for which, as it turned out, the municipal government had only reserved 100 ducats [c. 315 guilders]; ultimately Jordaens had to settle for 500 guilders.[32] Rembrandt seems to have been involved in similar sorts of affairs more often than other painters.

Valore di stima

It seems that Rembrandt tried to have the monetary value of his work determined solely by quality and reputation, the *valore di stima*, as opposed to hours of labour spent, leaving it to the client/connoisseur's judgement what the painting was worth upon completion of the work. Rembrandt often expected exceptional sums – but he did not always succeed – at least not in the cases known to us.[33] This was already the case with his first important commission, the *Passion* series for the stadtholder Frederick Henry – of which he might have made the first painting on his own initiative, offering it (through Huygens) to the stadtholder. He grossly over-estimated the value of the paintings, but simultaneously made it clear that he would adjust the price to whatever the court was willing to pay him ('I shall be satisfied with what His Excellency pays me'). It appears from the well-known correspondence with Constantijn Huygens that Rembrandt initially, in 1636, thought that he 'certainly deserved' 1200 guilders a piece for the first three paintings.[34] He eventually received 600 guilders each. In 1639, he believed that the last two paintings 'will be considered of such quality that His Highness will now even pay me not less than a thousand guilders each', but he added: 'should His Highness consider that they are not worth this, he shall pay me less according to his own pleasure'.[35] Also for these paintings he was rewarded 600 guilders each, which caused Rembrandt to write the self-assured but bitter words: '... if His Highness cannot in all decency be moved to a higher price, though they are obviously worth it, I shall be satisfied with 600 Carolus guilders each ...'.[36] By writing 'they will be considered of such quality ...' Rembrandt makes it clear that he does not want to calculate in terms of labour, but exclusively in terms of the high quality of the paintings and the reputation of its maker, the final decision being up to the client, whom he expects will pay substantially for the works. Rembrandt also wanted it to be understood that the long time he worked on those paintings should not be thought of as time devoted to manual labour, as was still usually the case; the cause of the prolonged genesis was that '*die meeste ende die natuereelste beweechgelickheijt in geopserveert is*' (the most natural motion and emotion has been observed).[37] Hence, according to Rembrandt, it was entirely due to the intellectual factor in the process of creation. However, he had far overreached; his reputation at the court and the willingness to pay up for this were not what he expected. However, he ultimately understood that he had to swallow some of his pride and be satisfied with what he could get. As a matter of fact, seven years later, in 1646, he did succeed in receiving 1200 guilders a piece for two additional paintings, but we do not know what he himself was asking for the pieces at the time. Compared to the 500 guilders which painters like Pieter de Grebber, Salomon de Bray, Theodoor van Thulden and Jacob Jordaens probably received for triumphal scenes in the Oranjezaal that were more than two meters high (undoubtedly the price for these works was agreed to in advance),[38] the sums Rembrandt received were indeed extravagant for paintings of less than a meter high.[39]

Delaying the delivery of commissioned works, as Malvasia pointed out in regard to Reni's market strategies, could have been 'a shrewd device for making his works more desirable and consequently more esteemed because they were so difficult to obtain'.[40] That Rembrandt had a similar attitude seems to be confirmed by Houbraken who remarks: 'His art was so much admired and sought after in his own time, that, as the saying goes, one had to beg and throw in money to boot.'[41] Rembrandt's attempt to offer Constantijn Huygens a large painting seems to be another aspect of this *valore di stima* strategy. Mancini praised this method of 'giving' works of art, because it signalled good will, courtesy and honour, and he added that 'through this [way of negotiating] one sees extravagant prices and compensation in the great generosity of some gracious person or prince'.[42] Rembrandt's words in his letter to Huygens allow us to infer that the latter had told Rembrandt that the painting was not welcome. Huygens was probably much more frugal than Rembrandt expected,[43] and might have been afraid that Rembrandt counted on a princely sum for such a major painting; and/or he simply did not want to feel obligated to continue promoting Rembrandt's career.[44] Nonetheless, Rembrandt sent the painting (probably the *Blinding of Samson*) 'against my lord's wishes, hoping that you will not spurn [my gift] ...'[45] As with the other paintings, Rembrandt seems to have greatly misjudged the 'generosity of gracious persons and princes', but he insisted on delivering the painting anyway. The presence of a spectacular and eye-catching work in the house of someone who was as a spider in the web of courtly commissions and probably the key figure in a circle of elite connoisseurs,[46] was already a good enough reason to take the trouble.[47]

An exorbitant asking price may also have been the cause of Andries de Graeff's battle with Rembrandt, although we cannot be sure what actually caused their disagreement.[48] Hendrick Uylenburg 'and other good men' acted as arbiters in the case and decided on a payment of 500 guilders, which was still a very high figure. My guess is that Rembrandt simply over-estimated 'the generosity' of this 'gracious person' – a man from the top of the Amsterdam elite – to pay substantially extra for Rembrandt's reputation. In his dealings with Don Antonio Ruffo from Messina, Rembrandt eventually seemed to get his way. He was asking 500 guilders for the *Aristotle*, which he received. For the second painting, the *Alexander* that Ruffo commissioned, he asked the same price, but sent a painting of *Homer*, which Ruffo had not commissioned, along with it. For that one he wanted 500 guilders as well, if Ruffo would allow him to finish the painting. Ruffo complained about ugly seams he noticed in the *Alexander*, because the painting consisted of several pieces of canvas sewn together, and offered

Rembrandt 500 guilders for the two, adding that this was already five times as much as he would pay an Italian master for works of this kind; he maintained that the going rate was 25 ducats per head (62.5 guilders), and 50 (125 guilders) for a half-figure – which were the exact prices that Guercino charged, whom he must have had in mind. Rembrandt did not give in and responded rather impudently 'I believe there must be few connoisseurs (he probably used the word *liefhebber*) in Messina', by which he meant to say: people capable of judging the value of his work. He added: 'I am surprised that your Lordship should lament as much about the price as about the canvas', implying that a prestigious patron should be willing to pay this kind of price.[49] This is in great contrast to Mattia Preti and Guercino's attitude, who were always ready to please Ruffo. Guercino received 150 guilders for the companion piece to the Aristotle that he had painted for Don Antonio (the *Cosmographer*), which was a bit more than usual because, as he wrote, 'it is of exceptional size for a figure in half-length'. Rembrandt behaved more like the notorious Salvator Rosa who demanded the extraordinary price of 1500 guilders for two paintings of *Pythagoras*, a price which Ruffo tried to bargain down. The artist responded to the patron's agent that he would rather die of hunger than dishonour his reputation.[50] Don Antonio eventually conceded, as he seems to have done with Rembrandt as well. These were artists who were extremely assertive about the high quality of their art and the monetary value of their name and reputation. In Italy, this might have worked with artists like Reni and Rosa, but in Holland it seems to have been more problematic.

Fascinating documents, discovered only very recently, that record an exceptional commission of two altarpieces for a church in Genoa in 1666/7 fit this image perfectly.[51] The Genoese nobleman Francesco Maria Sauli wanted Rembrandt first to paint two *modelli* (one an *Ascension of the Virgin*) before granting him the full commission. The negotiations were conducted by a certain Gio Lorenzo Viviano, captain of a ship then harboured in Amsterdam, who was assisted by two of Sauli's business agents. Viviano and the agents complained several times in their letters to Sauli that it took Rembrandt an endless amount of time to finish the *modelli*, which he had promised to complete within a month, and that one could not rely on the word of this difficult and eccentric artist. They also thought that Rembrandt asked an outrageous price for the *modelli*, causing them to wonder what the large paintings would cost and how long it would take to finish them! However, Sauli was undaunted by this discouraging information and clearly wanted to move forward with the commission. The price was indeed outrageous. At a certain point, the captain was in despair and wrote that he did not know how to manage Rembrandt, as the paintings were still not finished, and moreover, Rembrandt suddenly wanted 3000 guilders, despite his original request of 1200 guilders. In the end, after eight months of constant pressing and urging of the artist, the paintings were finished; the price they had agreed upon was 1023.15 guilders. In the context of this essay, the most telling part of the correspondence is the agents' report that Rembrandt apologizes for the delay with the contention that he cannot finish the paintings in a shorter time, 'applying himself to this task with the utmost mental commitment.'[52] To this they added that 'he wishes to acquire fame and honour in our parts.'[53] Concerning the substantial compensation, they write that Rembrandt 'wants a lot of money, because he maintains that he is someone who has knowledge of the art of painting and therefore stands his ground.'[54] The pattern described above is confirmed again by this example. It demonstrates Rembrandt's exceptional conviction about his stature as an artist and the quality and high monetary value of his art, while highlighting his inability or unwillingness to conceal his contempt for those who disagree with him. He, as a renowned artist, is the one who has true knowledge of art.[55] The long time it may take to finish the works is due to mental exertion and for this reason, patrons must simply be patient. His goal is to acquire honour and fame, but he tends to overrate the monetary value related to his fame as an artist. His unaccommodating attitude, caused foremost by his strong sense of artistic autonomy, made him a very difficult painter to deal with. Sauli, as a matter of fact, seems to be the kind of patron who was accustomed to this and knew that it was he who had to decide about the paintings' value in the end: 'he [Rembrandt] will have to be satisfied with what is reasonable and we for our part will not deviate from what is customary and from what the work is worth. He will have to explain exactly what he wants when he delivers the models or drawings, and then it will be up to us to respond,' Sauli writes. Italian princely connoisseurs probably knew better how to handle this type of artists than patrons from the Dutch burgher elite.

But what about Rubens? After listening to someone praising Rubens's great wealth, style of living and grand image, Guido Reni would have declared, according to Pietro da Cortona, that he, Reni, painted 'for glory and immortality, whereas Rubens busied himself painting for lowly interests and hankering for worldly gain'.[56] Natasja Peeters in her article in this volume, in which she analyzes how Rubens determined the prices of some 30 altarpieces created by the master and his workshop, demonstrates that things were not that simple. Although Rubens himself had written that 'one evaluates pictures ... according to their excellence, their subject and number of figures', and Jan van Vucht, in a letter to Balthasar Moretus, insisted that '... for 200 or 250 florins, he does not do much, unless you are content with a composition with one or two figures', which in turn reminds us of Guercino's pricing strategy, Peeters shows that there were remarkable differences in price between altarpieces that were seemingly similar in size and in the number of figures. She concluded that with the pricing, intangible factors, such as personal relations and the wealth of the patron, also played a large role. She did not find any correlation between pricing and the number of figures in the case of these altarpieces. Rubens's prices for altarpieces, which doubled in the later years of his career, had more to do with his reputation and his 'excellence' than numbers of figures or size, Peeters contends. The 'connoisseurial' appreciation of his 'excellence' certainly had a price. Rubens, according to Balthasar Moretus, even sent less competent connoisseurs to a lesser and cheaper artist (cf. Natasja Peeters essay in this volume, pp. 97-124).

By the master's own hand

A daunting issue that inevitably comes into play when discussing the value of seventeenth-century paintings, is the extent to which a painting is actually by the master's own hand, or a collaborative work, a copy, or a copy retouched by the master. Peeters assumes that the level of studio participation could also account for some of the lower prices in her sample of altarpieces, but it seems impossible to assess to what degree. In the case of retouched workshop 'products', there is a bit more clarity, because of the fascinating and well-known correspondence between Rubens and Sir Dudley Carleton. The letter in which Rubens explains rather precisely what he did entirely himself and what was done by collaborators or pupils, is extensively discussed in Anna Tummers's article in this volume (pp. 31-66), where she demonstrates, among other things, that in earlier discussions of Rubens's comments in connection with the question of what authenticity meant during that period, one often arrived at conclusions that were not entirely correct. She infers from the letters that not only Rubens, but also his client Carleton were not that concerned whether a painting was entirely by Rubens's own hand.

In their groundbreaking article on 'Pricing Invention', De Marchi and Van Miegroet also referred to this correspondence to point out the differences in prices between extensively retouched studio copies and paintings that were, according to Rubens, done entirely by his own hand. [57] However, and this is in line with Tummers's argument, I would like to add that, in contrast to what De Marchi and Van Miegroet maintained, it seems more remarkable how almost negligible those differences actually are. De Marchi and Van Miegroet set out to demonstrate that in the seventeenth century 'invention' became an important economic factor, reason why a '*principaal*' (a work that is not a copy) is more expensive than a copy – even if the copy is by the hand of the master himself. To this purpose they adduce the fact that Rubens recommends all the paintings he offers Carleton for sale as being 'by his own hand', but that the prices of the works he described as copies retouched by him – and which were, according to Rubens as good as the works that were entirely autograph – were priced considerably lower. However, I would argue that other conclusions are possible if one examines the list carefully.[58] 'A Sebastian, nude, by my own hand' of 7 x 4 foot, had the same price tag as the only slightly larger 'Susanna, done by one of my pupils, but then entirely retouched by my hand' of 7 x 5 feet, (both 300 guilders). The authors argue that a retouched copy of the *Last Judgement* was much less expensive (1200 guilders) than the original and they attribute this to the fact that in this case one did not have to pay for the invention.[59] However, Rubens described this work as 'begun by one of my pupils, after one which I did in a much larger size for the Most Serene Prince of Neuburg, who paid me 3500 florins cash for it; but this one, not being finished would be entirely retouched by my own hand, and by this means would pass as original.' A simpler explanation is that the original was, first of all, considerably larger, as Rubens himself explicitly points out, and secondly, that the incredible price he received for that painting – which Rubens undoubtedly mentioned to show Carleton that he was giving him a bargain – must have been an inflated price paid by a prince-connoisseur. But more importantly, it would take Rubens much less of his costly time to touch up a copy painted by a pupil than to paint an original. Remarkably, the 13 x 9 foot painting was still by far the most expensive that Rubens offered Carleton, more than twice as much as a 'Daniel among many lions ...Original, entirely by my hand' of 8 x 12 foot. For Rubens, it must have been of paramount importance that these retouched paintings looked as good as his originals – a difference in quality would not have been discernible. On the surface the paintings would reveal the inimitable hand of the master and they were, as much as the 'originals', his intellectual property. When he pointed out that 'well-retouched copies ... show more for their price', he merely meant that these were less expensive because it had taken him much less time to produce, not that retouched paintings would necessarily be of a lower quality. A connection between 'original' and 'invention' does not seem to be an issue here.

The fact that Jan Brueghel II charged half the price for copies which were made by himself and not by an assistant, as is recorded in his diary, plays an important role in De Marchi and Van Miegroet's argument that invention became an economic basis for a distinction between original and copy. However, it seems to me that this cannot be inferred from these examples. A more likely reason is that the number of days spent on a copy (Brueghel calculated 5 to 6 guilders a day) is considerably less than what he needed for painting a '*principaal*'. Apart from the fact that a '*principaal*' was more expensive because it could be used for 'exclusive' copying,[60] the difference in price with a copy was, in my opinion, not so much due to a clear distinction between the origination of the creative individual (invention) and the manual execution, but largely to costs involving the talent and reputation of the artist who had to work much longer on a new painting.[61] Remarkably, copies were sometimes valued as highly. An interesting case is the following entry by the previously mentioned Van Wyttenhorst about a copy after Cornelis van Poelenburch: 'the Magi, at first very accurately copied by Steenbergen and afterwards totally overpainted by Poelenburch; first paid 36 guilders for copying and afterwards one 100 guilders for the overpainting'.[62] This painting, a copy by an assistant and overpainted by Van Poelenburch, was one of Wyttenhorst's most expensive paintings. It must have been the hand of the master himself that determined the price. That it was not a new invention does not seem to have mattered. If a copy was by a renowned master, as we know from famous copies by Andrea del Sarto after Raphael, Ludovico Carracci after Parmigianino, Rubens after Titian or Mignard after Reni,[63] they could have been as expensive or even more. We find this same situation also in Van Wyttenhorst's inventory, where he describes two copies by Cornelis van Poelenburch after landscapes with biblical scenes by Adam Elsheimer, in both instances, adding: '... is valued more highly than the *principael*.'[64]

The master's touch plays a considerable role in discussions about early modern attitudes towards authenticity and authorship, a subject on which scholarly opinions differ widely. Anna Tummers examines the many problems connected with this challenging topic in the above mentioned essay in this volume (pp. 31-66), in which she analyzes the available evidence. She introduces previously overlooked primary sources and places these in a broader perspective, examining how important it was for seventeenth-century painters and connoisseurs that a painting was done entirely by the master under whose name it was sold. A painter could consider works that were not entirely painted by himself as being 'by his own hand'. As we have already seen, for Adriaen van der Werff, to name just one example, the fact that his brother Pieter actually had a large share in the production of a particular painting and not the other, did not make any difference in the selling price. In each of these cases, Adriaen van der Werff painted the finishing touch and guaranteed their quality. Tummers argues that it was the quality that counted, which means that a painting did not needed to be entirely autograph. She demonstrates that the master's touch was considered of great importance for the connoisseur in discerning good paintings from copies and studio productions. But she also shows that they were not that preoccupied with the question of whether or not the painting was entirely autograph. In many cases, they would have assumed that the less important parts were done by assistants anyway, which called for a 'hierarchical' way of looking at the works, where one had to focus on the key elements in a painting.

The buyer's opinion

Naturally, clients took it for granted that the master's work was of higher quality than the assistant's, even if the 'identity' of a great artist was not yet an issue. This easily led to potential tension between the interests of producers or sellers and clients. In early contracts for altarpieces we find already stipulations that the master had to paint it 'with his own hand' and thus without the assistance of pupils – the first case Liesbeth Helmus records is a contract from 1498.[65] In another contract it is stipulated that the master who received the commission should do the most important parts himself, such as 'all the naked parts [i.e., faces, hands, etc.] and the most important sections' (*alle de naecten ende 't principael werc*). In 1520, this led to a lawsuit because the painter of an altarpiece, Albert Cornelis, disagreed with his patrons about what this meant. He had done the faces with his own hand, saying that he was obliged 'to produce only the faces with his own hands, because here lies the most art' (*zelve metter handt te makene dan de aenzichten, daar de meeste const an licht*).[66] In fact, this is not so different from the seventeenth-century customer who felt cheated because he bought a painting for 17 guilders, after having been told by a dealer that it was an excellent work by a certain master, but was then informed by the artist himself – who was later consulted by the apparently suspicious buyer – that it concerned a painting by his humblest pupil, and that he sold it to the dealer for only 5 guilders and would never have let it pass as a work of his own.[67] In both cases, it is the hand of the master himself that guaranteed the best quality for the customer, but in this last case, the owner of the painting was obviously not an expert capable of making a judgement about such matters. However, this client was lucky that he could still return to the painter of the work. When a work of art was by an artist who was dead, one had to rely on one's own knowledge and experience or on that of an expert or dealer. Jonckheere's book *The Auction of King William's Paintings* contains numerous examples of foreign collectors who relied completely on the knowledge and expertise of their agents in Holland when buying 'Old Master Paintings'.[68] Others, however, did their research and consulted independent connoisseurs, as Jonckheere argues in his essay in this volume (pp. 69-95).

Contracts for fifteenth and sixteenth century altarpieces often included stipulations that a committee of guild members would upon completion judge whether the price was justified by the quality of the altarpiece. However, those who did the assessing of the quality and value of paintings (and the aspects that contributed to that value), changed significantly over the course of the sixteenth century – and this happened first in Antwerp – a period in which religious and secular panel paintings became commodities in an increasingly market-oriented society, commodities to be appreciated and enjoyed by burghers as decorations for their private homes. The tensions that arose between Amsterdam guild members and art dealers who had come from the Southern Netherlands in the early seventeenth century, seems to have been part of this process of change. In 1608, shortly before the signing of the Twelve Years' Truce, and continuing during the next few years, a large number of paintings from Antwerp apparently flooded the Dutch market and was sold at auctions.[69] The established painters demanded that the city council immediately enact measures to contain this influx from the south. They complained that these paintings were being sold for much more than their value through 'cunning and ungodly importunity', because the 'majority [are] poor copies'. Stimulated by profit, they contended, these interlopers obtain as many paintings as possible in Antwerp and the surrounding area, 'such that a multitude of paintings is presently at [their] disposal, in order to be sold here in the above-mentioned manner'. The Amsterdammers were convinced that 'in a short time this city, yea, the entire country will be filled with rubbish and inferior apprentices' work', adding that 'the good burghers here, who by and large have little knowledge of painting, [are being] deceived'.[70] In a petition dating from 1613, the sellers were said to withdraw the better works when bids were too low, 'such that the country was being inundated mostly by copies and other worthless rubbish occasioning the ridicule of all distinguished art lovers and the noticeable disrepute of art'. Although the guild members cited the inferior quality of the works as the main reason for their concern, capitalising on customers' fears relating to the unwitting purchase of copies instead of an 'original' (*principaal*), their real objection (and panic) had, in my opinion, to do with the fact that the intruders were successful. Evidently, there was no shortage of customers for the imports from Antwerp. These paintings sold readily for prices the Amsterdam guild members felt were far too high. In other words, they were in great demand – despite the disparaging judgement of the dean and headmen – by a public that was willing to pay more than they were worth, at least, according to local painters, who wanted to protect heir own production.

The question is whether the quality of the imported paintings was, indeed, as inferior as their critics would have us believe. They were inexpensive compared to the paintings that established local painters tended to produce, and undoubtedly, that was a significant enough threat. The paintings were probably cheaper because they were made using different production methods, for example, by means of less time-consuming and labour-intensive techniques. This alone was enough for the Amsterdam guild members to label them as rubbish, apprentices' work and copies; this was the most obvious vocabulary for expressing scathing censure.[71] Moreover, when these works sold for prices higher than the guild members deemed appropriate based on criteria of technical execution and time invested, the traditional way in which they assessed prices was entirely overturned. For those who imported this 'Brabant rubbish', apparently 'what the fool was willing to bid for it' was all that mattered. Suddenly the artists themselves were no longer determining the price based on conventional rules of thumb; it was now the dealers and their clients who determined the monetary value of works of art and they did so on much more imponderable grounds such as subject matter and '*handeling*'(manner of painting), factors which became dependent on trends and fashions in taste. And one wonders whether the buyers were indeed mostly burghers 'who by and large [had] little knowledge of paintings'. There were plenty of knowledgeable individuals in attendance at the auctions, which probably only further incited the fierce response of the guild. The same names appear over and over again, especially of Amsterdammers of Southern Netherlandish – usually Antwerp – origin, who were often registered as painters, but were presumably primarily active as dealers.[72] They probably sold the works chiefly among their own circle – that is to Southern Netherlandish immigrants, who were now in a position to purchase a type of art that was already familiar to them. In this way, new standards for quality and value were established for new types of paintings by new audiences. From this time onward, competing notions about who had the expertise to actually judge paintings – practising artists or art lovers/connoisseurs – would continue to rage. In her second article in this volume (pp. 127-147), Anna Tummers examines this fascinating discussion, analysing such issues in theoretical sources and connecting the diverging opinions to practices on the art market; in both cases, the amateur-connoisseurs became more prominent as the century progressed.

Karel van Mander was already somewhat uncomfortable with the phenomenon that new parties were able to establish the value of paintings, which went hand in hand with the increased popularity of various emerging genres of paintings. This is especially apparent when he begins describing the life of David Vinckboons with a peculiar exhortation in which he states in a rather roundabout way that, because 'his own understanding or judiciousness might not be good enough in itself to write with discrimination and proper discretion about the practitioners of our art or their works', he makes it a habit, when he enters the houses of art lovers, 'to take heed and note which artful works and by whose hand have been gathered and been valued there as being special and excellent'. Thus, he not only follows his own understanding, but also 'the consensus of the connoisseurs', and for that reason, he cannot, he notes, omit David Vinckboons.[73] Especially when discussing the painters specialising in the new genres – from Pieter Bruegel and Gillis van Coninxloo, to Jacob Grimmer, Pieter Baltens, Cornelis Molenaar, Hans Bol, Hendrick van Steenwijck and David Vinckboons – Van Mander emphasises that they were popular among art lovers. Apparantly, it was the appreciation of art lovers that determined their reputation; thus, Van Mander felt compelled to hide behind their assessments when he discussed Vinckboons.

The assessments of art lovers, who were often also 'amateur dealers' must have been crucial for the many young painters beginning their careers in the early seventeenth century. To be 'held in great esteem by art lovers' (*bij den liefhebbers in grooter weerden ghehouden*)[74] – which also meant being able to command higher prices – must have become imperative. A few decades later, in 1642, it seems obvious to Jan Orlers, himself an art lover, that the admiration of art lovers and the value they attached to a painter's work were the criteria that one should use to select a painter as an important asset to the fame of the city, and to be praised in his prestigious *Description of the City of Leyden.*[75] To Orlers, it was fairly evident that Jan van Goyen was the greatest landscape painter of his time, since his renown 'can be evidenced by many paintings which are held in high value by all art lovers'; and the greatness of Gerrit Dou can be affirmed because 'his work is highly valued by art lovers and is sold for high prices'. In that same year, Philips Angel made clear that the criteria of what made a good painter were the things that art lovers liked to see and found attractive.[76]

It is obvious that these art lovers needed knowledge to discern the differences in quality, or they needed the help of reliable middlemen who could provide the necessary insight. The fear of buying a lemon must have intensified as the prices of reputed masters diverged more significantly from those of second- and third-rate masters, and as more mediocre and bad copies entered the market. This fear was expressed by the St. Luke's Guild in The Hague, which, in 1632, filed a complaint with the city government about art dealers who were not members of the guild and who 'deceitfully sell art to a lot of people, cheating them with works that are often copies and rubbish, but selling these as excellent art'.[77] Whether they were right about the inferior quality of the works sold by those dealers – naturally it was their purpose to protect their own membership – is of less importance than the fact that they zeroed in on this fear, just as the Amsterdam guild had done a few decades earlier. After all, prices could vary wildly, not only between the paintings of reputable masters and the works of less reputable masters or even anonymous paintings, but also between the works of one and the same master; the range could be incredible. No wonder that art lovers who forked over large sums for works of well-known masters, became increasingly anxious about being swindled with copies or works by pupils or imitators.

Neil De Marchi and Ed Romein both apply the economic theory of Akerlof who observed the used car market to demonstrate that increased uncertainty among the buyers regarding quality because the sellers fail to share certain information with buyers, can have the effect of bad products driving good products off the market, which can eventually lead to a collapse of the market.[78] Ed Romein went so far as to argue that, because of uncertainties about quality in the Leiden art market in the 1630s, caused by an incongruity of information between buyers and sellers of paintings and consumer anxiety regarding bad paintings, the art market stopped functioning properly (many painters left Leiden during this period)[79] and was in need of criteria of quality, which the traditional guilds were no longer able to supply. A new organisation – which they called eventually a St. Lukes guild – was established in 1644, which, according to Romein, was meant to stimulate the sharing of information and augment the interaction between artists, dealers and art lovers. During this same period, a selective canon of good painters against which others could be gauged was established by Jan Orlers, while Philips Angel created a set of criteria to assess good paintings, criteria that were grounded in the shared judgements of connoisseurs. Both Orlers and Angel related quality to the appreciation of the market and advocated Gerrit Dou's fine and 'mannerless manner',[80] thus stimulating the emergence of the Leiden 'fine painters'. Although I am not entirely convinced that it all fits together so neatly, Romein made some very intriguing points in this area.

One of the results of the prestigious city descriptions by authors like Jan Orlers, Samuel Ampzing and Theodoor Schrevelius, in which renowned painters – living or dead – of a city were celebrated even more extensively than great scholars and theologians were,[81] was that their names – even in their lifetime – became canonised, a process which had been started in the sixteenth and early seventeenth centuries by Vasari (1550) and Van Mander (1604). Reputation by name must have become more and more important in the course of the 17th century, which went hand in hand with identifiability by genre, subject matter and 'manner of painting' (*handeling*). Inventories and sales from the early part of the century do not reveal many names; however, in the larger cities of Holland this increased rapidly.[82] By the 1650s, one notices an amazing increase in the need and ability to name works of art. Hendrik Bugge van Ring, to name an art lover who owned a huge number of paintings and must have been present when his inventory was made (1667), was able to name no less than 98 different artists by whom he had paintings hanging in his house; he was also precise in naming copies and attributions he was not sure of.[83] It was important not only for the truly talented artists to distinguish their work from that of others, but also among the humbler artists we can observe many painters pursuing their own recognisability in subject matter and manner, rather than merely imitating better-known artists, the result of which was that an immense variety of work could be seen in the art market. Toward the middle of the seventeenth century, there were numerous painters with limited gifts who created their own niche by way of signed paintings with specific subjects in a characteristic manner that were available for low prices. We still know an amazing number of well-defined oeuvres developed by relatively minor artists working during this period.

Thus, this market situation meant that painters, in the words of De Marchi and Van Miegroet, had to make 'creative moves to secure some (temporary) differential advantage'. It seems that 'successful artists ... in addition to having talent, had a sophisticated, positive understanding of the market as a forum for experimentation, rather than seeing it as a threatening place ...'.[84] To be the pupil of a famous master, must have been a good start toward the acquisition of a reputation. Malvasia's remark that 'the very fact of having such a great master bestowed good fortune on Reni's pupils', probably was also true for many of Rembrandt, Bloemaet, Dou or Van Poelenburch's pupils, to name a few. If they were ambitious, these pupils, after leaving their master's studio, had to find a way to show off their prestigious backgrounds while simultaneously developing a recognisable style of their own.

The talent and skill with which painters were able to suggest a convincing lifelikeness and the inventiveness with which they made their work identifiable through a certain range of subjects, motifs and manners, including a personal touch of the brush, constituted an important part of their 'capital'. It sounds entirely believable that Frans Hals, as Houbraken recounts, used 'to paint the underlayers of his portraits in a meltingly soft way, after which he brought in the touch of the brush, saying: 'And now the characteristic touch of the master has to be added.'[85] But for connoisseurs, it was not just a specific handling of the brush that was an important guide for distinguishing quality. As Romein argued, developing a 'fine' technique, in which the brushstroke was invisible, was another possible strategy to pursue. Art lovers then had to use criteria such as correct anatomy, perspective, colouring (especially of flesh), powerfully organised light and shadow, differentiation in reflection of light on surfaces to suggest materials, and the measure of refinement in a smooth and meticulous rendering of the wealth of 'illusionistic' details, without interference of a particular way of handling the brush. According to Angel, who enumerated these criteria, the standards for this style were set by Gerrit Dou, who, in his view, knew how to apply this technique with a curious looseness, never lapsing into stiffness and unnaturalness – still an acute and apposite observation.

Regrettably, in the Netherlands, one-liners like Reni's, that he was a better artist than Guercino because he sold better and had more followers, were not written down. However, painters like Rembrandt, Dou, Van Poelenburch and Van Goyen, must have also been very much aware that they were the market leaders who created a hallmark style that became highly popular among certain groups of art lovers. They were the ones that attracted many followers supplying the same type of paintings for a lower price or making copies of their works. Unlike Dou and Van Poelenburch, the fashion Van Goyen created did not last: while the prices of second-hand Dous and Poelenburchs soared after their deaths, the value of Van Goyen's paintings, as did the works of all paintings by artists of the 'monochrome' trend, declined rapidly.[86] In the late seventeenth and eighteenth centuries, Van Goyen's name would almost completely disappear from the art market (the works themselves did not, however, since they are still around in large numbers). Trends and fashion – during the painter's lifetime as well as after – would have been powerful incentives for increase or decrease prices. As Jan de Bisschop wrote when he disapprovingly referred to the 'naturalistic' trend in Dutch art: 'every age ... has its fashions [he uses the word *mode*], which are introduced by one or more masters held in high esteem at the time and therefore capable of making an impact'.[87] This is, I believe, what the amateur and economic theorist Bernard Mandeville meant by 'time of his age' – the period in which an artist worked – when he enumerated the criteria that define art market prices for second-hand paintings.[88] The other criteria he mentioned are already familiar: the name of the master, the prestige of those owning the works and the length of time the works have been in the possession of 'great families', as well as the scarcity of the artist's works.

The second-hand market

For art lover-connoisseurs and dealers this meant that, especially when selling or buying second-hand works, they not only needed to be able to put names on works of art, but also to rank them in terms of name, reputation and quality on the basis of experience and knowledge of alternatives while using criteria that were current to a certain period of time.[89] However, the goals of these two groups were different. In his article in the present book, Koenraad Jonckheere (pp. 69-95) focuses on auctions in the late seventeenth and early eighteenth centuries, a period in which the market for second-hand paintings by 'dead' masters expanded enormously and became far more important than that of living masters. He emphasises the conflicting interests of art dealers, on the one hand, and connoisseurs, on the other, and examines how dealers, auctioneers and connoisseurs attributed works of art, demonstrating that there was a marked difference between their respective attitudes towards attribution and the practices they applied. The sellers, not bothering with authenticity and more precise information, used 'brand names' to categorise in order to better guide amateurs through the vast art market. They left it up to the elite amateur-connoisseurs to assess a work's quality and challenge attributions. The latter group gathered and shared information – in which a good provenance played an important role. Thus, to understand the value of attributions in late seventeenth-century or early eighteenth-century catalogues it is important to make distinctions between art dealers/auctioneers and amateur-connoisseurs, he argues.

De Marchi and Van Miegroet (pp. 149-174) in their essay focus on the period immediately following the one discussed by Jonckheere. They observe that, in the course of the eighteenth century, new relations and new roles for art dealers and connoisseurs began to take shape in an increasingly complex art market. Examining the dealings in seventeenth-century Netherlandish art on the eighteenth-century Paris art market, they focus on the art dealers Gersaint and Lebrun, who, they argue, assumed both roles: that of the auctioneer/dealer and that of the connoisseur, endeavouring to satisfy both connoisseurs and new collectors. The dealers made themselves knowledgeable and obliterated the knowledge gap between connoisseurs and art dealers, and made the sales far more transparent than before, revealing information and knowledge about attribution, condition and provenance. This is exactly the opposite of what happened on the Dutch art market around 1700 where auctioneers kept their knowledge secret, as Jonckheere argues.

Together, the following articles demonstrate that the study of changing practices on the art market in relation to the artist's, dealer's and art lover's ideas and attitudes toward evaluating works of art yield many new insights, while simultaneously stimulating new areas of research.

* I am grateful to Marten Jan Bok who made many valuable comments and whose expertise greatly enriched this essay.

1 Marten Jan Bok, 'Pricing the Unpriced: How Dutch Seventeenth-Century Painters determined the Selling Price of their Work', in: Michael North and David Omrod (eds.), *Art Markets in Europe, 1400-1800*, Aldershot 1998, pp. 102-111, esp. p. 104.

2 Richard E. Spear, *The "Divine" Guido: Religion, Sex, Money and Art in the World of Guido Reni*, New Haven and London 1997, p. 212; for the second quotation, see also the article in this volume by Anna Tummers, pp. 31-66. From: Giulio Mancini, *Considerazioni sulla pittura*, A. Marucchi and L. Salerno (eds.), Rome 1956-1957.

3 Neil De Marchi and Hans Van Miegroet, 'Art, Value and Market Practices in the Netherlands in the Seventeenth Century', *The Art Bulletin* 86 (1994), pp. 451-464, esp. p. 451.

4 See Koenraad Jonckheere, *Kunsthandel en diplomatie. De veiling van de schilderijenverzameling van Willem III (1713) en de rol van het diplomatieke netwerk in de Europese kunsthandel*, Dissertation, Universiteit van Amsterdam 2005, pp. 199-206. (English edition: Koenraad Jonckheere, *The Auction of King William's Paintings (1713). Elite international Art Trade at the End of the Dutch Golden Age*, Oculi: Studies in the Arts of the Low Countries. 11, Amsterdam 2008.)

5 Jeffrey Muller, 'Measures of Authenticity: The Detection of Copies in the Early Literature on Connoisseurship', in *Studies in the History of Art, National Gallery of Art* 20, 1989, pp. 14-151.

6 Jaap van der Veen, 'By His Own Hand, The Valuation of Autograph Paintings in the Seventeenth-Century', in: Ernst van de Wetering et al., *A Corpus of Rembrandt Paintings*, Dordrecht 2005, vol. 4, pp. 1-41.

7 Bok, Pricing the Unpriced (note 1); De Marchi and Van Miegroet, *Art, Value and Market Practices* (note 3); Neil De Marchi and Hans Van Miegroet,

'Pricing Invention: 'Originals', 'Copies', and their Relative Value in Seventeenth Century Netherlandish Art Markets, in: Victor Ginsburgh and P.-M. Menger (eds.), *Recent Contributions to the Economics of the Arts,* Amsterdam 1996, pp. 27-70.

8 Ed Romein, 'Knollen en citroenen op de Leidse kunstmarkt: over de rol van kwaliteit in de opkomst van de Leidse fijnschilderstijl', *De Zeventiende Eeuw* 17 (2001), pp. 75-94; Elizabeth A. Honig, 'The beholder as a work of art: A study in the location of value in seventeenth-century Flemish painting', *Nederlands Kunsthistorisch Jaarboek* 46. *Beeld en Zelfbeeld in de Nederlandse kunst* (1995), pp. 253-297.

9 Spear, *The "Divine" Guido* (note 2), p. 213.

10 Quoted by Spear, *The "Divine" Guido* (note 2), p. 212.

11 As Marten Jan Bok pointed out, it is often worthwhile to realise the original meaning of a word. Implicit in the word 'honorarium' is 'honour'; the concept is closely related to the culture of honour among the nobility. For a gentleman it was dishonourable to work for money. To consider painting as a liberal art, rather than a handicraft, is linked to this world of honour, exchange of favours, gifts, etc. See Marten Jan Bok, 'Familie, vrienden en opdrachtgevers', in: J. Huisken et al. (eds.), *Jacob van Campen: het klassieke ideaal in de Gouden Eeuw,* Amsterdam 1995, pp. 26-52, esp. p. 46.

12 Spear, *The "Divine" Guido* (note 2), p. 242.

13 Spear, *The "Divine" Guido* (note 2), p. 221.

14 Joachim von Sandrart, *Academie de Bau-. Bild- und Mahlerey-Künste* (ed. A.R.. Peltzer), München 1925, p. 196; Arnold Houbraken, *De groote schouburgh der Nederlantsche konstschilders en schilderessen,* Amsterdam 1718-1721, 3 vols., vol, 2, p. 4; Eric Jan Sluijter, *Leidse Fijnschilders. Van Gerrit Dou tot Frans van Mieris de Jonge 1630-1670,* Leiden (Stedelijk Museum De Lakenhal) 1988 (exh. cat.), p. 26 and 27.

15 O. Naumann, *Frans van Mieris the Elder,* Doornspijk 1981, cat. no. 192, Sluijter. *Leidse Fijnschilders* (note 14), p. 27.

16 Guido M.C. Jansen, 'De Notitie der gelijxe schilderoeffening van Henrik van Limborch (1681-1759)', *Bulletin van het Rijkmuseum* 45 (1997), pp. 27-67, esp. p. 32-33. For the transcription of Van Limborch's account book, see pp. 46-67.

17 Bok, *Pricing the Unpriced* (note 1), p. 108. For Van der Werff's account book (only over the years 1716-1722), see Barbara Gaethgens, *Adriaen van der Werff.* 1659-1722, Munich 1987, pp. 442-444.

18 Only one painting made in the years recorded in this account book was entirely done by Adriaen. In the other paintings Pieter's share of the work varied between 20 and 60 percent (in many cases around 25 percent).

19 Johan van Gool, *De nieuwe schouburg der Nederlantsche kunstschilders en schilderessen: waer in de levens- en kunstbedryven der tans levende en reets overleedene schilders, die van Houbraken, noch eenig ander schryver, zyn aengeteekend, verhaelt worden,* The Hague 1750-1751, vol. 1, p. 237. Van Gool explicitly mentions that 'he [Pieter] had finished his work, the knight [Adriaan] painted over it in wet' (schilderde ... het in 't nat over).

20 For a complete transcription and a valuable and exhaustive analysis of Wyttenhorst's exceptionally precise inventory, see Marion Boers, 'De schilderijenverzameling van baron Willem Vincent van Wyttenhorst', *Oud Holland* 117 (2004), pp. 181-243, esp. pp. 198-208 on the prices.

21 Eric Jan Sluijter, 'Jan van Goyen als markleider, virtuoos en vernieuwer', in: C. Vogelaar (ed.), *Jan van Goyen,* Leiden (Stedelijk Museum de Lakenhal) 1996 (exh. cat.), pp. 38-59. esp. pp. 39-48. In a few cases involving large commissioned paintings , Van Goyen worked in a more elaborate style, which means that the result was more expensive. Sluijter, *Jan van Goyen* (note 20), pp. 44-45.

22 Jan Jansz. Orlers, *Beschrijvinge der stadt Leyden.* Inhoudende 't begin, den voortgang, ende den wasdom der selver: de stichtinge vande kercken, cloosteren, gasthuysen, ende andere publijcque gestichten, etc. [...], Leiden 1641, pp. 373-74 (Van Goyen), p. 375 (Rembrandt). See Sluijter, *Jan van Goyen* (note 21), p. 39.

23 Quoted by Boers, *De schilderijenverzameling* (note 20), p. 208; Houbraken, *De groote schouburgh* (note 14), vol. 2, pp. 112-113. His pupil Justus van Huysum provided Houbraken with this information.

24 Marion Boers-Goosens, 'Prices of Northern Netherlandish Paintings in the Seventeenth Century', in: A. Golahny et al. (eds.) *In his Milieu. Essays on Netherlandish Art in Memory of John Michael Montias,* Amsterdam 2006, pp. 59-73, esp. p. 63.

25 Quoted by De Marchi and Van Miegroet, *Pricing Invention* (note 7), p. 59 from Katlijne Van der Stighelen, 'De (atlier-)bedrijvigheid van Andries Snellinck (1587-1653) en co', *Jaarboek Koninklijk Museum voor Schone Kunsten Antwerpen* (1989), p. 305.

26 De Marchi and Van Miegroet, *Pricing Invention* (note 7), pp. 54-56. The documents on Jan Breugel II were published by J. Denucé, *Brieven en documenten betreffend Jan Bruegel I en II,* Antwerp 1934, p. 93.

27 Van Everdingen received his first commission in 1641: a militia piece of the officers of the Old Civic Guard (Oude Schutterij) in Alkmaar; see Paul Huys Jansen et al. (eds.), *De zestiende en zeventiende-eeuwse schilderijen van het Stedelijk Museum Alkmaar, Alkmaar* 1997, no. 23.

28 Boers, *De schilderijenverzameling* (note 20), p. 227.

29 Boers-Goosens, *Prices of Northern Netherlandish Paintings* (note 24), pp. 64-65.

30 Boers-Goosens, *Prices of Northern Netherlandish Paintings* (note 24), pp. 63-64. For the documents, see Jan Jacob de Gelder, *Bartholomeus van der Helst*, Rotterdam 1921, p. 144, doc. 87. Also in A. Bredius, *Künstler-Inventare: Urkunden zur Geschichte der Holländischen Kunst des XVIten, XVIIten und XVIIIten Jahrhunderts*, The Hague 1915-1921, vol. 1, pp. 299-301.
31 Bredius, *Künstler-Inventare* (note 30), vol. 2, pp. 671-79.
32 Quoted by Boers-Goosens, *Prices of Northern Netherlandish Paintings* (note 24), pp. 63, from De Nora de Poorter, 'Seriewerk en recyclage: Doorgedreven efficiëntie in het geroutineerde atelier van Jacob Jordaens', in: H. Vlieghe (ed.), *Concept, Design, and Execution in Flemish Painting. 1500-1700*, Antwerp 2000, pp. 229-30.
33 About Rembrandt's troubles with clients, see especially Paul Crenshaw, *Rembrandt's Bankruptcy: The Artist, His Patrons, and the Art Market in Seventeenth-Century Netherlands*, Cambridge 2006, chapter VI.
34 H. Gerson, *Seven Letters by Rembrandt*, The Hague 1961, p. 30. Rembrandt demanded 200 pounds, without specification. However, this would have been 200 Flemish pounds (=1200 guilders).
35 H. Gerson, *Seven Letters* (note 34), p.46.
36 Ibid. (note 34), p. 62.
37 Ibid. (note 34), p. 34.
38 It is not certain that they received 500 guilders; this figure is the 'estimate' (raminge) which Jacob van Campen made of the expenses (Friso Lammertse in A. Blankert, *Hollands Classicisme in de zeventieuwe-eeuwse schilderkunst*, Rotterdam and Frankfurt a/M 1999, p. 95; See for the document D.F. Slothouwer, *De paleizen van Frederik Hendrik*, Leiden 1945, p. 315.)
39 One would think that Houbraken's wry remark that, in the period when Flinck was his pupil, everyone had to paint in Rembrandt's manner if one wanted to please the world – in other words, that Rembrandt's style was high fashion – would have been valid for the 1630s only. Indeed, the number of followers diminished after the mid 1640s, when other styles became more fashionable, but his reputation was at this time obviously still on a remarkably high level.
40 Spear, *The "Divine" Guido* (note 2), p.211.
41 Houbraken, *De groote schouburgh* (note 14), vol. 1, p. 269.
42 Spear, *The "Divine" Guido* (note 2), p. 212.
43 Inge Broekman will demonstrate in a chapter of her dissertation on Huygens as connoisseur and collector that Huygens himself rarely seems to have bought expensive paintings.
44 On the symbolic value of gifts, see Michael Zell, 'The Gift Among Friends: Rembrandt's Art in the Network of His Patronal and Social Relations,' in: A. Chong and M. Zell, *Rethinking Rembrandt*, Boston (Isabella Stewart Gardner Museum) 2002 (exh. cat.), pp. 173-194, esp. p. 182.
45 Gerson, *Seven Letters* (note 34), p. 50.
46 On Huygens as a member of a circle of elite connoisseurs, see: Herman Roodenburg, 'Visiting Vermeer: Performing Civility', in: A. Golahny et al (eds.), *In his Milieu. Essays on Netherlandish Art in Memory of John Michael Montias*, Amsterdam 2006, pp. 385-394.
47 The emulative reference to Rubens's gruesome Prometheus, which could be found for some time in The Hague in Sir Dudley Carlton's collection might have been a calculated strategy to show The Hague connoisseurs that he was able to surpass Rubens in the representation of extreme passions (see Eric Jan Sluijter, *Rembrandt and the Female Nude*, Amsterdam 2006, p. 260). However, also in this respect, he might have misjudged Huygens: sending a painting with such an atrocious subject as a present to a gentleman, might have been taken as an offence.
48 See Crenshaw's outstanding discussion of all the possible reasons for this dispute: Crenshaw, Rembrandt's Bankruptcy (note 32), pp. 111-120.
49 Ibid. (note 32), p.132.
50 Ibid. (note 32), p. 131.
51 The new documents, discovered by Lauro Magnani, were presented at a small symposium at the Rembrandthuis on June 13, 2008, and they were published in: L. Magnani, '1666. Een onbekende opdracht uit Genua voor Rembrandt', *Kroniek van het Rembrandthuis* (2007), 2-17 (published June 2008).
52 Magnani, '1666', p. 6: 'pur applicando tutto il suo spirito all'opera non può perfettionarla in quella brevità [che] si desiderebbe'. In the article by Magnani this is translated with 'although he has thrown himself into the work heart and soul'. However, this translation is too superficial for contemporary language; it only says that Rembrandt worked with great dedication. In my opinion, Rembrandt informed them that he is using all his mental powers as an artist while working on these new and important inventions and that this takes a great amount of time.
53 Ibid., p. 6: 'vuol in questa occasione acquistare in cotteste parti lode et honore.'
54 Ibid., p. 5, 'Pretende molto denaro però si rimesso in persona intelligente di pittura per stare a suo giudizio.'
55 See also Crenshaw, *Rembrandt's Bankruptcy* (note 32), chapter 6.
56 Spear, *The "Divine" Guido* (note 2), p. 213.
57 De Marchi and Van Miegroet, *Art, Value and Market Practices* (note 3), pp. 40-41.
58 For an English translation, see Ruth Saunders Magurn (ed.), *Letters of Peter Paul Rubens*, Evanston 1991, pp. 60-61.
59 De Marchi and Van Miegroet, *Art, Value and*

Market Practices (note 3), p. 58; they also ignore the great difference in size when they calculate the ratio between original and copy.

60 As Marten Jan Bok pointed out to me, the word 'principaal' comes from accounting and refers to the 'principal money' from which interest is harvested. In painting, the 'principaal' is worth more, because it could be used for 'exclusive' copying as long as the distribution of the image could be controlled by the owner, and because better copies could be made from a 'principaal' than from a copy.

61 Interestingly, Guercino even charged the same amount for copies he made himself as for the originals, but much less for copies by assistants; in his efficient manner of pricing, there was obviously no place for invention;
See Spear, *The "Divine" Guido* (note 2), p. 215.

62 Boers, *De schilderijenverzameling* (note 20), p. 217.

63 Spear, *The "Divine" Guido* (note 2), pp. 263 and 269; Muller, *Measures of Authenticity* (note 5), p. 145.

64 Ibid. (note 2), p. 217.

65 Quoted in Liesbeth Helmus' dissertation on fifteenth- and sixteenth-century contracts for altarpieces in the Northern Netherlands, which will be published in 2008 (Liesbeth Helmus, *Schilderen in opdracht. Noord-Nederlandse contracten voor altaarstukken 1450-1570*).

66 About the complicated genesis of this altar, see Dorien Tamis, 'The Genesis of Albert Cornelis's "Coronation of the Virgin" in Bruges', *The Burlington Magazine* 172 (2000), pp. 672-680.

67 It concerns a painting by Isack van Duijnen (1686); see also Anna Tummers' article in this volume pp. 31-66. For the document, see Van der Veen, *By His Own Hand* (note 6), doc. 28.

68 Jonckheere, *The Auction of King William's Paintings* (note 4).

69 For the following case, see more extensively: Eric Jan Sluijter, 'Over Brabantse vodden, economische concurrentie, artistieke wedijver en de groei van de markt voor schilderijen in de eerste decennia van de zeventiende eeuw', *Nederlands Kunsthistorisch Jaarboek 50. Art for the Market 1500-1700* (1999), pp. 113-144, especially pp. 118-121
(see for English translation: http://home.medewerker.uva.nl/e.j.sluijter)

70 Fr.D.O. Obreen (ed.), *Archief voor Nederlandsche Kunstgeschiedenis*, Rotterdam 1877-1878, vol. 3, pp. 164-165.

71 See also Neil De Marchi, 'The role of Dutch auctions and lotteries in shaping the art market(s) of 17th century Holland', *Journal of Economic Behavior & Organization* 28 (1995), pp. 203-221, esp. pp. 206-212. De Marchi took this literally and assumed that it concerned indeed rubbish, copies and works by pupils. For this reason, he applied Akerlof's theory concerning the fear of 'lemons' (see below, note 73). However, the success of the auction sales and the probable expertise of the buyers (that is to say, the buyers at the sales mentioned below – we do not know if there were other illegal sales), apart from the fact that the market did not collapse but started to grow rapidly, points in another direction.

72 Montias, J. Michael, *Art at Auction in 17th century Amsterdam*, Amsterdam 2002, pp. 41-51 and Sluijter, *Over Brabantse vodden* (note 64), p. 140 and note 46.

73 Karel van Mander, *Het Schilder-Boeck*, Haarlem 1604, fol. 299r.

74 Van Mander wrote this about, for instance, Jacob Grimmer, Cornelis Molenaer (Schele Neel [Cross-eyed Neil]) and Joos van Liere (Van Mander, *Schilder-Boeck* (note 68), fol. 256v and 257r. Orlers would write something similar several decades later about Van Goyen. See Orlers, *Beschrijvinge der stadt Leyden* (note 21), p. 373. With regard to strategies of innovative behaviour on a competitive art market, see De Marchi and Van Miegroet, *Art, Value and Market Practices* (note 3), pp. 451-464. Also see: Marten Jan Bok, *Vraag en aanbod op de Nederlandse kunstmarkt, 1580-1700*, Utrecht 1994, p. 190. For the concept of 'liefhebber (art lover)', idem, p. 73-75

75 Eric Jan Sluijter, *Verwondering over de schilderijenproductie in de Gouden Eeuw*, Amsterdam 2002, pp. 16-17.

76 For the relevant passages, see passages in Angel's text, see Eric Jan Sluijter *Seductress of Sight. Studies in Dutch Art of the Golden Age*, Zwolle 2000, p. 9 and 223-258.

77 Romein, *Knollen en citroenen* (note 8) , p. 77.

78 De Marchi, *The role of Dutch auctions* (note 66), pp. 203-221 and Romein, *Knollen en citroenen* (note 8) pp.79-82.

79 Dudok van Heel argued that many artists left Leiden in the early 1630's because of the oppressive political and economic climate: S.A.C. Dudok van Heel, *De jonge Rembrandt onder tijdgenoten: godsdienst en schilderkunst in Leiden en Amsterdam*, PhD Dissertation Radboud Universiteit Nijmegen 2006, pp. 195-197.

80 Angel thought of Dou's work as not having a recognizable 'manner' (see Sluijter, *Seductress of Sight* [note 71], p. 245).

81 Sluijter, *Seductress of Sight* (note 71), pp. 210-205. Sluijter, *Verwondering over de schilderijenproductie* (note 70), pp. 13-15.

82 A good example would be the Leiden inventories selected by Willemijn Fock (she only selected the ones that included a lot paintings, 12 inventories from every ten years). C. Willemijn Fock, Kunstbezit in Leiden in de 17de eeuw', in: Th.H. Lunsigh Scheurleer, C.W. Fock and A.J. van Dissel (eds.), *Het Rapenburg. Geschiedenis van een*

Leidse Gracht, vol. Va, Leiden 1990, pp. 3-36. As a matter of fact, this is not true for cities outside the province of Holland: see the recent study of Leeuwarden by Piet Bakker, *Gezicht op Leeuwarden. Schilders in Friesland en de markt voor schilderijen in de Gouden Eeuw*, Amsterdam 2008. See also below, p. 38.

83 Eric Jan Sluijter, '"All striving to adorne their houses with costly peeces". Two Case Studies of Paintings in Wealthy Interiors', in: Mariët Westermann (ed.), *Art & Home: Dutch Interiors in the Golden Age, Denver* (Denver Art Museum) 2001 (exh. cat.), pp. 102-127, esp. p. 119.

84 De Marchi and Van Miegroet, *Art, Value and Market Practices* (note 3), pp. 459-460.

85 Houbraken, *De groote schouburgh* (note 14), vol. 1, p. 92.

86 See the list of maximum, minimum, average and median prices paid at auction for these painters in the 1676-1739 period in Jonckheere, *The Auction of King William's Paintings* (note 4), appendix A2, pp. 229-233.

87 Sluijter, *Rembrandt and the Female Nude* (note 47), p. 197.

88 De Marchi and Van Miegroet, *Art, Value and Market Practices* (note 3), pp. 454-455. They assume that it refers to the period within an artist's oeuvre.

89 De Marchi and Van Miegroet, *Art, Value and Market Practices* (note 3), p. 460.

Chapter 1
Anna Tummers

'By His Hand': The Paradox of Seventeenth-Century Connoisseurship*

Introduction

The question of whether seventeenth-century painters and connoisseurs had a different understanding of authenticity than we do today, has been the cause of much debate. Several scholars have even wondered if present-day connoisseurship is anachronistic in its efforts to distinguish the hand of a seventeenth-century master from those of his assistants and pupils. For was it not common for a seventeenth-century master to collaborate with his assistants and to sell the various studio products under his own name?

Nowadays connoisseurs tend to differentiate sharply between what is believed to be purely autograph work with paintings done in part or entirely by assistants, which can make for a price difference of several millions of dollars.[1] Yet, among scholars there is no consensus as to whether such a distinction agrees with seventeenth-century categories of thought.

Seventeenth-century connoisseurs were certainly interested in attaching names to paintings. In fact, attributing pictures seems to have been an entertaining pastime among the upper echelons of society in Europe. For example, the British King James I reputedly removed the labels from his paintings to see if his courtiers could guess the artists.[2] A letter sent from Paris by the Dutch scientist and art lover Christiaan Huygens to his brother Constantijn in The Hague shows that these rather playful attribution debates were not an exclusively British phenomenon. After visiting the Flemish dealer Valcourt with a group of Parisian connoisseurs, Christiaan wrote to his brother on 1 June 1668:

'You would have had unparalleled pleasure to see [the collector-connoisseur] Jabach determine the authenticity of those [Valcourt's] pieces with a magisterial complacency;

only to conclude in the end that out of 300 drawings that were given to Raphael there were but two originals. I would give a good thing to see him censure yours and that you were [listening in from] behind the tapestry. When we were at his place, there was also no shortage of 'controllers', of which I was one of the minor figures, who challenged the attribution of what he [Jabach] believed to be true Giulio Romanos and Raphaels, which drove him into a rage that made us all laugh, so much so that there would be hardly any comedy that would equal such a conference'. [3]

Christiaan's account is so vivid that it is not hard to imagine the excitement of these early connoisseurs. However, the precise considerations and assumptions of these gentlemen remain elusive. On what grounds exactly would they have attributed and de-attributed pictures? What elements were seen as particularly telling? Would they have differentiated between different types of studio products, and if so: how?

It is very rare indeed that one can find evidence of early connoisseurs weighing arguments when making an attribution. An imaginary dialogue written in 1677 by the Parisian writer and collector Roger de Piles, suggests that some of these early experts may have been quite sophisticated in their judgements. The protagonists discuss even how feasible and necessary it is in their opinion to attach a name to a painting; for example: how difficult it can be to recognise works made in a transitory period in which an artist changes his style; or how impossible it is to even know all the painters from the past – especially those who worked for others and never really acquired their own reputations.[4] Yet primary sources addressing these issues are scant. Also, it is only in very exceptional instances that we know with any certainty what pictures exactly these early connoisseurs were discussing, and that we can thus clarify their comments by matching their accounts to the very pictures at which they must have been looking.[5]

Reconstructing seventeenth-century views on authenticity is mostly a matter of critically analysing and connecting circumstantial evidence: relevant passages in guild statutes, notarial deeds, personal writings, art theoretical treatises, probate inventories and sales catalogues, and match these to what we can see in pictures wherever possible.[6] Interestingly, the available sources seem rather ambivalent. On the one hand, surviving guild statutes indicate that it was common practice for master painters to sell works produced in collaboration with their studio assistants under their own name, as we will see. However, on the other hand, some early art theoretical treatises that discuss attribution practices advise art lovers to look for brush marks that seem distinctively individual, much like someone's handwriting, which suggests they were indeed interested in attributing pictures to a specific hand.

It is this seeming contradiction that I propose to call the paradox of seventeenth-century connoisseurship. After first analysing the scholarly debate, I will have a closer look at seventeenth-century sources and introduce some new source material into the discussion in order to better understand the seventeenth-century appreciation for authenticity, and the practice of both signing and attributing pictures. The underlying goal is to bridge contradictions in previous interpretations in this field and, in doing so, provide a clearer frame of reference for attributions to seventeenth-century Dutch and Flemish masters such as Rembrandt, Rubens and Honthorst. Although commercial and social interests must have played an important role in seventeenth-century attribution practices (as they do today), I will not speculate much about their impact in this essay, focusing mostly on the more general question what types of distinctions were made and what their implications are for present-day connoisseurship.[7] Also, I will not pay much attention to the question of how the insights of painters may have differed from those of buyers since – as we will see – there is little reason to assume that their insights as to these general distinctions would have differed strongly.[8]

The debate: Autograph pictures, the holy grail of present-day connoisseurs?

Ernst van de Wetering, the head of the Rembrandt Research Project, phrased the issue most poignantly in 1992 when he gave a lecture entitled 'The Search for the Master's Hand: An Anachronism?' at the 28th International Art History Congress in Berlin. If seventeenth-century viewers would have found it self-evident to regard all works produced in a studio as works by the master who headed the studio, even if they were carried out by others, then, he pointed out: 'the idea at the basis of the Rembrandt Research Project, namely that there is a need to isolate works of Rembrandt's hand from that of his pupils and assistants, would be a complete anachronism, a wrongly applied projection of the 19th-century cult of genius to everyday 17th-century workshop practice.'[9]

Earlier in 1984, he had addressed the same concern in the second volume of *The Corpus of Rembrandt Paintings*, stating that there was too little evidence to draw any conclusion with certainty.[10] However, in the meantime several other scholars had been pondering the same issue and voiced different opinions. In 1988, Svetlana Alpers' book *The Rembrandt Enterprise* was published, in which she analysed Rembrandt as a talented artist and entrepreneur who created pictures that give the *effect* of individuality together with his studio, thus not necessarily with his own hands.[11] Referring to the Rembrandt Research Project, she pointed out that it seemed that Rembrandt had not collaborated much with his assistants on particular works, yet she emphasised that the master liked to have his name attached not just to his own works but also to works done by others in his studio.[12] Therefore, she stated, the master's oeuvre cannot simply be reduced to his autograph works.[13]

Also, Eddy de Jongh had briefly touched upon this matter when he analysed the attribution debate that was sparked by the Frans Hals overview exhibition of 1990.[14] As the lack of consensus in the definition of Frans Hals's oeuvre became painfully clear (Seymour Slive approved 222 paintings, while Claus Grimm only agreed with 145 of these), De Jongh wondered if what he called the '19th and 20th century fixation on authenticity' can be historically justified. In his view, a seventeenth -century viewer would have certainly been aware of the difference in value between originals and copies, and an occasional connoisseur may have had a preference for works done entirely by the hand of a famous master. However, he suspected that in general it was rule rather than exception in seventeenth-century studios that painters collaborated with their assistants; it seemed quite probable that in various instances the only autograph detail in a picture from Frans Hals's studio would have been the master's monogram *FH*.

In his 1992 lecture, Ernst van de Wetering weighed evidence both in favour and against the idea that seventeenth-century painters and their clientele had a preference for autograph paintings by the master, without however reaching a definitive conclusion. On the one hand, Van de Wetering argued, it was perfectly normal for pupils and assistants to work in the style of their master. However, that did not mean that various types of studio products were interchangeable in his view; and he claimed that there was a 'substantial amount of documents which indicate that the aspect of *autographness* was relevant in 17th century Holland' (which Jaap van der Veen was in the process of assembling and interpreting).[15] But he suspected that master painters may have worked in close collaboration with their studio all the more easily since many art buyers could not easily recognise poor quality pictures.

At the Berlin conference Claus Grimm also addressed this issue - the scholar who had not only sparked the Frans Hals attribution debate in 1990 but who had also just published a book on Rembrandt's portraits (1991) in which he narrowed down the selection of autograph works even further than the Rembrandt Research Project had done. In his lecture *The Question about Autographness and the Practice of Attribution*, Grimm emphasised that much research remained to be done in order to get a clearer idea of seventeenth-century workshop practice and better standards for current attributions to old masters.[16]

Close inspection of just a few pictures by Rembrandt led Grimm to conclude that the master must have collaborated with his assistants in different ways. He pointed to the built-up of the paint in the man's face in *The Shipbuilder and His Wife*: in the shadow part at right, a relatively thin first layer is applied somewhat hesitantly, presumably by an assistant. It is topped by confident strokes which Grimm identified as corrections by the master. (fig. 1). By comparison, another group portrait done in the same year, the *Anatomy Lesson of Doctor Tulp* (1633), does not show a similarly sharp distinction in its built-up; instead, it seems to have been worked up much more coherently and smoothly (fig. 2). This led Grimm to conclude that Rembrandt sometimes, but not always, had assistants execute the general building-up of the top layer, while adding the light and shadow parts himself. In a third example taken from the same year, Rembrandt's *Portrait of the Remonstrant Minister Johannes Uytenbogaert* (fig. 3), Grimm pointed out the differences in style and execution between Uytenbogaert's face and the definition of the hands. This, according to Grimm, indicated that the different parts were executed by different hands, that is: the head by the master and the hands by an assistant.[17]

What should we conclude from all this? Would such collaborations have been the rule or the exception? The exact extent of collaboration in Rembrandt's studio remains an issue of much debate. On the one hand, a number of specialists believe that Rembrandt tended to distinguish rather sharply between his own paintings and those done by students and assistants, and that he would have priced them accordingly (even though he may have also sold non-autograph works as 'Rembrandts'). In particular Josua Bruijn stated that Rembrandt hardly ever collaborated with his pupils and assistants on the same composition, and Ernst van de Wetering wrote that such collaborations occur almost exclusively in portraits created before 1642. [18] However, there have also been other scholars like Grimm who believe that Rembrandt's studio output and his working practices may have been more diversified.

In 1995, Arthur Wheelock distinguished four different types of collaborative works produced in Rembrandt's studio: works done by an assistant on the basis of a sketch or drawing by the master, works blocked in on a canvas by the master and worked up by an assistant (such as the National Gallery's of Art's *Man in Oriental Costume*, c. 1635), portraits done by the master in which the costume and even the hands are done by an assistant, and lastly works produced by pupils or assistants and retouched by the master.[19] Also, Walter Liedtke made a plea for a thorough re-evaluation of Rembrandt's studio practices in 2004; in his view, the input of students and assistants, in many instances, has not been properly recognised.[20]

These differences of opinion regarding the studio practice of the most studied painter from the Dutch Golden Age, illustrate just how little is certain about the historical context in which these pictures were made. It makes the question of how

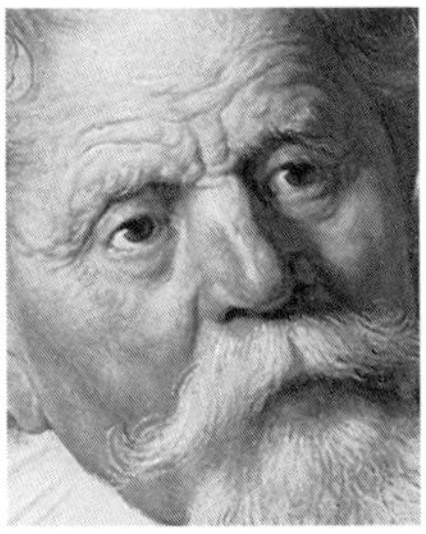

1.

2.

3.

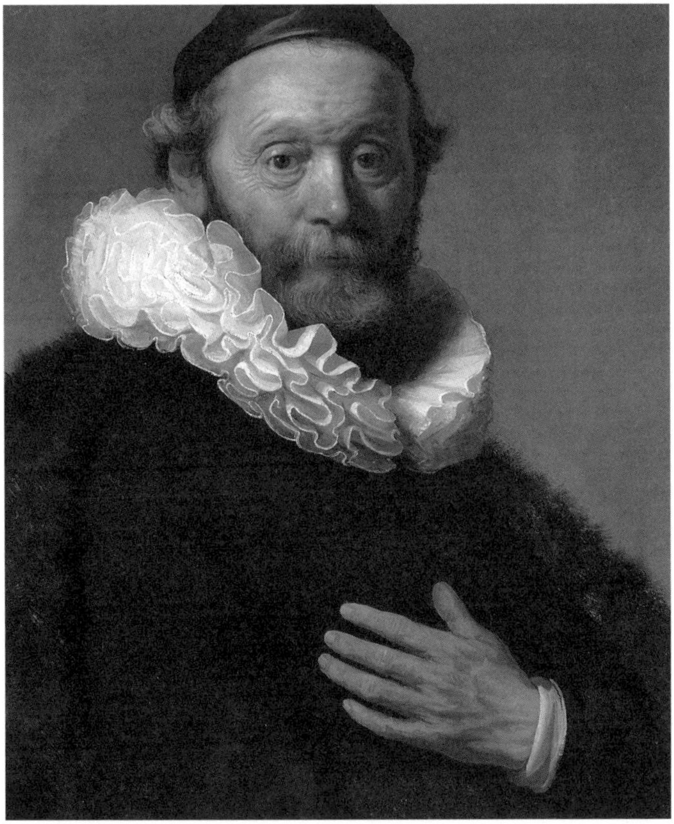

1. Rembrandt, see colorplate p. 177 (entire painting)
The Shipbuilder and his Wife [detail], 1633
The Royal Collection, Her Majesty Queen Elisabeth II, London

2. Rembrandt, see colorplate p. 178 (entire painting)
The Anatomy Lesson of Doctor Tulp [detail]
1633, Royal Cabinet of Paintings The Mauritshuis, The Hague

3. Rembrandt, see colorplate p. 178 (entire painting)
Portrait of the Preacher Johannes Uyttenbogaert [detail]
1633, Rijksmuseum, Amsterdam

seventeenth-century painters and connoisseurs would have thought about issues of authenticity all the more relevant. Do seventeenth-century sources give us any indication as to what types of pictures to expect? Can we safely assume, for example, that most seventeenth-century master painters created at least a part of their oeuvre entirely by their own hand? And that present-day connoisseurs can thus take an autograph 'core oeuvre' as a point of departure for their attributions? Or is such a core oeuvre much like the holy grail: highly desirable (for the amount of certainty it would give in matters of attribution), yet eternally elusive? [21]

At the time of the Berlin conference, many primary sources had not yet been extensively studied, in particular, archival documents and art theoretical texts. Since then, Jaap van der Veen has written a thorough analysis of Netherlandish archival documents and probate inventories in relation to issues of authenticity: 'By his Own Hand, The Valuation of Autograph Paintings in the Seventeenth-Century', which was published in *A Corpus of Rembrandt Paintings*, volume IV (2005).[22] In the appendix, he listed and transcribed 36 relevant notarial documents. These documents mostly concern pictures by or after Netherlandish masters (including Porcellis, Bloemaert, Jordaens and Den Uyl) and also some paintings by or after Italian masters such as Titian and Caravaggio.

One of the difficulties with the interpretation of this material is that most of these notarial deeds deal with the status of particular paintings as either an 'original' (*principael/origineel*) or a 'copy' (*kopie*).[23] The same holds true for seventeenth-century inventories and sales catalogues. '*Principael*', the most commonly used word for 'original', simply meant that the work was not a copy, but did not encompass a claim as to the execution; it could well have been painted by several hands.[24]

In the case of the 36 documents accumulated by Jaap van der Veen, only six make a specific claim as to the execution of a work.[25] These six documents state that a certain work is done entirely 'by the hand of the master' and sometimes even specify that it was done 'without help from others'. This seems to suggest that there was indeed an interest in purely autograph works. Jaap van der Veen believes that this was the case among well-to-do burghers who could afford the better paintings (there seems no reason to assume that issues of authenticity would have been of great concern to the producers and buyers of cheap pictures). Furthermore, he speculates that the interest in autograph works may have increased throughout the century, reaching a high point around 1650, and that the less commonly used term for 'original' (*origineel*) may have implied that a certain work was autograph.[26] Therefore he concludes that the premise of the Rembrandt Research Project to distinguish the master's hand from those of his assistants and pupils is in fact not anachronistic.

However, there is also another way to interpret the evidence that Jaap van der Veen has gathered. For similar statements about pictures, namely that they were done 'by the hand of the master' also occurred in other countries, most notably in Italy. However, scholars of Italian art believe that these should not be taken literally; the Italian equivalent of this phrase '*fatto di suo mano*' had a certain legal validity and was more of a guarantee of personal, moral responsibility than necessarily of physical involvement.[27] Could the same be said of the Netherlands? Did painters' names function mostly as guarantees of a certain style and quality?

In the following I will try to bridge some of the contradictions in current interpretations by re-evaluating some existing evidence, by bringing some additional research into the discussion and by introducing a number of previously overlooked primary sources, mostly taken from a still relatively little explored field, that of the art theoretical discourse. First, I will explore seventeenth-century categories of thought by looking at the importance attached to painters names in general, and by analysing the types of distinctions made in seventeenth-century inventories and notarial deeds, in particular the distinction between works identified as by a master and those given to a pupil. Subsequently, I will discuss what evidence exactly suggests that master painters sold entirely autograph pictures, whether or not buyers may have had a special interest in these, and what – if anything – we could deduce from master painters signing habits. Secondly, I will look into seventeenth-century texts on connoisseurship, especially at insights as to attributing pictures. Do these texts indicate that seventeenth-century connoisseurs were as keen as we are today to recognise the master's hand or did they have somewhat different priorities?

The master's name and its implications

No longer the anonymous craftsmen they had often been in medieval times, in early modern Europe, successful artists were able to gain an increasing amount of fame and independence for themselves. They appeared from behind their works and placed themselves in the foreground, attracting attention to themselves by signing their works, initially, mostly with monograms, and later with their names spelled out in full. If they were really famous, just their first names would have sufficed: Michelangelo, Titian, Raphael, Rembrandt ....[28]

The artist's position changed most rapidly in Italy. In 1501, after having tried to give the painter Gentile Bellini a specific commission, Isabella d'Este eventually let him decide for himself what scene from classical history or mythology he would paint for her.[29] Another collector, Federico Gonzaga, went a step further, in his 1527 request to Michelangelo; he had no requirements at all as to the subject matter, format or medium; all he wanted was that the work was'of his [Michelangelo's] genius', 'an example of his unique ability'.[30]

In the Netherlands, the artist's reputation as the creator of 'unique' works also gained weight, and gradually increased over time. Tellingly, around 1600 print collectors started to organise their prints by artists' names, whereas sixteenth-century print collections had usually been grouped by subject.[31] As the art market boomed in the early seventeenth century, more artists than ever began signing their works, often still with monograms, yet increasingly with their full names, emphasising their role as individual creators.[32] Although the signing habits of painters could vary considerably (Rubens, for example, barely signed his works at all), the general knowledge of artists names increased greatly. Witness the dazzling variety of artists names mentioned in probate inventories throughout the century, for instance (see below).

But, despite this growing emphasis on the artist's individual name, its use was not very individualised in early modern Europe. A striking example comes from Vasari's biography of the renaissance master Giulio Romano, in which he describes an artwork as follows: 'It was the best carton that he [Giulio] had ever made, and it was executed by Fermo Guisoni, who has since then become an excellent master himself.'[33] A work could count as being by a master if it was done under his supervision and after his design, and it was common for masters to collaborate with their assistants not only on large-scale commissions but also on modestly-sized paintings. For example, when Giulio himself was not yet an independent master, his master Raphael reputedly used his assistance in all of his greatest works, including his famous panel paintings *Portrait of Leo X with two Cardinals* (Uffizi, Florence) and his *Portrait of Giovanna of Aragon* (Louvre, Paris).[34]

It was also common in the Netherlands of the early seventeenth century for masters to attach their names to paintings that were in part or largely executed by their pupils and assistants. Witness, for example, a laudatory poem on Van Mander's *Schilderboeck* (1604). The writer likens Van Mander's book to a picture of Pittura, the personification of the art of painting. This metaphorical portrait has benefited from many contributions in the form of painted jewellery, much in the same way that Van

Mander benefited from those who brought the art of painting to greater heights and thus enriched the art of painting. However, Van Mander deserves to sign the work as an 'original' (*principael*), since he is responsible for the most impressive part: a crown of pearls on Pittura's head. He would have made 'a mistake' (*faut bedrijvet*), 'if he had not written his name at the bottom of the work' (*Soo hy sich self daer onder niet en schrijvet*).[35] Admittedly, a lot of research remains to be done as to specific master's studio habits. However, on the basis of the available evidence, we can already conclude that the master's signature could function as a 'trademark', a 'logo of a studio style' or even as a 'brand name', in the terms coined by Svetlana Alpers, Ann Jensen Adams, Koenraad Jonckheere and Tine Nygaard respectively (see also Koenraad Jonckheere's essay, pp. 69-95).[36] However, it was not a guarantee that a work was painted solely by the hand of the master himself.[37]

But if a painter's name did not guarantee that the work was executed by the master himself, then how did seventeenth-century painters and connoisseurs classify different types of studio products? Did seventeenth-century painters and their public differentiate between various types of studio products? And what role, if any, did signatures play in this respect?

Distinctions in seventeenth-century inventories and notarial deeds

Seventeenth-century inventories and notarial deeds give a fairly coherent view of seventeenth-century categories of thought. As briefly mentioned above, artists names appear with increasing frequency in probate inventories from the beginning of the seventeenth century, not only in those inventories belonging to painters and collectors but also in those of burghers who owned but a modest amount of works. So far, research of inventories in Delft, Amsterdam, Antwerp, Haarlem, Leiden and Dordrecht indicate similar patterns.

While in sixteenth-century inventories the creators of pictures were seldomly mentioned, the number of pictures that was attributed to a particular master rose around the turn of the seventeenth century. In Antwerp, for example, the numbers of pictures that were identified as originals by a specific master rose steadily to about a quarter of all pictures between 1601 and 1620.[38] From the beginning of the seventeenth century the number of attributed pictures also increased in Amsterdam, while in Delft, the 1640s and 1650s in particular witnessed a growing number of specific attributions in inventories.[39] In Leiden, the number of attributed pictures in a sample of collectors inventories from the 1650s and 1660s was particularly high, amounting to about 40 percent of all the works mentioned.[40]

Admittedly, the specific implications of these early attributions in inventories can be tantalisingly hard to interpret as we often cannot identify the works mentioned and relatively little is known about the notaries and experts that compiled these lists.[41] Moreover, the general boom in the production of paintings, and increasing numbers of works that were signed must have also influenced the listings. Yet, some general patterns are unmistakable. Firstly, there was a growing awareness of both the names of specific masters painters and their hallmark styles. An inventory of the Leiden collector Hendrik Bugge van Ring even mentions as many as 98 different painters' names, and specifies that two pictures by respectively Jan Steen and Gerrit Dou were done 'in their youth' (*in sijn jonckheyt*).[42] Secondly, a number of different descriptive terms were used to classify works.[43] Basically, two main distinctions were made, which partially overlap. Pictures were often labelled as either an original, a copy or a work in a certain master's style (see below). Another distinction concerned the master's share: the overwhelming majority of the attributed works is given to master painters, but in a few rare instances, a picture is identified as by a pupil (*discipel*) of a master and/or mentioned as retouched (*geretokkeert*) by the master. Before discussing these distinctions further, I will briefly indicate what other descriptive terms can be found. Especially artist's inventories also occasionally contain terms indicating that a picture was unfinished. For example, pictures were described as '*gemodelt*' / '*gebootst*' (sketched), '*gedoodverwet*' (underpainted), or simply as '*niet opgemaect*' (not completed). Lastly, one can also find descriptive terms indicating the quality of a work, often in very general terms. For example, the 1682 inventory of the painter Claes Moyaert mentions 11 '*sleghte schilderijen*' (mediocre paintings), while the above mentioned inventory of the collector Hendrik Bugge mentions two pictures by an unidentified yet 'good master from the province of Brabant' (*een goet Brabants meester*).[44]

As to the distinction between originals and copies, the term 'original' (*principael / origineel*) meant that a certain work was a new creation, thus not a copy. It was used for works attributed to master painters; new compositions invented by pupils were usually described as simply a 'piece' (*stuckje*).[45] A copy, on the other hand, was based on a prototype, and therefore generally a cheaper type of picture. As Hans Van Miegroet and Neil De Marchi have shown, copies were valued at about 50 percent of the price of an original when done by the same master as the original.[46] However, this does not mean that copies could not occasionally be valuable. The 1659 inventory of the well-informed collector baron Willem Vincent van Wyttenhorst specifies that two copies by Cornelis van Poelenburch after originals by Adam Elsheimer were even 'held in higher esteem than the original' (*wort hooger als het principael geacht*).[47] Lastly, pictures could also be described as 'in the manner' (*aert, handelinge, manier*) of a particular master. Usually the maker of such works is not identified and their price estimates were low, although there were exceptions. A document related to the inventory of the painter Cornelis Dusart, dated 7 March 1703, mentions two paintings 'done in the manner (*manier*) of Berchem by Dusart's pupil Wynand de Haas, which were estimated at 20 guilders, which was double the price of a small picture of a smoking figure by Jan Steen mentioned in the same document.[48]

As mentioned earlier, the most commonly used term for 'original', 'principal' only specified that the picture was not a copy and thus did not make any claim as to whether a work was autograph or not.[49] In my opinion, the less commonly used term for 'original' ('*origineel*') had the same meaning.[50] Jaap van der Veen suspected that 'original' may have implied that the work was purely by the hand of the master on the basis of a passage in Junius's treatise *The Painting of the Ancients*, in which he describes the connoisseurs of his time: '...most are wont to prove their knowledge of art by being able to immediately distinguish originals from copies. The works that the excellent masters themselves have made after life, are here referred to as original pieces.'[51] However, this passage is so unspecific – Junius contrasts originals by masters and copies by pupils in a very general way, without mentioning any other type of painting – that the reasoning becomes circular: if 'original' implied that a picture was autograph, then the occasional use of the term would illustrate that there was an interest in purely autograph pictures. As I have not come across a seventeenth-century use of the term '*origineel*' which clearly differentiates its meaning from the term '*principael*', I subscribe to the conclusion of the linguist Lydia de Pauw-de Veen, namely that these terms were used interchangeably.[52] Of course, this does not exclude the possibility that some originals may have been purely autograph. However, before discussing the questions of how common it may have been for painters to create purely autograph works and if connoisseurs and art theorists had a particular preference for these, I will first look more closely at the distinction made between masterpieces and works by pupils.

Master, pupil or 'retouched'

By far most attributions in seventeenth-century inventories concern master painters, although occasionally, especially in inventories belonging to artists and dealers, a picture is identified as a work by a pupil (*discipel* or '*leerling*'). For example, the 1669 inventory of the Amsterdam collector Laurens Mauritsz Douci identifies a picture as 'A cave by a pupil of Karel van der Hooch' (*Een grot van een discipel van Karel van de Hooch*), estimated at the relatively low price of 8 Carolus guilders.[53] This differentiation between works by masters and those by pupils indicates that not all paintings produced in a master's studio could pass under his name. In fact, the master's name must have guaranteed at least a minimum level of quality.

The same conclusion can be drawn from a variety of contracts and notarial deeds, which both suggest that a variety of pictures could pass under artist's name, and that there was a bottom line in terms of quality. For example, when the painter Isack van Duijnen was confronted with a buyer who believed he had just bought a good picture by Van Duijnen, the painter reputedly replied: 'that is not by me, but by one of my worst pupils, I pity you, for you have been deceived. Broekman [the dealer] bought it from me for five guilders and I did not want to pass it off as a painting by me'.[54] A carefully phrased judgement by Jacob van Ruisdael when asked in 1661 if a certain picture was by Porcellis similarly suggests that a certain amount of input by others would be acceptable in a work sold under Porcellis's name but also that there was a definitive bottom line, judging that : 'if the before-mentioned Porcellis has started this work ... the piece is nowadays altered to such an extent, that it would be inapt to sell it as a Porcellis'.[55] Together with the other painters that were consulted on this issue, he stated that the picture was simply 'not worthy to be sold ... as a piece by Porcellis'.[56]

In a work contract drawn up in 1648 for the prolific painter Jacob Jordaens, this line of thought is explained even more explicitly. Jordaens was to produce 35 ceiling paintings for the Swedish court, which would be painted 'partly by himself and partly by others, as Jordaens can most aptly judge himself. And that which will be painted by others, he is obliged to paint over to such an extent, that it will be considered Jordaens's own work and therefore be entitled to bear his name and signature.'[57] Moreover, the Rotterdam painter Johannes van Vucht agreed in 1635 to deliver paintings which 'will be allowed to pass as work by Van Vucht, such as he has previously delivered to [the art dealer] Van Waesberge, and signed with his own hand'.[58] Similar statements can be found in a variety of artistic commissions drawn up throughout Europe, witness, for example, a commission given to the Italian sculptor Bernini by the French minister of State Colbert on 9 December 1669. Bernini was to use students from the newly founded French Academy in Rome in the execution of an equestrian statue of King Louis XIV. But Bernini had to execute the head himself and apply the final touches so that 'one can say with truth that the work is entirely by you'.[59] Similarly, Rubens used the phrase 'by my hand' to describe works which he had in fact not painted entirely by himself, as we will see.[60]

Phrases such as 'the master's own work' or work 'by his hand' thus denoted a quality distinction. Where exactly the line was drawn between a work that could count as by the master's hand, worthy of carrying the master's signature, and one identified as by a pupil and/or as retouched by the master must have depended on the individual master and his personal judgement. It is very rare that we can identify a painting that is listed in a seventeenth-century document as by an anonymous 'pupil' and/or as retouched by the master. However, the little available evidence suggests that works described as by a 'pupil' and/or as 'retouched' must have differed noticeably from the master's usual level of quality.

This can be deduced from statements in contracts and notarial deeds explaining that if a work was retouched substantially enough, it could, in fact, count as by the master, such as the above cited examples of Jordaens and Van Vucht illustrate. Thus, if a work was explicitly identified as 'retouched', it must have been a cheaper kind of picture. Rubens, for example, sold retouched student copies for cheaper prices than his higher quality pictures. As he explained in a letter to the British collector Dudley Carleton, 'retouched copies ... show more for their price' (see also below, p. 43 and Natasja Peeters' essay, p. 120).[61] The mention of six retouched paintings in Rembrandt's inventory of 1656 (drawn up during the master's lifetime) suggests that Rembrandt also produced cheaper pictures.[62]

As to pupil work, the terms used in such descriptions seem telling: '*leerling*' or '*discipul*'. These were pupils training with their first or second masters. Although the term '*discipul*' seems to have generally indicated a more advanced student than the term '*leerling*', the use of these terms varied a bit.[63] For example, an elaborate draft statute of the Haarlem painter's guild dated 1631, uses the terms '*leerling*' and 'disciple' interchangeably to refer to pupils in their first three years of training, and distinguishes them sharply from paid assistants or journeymen (in Dutch '*werckgesel*' or '*vrije gast*'). In order to become an independent master, one had to work at least three years as a pupil ('*leerling*' or '*discipul*') and subsequently at least one year as journeyman ('*werckgesel*' or '*vrije gast*') for a master, according to this draft statute.[64]

Interestingly, no seventeenth-century document lists a painting as by a '*gesel*' or paid assistant of a certain master painter, which to me suggests that their share in the studio production must have commonly counted as 'by the master' if it was done in the master's style. In some instances, these journeymen or paid assistants even worked quite independently, creating works of their own invention and signing these with their own names. In Haarlem, this was not uncommon; witness paintings by Judith Leyster and Pieter de Grebber which these artists signed before they became independent masters.[65] As master painters had to pay the guild a much higher contribution for having journeymen (paid assistants) than for having pupils it seems in any case unlikely that they would have sold a journeyman's work while calling it the work of a '*werckgesel*' or '*vrije gast*'.[66]

To conclude, the seventeenth-century distinction between works that could pass as by a certain master and those ascribed to usually nameless 'pupils' of his cannot be equated to the present-day tendency to separate purely autograph work from works which were partially or entirely done by pupils and assistants. Although it may not be possible to reconstruct exactly where a seventeenth-century master would have drawn the line, the quality of 'pupil work' must have contrasted with the usual quality of pictures sold under the master's name.

Further distinctions: a preference for autograph pictures?

The fact that various types of studio collaborations – though certainly not all studio products – could leave the studio under the master's name, raises the question of whether these then all enjoyed a similar value. Did master painters make further quality distinctions? To what extent were contemporary buyers aware of the different types of studio collaboration? Did painters keep their working methods a secret or were they relatively open about their practices? And is there any evidence that painters or buyers had a special interest in autograph works done by the master alone or was the master's name indeed merely a guarantee of a certain involvement and quality?

As with the exact type of studio collaboration, the openness of master painters about their studio practices must have varied from one master to the next. And although some connoisseurs were able to confidently recognise the master's hand (see below), certainly not all buyers had such a keen eye and some in fact did not realise that a signed work was not necessarily painted by the master himself. A curious document in the Delft archive illustrates such a misunderstanding. In 1644, a certain Sybert Dogger, the owner of a painting signed by Willem van Aelst, claimed in an official bet that his picture was by this master and referred to the signature to prove his point. He was challenged by Adam Pick, a little-known painter of farm scenes, who stated he could demonstrate that, despite the signature, the work was not painted by Van Aelst and that the latter had not even touched it.[67] Interestingly, Dogger seems unaware of the possibility that master painters could sign works that were not or not entirely executed by themselves, and that signatures could even be falsified. Pick, on the other hand, who had himself been a pupil of Van Aelst, was clearly not impressed by the signature.

Four legal statements that Jaap van der Veen gathered even address the question of whether or not a certain picture was executed entirely by the master himself.[68] In a document dated 1606, a certain Mr. van Leeuwen declared he would provide two 'originals' (*principaele stukken*) one by Abraham Bloemaert and one by Gillis van Coninxloo and that 'no-one but the afore-mentioned two masters had worked on the afore-mentioned pieces'.[69] Moreover, Ambrosius Bosschaert in 1615 declared that he had created a flower still life entirely by his own hand 'without having anyone else contribute with their hand or work on it'.[70] Similarly, Jan Miense Molenaer in 1653 declared that two paintings – a peasant scene and one with a stone surgeon – had been made by him 'without anyone else having contributed something to these'.[71] Lastly, in a document dated 1658, two witnesses declared that Bartholomeus van der Helst had stated that he had painted a certain picture of Diana and that it was an original, not a copy. When he was subsequently asked if anyone else had contributed to the piece, he shook his head.

While Van der Helst may have been lying – since he only shook his head, he could always say that he had never actually said so – these sources are nonetheless telling. On the one hand, these documents indicate that it was not self-evident that a work signed and sold as by a certain master was indeed entirely executed by that master. On the other hand, they suggest that at least some painters deliberately created purely autograph works and in doing so provided both seventeenth-century buyers and present-day connoisseurs with the certainty that at least some of their works can be expected to have been done solely by their own hand. Moreover, at least four owners were so keen on proving that their work was indeed by a specific master that they demanded a written guarantee, an 'expert-opinion' or '*Gutachtung*' avant-la-lettre.

As to how exactly painters presented their pictures when selling them to customers, very little is known. One unique exception is the correspondence between Peter Paul

Rubens and the British ambassador to the Netherlands, Sir Dudley Carleton. In exchange for Carleton's collection of antique sculptures, Rubens offered him a choice of a number of 'paintings by [his] hand' which he had available in his studio, in such a way that the total value of the pictures would match that of the antique sculptures.[72] As Carleton did not have the opportunity to see the paintings for himself, Rubens described the pictures fairly extensively in a letter dated 28 April 1618. Although all of the pictures counted as 'by Rubens's hand', they were not literally painted just by him. In fact, Rubens distinguished five different types of studio products: originals by his hand, originals by his hand with a contribution by a specialist (an animal by Snyders or a landscape by an unidentified landscape specialist[73]), copies by pupils after his own work that were retouched by himself, one unfinished copy by a pupil that Rubens promised to finish so well that it would count as an original by his hand, and lastly, works started by pupils and retouched by Rubens himself.

Interestingly the copies and works begun by pupils which were subsequently worked on by the master himself do not differ much in price from originals by Rubens' hand. For example, a single-figure 4 x 7 foot painting of Saint Sebastian by Rubens was the same price of 300 guilders as a single-figure 5 x 7 foot painting of Susanna, which was started by a pupil and retouched by Rubens. A worked-up copy of a Lion Hunt (8 x 11 feet) carried the same 600 guilder price as a slightly larger original painting of Daniel in the Lion's Den by the master himself (8 x 12 feet). Because we can only identify the last work, it is hard to say what could explain this remarkable price difference; perhaps the picture of the hunt contained more figures (on the pricing of Rubens' pictures, see also essay Natasja Peeters below, esp. p. 107 ff). In general, the relatively similar prices indicate that Rubens considered all these works to be of good quality.[74]

Carleton subsequently chose works Rubens described as by his own hand and the ones he did with specialists.[75] For this reason, the correspondence between Carleton and Rubens has been interpreted as unique evidence that at least one affluent art lover had a preference for purely autograph originals.[76] However, it seems more accurate to state that among the works that could count as by Rubens' hand, Carleton picked the works of the highest quality whether these were technically entirely by Rubens' hand or not. For Carleton did not seem to mind the hand of another master or a specialist assistant; he picked a painting of Prometheus with an eagle by the animal specialist Snyders, as well as a painting of leopards with a landscape by an unnamed specialist. Moreover, he did not protest when Rubens let him know that his landscape specialist had worked up parts of several pictures that the master had described as purely by his own hand: 'According to my habit, I have taken a specialist gentleman to finish the landscapes only to increase the taste of Your Excellency but in the other parts please be assured that I have not allowed a living soul to touch these works', Rubens wrote on 28 May 1618.[77] By that time, Carleton had also accepted a worked-up copy (the *Lion's Hunt*) and a work started by a pupil (the *Susanna*) as part of the exchange, after Rubens promised he would retouch them so extensively that they would have the same 'quality' (*bontà*) as originals by his hand.[78]

When describing the various pictures to Carleton, Rubens indicated subtle gradations in quality and price among works that all counted as 'by his hand'. As to what extent other masters differentiated between pictures they sold under their own names, much research remains to be done. It seems likely, however, that master painters who collaborated with pupils and or assistants in various ways like Jordaens and Van Miereveld would have made similar price and quality distinctions. Interestingly, one such master, Gerrit van Honthorst, seems to have indicated variations in the quality of his paintings by altering his signature.

Quality distinctions reflected in the signature

In the paintings Gerrit van Honthorst produced for the Oranjezaal in Huis ten Bosch, he used two distinct signatures: his name 'GvHonthorst' and 'GvHonthorts fe[cit]', the latter reads in latin: made by Gerrit van Honthorst. (figs. 4, 5 and 6) Jolanda de Bruijn, who extensively researched three of the five works which Honthorst was commissioned to make for the Oranjezaal, *Allegory on the Marriage of Frederik Hendrik and Amalia van Solms*, *Wiliam II's Reception of Mary Stuart upon her Arrival in the Netherlands*, and *Frederik Hendrik's Steadfastness,* noticed distinct differences in execution between these three pictures. She considered *Frederick Henry's Steadfastness*, signed with the longer signature, to be more skilfully and efficiently executed than the other two works: the figures were well-rounded, showing subtle gradations in skin colour, including a bluish middle tone, which were largely lacking in the other works. She thus speculated that the signature 'GvHonthorst' indicated studio products of lesser quality than the painting signed 'GvHonthorts fe[cit]'.[79] While the master in both instances must have obviously thought the pictures worthy of carrying his name, he seemed much more closely involved in the actual execution of the work signed with the longer signature.

Although Honthorst's most recent oeuvre catalogue does not distinguish various quality levels among the pictures attributed to Honthorst, this seems a worthwhile pursuit.[80] Out of the 295 history paintings and pastoral scenes labelled authentic, 31 carry the longer 'GvHonthorst fe[cit]' signature, including some of his most famous masterpieces such as his *Saint Sebastian* (National Gallery London) and the *Merry Fiddler* (Rijksmuseum, Amsterdam).[81] If authentic, these signatures seem certainly worthy of further study. Interestingly, only about 14 of the 224 portraits attributed to Honthorst in the catalogue carry the 'GvHonthorst fe[cit]' signature, which could possibly mean that the master was less closely involved with the many portraits produced in his studio.[82]

While Honthorst's practice may at first sight seem rather curious, an anecdote which was mentioned by several seventeenth-century art theorists, explains it. Already in antiquity, artists reputedly used their signature to indicate distinct quality levels. According to the ancient writer Pliny, some of the most famous painters and sculptors had inscribed the majority of their works with a signature disclaiming finality, such as 'Apelles faciebat' (being made by Apelles) or simply 'Polyclitus'. Reputedly, they did so out of modesty to indicate that these artworks were not finished. Moreover, it gave them a means to save their face should one such work be criticized. They could claim they would have made a desired correction if only the work had not been taken from them by forces beyond their control. According to Pliny, solely three artworks were known to carry a signature implying completion ('X fecit', 'Made by X'), testifying of the supreme confidence the artists had in these particular pieces.[83] In the seventeenth century, this story was recounted by Karel van Mander, Etienne Binet and Franciscus Junius among others.[84]

Thus far, the signing habits of seventeenth-century Netherlandish painters have not been studied in relation to this story. Netherlandish painters all regularly used Latin phrases when signing their works, and many of them probably realised the connotations of the different Latin phrases. In the case of Honthorst, his signing habits match the art theoretical account so literally that he must have known the story. It would be interesting to know in how far other painters (especially those heading larger workshops) used distinct signatures to distinguish between various levels of quality of their paintings, and how possible distinctions would have been reflected in the price. Also, could the addition of 'f' after the artist's name, which is commonly interpreted as an abbreviation of '*fecit*', also stand for '*faciebat*', and indicate a deliberate attempt by the painter to not specify exactly how finished he judged the work to be?

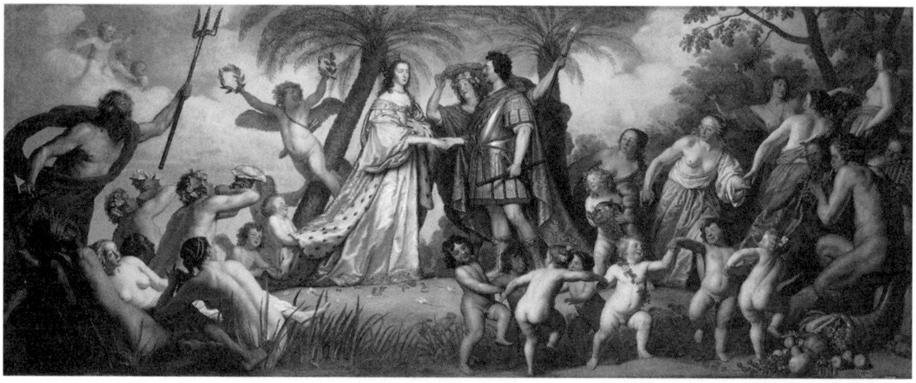

4.

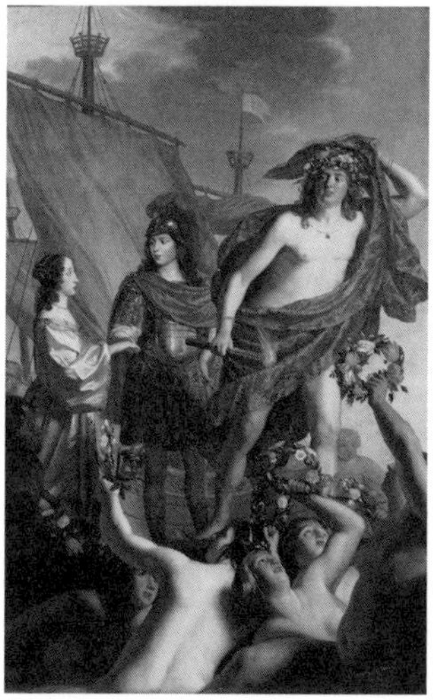

5.

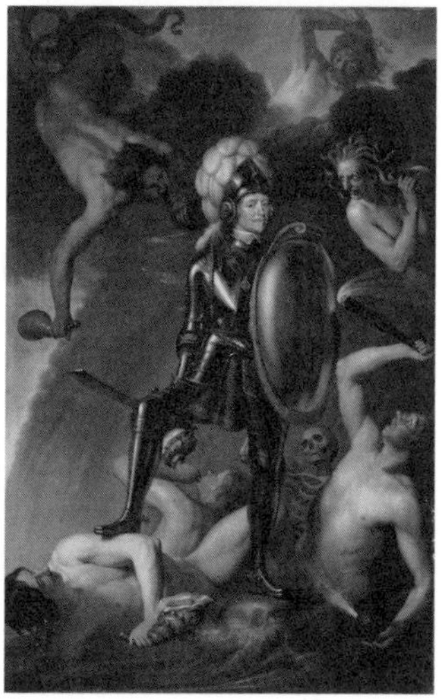

6.

4. Gerrit van Honthorst, see colorplate p. 180
Allegory on the Marriage of Frederik Hendrik and Amalia van Solms, 1651
Oranjezaal, Huis ten Bosch

5. Gerrit van Honthorst, see colorplate p. 180
Wiliam II's Reception of Mary Stuart upon her Arrival in the Netherlands, 1649
Oranjezaal, Huis ten Bosch

6. Gerrit van Honthorst, see colorplate p. 180
The Constancy of Frederik Hendrik, after 1649
Oranjezaal, Huis ten Bosch

Seventeenth-century insights as to attributing pictures

Studio practices and signing habits are of course crucial when trying to recognise the master's hand and to attribute seventeenth-century pictures. Various seventeenth-century sources on connoisseurship throw some further light on contemporary ideas about authenticity, for they give an impression of seventeenth-century attribution practices, and therefore help to answer the question of whether these early connoisseurs faced problems that are similar to what we face today. What elements did they consider particularly revealing? How did seventeenth-century connoisseurs go about attributing paintings that were not necessarily painted by the master alone? Were they able to distinguish between different hands within a painting? And did they care to distinguish workshop assistance?

Manner

Although the design of pictures could be of great importance when attributing pictures, many specific recommendations in the early literature on connoisseurship focus on the execution.[85] Most early writers on connoisseurship believed that a painter's characteristic manner could best be recognised in areas that are executed with a certain boldness and resolution. Such areas were seen as particularly hard to imitate, which also explained why paintings done in a bold or free manner were more easily distinguished from copies than pictures done in a very precise and fine manner. As a general rule of thumb, the painter's characteristic handwriting was to be found in those passages in which the painter did not follow nature too closely but relied on his imagination and inborn talents. The advice on which areas tended to be particularly telling varied a bit from one author to the next. In the first draft of his chapter on 'judging pictures' (*Considerazioni sulla Pittura*, c. 1617-19) Giulio Mancini pointed out muscles and draperies as examples, but with an ellipsis he indicated that he intended to elaborate his thoughts later. In the more elaborate version written in c. 1620, Mancini stated that locks of hair, ringlets in beards, the definition of eyes as well as confidently applied light and dark accents in the folds and highlights of drapery were all good examples of areas where the master's manner and resolution could be recognised. Mancini himself did not give a specific example of these confident drapery folds; however, his analysis seems applicable to the execution of drapery in Jan Steen's paintings, particularly the characteristic accents that Van Dantzig labelled the 'mussel stroke'(fig. 7).

Two decennia earlier, Karel van Mander was even more explicit. In his view, a painter's characteristic 'spirit' (*gheest*) could best be recognised in the depiction of 'leaves, hair, air and draperies' (*bladen, hayr, locht, en laken*). He added that, out of these elements, the depiction of draperies was the most dependent on the painter's spirit – presumably because the painter here enjoyed the greatest freedom of invention and execution, since draperies can be depicted in a sheer endless variety of shapes, textures and colours.

When Van Mander discussed the uniqueness of an artist's manner of painting,[86] he indeed frequently focussed on characteristic details such as the depiction of hair and a drapery. For example, when comparing Lucas van Leyden's prints to similar works by Dürer, Van Mander observes that Lucas van Leyden had 'a different, sweeter, more continuous manner of incision with which he depicted his receding and flowing drapery'.[87] (fig. 8 and fig. 9)

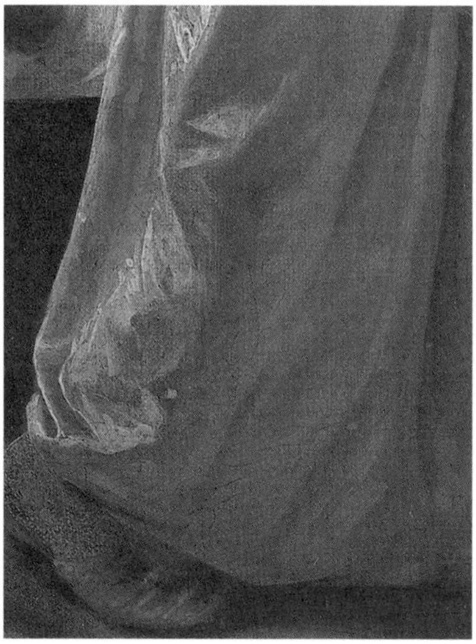

7.

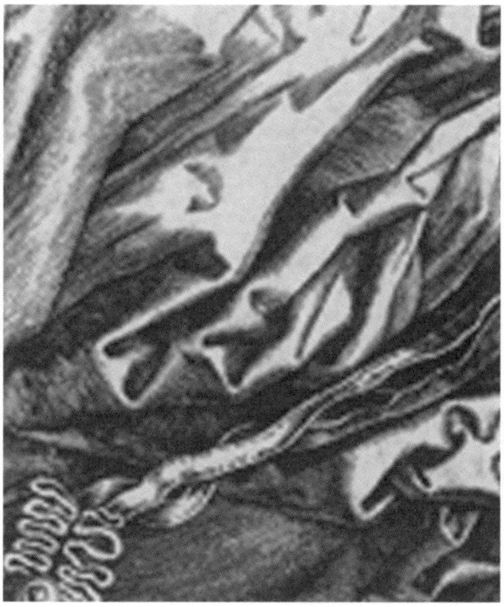

8.

7. Jan Steen, see colorplate p. 179 (entire painting)
Merry Family (*So de Oude Songen, Pijpen de Jonge*) [detail], 1668
Rijksmuseum, Amsterdam

8. Albrecht Dürer, see plate p. 181 (entire painting)
Melancholia [detail of the drapery figure Melancholia], 1514
Rijksmuseum, Amsterdam

9. Lucas van Leyden, see plate p. 181 (entire painting)
The Holy Family [detail of the drapery figure right foreground], 1506-1510
Rijksmuseum, Amsterdam

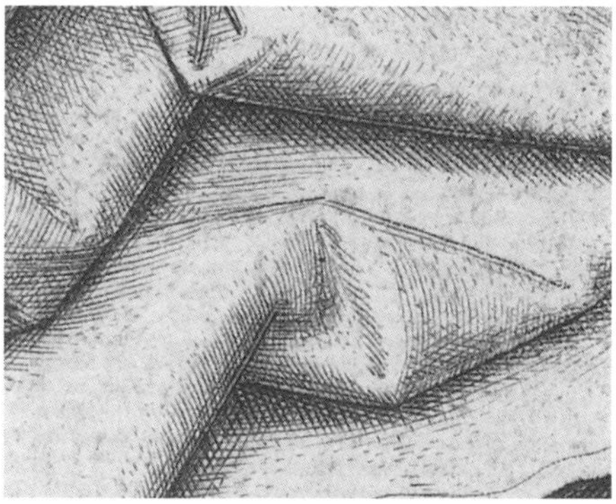

9.

Moreover, when discussing Holbein, Van Mander notes that this painter had a certain 'firmness in drafting and painting' which one can see in all his works, and an orderly way of building up his works which was 'very different from other painters'. He explained this by pointing out how Holbein depicted hair or a beard: he would first paint the area in general terms with perfectly accurate shadows, and once this layer was dry, he would paint the hairs or beard very naturally over it with a free-flowing brush.[88] (fig. 10)

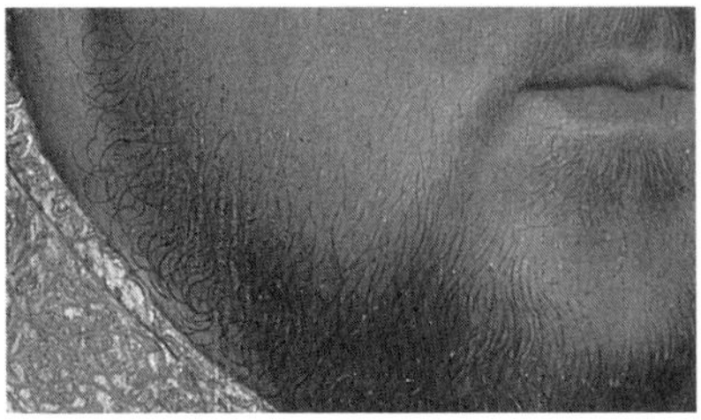

10. Hans Holbein, see colorplate p. 182
(entire painting)
Henry VIII, [detail], c. 1536
Thyssen-Bornemisza Collection, Madrid.

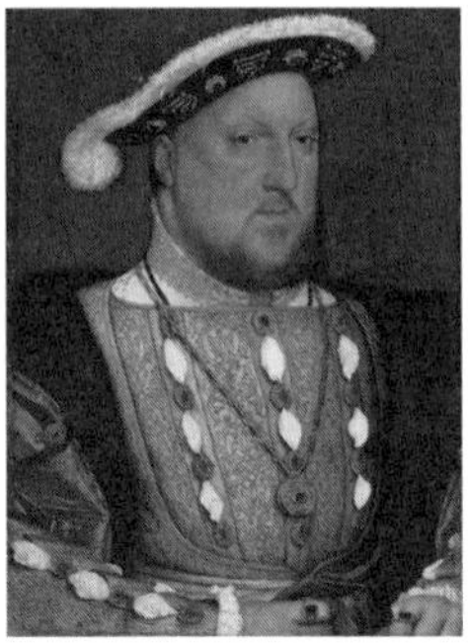

10.

As to the depiction of leaves, it seems important to realise that in Van Mander's time, Netherlandish painters did not often base their depictions of trees on close observation of natural trees but preferred to invent a manner that would convincingly evoke nature.[89] Having a convincing manner and matching brush technique to suggest leaves in painting remained important throughout the century; compare, for example, Jacob van Ruisdael's hallmark dense foliage with Meindert Hobbema's airy depiction of leaves, often silhouetted against the sky. However, very few painters (Jacob van Ruisdael being one of the exceptions) combined their specific manner with botanical accuracy. (fig. 11 and fig. 12)

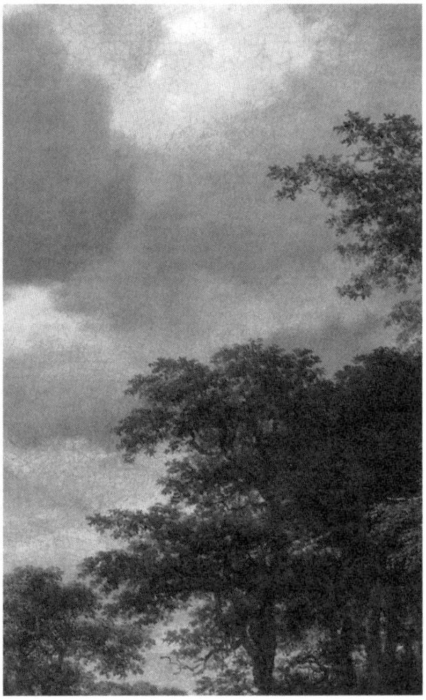

11.

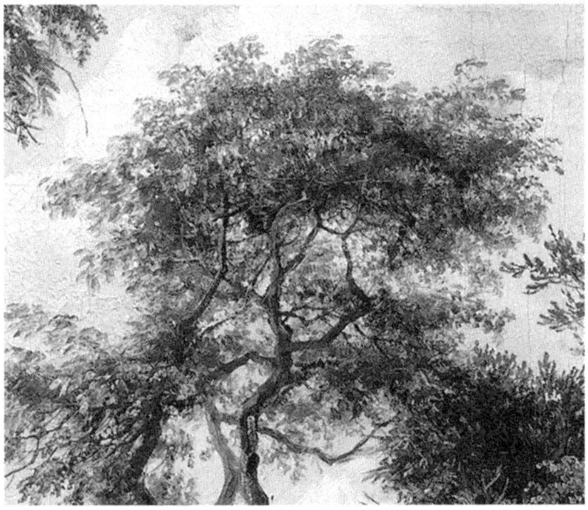

12.

11. Jacob van Ruisdael, see colorplate p. 183
(entire painting)
Forest Scene [detail of the foliage], c. 1655
National Gallery of Art, Washington, D.C.

12. Meindert Hobbema, see colorplate p. 183
(entire painting)
Farm in the Sunlight [detail of the foliage], c. 1668
National Gallery of Art, Washington, D.C.

By the mid-seventeenth-century, Van Mander's observation that a painter's characteristic spirit could readily be recognised in the depiction of leaves, was fairly widespread knowledge; Charles Alphonse du Fresnoy's dictionary of painting terms lists 'the touch of trees' (*de slag van bomen*): 'One says that the trees in this landscape have been depicted with a very recognisable touch, or this Painter hits his trees well.'[90]

As noted above, the insights as to exactly which elements were 'telling' varied somewhat from one author to the next. For example, Cornelis de Bie believed that light and dark accents in the paintings of Gerrit van Honthorst were particularly 'spirited' (*gheestig*)", while Paul Fréart de Chantelou recorded in his diary that Bernini believed that the depictions of hands were especially revealing.[91] However, all these characteristics seem to have one common denominator: an inventive and resolute execution.

The paradox of seventeenth-century connoisseurship

So far, the elements discussed as important are those which show distinctly individual brush marks. Indeed, much like handwriting specialists looked for resolute turns and curves in free-hand writing, so aspiring connoisseurs were advised to look for characteristic habits of the brush.[92] This practice of singling out the individual handwriting of the painter seems to be in sharp contrast with what is known about seventeenth-century studio practices. For how can the practice of singling out individual hands be reconciled with the habit of master painters to also sign works that they had not necessarily executed entirely by themselves? It is this seeming contradiction that I call the paradox of seventeenth-century connoisseurship.

While some of the above-mentioned advice seems to suggest that at least some early modern connoisseurs were primarily looking for individual habits of the brush and thus for individual hands, there is reason to believe that their thinking was, in fact, not necessarily at odds with contemporary studio practice; that their search for the master's characteristic touch did not necessarily mean they were looking for purely autograph works. In my opinion, two passages in Junius and Hoogstraten's treatises are particularly telling in this respect. Although both authors have been mentioned before in relation to seventeenth-century studio practices, these passages have not yet been studied in this context. When discussing how a knowledgeable art lover should look at a painting, Junius stresses the fact that not all of the elements in a painting were equally important. Therefore he advises his readers to not pay undue attention to unimportant areas, to the mere '*byworke*' or '*parerga*' as these were called in Latin: 'because the Artificers goe over these workes slightly and with a light hand, so it is that we doe likewise for the most part examine them more negligently.'[93]

Some 40 years later, Samuel van Hoogstraten repeated Junius's warning and used his practical experience as a painter to clarify the reasoning: 'It is certainly amusing to listen in when sometimes ignorant yet conceited art lovers, wanting to point out the best part of a certain piece, pick out something so ordinary, which the Master executed practically in his sleep, or at least while he was resting from his more important tasks. The ancients saw these as excesses or extras to the important tasks, and they called these *Parerga*; in the works of great Masters these are usually done by pupils and novices, or by some others, who were able to create these.'[94] According to Van Hoogstraten, the workshop practice should thus be taken into account when looking at a painting; erudite art lovers (connoisseurs) should focus on the masterly passages, not on the subsidiary work.

Contrary to Junius, however, Samuel van Hoogstraten had, as noted, first-hand experience as a painter. He had trained with Rembrandt and it is tempting to think that his treatise, which often seems to reflect Rembrandt's thinking, also does when he is discussing *parerga*. His statement that all great masters used assistance in their work is, in any case, revealing. It was a practice of which Hoogstraten approved, as he also stresses elsewhere: 'I will gladly allow a master to use the assistance of others, who are experienced in 'subordinate passages (*bywerk*)' in major works; but he who wants to rightfully carry the name of Master of History Painting should also know how to do the 'subordinate passages (*bywerk*)' [himself] in case this is urgently needed.'[95]

The distinction between masterly and subordinate passages is, in my opinion, very important. Interestingly, the passages that were labelled by the different early art theorists as particularly telling when trying to attribute a picture, show parallels with what was seen as 'masterly' and 'difficult', as we will see below, passages which were in fact often executed by the master. Although the specific areas that the different art theorists singled out as illustrative could also refer to secondary passages – in particular leaves and draperies were not necessarily key elements in a seventeenth-century painting – their description of how a master's characteristic style can be recognised suggests that such elements were only considered important if executed soundly. In the history paintings that Rubens sent to Carleton, for example, the figures, not the background landscapes, were key elements; and I suspect it was for this reason that he had his landscape specialist (probably a paid assistant since he is not mentioned by name) finish these secondary passages and assured Carleton that the other (read: key) parts were entirely by himself. In any case, it looks like seventeenth-century connoisseurs, contrary to later thinkers,[96] did not, in principle, judge all areas of a painting equally important. Instead, when analysing the brushwork the art theorists and connoisseurs whose thoughts have come down to us, all seem to have been looking for bold, resolute and spirited strokes, that is: for touches showing mastery.

Masterly passages

In the art theoretical literature a certain looseness and boldness in the execution of both sketches and finished paintings was associated with mastery. Willem Goeree, for example, explains in his treatise on the art of drawing of 1668 that a finely executed drawing done in the '*reusel*' technique (with parallel strokes one immediately next to the previous one so the result looks uniform) will not look 'masterly' (*meesterlijk*) unless it also contains some quickly and loosely applied accents.[97] Even Philips Angel who generally believed it was better for painters to imitate nature as closely as possible rather than to develop a manner of painting, still strongly praised the 'curious looseness' (*curieuse lossicheyt*) in the brushwork by his favourite painter, Gerard Dou.[98]

Vasari and Van Mander described masterly applied loose strokes not only as difficult to execute, but also as difficult to imitate and, therefore, all the more characteristic of the artist who had created them. Van Hoogstraten also praised the difficulty and mastery evident in loosely executed masterpieces.[99] In France, art lovers even called freely and loosely applied brushwork 'artistically touched' (*artistement touché*).[100] The interest in loose brushwork is further underscored in the amount of terms used to indicate bold and resolute brushwork; Abraham Bosse, for example, uses no less than four different terms: 'artistically touched, sketchy, forceful and proud' (*artiste, croqué, sevelt,* and *fier*).[101]

Together with the design of a picture, the accents that were applied while working up a painting after the main parts had been painted in, were seen as some of the most difficult parts of the painting. This is evident, for example, in a passage from a 1621 French book on eloquence, which aims to give the reader a quick overview of the knowledge necessary to talk eloquently about art: 'The profile, the gestures, the symmetries and proportions, the faces and expressions are those which give a sound to the brush and they are the principle elements in the entire enterprise. The inside is easy to make, but the profile, the last touches and heightening are necessarily the most difficult.'[102] Abraham Bosse similarly stresses how the contours and light and dark areas are often hard to execute: 'a large part of that which makes an element appear in the round and to move away from the viewer and seem to disappear, as well as the contours are all rather difficult to do well.'[103]

It seems logical that master painters would execute such difficult areas singlehandedly and that they would finish and retouch pictures which were (partly) done by pupils and assistants especially in these areas.[104] Interestingly, it is exactly these features, that is: the light and dark accents and final touches which Mancini and De Bie among others singled out as particularly characteristic when describing a painter's personal style, as areas where one can expect to see the master's resolute handling of the brush.[105] According to the painter and art theorist Arnold Houbraken, Frans Hals even had a habit of calling these final touches 'the recognisable features of the master' (*het kennelyke van de meester*).[106]

In fact, it seems like the vocabulary of early modern connoisseurs was mostly geared towards discerning masterly elements in a painting, witness, for example, the terms which De Chambray described as typical of the connoisseurs of his day:

'The Freshness and Loveliness of the Colouring, the Freedom of the brush, the bold Touches, the Colours thickly impasted and well nourished, the separation of the Masses, the Draperies well cast, the rare Folds, the Masterful Strokes, the Grand Manner, the Muscles strongly felt, the beautiful Contours, the beautiful Tints, and the Softness of the Flesh tones, the beautiful Groups, the beautiful Passages, and a great many other chimeries of this kind.'[107]

The flesh tones – mentioned by De Chambray in connection with 'softness' – were also considered hard to paint. In France, there was even a specific expression for the depiction of flesh tones, as Etienne Binet explained in 1621: 'The painter has a good touch, that is to say, he is good at depicting bare skin, that is to say, of the face, of the hands and of the feet for the rest is clothed.'[108] Not surprisingly, perhaps, in seventeenth-century portraits, the face and hands (areas of exposed flesh tones) were commonly painted by the master himself, while pupils and assistants occasionally helped with the secondary elements, such as the clothing and the background.[109]

Beyond the paradox

Although primary sources on seventeenth-century connoisseurship are relatively scarce and there is no reason to assume that all seventeenth-century connoisseurs would have agreed on what elements exactly were the most telling when attributing pictures (if only because master painters' studio practices and styles could vary considerably), the surviving sources seem coherent enough to formulate a hypothesis.

I suspect that an awareness of contemporary studio practices made knowledgeable connoisseurs focus all the more on masterly aspects, that is, more on the main elements than on the subsidiary work (‘*bywerk*’) and more on the difficult and resolute brushwork than on subordinate passages.[110] Also, I suspect that this made the overall quality of the picture all the more important. As we have seen, a picture was worthy of carrying the master’s name if it was made under a master’s supervision and of high enough quality whether or not it was entirely executed by the master himself. It is interesting how many sources on early attributions underscore this reasoning; witness, for example, the largest attribution controversy of the seventeenth century: the Uylenburgh case.

In 1671, the Amsterdam dealer Gerrit Uylenburgh had sold 13 old master paintings to the German Elector of Brandenburgh.[111] Uylenburgh believed the works to be originals by masters such as Michelangelo, Holbein, Titian and Palma il Giovane; however, once the paintings arrived in Berlin, the Elector’s court painter Hendrick Fromantiou dismissed 12 of them as copies.[112] Subsequently, the paintings were returned to the Netherlands and toured the country while both Uylenburgh and Fromantiou collected expert opinions on the status of the pictures.

When asked whether the contested pictures were indeed done by the master under whose name they were sold, most painters and connoisseurs did not answer the question directly, but instead stated that the pictures were either good or not good enough to be sold under the various master’s own names. For example, Philips Koninck reputedly responded that he thought the pictures were ‘painted with virtue and art’ and ‘worthy of carrying the name of the masters under whose name they were sold and that they were estimated and judged to be so by unbiased connoisseurs of Italian art and painters’.[113] Dirck Santvoort and Anthonie de Grebber judged the pictures worthy of hanging in a cabinet of Italian pictures[114], while, on the other hand, the heads of the painters guild in The Hague considered the quality of the pictures ‘not worthy to carry the name of a good master, much less those of such exquisite masters as the ones under whose name they were sold’.[115] Similarly, a number of Antwerp specialists believed the works were ‘not notable [enough] to be sold by such masters’.[116]

Comparable comments can be found in other legal statements. For example, a picture in the manner of the still life painter Den Uyl the Elder was judged ‘not beautiful enough’ (*niet fray genoech*) to be by the master in 1650.[117] Moreover, in the case of a painting in the manner of Porcellis, four painters including Jacob van Ruisdael and Allart van Everdingen, concluded that the painting was not ‘worthy’ (*waerdich*) to be sold as a Porcellis.[118]

These kinds of general quality assessments could also be explained by the possibility that the specialists involved did not have sufficient knowledge of the painter’s specific manner to produce a more accurate assessment. This may indeed have been true, especially in the Uylenburgh case, which concerned exclusively Italian pictures.[119] But even if that was the case, that in itself would also be interesting. For, if it was in any way common to officially record opinions of painting specialists who did not necessarily know much about the specific manners of the painters under whose name contested works had been sold, then to these seventeenth-century viewers quality apparently mattered much more than the specific recognition of the master’s hand. Interestingly, this is also the impression one gets from the high-end market for paintings in the second half of the seventeenth century. Both attributed and unattributed paintings fetched high prices; apparently the increased interest in painters’ names did not mean that the highest end of the market was reserved for attributed works (see below, Koenraad Jonckheere's essay).

The interest in quality even without knowing a painter's name is also evident in a diary entry from Constantijn Huygens Jr., in which he described the art collection of the Elector of Brandenburg, which he saw in 1680 in Berlin. One of the works he found noteworthy he described as 'a good portrait of a woman by the master who made the two figures near a table in the collection of Mr. van Ommeren'.[120] Apparently, Huygens thus memorised the characteristics of paintings he found interesting even without knowing the artist's name.[121]

Collaborations

Although seventeenth-century connoisseurs were, in various cases, able to distinguish different hands within a certain painting, they did not always do so. The desire to identify individual hands seems to have been related to the type of collaboration evident in the picture. Recognising the input of two different masters in one painting was a very different matter from identifying anonymous studio assistants in a well-known master's work.

In art theoretical treatises we can find various examples of paintings mentioned as by a certain master, which were certainly not done solely by this painter. When Van Mander discusses the famous *Portrait of Pope Leo X with Two Cardinals* (c. 1518, Uffizi, Florence) which Raphael painted with the aid of Giulio Romano, he repeats most of Vasari's account, yet fails to mention the input of Giulio Romano. In Vasari's account, Giulio plays a key role since he is fooled by a copy of the portrait thinking he recognised his own brushwork (though what it was exactly that he painted remains unclear). To Van Mander however, Giulio's involvement was apparently not worth mentioning, and he discusses the portrait simply as a 'Raphael'.

When discussing Holbein's painting of *Henry VIII and the Barber Surgeons* (fig. 13), Van Mander's reasoning becomes even more explicit. Van Mander observes that 'There are some people who believe that this work has not been completed in its entirety by Holbein himself. But that after Holbein's death it was completed by someone else; however, if this was the case, this painter has imitated Holbein's manner (*handelinghe*) so sensibly (*verstandig*) that neither a Painter nor an Art expert would distinguish different hands.'[122]

The attribution discussion that Van Mander (and later Von Sandrart also [123]) mentions, is very interesting for several reasons. It is often stated that early connoisseurship developed at a time when the practice of art collecting became more widespread and the art market flourished. And while this was certainly the case, it seems important to remind oneself that this relation was not mutually exclusive; that is to say: attributions and quality judgements were not necessarily made in the context of the art market. Holbein's picture in the Hall of the Barber Surgeons Guild was obviously not for sale, and its attribution or partial de-attribution was not a prelude to giving the work a price tag. The attribution of this large, prestigious work was an end in itself, an interesting topic for intellectual debate.

Van Mander's conclusion is also revealing. Even if the picture is partly done by another hand, he writes, as long as it is well done he does not care to distinguish different hands and neither would, according to him, another painter or art expert.[124] Unfortunately, it is hard to judge the brushwork in this painting since the work has

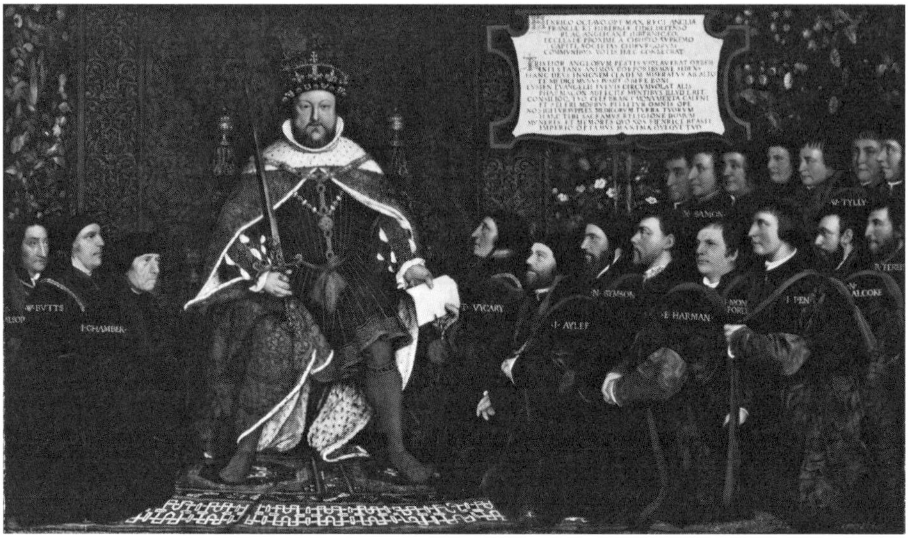

13.

Hans Holbein, see colorplate p. 184
Henry VIII and the Barber Surgeons, begun 1541-43
Hall of the Barber-Surgeons Guild, London

been very heavily restored after it was severely damaged by the Great Fire of London in 1666. However, in this particular instance, we know for sure that the picture was finished after Holbein's death in 1543, since two men depicted in the top row on the right, Mr. X. Salmon and Mr. W. Tully, only became wardens of the guild after Holbein had passed away.[125]

The people who in Van Mander's time stated that the work was finished after Holbein's death were thus right. In my opinion, it is telling that the early seventeenth-century debate focused on a possible contribution to the work done when the master himself could no longer supervise the work. Had the work been completed under Holbein's supervision, I very much doubt there would have been any discussion at all.[126]

Even though this work was completed after Holbein's death, Van Mander believes that no one knowledgeable about the arts would have minded. A similar view can be found in Giulio Mancini's *Considerazioni*. When discussing quality in art, Mancini uses the *Sala di Costantino* as an example of an exquisite Raphael painting.[127] However, it was common knowledge at the time that this room had largely been completed after Raphael's death, a fact that Vasari had discussed extensively in his *Vite*.[128] Mancini knew Vasari's treatise very well, as he wrote a concise comment about it. Moreover, he worked, as the personal physician to the Pope, in the very building in which this fresco series can still be seen. In short, he must have been well aware of the execution process. But, in his view, a work done after Raphael's designs by his own assistants could simply be called a 'Raphael'.

Seventeenth-century connoisseurs were not necessarily against identifying studio input; especially if a picture produced in a master's studio was not worthy of carrying the master's name or when differentiating between various quality levels, the relative shares of master and pupil could be relevant.[129] And if a certain pupil had executed a specific figure in a painting by his master, this might occasionally be worthy of mention. For example, when Van Mander discusses a painting by Maarten van Heemskerk, he somewhat casually mentions that 'the angel is very exceptionally and ornately executed: the lower lips are purplish, which have been done by Jacob Rauwert who lived with him [Van Mander] at the time, as I have heard.'[130] A curious contribution by an assistant could thus, in some instances, be noteworthy, but, in general, seventeenth-century connoisseurs did not seem to have been particularly interested in identifying studio input in great detail. The remarkable absence of mentions of such collaborations in inventories, notarial deeds and personal writings suggests that connoisseurs did indeed examine subordinate passages 'negligently' as Junius and Hoogstraten advised.

As to recognising the hand of two different masters in one painting, this was a pursuit that already intrigued connoisseurs in the early seventeenth-century. Especially in the Southern Netherlands, where specialist collaborations were widespread, the interest seems to have been considerable. For example, in Antwerp, roughly one percent of the attributions recorded in inventories between 1611 and 1650 concerned attributed collaborations, in a sample researched by Elisabeth Honig.[131] In the North, collaborations between two masters also occurred, especially in landscape and architectural paintings in which the figures were sometimes added by another master.[132] However, in the North, the opinions seem to have been divided on the artistic merits of these collaborations. For example, Willem Goeree warned his readers in 1670 that it was better to paint the figures oneself than to have these added by another master. Even if the other master painted better figures, the painting as a whole would not necessarily be improved, according to Goeree, since additional figures usually did not agree with the '*houding*' in a painting, that is: the subtle use of colours, shadows and light to create a sense of pictorial depth.[133]

A fascinating account of the interest in recognising the hands of two different masters within a certain picture comes from a letter by Toby Matthew to Sir Dudley Carleton on 25 February 1617. In this letter, Matthew discusses a hunting piece by Rubens in which Carleton and Matthew thought they had recognised the hand of Snyders:

'Concerning the causinge of anie part thereof to be made by Snyders, that other famous Painter, Y[ou]r L[ordshi]p and I have been in an errour, for I thought as y[o]u doe, that his hand had been in that Peece, but sincerely and certainly it is not soe. For in this Peece the beasts are all alive, and in act of eyther escape or resistance, in the expression whereof Snyder doth infinitlie come short of Rubens, and Rubens saith that he should take it in ill part, if I should compare Snyders with him in that point. The talent of Snyders, is to represent beasts but especiallie Birds altogether dead, and wholly w[i]thout anie action ...'[134]

Less than a year later, however, Rubens seemed to contradict himself when he informed Carleton that the eagle in his picture of Prometheus was done by Snyders (fig. 14. Peter Paul Rubens and Frans Snyders, *Prometheus*, ca. 1611-1612, completed by 1618, Philadelphia Museum of Art).[135] It was a picture that Carleton acquired as part of the collection of works he exchanged with Rubens[136] and the eagle in this picture is certainly not represented 'without anie action'; quite the opposite, it looks very dynamic. To reconcile these contradictory accounts, one could state, as Peter Sutton has done, that the eagle must have been designed by Rubens and subsequently executed by Snyders, which would explain the expression of energy.[137] After all, Snyders' individual paintings do look somewhat stiff and lack a comparable dynamism. In fact, this kind of assessing of the possible merits and characteristics of these two masters may have been exactly the type of activity that would have delighted a seventeenth-century connoisseur like Carleton.

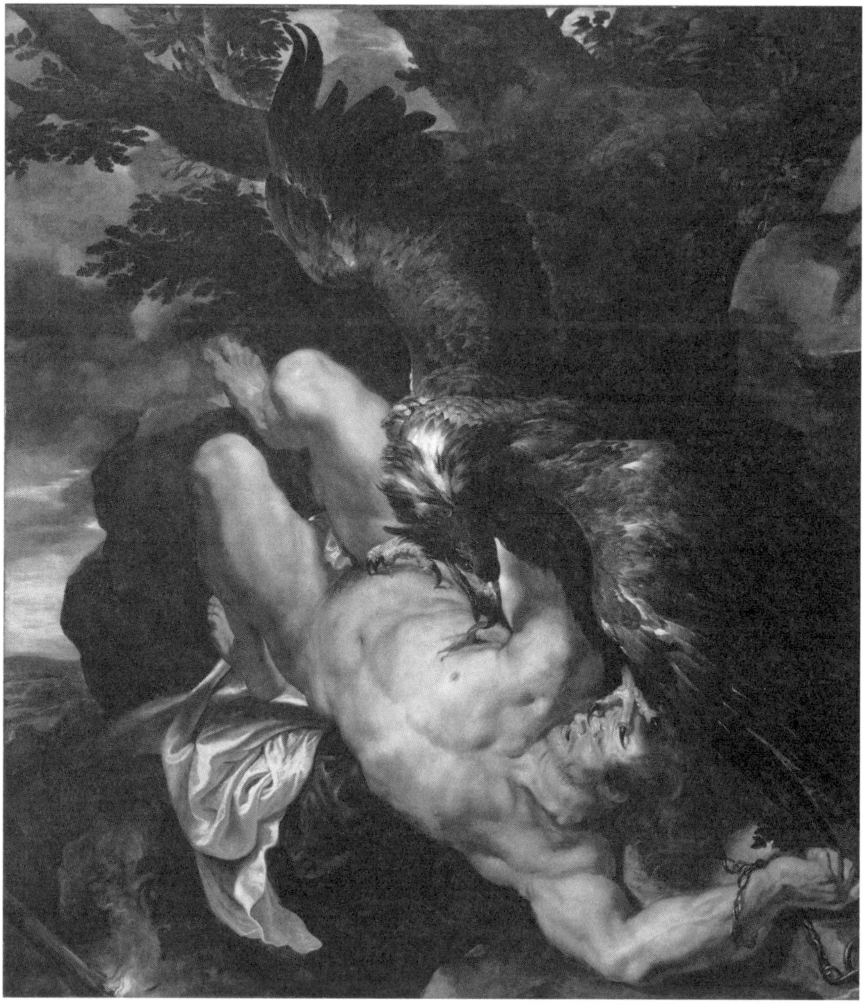

14.

Peter Paul Rubens and Frans Snyders
Prometheus, c. 1611-1612
Philadelphia Museum of Art, Philadelphia

Conclusion

Like present-day experts, seventeenth-century painters and connoisseurs were keen on attaching names to pictures. However, their ways of labelling pictures differed somewhat from ours. Master painters could claim pictures as their own and even describe works as 'by their hand' which they had not literally painted themselves, as Rubens, for example, did. Moreover, the term 'original' (*principael* or *origineel*) did not mean that a picture was executed by the master alone. They did distinguish works worthy of carrying their name from those they sold anonymously as by a 'pupil' (*leerling* / disciple) and/or works they had merely 'retouched' (*geretukkeert*), though if done well these last works could also simply be considered paintings by the master. Input from a 'paid assistant' (*gesel*) would have presumably counted as by the master if done in the master's style. Furthermore, it seems likely that many a master painter made quality distinctions between the works that counted as by their hand, possibly using Latin phrases to indicate different quality levels, like Apelles and other ancient painters had reputedly done. For example, Gerrit Honthorst seems to have added '*fecit*'(has made) to his signature to indicate the highest level of quality. In studios, the highest quality presumably stemmed from a closer involvement by the master himself; these pictures could be autograph, however, this was not necessarily the case (witness Rubens's correspondence). Although the main seventeenth-century categories of thought (that is: the distinctions between originals and copies and between masterpieces, works by pupils and retouched works) do not represent a special interest in purely autograph pictures by the master, this does not, however, exclude the possibility that such works were (occasionally) made and that some buyers may have had a special interest in these. In fact, a handful of documents indicates that at least some painters (namely Ambrosius Bosschaert, Jan Miense Molenaer, Abraham Bloemaert, Gillis van Coninxloo, and possibly Bartholomeus van der Helst) created one or more autograph pictures and that four buyers wanted to have certainty as to the execution of one such work.

Early modern art theorists also suggest that seventeenth-century connoisseurs were keen on recognising the master's touch. However, they do not seem to have been particularly preoccupied with deciding whether or not a picture was entirely autograph. Several seventeenth-century art theorists recommended that readers look for distinctively individual brushwork in order to recognise a master's hallmark style, which at first seems to imply that seventeenth-century attribution practices could have been at odds with contemporary studio practice. It is this seeming contradiction that I have called the paradox of seventeenth-century connoisseurship. However, upon close study, it looks like seventeenth-century attribution practices (in as far as these can be reconstructed on the basis of the surviving texts on the topic) were not necessarily at odds with studio habits. Interestingly, both Franciscus Junius and Samuel van Hoogstraten emphasise the importance of focusing on key elements in a painting while looking at the secondary passages more heedlessly. Van Hoogstraten further explained his advice by adding that great masters commonly had their pupils and assistants execute the secondary elements. My hypothesis is that this somewhat hierarchical way of looking at the situation was quite common among connoisseurs. For example, witness the emphasis early writers on connoisseurship put on masterly passages, and the absence of primary sources that distinguished studio input in pictures worthy of carrying a master's name. Although an occasional art buyer may have had a particular preference for purely autograph pictures, this does not seem to have been a very widespread concern; if we are to believe Karel van Mander and Samuel van Hoogstraten, knowledgeable art lovers did not mind contributions by other hands if these were done well and /or only concerned secondary elements. By comparison, connoisseurs seem to have been generally more interested in recognising the hands of two different masters if they had collaborated on the same composition (and I suspect that in doing so they focused again on masterly elements).

As to present-day connoisseurship, do seventeenth-century categories of thought (in so far as they can be reconstructed on the basis of the sources I studied) call for thorough revisions of the oeuvre catalogues of seventeenth-century painters? Possibly yes. In my opinion, the seventeenth-century sources studied here raise three important questions, which deserve further study (though they may prove to be hard to answer in individual cases). The need to rewrite existing oeuvre catalogues depends on the outcome of these questions. Firstly, to what extent did seventeenth-century painters such as Honthorst and Rembrandt consciously produce works of various levels of quality? Secondly, the relatively modest amount of evidence that suggests painters created purely autograph pictures calls for caution when attributing paintings entirely to the hand of a master or entirely to the hands of his pupils and assistants. Moreover, this warrants the question of what exactly was the master's share in the various studios? Thirdly, if the point of departure for attributions to a specific master is no longer a group of works which is considered to be entirely autograph, but rather the key characteristics in documented or firmly attributed works, such as the design and the execution of the main areas and accents, does this lead to a different understanding of the master's hallmark style and his oeuvre? If the answer to any of these questions leads to new insights about a seventeenth-century painter, there is cause for a revision.

* I would like to thank Marten Jan Bok, Koenraad Jonckheere, Arjan de Koomen and Eric Jan Sluijter for their insightful comments on earlier drafts of this essay.

1 Jephta Dullaart (Sotheby's Amsterdam) kindly informed me that currently at auctions, a good 'Rembrandt studio' painting is valued at about 5-10 percent of the price of an 'autograph Rembrandt'. This basically means that a 'Rembrandt studio' picture tends at best to fetch a price in the range of six figures, while paintings considered to be entirely autograph Rembrandts start at about $5 million.

2 According to an agent of Pope Urban VIII, Inigo Jones boasted about being able to correctly attribute all the works. See Jonathan Brown, *Kings and Connoisseurs: collecting art in seventeenth-century Europe*, Princeton 1995, p. 47. A further indication that attributing paintings was considered an entertaining pastime comes from Franciscus Junius, who argued in his *The Painting of the Ancients* that analysing pictures was a better and more innocent pastime than gambling, see Franciscus Junius, *The Literature of Classical Art, Vol. I. The Painting of the Ancients, according to the English translation (1638)*, Keith Aldrich et. al. (eds.), Berkeley, Los Angeles and Oxford 1991, pp. 72-74.

3 'Vous auriez un plaisir nonpareil à voir comme Jabach determine sur l'authenticité de ces pieces avec une suffisance magistrale; concluant enfin que de 300 dessins qu'on donnait pour des Raphael il n'en avoit que 2 d'originaux. Je donnerois quelque chose de bon pour le voir censurer les vostres et que vous fussiez derrière la tapisserie. Quand nous fusmes chez luy, il ne manqua pas d'y avoir des controlleurs, dont j'estois des moindres, qui luy contestoient des pieces qu'il donnoit pour veritables Julio Romano et Raphael dont il se mettoit dans une colere a nous faire rire tous, tellement qu'il n'y a point de comedie qui vaille une pareille conference.' Letter from Christiaan Huygens to his brother Constantijn, dated 1 June 1668, cited in: F. Grossman, 'Holbein, Flemish Paintings and Everhard Jabach', *The Burlington Magazine* 93 (1951), pp. 16-25, esp. p. 18. Christiaan Huygens, *Oeuvres Complètes*, 22 vols., The Hague 1888-1950, vol. 6 [1895], p.47.

4 Roger de Piles, *Conversations sur la Connoissance de la Peinture*, Paris 1677, pp. 5-7. De Piles is also aware of the difficulty of attributing works to masters who adjusted their manner depending on the subject they were painting. See my forthcoming Ph.D. thesis *The Fingerprint of an Old Master: On the Attributions of Paintings by Rembrandt, Rubens and their Contemporaries* (esp. Chapter IV), University of Amsterdam 2008.

5 See below, fig. 13, p. 54 and fig. 14. p. 56.

6 Sales catalogues will be discussed by Koenraad

Jonckheere, see pp. 69-94 below. [As he argues, commercial interests seem to have quite strongly influenced the connoisseurship in sales catalogues.]

7 On the trustworthiness of the judgements of painters and connoisseurs, see also *The Painter versus the Connoisseur*, below in this volume, pp. 127-145; see pp. 69-94 (Koenraad Jonckheere's essay in this volume) for a discussion of dealers interests. Neil De Marchi and Hans Van Miegroet trace larger developments in the mentality of art sellers as the art market evolved, see pp. 149-174.

8 By contrast, auctioneers in the later seventeenth-century did use different standards when attributing pictures, see Koenraad Jonckheere's essay, pp. 69-94 below.

9 Ernst van de Wetering, 'The Search for the Master's Hand: An Anachronism? (A Summary)', in: Thomas W. Gaetgens (ed.), *Künstlerischer Austauch / Artistic Exchange, Akten des XXVIII. Internationalen Kongresses für Kunstgeschichte Berlin, 15-20 Juli 1992*, Berlin 1993, pp. 627-630, esp. pp. 627-28.

10 Josua Bruyn et al., *A Corpus of Rembrandt Paintings*, The Hague 1986, vol. 2, pp. 60-76, esp. pp. 89 & 90. The issue itself was not new; it had also been discussed, for example, by Frits Lught in his article 'Italiaansche kunstwerken in Nederlandsche verzamelingen van vroeger tijden', *Oud Holland* 53 (1936), pp. 97-135, esp. pp. 110-112 and by Albert Blankert in his monograph on Ferdinand Bol. See Albert Blankert, *Ferdinand Bol: 1616-1680: een leerling van Rembrandt*, Ph.D. Dissertation University Utrecht 1976, pp. 14 and 18.

11 Svetlana Alpers, *Rembrandt's Enterprise: The Studio and the Market*, Chicago 1988. On Rembrandt's marketing abilities, see also Marten Jan Bok, 'Rembrandt's Fame and Rembrandt's Failure. The Market for History Paintings in the Dutch Republic', in: *Proceedings of the International symposium Rembrandt and Dutch History Painting in the 17th Century. Tokyo, 13-14 September 2003*, Tokyo 2004, pp. 159-178.

12 Alpers, *Rembrandt's enterprise* (note 11), pp. 69 and 143 (note 24). Alpers refers in this context to a statement by Houbraken that Flinck's work was sold under Rembrandt's name. In 1991, Josua Bruyn pointed out that quite a few works listed as being by Rembrandt in the artist's inventory of 1656 appear to be studio works, see Josua Bruijn, 'Rembrandt's Workshop: Its Function and Production', in: *Rembrandt, the Master & his Workshop*, Berlin, Amsterdam and London 1991 (exh. cat.), pp. 68-89, esp. pp. 70-71; see also Arthur Wheelock, *Dutch Paintings of the Seventeenth Century: The Collections of the National Gallery of Art Systematic Catalogue*, Washington, D.C. (National Gallery of Art) 1995 (coll. cat.), pp. 208 and 209 (note 27).

13 Alpers, *Rembrandt's enterprise* (note 11), p. 122.

14 Eddy de Jongh, 'De dikke en de dunne Hals', *Kunstschrift* 34, 2 (1990), pp. 2-3.

15 Van der Veen's research is discussed below.

16 Claus Grimm, 'Die Frage nach der Eigenhändigkeit und die Praxis der Zuschreibung', in: Thomas W. Gaetgens (ed.), *Künstlerischer Austauch / Artistic Exchange, Akten des XXVIII. Internationalen Kongresses für Kunstgeschichte Berlin, 15-20. Juli 1992*, Berlin 1993, pp. 631-648.

17 This is also the conclusion drawn by Wouter Kloek and Guido Jansen in *Rembrandt in a new Light, Presentation of Seven Restored Paintings by Rembrandt*, Amsterdam (Rijksmuseum) 1993 (exh. pamphlet), who state that among other things the lack of wrinkles in the hands seems unusual for Rembrandt.

18 Bruyn explained his view as follows: 'On the whole, one may say that with Rembrandt design and execution were closely bound up. Instead of making use of sophisticated workshop procedures which could in part replace the share of the master's hand, he seems to have allowed invention and execution to be separated only in the early stages of an assistant's activities. Later, they would be welcome to their own design and only rarely did they intervene with his own work.' Bruyn, *Rembrandt's Workshop* (note 12), pp. 68-89, esp. pp. 83-85. Also quoted in Wheelock, *Dutch Paintings of the Seventeenth Century*, (note 12), p. 209; Bruyn et al., *A Corpus of Rembrandt Paintings* (note 10), vol. 2, pp. 49-90. Ernst van de Wetering et al., *A Corpus of Rembrandt Paintings*, Dordrecht 2005, vol. 4, 'Preface', p. XXII. See also Tine Nygaard, *Rembrandt? The Master and his Workshop*, Copenhagen (Statens Museum for Kunst) 2005 (exh. brochure), p. 39: 'we tend towards the view that in general, Rembrandt distinguished quite sharply between works by himself and those done by his students – in terms of price, too. We imagine that Rembrandt, the pupils at his workshop, and the customers all knew who painted what, and that the prices were set accordingly. Rembrandt's signature was a brand name for the students, and for that reason it sometimes appears on works done by pupils. This does not, however, make such works forgeries.'

19 Wheelock refers to several primary sources which mention pictures that were '*geretukeert*' (retouched) by Rembrandt, including his 1656 inventory which also mentions one painting which was '*gemodelt*' (designed) by Rembrandt. Athur Wheelock 'Issues of Attribution in the Rembrandt Workshop', in: Wheelock *Dutch Paintings of the Seventeenth Century* (note 12), pp. 205-210, esp. p. 207.

20 Walter Liedtke, 'Rembrandt's 'Workshop' Revisited', *Oud Holland* 117 (2004), pp. 48-73, esp. p. 57.

21 Grimm suspected that there was no reason to believe that seventeenth-century masters created a core oeuvre of entirely autograph pictures, which led him to say that if the opposite could be proven to be more probable, most monographic studies of old masters would have to be re-edited, now with the dual purpose of both establishing the output of the old master's workshop, and of analysing the share of the master himself in the workshop production, see Grimm, *Die Frage* (note 16), p. 643.

22 Jaap van der Veen, 'By His Own Hand, The Valuation of Autograph Paintings in the Seventeenth-Century', in: Van de Wetering et al., *A Corpus of Rembrandt Paintings* (note 18), vol. 4, pp. 1-41.

23 Van der Veen, *By His Own Hand* (note 22), docs. 2, 3, 5, 6, 8, 9, 10, 14, 16, 17, 21, 22, 25, 27, 31, 33, 34, 35, 36.

24 Ibid. (note 22), p. 2. See also below, p. 38.

25 Ibid.(note 22), docs. 1, 4, 5, 19, 20, 22. (dated respectively: 1606, 1615, 1616, 1653, 1649 [sic], and 1658)

26 See Ibid. (note 22), esp. pp. 2, 3, 8, 14, and 28. On the meaning of the term *'origineel'* see also below, pp. 39-40.

27 The first scholar to analyse these phrases was Charles Seymour. See Richard Spear, 'Notes on Renaissance and Baroque Originals and Originality', in: Kathleen Preciado (ed.), *Retaining the Original: Multiple Originals, Copies, and Reproductions*, Washington National Gallery of Art Studies in the History of Art. 20 (1989), p. 98; and Richard Spear, *The "Divine" Guido: Religion, Sex, Money and Art in the World of Guido Reni*, New Haven 1997, esp. 'Di Sua Mano', pp. 253-274.

28 While Michelangelo, Raphael and Titian (predominantly) signed their works using their full names, they were known by their first names. Rembrandt signed most consistently using just his first name from the early 1630s onwards. Ann Jensen Adams gives a good overview of the development of signatures and their cultural historical implications, see Ann Jensen Adams, 'Rembrandt f[ecit]. The Italic Signature and the Commodification of Artistic Identity', in: Thomas W. Gaetgens (ed.), *Künstlerischer Austauch / Artistic Exchange, Akten des XXVIII. Internationalen Kongresses für Kunstgeschichte Berlin, 15-20. Juli 1992*, Berlin 1993, pp. 581-594.

29 'Qualche istoria o fabula antiqua aut de suo inuentione ne finga una che rapresenti cosa antiqua e de bello significato.' Letter dated 28 June 1501, State Archive of Mantua, Copia lettere Isab., Busta 2993, letter 188. See J. M. Fletcher, 'Isabella d'Este and Giovanni Bellini's "Presepio"', *The Burlington Magazine*, 113, 825 (1971), pp. 703-713.

30 'una cosa fatta di mano sua o sia di sculptura o di pittura ... Et se per caso vi dimandasse che subietto voressimo, gli direti che non cercamo ne desideramo se non un'opera dell'ingegno suo ... un exempio della sua singularissima virtù.' Federico Gonzaga stipulated his request in a letter to his agent in Florence: Giovanni Borromeo. See Alessandro Luzio, *La Galleria dei Gonzaga venduta all'Inghilterra nel 1627-28*, Rome 1974 [1913], pp. 246-247.

31 See William W. Robinson, '"This Passion for Prints": Collecting and Connoisseurship in Northern Europe during the Seventeenth Century', in: Clifford S. Ackley (ed.), *Printmaking in the Age of Rembrandt*, Boston and St. Louis 1981 (exh. cat.), pp. xxvii-lviii, esp. p. xxxiv ff.

32 On the different ways of signing, see also below. Rembrandt seems to have signed 90 percent of the works he is believed to have produced between 1632 and 1642; by comparison, Raphael signed only 14 of the 156 paintings that he is believed to have produced. See Jensen Adams, *Rembrandt f[ecit]* (note 28), p. 581.

33 Translation taken from Giorgio Vasari, *The Lives of the Artists*, ed. by J.M. Dent, London 1966 [1963], p. 110.

34 The *Portrait of Giovanna of Aragon* was later transferred to canvas.

35 'Waer in hy dan maer een groof faut bedrijvet, / Soo hy sich self daer onder niet en schrijvet / Als principael: want hebben sy dit Beeldt, / Elck nae sijn macht, verciert end' bejuweelt, / D'een met een ringh, en d'ander met een keten, / Dees met een bagg', en die, ist wel te weten / Met wat ghesteent: soo heeft van Mander haer / Versorght een Croon van enckel peerlen claer.' *Ode, op het Schilder-Boeck van den Const-rijcken Carel van Mander*, by: A.V.M.; See Karel van Mander, *Het Schilder-Boeck*, Haarlem 1604, fol. *7r.

36 Jensen Adams, *Rembrandt f[ecit]* (note 28), p. 590; Nygaard, *Rembrandt?* (note 18); Koenraad Jonckheere in his essay in this volume. Catherine Scallen uses the term 'trademark' in her book *Rembrandt, Reputation, and the Practice of Connoisseurship*, Amsterdam 2004, p. 327 and note 10, p. 380.

37 Placing one's signature onto a painting could even be considered a means of appropriating a work from another master. Witness a remarkable incident in Hasselt, Overijssel: When the nowadays little-known painter Adam van de Plancke painted the picture *The Judgement of Count Willem de Goede* for the Hasselt town hall, the local painter's guild filed a complaint because Van der Plancke was not a member of the guild and thus had no right to receive the commission from the city. The issue was resolved by having a local painter sign the work and municipal authorities paid the guild a fine, see J. Verbeek, 'De beeldende kunst in Overijssel', in: *Geschiedenis van Overijssel*, Deventer 1970, p. 339.

38 Elisabeth Honig, 'The Beholder as Work of Art: A Study in the Location of Value in Seventeenth-Century Flemish Painting', *Nederlands Kunsthistorisch Jaarboek* 46 (1995), pp. 253-297, esp. pp. 294-295.

39 J. Michael Montias, *Artists and Artisans in Delft: A socio-economic Study of the Seventeenth Century*, Princeton 1983, pp. 218, 227 and 247-258; J. Michael Montias, *Vermeer and his Milieu, A Web of Social History*, Princeton 1989, p. 245 ; In Dordrecht, artists' names appeared mostly in inventories from the 1650s and later; however, many notarial deeds have gone missing, see John Loughman, 'Een stad en haar kunstconsumptie: openbare en privé-verzamelingen in Dordrecht', in: *De Zichtbaere Werelt*, Dordrecht (Dordrechts Museum) 1992 (exh. cat.), pp. 34-64, esp. pp. 45-46; Van der Veen, *By His Own Hand* (note 22), pp. 4 and 15ff. By contrast, a recent analysis of inventories from the province of Friesland shows a relatively large share of cheap pictures and relatively little interest in painters' names; presumably, connoisseurship was concentrated in large urban centres. See Piet Bakker, *Gezicht op Leeuwarden. Schilders in Friesland en de markt voor schilderijen in de Gouden Eeuw*, Ph.D. Dissertation University of Amsterdam 2008.

40 Willemijn Fock, 'Kunstbezit in Leiden in de 17de eeuw', in: Th.H. Lunsingh Scheurleer et al. (eds.), *Het Rapenburg. Geschiedenis van een Leidse gracht*, Leiden 1990, vol.Va, pp. 3-36, esp. p. 5. Fock's analysis is based on a random sample of ten collectors inventories per decennium.

41 Montias assumed that the expertise of notaries varied considerably. Jaap van der Veen questions how much the inventories reflect the knowledge of the notaries that often composed them, as these notaries may have profited from existing inventory lists, from knowing the owner of the works and from signatures and monograms on the pictures (which are sometimes literally transcribed). Van der Veen, *By His Own Hand* (note 22), p. 16 esp. note 82. See also J. Michael Montias, 'Review: *De wereld binnen handbereik: Nederlandse kunst- en rariteitenverzamelingen. 1585-1735, Simiolus* 22 (1993), pp. 99-105, esp. p. 103, note 16.

42 See Eric Jan Sluijter, *All striving to adorne their houses with costly peeces.* Two Case Studies of Paintings in Wealthy Interiors', in: Mariët Westermann (ed.), *Art & Home, Dutch Interiors in the Golden Age*, Zwolle and Denver 2001, pp. 102-127, esp. p. 119.

43 Given the large amount of surviving inventories and the many variables regarding the circumstances in which the inventories were compiled, an in-depth quantitative analysis requires a separate study. However, a number of general conclusions regarding the terms that did and did not exist and the frequency with which terms were used, can already be drawn, see below.

44 A. Bredius, *Künstler-Inventare: Urkunden zur Geschichte der Holländischen Kunst des XVIten, XVIIten und XVIIIten Jahrhunderts*, The Hague 1915-1921, vol. 1 [1915], pp. 258-259; Sluijter, *All striving to adorne their houses* (note 43), pp. 102-127, esp. p. 119.

45 In the 1687 inventory of the art dealer Hendrick Meyeringh we find for example '133. Een stuckje van de discipulen van Sonjé', Bredius, *Künstler-Inventare* (note 44), vol. 1, p. 340.

46 See Neil De Marchi and Hans Van Miegroet, 'Pricing Invention: "Originals", "Copies", and their Relative Value in Seventeenth Century Netherlandish Art Markets', in Victor Ginsburgh and P.-M. Menger (eds.), *Recent Contributions to the Economics of the Arts*, Amsterdam 1996, pp. 27-70.

47 Marion Boers-Goosens, 'De schilderijenverzameling van baron Willem Vincent van Wyttenhorst', *Oud Holland* 117(2004), pp. 181-243, p. 217, nos. 37 & 38. Wyttenhorst also mentions a copy after Poelenburch by a certain Steenbergen, which was subsequently reworked by Poelenburch himself. He specifies that he paid Steenbergen 36 guilders and Poelenburch 100 guilders for this piece, which makes the picture more expensive than many an original by Poelenburch. See ibid. p. 217, no. 152.

48 Bredius, *Künstler-Inventare* (note 44), vol. 1, pp. 54-55. This document also mentions a painting in the manner of Berchem by Van der Meer. 'Een Capitaal stuk van van der meer (in) den aert van Berghem met menschen, beesten en lantschap'.

49 See above, p. 36.

50 Eric Jan Sluijter kindly informed me that the term '*origineel*' was mostly used in the Southern Netherlands.

51 Junius, *The Painting of the Ancients* (note 2), pp. 305-306. In the Dutch version: '... plagten de meeste haerer Konst-kennisse daer in voornaemelick te bewijsen, datse d'originelen staend-voets van de copijen weten t'onderscheyden. 'd'Oorspronckelicke wercken die de treffelicke Meesters nae 't leven selver ghemaect hebben, worden alhier door den naam van orginele stucken te verstaen ghegeven'; quoted in Van der Veen, *By His Own Hand* (note 22), p. 2.

52 Lydia de Pauw-de Veen, *De begrippen 'schilder', 'schilderij' en 'schilderen' in de zeventiende eeuw*, Brussels 1969, pp. 107-111.

53 The attributions and taxations in this inventory are done by the painter Ferdinand Bol and the dealer Gerrit Uylenburgh, see Bredius, *Künstler-Inventare* (note 44), vol. 1, p. 425. See, for another example, also note 45 above.

54 'dat is van mij niet, maer van een van mijn slechtste discupels, ick beclaeg je, u bent bedrogen. Broekman heeft het van mij gecocht voor vijff guldens en ick wil dat voor mijn schilderij niet laten gaen'. *Oud-Holland* 9 (1891), p. 148-149; Van der Veen, *By His Own Hand* (note 22), doc. 28 (dated 1676).

55 'Verclaert Jacob van Ruisdael, dat bij aldien den voorsz. Parcellus het voorsz. stuck schilderije begonnen heeft, dat hij oordeelt hetselve tegenwoordig sodanich is toegestelt, dat het onbequam is om voor een stuck van Parcellus gelevert [te worden].' *Oud-Holland* 6 (1888), pp. 21-24; Van der Veen, *By His Own Hand* (note 22), doc. 24.

56 'Verclaren sij getuygen noch al t'samen t'oordelen dat dienvolgende het voorsz. stuck schilderij niet waerdich is voor een stuck van Parcellus gecocht en gelevert te werden.' Ibid. (note 55).

57 '... well ende curieuslijck ten deele zelffs te schilderen ende ten deele door andere, sooals het bequamst door hem Jordaens goet gevonden sal worden. Ende 't gene door andere geschildert sal wesen blijft hij gehouden zoo te overschilderen, dat het voor zijn signors Jordaens eygen werck gehouden sal worden ende oversulckx zijnen naem ende teeckininge daer onder stellen.', Antwerp, City Archives, not. H. van Cantelbeck Jr, NA 3399, dd. 21 April 1648; F.J. Van den Branden, *Geschiedenis der Antwerpsche schilderschool*, Antwerp 1883, p. 828; R.-A. d'Hulst, *Jacob Jordaens*, Antwerp 1982, p. 30. Van der Veen, *By His Own Hand* (note 22), p. 14. Jordaens explained his workshop practice also himself in similar terms. See Van der Veen, *By His Own Hand* (note 22), pp. 13 and 14 (note 67); M. Rooses, *Jordaens' leven en werken*, Amsterdam 1906, p. 139. Since Jaap van der Veen assumes that well-to-do buyers had a preference for autograph paintings, he believes that Jordaens' workshop practice may have been shocking to the buyers. However, the documents give no reason for this assumption; on the contrary, the statement that Jordaens himself could judge most aptly how to use his assistants, indicates that the patron had faith in Jordaens' judgement and the resulting quality of the work.

58 '... sullen vor hem Van Vuchts werck mogen passeeren, te weten soodaenich als hij aen hem Van Waesberge voor desen heeft gelevert ende met sijn eygen hant geteeckent', p. Haverkorn van Rijsewijk, 'Johannes van Vucht', *Oud Holland* 9 (1891), pp. 39-51, esp. p. 43. See also Van der Veen, *By His Own Hand* (note 22), p. 13.

59 '... et y mettre la dernier main, en sorte que l'on puisse dire avec vérité que tout cet ouvrage sera de vous.' Letter from Colbert to Bernini, 9 December 1669, cited in: Rudolf Wittkower, 'The Vicissitudes of a Dynastic Monument. Bernini's Equestrian Statue of Louis XIV', in: Millard Meiss (ed.), *De Artibus Opuscula XL, Essays in Honor of Erwin Panofsky*, New York 1961, pp. 497-531, esp. p. 521 (doc. 23). See also Spear, *Notes on Renaissance and Baroque Originals and Originality* (note 27), p. 98.

60 See below, p. 43.

61 M. Rooses and C.L. Ruelens, *Correspondance de Rubens et documents épistolaires concernant sa vie et ses œuvres*, vol. 2, p. 149 (letter CLXVIII): '... copie en ritocci ... luçono piu per il lor prezzo'.

62 Walter L. Strauss et. al., *The Rembrandt Documents*, New York 1979, doc. 1656/12, nos 25, 27, 28, 33, 295 & 301; for another early mention of a retouched Rembrandt, see Jaap van der Veen, 'Onbekende opdrachtgevers van Rembrandt. Jacomo Borchgraeff en Maria van Uffelen en hun portretten door Rembrandt, Jonson van Ceulen, Van Zijl, Van Mol en Jacob Backer', *Kroniek van het Rembrandthuis* 1998, pp. 14-31. Two pictures carrying inscriptions that they were retouched by Rembrandt, seem to indicate that such works were indeed quite different from pictures worthy of carrying the master's name: *Head of a Boy*, Amsterdam Rijksmuseum, Inv. no. A2391 (the now illegible inscription was once read as 'Rembrandt geretuceer ... [naar?] Lieve.. [i.e.: Lievens]') and *The Sacrifice of Isaac*, Alte Pinakothek, Munich [inscribed: '*Rembrandt. verandert. En over geschildert*']. Admittedly, the attribution of both these pictures remains an issue of debate and no works sold as by a 'pupil' in the seventeenth century have been definitively identified. However, if these works are in any way illustrative, the quality of 'pupil work' must have been rather poor. In fact, these works look so little like accepted Rembrandts that some scholars doubted whether Rembrandt had touched them at all. See Josua Bruyn et al., *A Corpus of Rembrandt Paintings*, The Hague 1989, vol 3, no. A 108; Christian L. Tümpel et al., *Het Oude Testament in de schilderkunst van de Gouden Eeuw*, Amsterdam (Joods Historisch Museum) 1991 (exh. cat.), cat. no. 9; Martin Royalton-Kisch, 'Rembrandt's sketches for his paintings', *Master Drawings* 27 (1989), pp. 128-145; Hubert von Sonnenburg reputedly recognised retouches in the Munich painting. See Van der Veen, *By His Own Hand* (note 22), p. 25 and note 136.

63 See Ronald de Jager, 'Meester, leerjongen, leertijd. Een anlyse van zeventiende-eeuwse Noord-Nederlandse leerlingencontracten van kunstschilders, goud- en zilversmeden', *Oud Holland* 37 (1999), pp. 215-222. See also Marion Goossens, *Schilders en de markt. Haarlem 1605-1635*, PhD Dissertation University of Leiden 2001, pp. 69-81, esp. pp. 77-79.

64 Fr.D.O. Obreen (ed.), *Archief voor Nederlandsche Kunstgeschiedenis*, Rotterdam 1877-1878, vol. 1, pp.222-293, esp. stipulations 3, pp. 239-240 and 6, pp.243-244.

65 Goossens, *Schilders en de markt* (note 63), pp. 89-90.

66 Ibid. (note 63), p. 73.

67 'Dat daerop bij de voorsz. requirant [Dogger] werden gepersisteert dat de voorsz. Van Aelst het immers hadde geschildert ende bij contrarie niet soude vertonen, daerbij voegde dat desselfs, Van Aelst' naem onder de voorsz. schilderij was staende. Sijluyden metten anderen alsoo daerop wedden, namentl. dat de voorsz. Pic seyde te sullen vertonen, dat het voorsz. stucje schilderij bij de voorsz. Aelst niet en was geschildert, nog geen handen daeraen gehadt hadde [...]

niettegenstaende den deposant Bronchorst hem Pic voor de voorsz. weddinge de naem van de voorn. Van Aelst hadde vertoont, alsoo de voorsz. Pic seyde: 'daer is niet aen gelegen al staet de naem daeronder, hij heeft 't selve evenwel niet gemaect'.' See Abraham Bredius, 'Drie Delftsche schilders: Evert van Aelst, Pieter Jansz. van Asch, en Adam Pick', *Oud-Holland* 6 (1888), pp. 289-298, esp. 290-291; Van der Veen, *By His Own Hand* (note 22), doc. 15.

68 Ibid. (note 22), docs. 1, 4, 19, and 22. Two other documents simply state that certain pictures were done 'by the own hands' of respectively Hendrick van Steenwijck and Pouwels [Paulus] Bril (docs. 5 and 20, dated repectively 1617 and 1649). First publication of these documents: *Oud-Holland* 34 (1916), pp. 161-162 (doc. 1); L.J. Bol, *The Bosschaert Dynasty. Painters of Flowers and Fruit*, Leigh-on-Sea 1960, pp. 27-28 (doc. 4); Van der Veen, *By His Own Hand* (note 22) (doc. 5); Bredius, *Künstler-Inventare* (note 44), I, p. 15 (doc. 19); Abraham Bredius, 'Kunstkritiek der XVIIe eeuw', *Oud-Holland* 7 (1889), pp. 41-44 (doc. 20); Bredius, *Künstler-Inventare* (note 44), II, pp. 401-402 (doc. 22).

69 'Hendrick van Leeuwen belooffde te leveren voor principaele stukken [...] endee gemaeckt te sijn 't eene van Bloemaert tot Utrecht ende 't ander van Coninxloo, sonder ymanden anders als d'voorsz. twee meesters aen de voorsz. twee stucken hebben gearbeyt'.

70 'een blompot [...] met sijn eygen hant gemaect heeft, sonder datter yemant anders de hant aen gehadt ofte gewerct heeft.'

71 'sonder dat bij ymant anders daeraen iets is gedaen.'

72 In the letter Rubens refers to all the paintings in the list as 'delle pitture de mia mano qui da basso nominate', which means that all works mentioned counted as by Rubens hand, as the master's own work. He subsequently makes further quality distinctions. See Adolf Rosenberg (ed.), *Rubensbriefe*, Leipzig 1881, pp. 42 ff, esp. pp. 43-44.

73 The fact that Rubens does not mention this specialist's name (see also letter of 28 May 1618, quoted below) suggests that he was not a master painter but rather a '*gesel*' or paid assistant.

74 Compare De Marchi and Van Miegroet, *Pricing Invention* (note 46), pp.27-70. According to their findings copies commonly amounted to only half of the price of originals, even if they were painted by the master himself as in the case of Breughel the Elder.

75 Unfortunately, one of these works, a Crucifix described by Rubens as 'perhaps the best thing I ever made' (*forse la meglio cosa chio facessi giamai*), turned out to be too large for Carleton's house, and he therefore removed it from his selection. See Rosenberg, *Rubensbriefe* (note 72), p. 44.

76 De Jongh, *De dikke en de dunne Hals* (note 14); Van de Wetering, *The Search for the Master's Hand* (note 9), p. 628; Van der Veen, *By His Own Hand* (note 22), p, 7.

77 'Ho preso secondo il mio solito un valenthuomo nel suo mestiere a finere li paesaggi solo per augmentar il gusto di V.E. ma nel resto la sia sicura ch'io non ho permesso animo vivente vi metta la mano', see Rubens's letter dated 28 May 1618 in Rosenberg, *Rubensbriefe* (note 72), p. 49.

78 Rosenberg, *Rubensbriefe* (note 72), p. 46; see also p. 45 where Rubens explains that the works he had described are not 'simple copies' and refers to the price as an indication of their quality.

79 Interestingly, she also noticed strong differences in execution between the two works signed with simply Honthorst's name. See Jolanda de Bruijn, *Honthorst fecit (?) : een onderzoek naar de atelierpraktijk van Gerard van Honthorst (1592-1656)*, MA thesis (unpublished) University of Amsterdam 2001, p. 63-111. While De Bruijn believed the 'Honthorst fec[it]'-signature indicated entirely autograph works, more recent research of his paintings in the Oranjezaal makes this very unlikely, see the entries on the six paintings by Van Honthorst by Margriet van Eikema-Hommes, Lidwien Speleers and Jolanda de Bruijn, and the chapter The painting technique of the twelve painters in the Oranjezaal, by Margriet van Eikema Hommes and Lidwien Speleers, in the forthcoming book on the Oranjezaal, edited by the Netherlands Institute for Art History (RKD), The Hague 2010.

80 J. Richard Judson and Rudolf E.O. Ekkart, *Gerrit van Honthorst, 1592-1656*, Doornspijk 1999. Marten Jan Bok kindly informed me that Hendrick Terbrugghen may have also used his signature to distinguish between various quality levels.

81 Judson and Ekkart, *Gerrit van Honthorst* (note 80), cat. nos. 11, 23, 76, 85, 99, 109, 120, 122, 137, 142, 143, 145, 171, 189, 192, 193, 208, 211, 215, 221, 222, 229, 236, 240, 241, 242, 249, 253, 255, 275 and 276. Please note that not all pictures discussed in the catalogue could be traced by the authors; therefore some paintings could not be properly studied.

82 Judson and Ekkart, *Gerrit van Honthorst* (note 80), cat. nos. 303, 307, 309, 332, 338, 401, 407, 422, 455, 458, 471, 495, 497 and 508. As with the history paintings and pastoral scenes, not all portraits could be studied in real life.

83 C. Pliny the Elder, *Naturalis Historia*, c. 77 A.D., *Praef.* 27: 'quare plenum verecundiae illud, quod omnia opera tamquam novissima inscripsere et tamquam singulis fato adempti. tria non amplius, ut opinor, absolute traduntur inscripta ILLE FECIT, quae suis locis reddam. quo apparuit summam artis securitatem auctori placuisse, et ob id magna invidia fuere omnia ea.'

84 Van Mander, *Het Schilder-Boeck* (note 35), fol. 80r; Etienne Binet, *Essay des merveilles de nature, et des plus nobles artifices*, with an introduction by Marc Fumaroli, Paris 1987 [1621], p. 353; Junius,

The Painting of the Ancients (note 2), p. 36. Junius also refers to Poliziano – *Observationes et Emendationes* – who in turn refers to Giovanni Lorenzi da Venezia, an antiquarian who states that several such formulations of completion are extant, see ibid., p. 44. See also Van Hoogstraten, *Inleyding* (note 94), p.320.

85 Roger de Piles for example distinguishes between the 'character of the hand' and the 'character of the mind', which one could look for in a picture. According to one of the protagonists in his Conversations, the first approach was useful but rather superficial. De Piles, *Conversations* (note 4), pp. 10-11. See also my forthcoming Ph.D. Dissertation *The Fingerprint of an Old Master, On the Attributions of Paintings by Rembrandt, Rubens and their Contemporaries.* (University of Amsterdam 2008), for a more complete overview of the various characteristics of pictures that art theorists considered important when attributing paintings.

86 This was not the prime purpose of Van Mander's book; in fact, the first and foremost aim was to elevate the status of painting as a liberal art. It was written for both young painters and art lovers. It is certainly not a manual for aspiring connoisseurs, although some passages in the treatise are nonetheless very revealing in this respect.

87 Van Mander, *Het Schilder-Boeck* (note 35), fol. 212r: 'Men siet oock in Lucas dinghen ... een ander soeter eenparige handelinghe van snede, daer zijn drijvende en vloeyende lakenen soo verstandich, als constich mede zijn uytgebeeldt, als men doet in ander van zijnen tijt, ghelijck ick achte my de verstandighe sullen toestemmen.'

88 Van Mander, *Het Schilder-Boeck* (note 35), fol. 223v: 'Desen uytnemenden Holbeen hadde in alle zijn wercken en handelinghe een seker vasticheyt in stellen, en schilderen, zijn dinghen al by order aenlegghende, en op doende, veel anders als ander Schilders: ghelijck onder ander, waer baerdt oft hayr over te comen hadde, schilderde hy doch volcomelijck alsoo't te wesen hadde, de schaduwen daer in recht waernemende, en maeckte als het droogh was baerdt oft hayr seer vloeyende en natuerlijck daer over.'

89 In printmaking it was not until the early seventeenth century that an artist developed a keen interest in botanical accuracy; Johannes Brosterhuizen's etchings of trees are the first in which specific species can be identified. See Huijgen Leeflang, 'Geen dromen of grillen van schilders, de bomen van Johannes Brosterhuysen (1596-1650)', *Kunstschrift* 4 (2004), pp. 24-29.

90 In the Dutch translation: 'De Slag van bomen / Men zegt de bomen van dit Landschap zyn zeer onderscheidentlyk getoest, of deeze Schilder slaat zeer wel zyn bomen.' Charles Alphonse du Fresnoy, *Termes de Peinture. Konstwoorden of spreekwyzen van de schilderkonst*, Amsterdam 1722 [first published Rome, c. 1647], p. 29.

91 Cornelis de Bie, *Het gvlden cabinet vande edel vry schilder const : inhovdende den lof vande vermarste schilders, architect , beldth wers, ende plaetsnyders van dese eevw*, Antwerp 1661, p. 164 over Gerard van Honthorst *'Soo gheestich is sijn Const ghediept en uyt ghehooght'*; De Bie's remark is reminiscent of Mancini's suggestion that confidently applied light and dark accents in the depiction of drapery can be particularly revealing; Paul Fréart de Chantelon, *Diary of the cavaliere Bernini's visit to France (1665)*, Anthony Blunt (ed.), Princeton 1985, p 251. A similar suggestion to look particularly at the execution of hands can be found in Anea Vico's treatise on coins of 1555, see Jeffrey Muller, 'Measures of Authenticity: The Detection of Copies in the Early Literature on Connoisseurship', in: Kathleen Preciado (ed.), *Retaining the Original: Multiple Originals, Copies, and Reproductions*, Washington National Gallery of Art Studies in the History of Art. 20 (1989), pp. 141-151, esp. p. 142.

92 The comparison with handwriting was already much in use in early modern times, see, for example, Giulio Mancini, *Considerazioni sulla Pittura, publicato per la prima volta da Adriana Maracchi con il commento di Luigi Salerno* (Academia Nazionale dei Lincei), Rome 1956, p. 134; and Abbé Du Bos, *Réflexions critiques sur la poésie et sur la painture*, Paris 1993 [1719], p. 297.

93 Junius, *The Painting of the Ancients* (note 2), p. 310. Earlier Mancini had also stated that when observing a painting one should start with the main figures and only afterwards look at the less important figures, see Mancini, *Considerazioni sulla Pittura* (note 92), pp. 135 ff & p. 329.

94 'Zeker 't is onvermakelijk te hooren, als somtijds onweetende, doch verwaende liefhebbers, het beste deel in eenich stuk willende aenwijzen, iets zoo gemeens uitpikken, dat by den Meester schier als slapende, of ten minsten van zijn voornaemen arbeyt rustende, gemaekt is. Deeze dingen zijn by de ouden als overmaet of toegift tot het voornaemste werk geacht geweest, en wierden van hen *Parerga* genoemt; en zijn by groote Meesters gemeenlijk door de hand van jongers en aenkomelingen, of van de geene, die daer een handwerk van konden, gemaekt.' Samuel van Hoogstraten, *Inleyding tot de hooge schoole der schilderkonst, anders de zichtbaere werelt: verdeelt in negen leerwinkels, yder bestiert door eene der zanggodinnen*, Rotterdam 1678, p. 76.

95 'Ik zal gaerne toestaen, dat een meester in groote werken hulp van anderen nemen, die in bywerk geoeffent zijn: maer die met recht den naem van Meester in Historyen draegen wil, moet ook raet weten, als 't nood doet, tot bywerk.' Van Hoogstraten, Inleyding tot de hooge schoole der schilderkonst (note 94), p. 72.

96 According to Hayden B. Maginnis it was Giovanni Morelli's most important contribution to connoisseurship that his emphasis on the execution of various details made experts focus not just on the key elements but on the entire picture, see Hayden B. J. Maginnis, 'The role of perceptual learning in connoisseurship: Morelli, Berenson and beyond', *Art history* 13, 1 (1990), pp. 104-117.

97 Willem Goeree, *Inleydinge tot de al-ghemeene teycken-konst*, Middelburgh 1668, p. 47.

98 See Eric Jan Sluijter, *Seductress of Sight: Studies in Dutch art of the Golden Age*, Zwolle 2000 [1993], pp. 244-258; Philips Angel, *Lof der Schilderkonst*, Leiden 1642, p. 52.

99 Van Hoogstraten, *Inleyding tot de hooge schoole der schilderkonst* (note 94), p. 27. According to Van Hoogstraten 'connoisseurs' (*kenders*) also very much appreciate rough sketches.

100 Abraham Bosse, *Sentimens sur la Distinction des diverses manières de peinture, dessin et gravure et des orginaux d'avec leurs copies*, Paris 1649, sommaire (with explanation of different terms used. 'Artiste & croquée' is explained as: roughly applied paint which looks unfinished from nearby and has been painted with much 'ease' (*facilité*). Bosse also uses the term '*sevelt*' for such loose brushwork, i.e., done with a 'strong, free and fluid brush' (*pinceau fort, libre et coolant*).

101 Bosse, *Sentimens sur la Distinction des diverses manières de peinture* (note 100), sommaire. All these terms appear in the introduction and are explained throughout the treatise.

102 'Le pourfil, les gestes, les symmetries et proportions, mines et bonnes contenances sont celles qui donnent bruit au pinceau, et le poinct principal de tout cet Estat. Le dedans se fait aisément, mais le pourfil, les derniers traits et l'arrondissement de la besongne est mal-aisée.' Binet, *Essay des Merveilles de nature* (note 84), p. 360. An explanation of what is understood by 'contenance' can be found under no. 9 on pp. 359-360: 'Donner contenances aux Images, et bonne mine, ouvrant la bouche, l'oeil, le ris, etc., Peindre l'esprit, les moeurs, les passions, etc.'

103 Bosse, *Sentimens sur la Distinction des diverses manières de peinture* (note 100), p. 57.

104 See above p. 40 (on contracts Bernini & Jordaens).

105 On passages by Mancini and De Bie, see above p. 46 and 49

106 Arnold Houbraken, *De groote schouburgh der Nederlantsche konstschilders en schilderessen*, Amsterdam 1718-1721, 3 vols., vol. I, p. 92. On the close connection made in art theory between retouchings and the master's recognisable 'ingenium', see also Spear, *The "Divine" Guido* (note 27), p. 265-266, who quotes an evocative passage from *Diálogos de la pintura* (1633) by the painter and art theorist Vicencio Carducho: 'after the assistant considers his work finished, the master retouches the painting again and perfects it. This is the last step and refinement which breathes spirit into a painting. Here, in these brush-strokes and fine finishing touches, the true master is revealed.'

107 'ils ont mesmes inventé un Jargon exprés, avec lequel ils exagerent magnifiquement par des gestes et des expressions fort amphatiques pour faire admirer, la Fraisheur et la Vaghesse du Coloris, la Franchise du pinceau, les Touches hardies, les Couleurs bien empastées et bein nourries, le Detachement des Masses, les Draperies bien jettées, les beaux Plis, let Coups de Maistre, la grande Maniere, les Muscles bein ressentis, les beaux Contours, les belles Teintes, et la Morbidesse des Carnations, les beaux Groupes, les beux Morceaux, et force autre autres beautez chimeriques de cette nature.' Roland Fréart de Cambray, *L'Idée de la Perfection de la peinture*, Paris 1662, pp. 61-63, cited and translated in Donald Posner, 'On the Mechanical Parts of Painting and the Artistic Culture of Seventeenth-Century France', *The Art Bulletin* 75 (1993), pp. 583-595.

108 'Le Peintre touche bien, c'est à dire, fait bien la carnation du nud, c'est à dire, de la face, de la main, du pied, car la reste est habillé.' Binet, *Essay des Merveilles de nature* (note 84), p. 364. There are many other sources which discuss the fleshtone as particularly hard to depict, see Ann-Sophie Lehmann, *Das unsichtbare Geschlecht: Studien zu einem Detail des nakcten weiblichen Körpers in der bildenden Kunst*, PhD Dissertation University Utrecht 1996; Eric Jan Sluijter, 'Goltzius, painting and flesh, or, Why Goltzius began to paint in 1600', in: Marieke van den Doel et al., *The Learned Eye: Regarding Art, Theory, and the Artist's Reputation. Essays for Ernst van de Wetering*, Amsterdam 2005, pp. 158-177.

109 See my unpublished paper 'Rembrandt en de atelierpraktijk bij het schilderen van portretten', University of Amsterdam 1995.

110 See above *Masterly Passages*, pp.50-51.

111 See Friso Lammertse and Jaap van der Veen, *Uylenburgh & Zoon, Kunst en Commercie in de Tijd van Rembrandt*, Dulwich and Amsterdam 2006 (exh. cat.), esp. pp. 79-102.

112 The one picture that was not contested and stayed with the Elector was Giuseppe de Ribera's *Executioner with the Head of Saint John the Baptist*, see the letter from Uylenbrugh in the Geheimes Staatsarchif, Berlin, 1 HA Rep. 76, Alt 111, nr. 167.

113 'deugtsaem en kunstich geschildert'; 'datze de namen van de meesters daerse voor verkocht sijn waerdich sijn te dragen en van onpartijdige Italiaense kunstkenders en schilders daer voren behouden geestimeert ende gehouden te werden' quoted in Lammertse and Van der Veen, *Uylenburgh* (note 111), p. 85.

114 Their opinion was shared by the painters Johanna van Aerssen van Wernhout, Caspar Netscher, Pieter Moninckx, Dirck Dalens, Johan von Sandrart, Johan Moninckx, Johan van Haensbergen, Martinus Mijtens, François van Santwijck en Daniel Haringh.

115 'niet weerdich te sijn te draegen den naem van een goet meester, veel min den van soodanige uytmuntende meesters daer deselve voor uytgegeven werden'; Gemeentearchief Den Haag, not. P. van Swieten, NA 932, fol.295r-v. Lammertse and Van der Veen, *Uylenburgh* (note 111), p. 87.
116 'niet considerabel sijnde om voor sulcken meesters verocht te worden'; quoted in Lammertse and Van der Veen, *Uylenburgh* (note 111), p. 88.
117 Van der Veen, *By His Own Hand* (note 22), doc. 17c (dated 28 April 1650): 'Doncker [=owner] seyde te sijn van den Den Uyl, waerop hij deposant vraeghende of het van den Ouden was, alsoo hij deposant [=Bleker, a connoisseur] daeraen twijffelde als zijnde niet fray genoech'.
118 'Verclaren sij getuygen noch al t'samen dat dienvolgende het voorsz. stuck schilderij niet waerdich is voor een stuck van Parcellus vercocht en gelevert te werden.' *Oud-Holland* 6 (1888), pp. 21-24; Van der Veen, *By His Own Hand* (note 22), doc. 24 (dated 9 June 1661).
119 Although many Italian pictures were sold in the Netherlands and collectors also owned more Italian pictures than can nowadays be found in the Netherlands. It is often too easily assumed that there was little knowledge of Italian art in the Netherlands, I think.
120 'un bon portrait de femme du maistre qui a fait les deux figures auprès dune table, qu'a Mr. van Ommeren'; see Constantijn Huygens, *Journaal van Constantijn Huygens,den zoon*, Utrecht 1876-1888, Vol. III, p. 35-38. See also Lammertse and Van der Veen, *Uylenburgh* (note 111), p. 81.
121 Moreover, the inventory of the Leiden collector Hendrick Bugge van Ring, drawn up during his lifetime, mentions two pictures by 'a good Brabant master' (*een goet Brabants meester*). See Sluijter, *All striving to adorne their houses* (note 42), pp. 102-127, esp. p. 119.
122 Van Mander, *Het Schilder-Boeck* (note 35), fol. 222r: 'Het zijn eenighe die meenen, dat dit werck by *Holbeen* self niet gheheel voldaen en is: maer dat nae zijn doot, het ghene daer noch aen ghebrack van yemandt anders voleyndight soude wesen: doch indient soo waer, heeft den opmaker den *Holbeens* handelinghe soo verstandigh connen volghen, dat het geen Schilder noch Const-verstandighe van verscheyden handen en souden oordeelen.'
123 Joachim von Sandrart, *Teutsche Academie der Bau-, Bild- und Mahlerey-Künste*, Nurnberg 1675-1680 [reprint Nördlingen 1994], vol. 1, p.250.
124 Von Sandrart states that if indeed part of the picture was completed after Holbein's death, this part is done so well that it is hard distinguish, see previous note.
125 John Rowlands, *The Paintings of Hans Holbein the Younger: Complete Edition*, Oxford 1985, pp. 148-149 (cat. no. 78).
126 In fact, John Rowlands thought that the execution of the work, even allowing for its present condition, suggests that Holbein employed a studio assistant extensively in the execution of this work. Interestingly, neither van Mander nor Von Sandrart discusses to what extent Holbein may have used assistance in this work when he was still alive.
127 Mancini, *Considerazioni sulla Pittura* (note 92), p. 330.
128 Giorgio Vasari, *Le vite de' più eccellenti pittori, scultori ed architettori*, ed. Milanesi, Florence 1880, vol. 5, pp. 527-531.
129 See p. 43 above (correspondence Rubens and Dudley Carleton).
130 'Den Engel is seer vreemt en cierlijck toeghemaeckt: de onderste slippen zijn purperigh, welcke ghedaen zijn van *Iacob Rauwaert*, die op die tijdt by hem woonde, also ick hem wel heb hooren verhalen.' Van Mander, *Het Schilder-Boeck* (note 35), fol. 246r.
131 Honig, *The Spectator as a Work of Art* (note 38), pp. 294-295; on the difference between the Nothern and the Southern Netherlands see also p. 285, notes 14 and 15.
132 Occasionally other types of collaborations are mentioned. For example, the inventory of the art dealer Johannes de Renialme lists a picture that was by Rembrandt and Dou, see Bredius, *Künstler-Inventare* (note 44), vol. 1, p. 235.
133 Willem Goeree, *Inleydingh tot de practijck der al-gemeene schilder-konst*, Amsterdam 1697 [1670], p. 100. Earlier in 1628, Jacques de Ville had stated that those artists which could both paint architectural perspectives and were able to depict figures proportionately (and thus did not need others to do this for them), deserved 'double honour'. Jacques de Ville, *T'Samen-spreekinghe betreffende de architecture ende Schilderkonst*, Gouda 1628, p. 13. On the term 'houding', see Paul Taylor, 'The Concept of Houding in Dutch Art Theory', *Journal of the Warburg and Courtauld Institutes* 55 (1992), pp. 210-232.
134 Max Rooses and Charles Louis Ruelens (eds.), *Correspondance de Rubens et documents épistolaires concernant sa vie et ses oeuvres*, 6 vols., Antwerp 1887-1909, II, doc. CXLVIII, p. 99. See also Honig, *The Spectator as a Work of Art* (note 38), p. 283. I would like to thank Ariane van Suchtelen for bringing this passage to my attention.
135 Rosenberg, *Rubensbriefe* (note 72), pp. 42-44 (letter 28 April 1618).
136 See above p. 43.
137 Peter C. Sutton, *The Age of Rubens*, Boston and Ghent 1993 (exh. cat.), pp. 238-241 (cat. no. 10).

Chapter 2
Koenraad Jonckheere

Supply and Demand: Some Notes on the Economy of Seventeenth Century Connoisseurship*

Introduction

A while ago, a large auction house contacted me about a sixteenth-century painting. They could not find the proper attribution. I suggested the name Huybrecht Beuckeleer, explaining that he was the son in law of Willem Key and the brother of Joachim. I could not be certain since little is known about this scion of the Beuckeleer family, and I therefore suggested that they should, at the very least, add a question mark after his name. The people at the auction house were appreciative of my suggestions, yet informed me that they were planning to call the painting 'Circle of Willem Key', adding that they assumed I would probably disagree. The painting had nothing to do with Willem Key's known oeuvre, but the auction house considered it wiser to use the more familiar name, and since I suggested his son in law Beuckeleer, the qualification 'circle of Willem Key' was, according to them, not completely inaccurate. This incident made me wonder about the economy of connoisseurship and the opposing interests of art dealers, art collectors and independent connoisseurs.

Connoisseurship on the art market is a pragmatic kind of connoisseurship, where the economic rule of supply and demand has a great impact. Scholars, normally, do not have to worry about such issues. Over the past few decades, they have illustrated in detail how complex an attribution can be (see also Anna Tummers' essay above).[1] Scholars today are familiar with the difficulties of attributing and, in general, tend to be very cautious. The art market does not always follow the trend.[2]

But how did seventeenth-century connoisseurs, active in the art market, deal with painters' names and attributions? Did they differentiate between a copy, a workshop copy and a '*principaal*'?[3] How important was authenticity for them? Money was at stake in the art market and the connoisseurship of art buyers might have been much more pragmatic than that of art theorists. The independent connoisseurship of writers such as De Piles or Richardson, whose ideas shaped our notion of seventeenth- and early eighteenth-century connoisseurship, was of a more theoretical nature.[4]

In this article, I would like to look at the complexity of attributions on the art market in the late seventeenth- and early eighteenth-century Netherlands. In doing so, I will not focus on descriptive sources such as Van Mander, De Bie or Houbraken, nor the writings of De Piles or Richardson, but on auction catalogues, probate inventories and other source material, such as letters, instead.[5] Let me clarify that goal. What I would like to do first is to investigate whether attributions in, for instance, auction catalogues are trustworthy and secondly to find out if it is possible to determine the value of such an attribution. In other words, are the names that are mentioned in late seventeenth-century and early eighteenth-century auction catalogues precise attributions, are they intended to be accurate, and is it possible to agree on a method that can help us determine the significance of such old 'attributions'? How complex is the behaviour of the auctioneer concerning attributions around 1700 and how often were these correct? In the second part of this article, I would like to analyse what the concerns of amateurs in the upper segment of the market were and how they made use of these auction catalogues. Did they pay much attention to authorship and did they take the attributions of the brokers-auctioneers for granted?[6]

In this article I will argue that the key to understanding attributions on the seventeenth-century Dutch art market, depends on making a differentiation between the connoisseurship of an art dealer, broker or auctioneer and the connoisseurship of an amateur in the arts.[7] These two groups, art dealers-connoisseurs and amateurs-connoisseurs, active in either the supply or demand side of the market, had conflicting interests and their 'connoisseurship' was, in my view, based on opposing principles. A division will thus make it possible to gain a better understanding of attributions by both art dealer-connoisseurs and collector-connoisseurs at the top end of the art market in the seventeenth and early eighteenth centuries.[8]

Art dealers and art lovers: A tense relation

The relation between art dealers-auctioneers and amateurs of the arts around 1700 was a tense one. Most art lovers or *liefhebbers*, as they were called, were not fond of auctioneers or art dealers. They often considered their attributions as implausible or incredible and took every chance they had to confront dealers.[9] In his unpublished book manuscript on art dealers (1730), the famous painter-writer Jacob Campo Weyerman, for instance, opened with an old Dutch saying: 'Every time God offers the world a merchant, the devil gives the world a broker'.[10] This proverb was referring to Jan Pietersz. Zomer and his colleagues. A few pages later Weyerman noted that 'a wise connoisseur would laugh himself to death if he ever heard how art dealers summed up the names of artists'.[11] He believed that the main concern of art dealers was making money, and not enjoying the intellectual pleasure of art. In the words of Weyerman, a good collector-connoisseur was never impressed by an art dealer or auctioneer's attributions. He made his own calls. Weyerman was not the only one who doubted the competence of art dealers and auctioneers. The gentleman-dealer Pieter de la Court, for instance, wrote Tsar Peter the Great to recommend him not to get involved with them.[12] He further advised the Tsar to have his own agents, buy at the auctions of honourable collectors, and not allow art dealers to interfere; because at least a painting in a respectable amateur's collection was bound to be an original. He, the famous collector Jan van Beuningen, in turn, did not value his obliged collaboration with Jan Pietersz. Zomer whom Van Beuningen accused of fraud and greed[13]. Jan Goeree, a well-known connoisseur, even published a poem attacking Jan Pietersz. Zomer: '*Dit is Jan Piet de makelaar, in de kunst een kakelaar*' (This is Jan Piet the broker, in the arts he is a joker) or '*Hier onder leyt Jan Knorrepot, Weleêr bygenaamd Zomer*' (Here lies Jan Moaner, formerly known as Zomer).[14]

Throughout his manuscript on art dealers, Weyerman makes a clear distinction between art dealers and auctioneers, on the one hand, and what he calls '*verstandige kunstkenners*' (wise connoisseurs) on the other.[15] The wise connoisseurs were the extremely wealthy collectors who, on occasion, sold paintings to friends, foreign princes or noblemen, but profiled themselves mainly as collectors. As such, they generously opened their collections up to other amateurs. Pieter de la Court and Jan van Beuningen are famous examples. It was people like them who, in Weyerman's eyes, were the real connoisseurs. Yet, they too had to make their purchases at auctions, which became one of the most important retail venues in the Netherlands in the seventeenth and eighteenth centuries. Not withstanding their apathy, wealthy amateurs systematically made use of art dealers to buy for them at the auctions or consummate deals with other art collectors. Art dealers often functioned as the agents of affluent collectors[16] and thus it is important to keep in mind the love-hate relationship between art dealers-brokers and the wealthy arts amateurs while reading the following section. It is equally important to remember that I am only discussing the top end of the art market here.

Part I. Supply: The Connoisseurship of Auctioneers

Introduction: Old Master names

We often do not realise how complex the implications of a painter's name can be (see also pp. 31-66 above, essay Anna Tummers). Before focussing on the behaviour of art dealer-auctioneers concerning attributions, it is important to sum up a few remarks concerning painter names. This should allow us to gain a better understanding of the attributions made by auctioneers, since the ways in which early modern painters used their own names is already a very confusing topic.

I believe that sixteenth- and seventeenth-century painters often deliberately caused confusion about their own names. Rubens, for instance, is famous for not signing his works, presumably to avoid discussions regarding his share in the actual production as has been suggested by Hans Van Miegroet and Neil De Marchi.[17] Rubens was certainly not the only one to have mystified the details of production in his workshop. Many painters in the sixteenth- and seventeenth-centuries Netherlands played with their own and/or their master's (often their father's) names. To illustrate the complexity of this phenomenon, I would like to bring up another example, namely that of Adriaen Thomasz. Key.[18] This sixteenth-century painter from Antwerp had, until recently, seldom been the subject of any studies and thus little was known about him. He was believed to have been the cousin of the better-known artist Willem Key, who was a friend and the counterpart of Frans Floris. Adriaen Thomasz. Key signed his portraits and religious oeuvre with his monogram ATK or with his full name Adriaen Thomasz. Key. Because he clearly worked in the style of Willem Key, most scholars, until recently, believed he was both a pupil and a cousin of Willem Key. However, although Adriaen Thomasz., as his paternal name indicated, was indeed Willem Key's pupil, he was no relation of Willem's. Adriaen Thomasz. signed his work using an AT monogram while he was still working in Willem Key's workshop and only later on, when he took over his master's workshop in 1568, added the name Key to his full signature and his monogram. He thus used the name 'Key' to brand his art.

This unrecognised fact is quite intriguing. From an economic point of view, it is clear that Adriaen Thomasz. and his clientele were fully aware of the fact that Willem Key's last name stood for a certain style and a certain material quality and that Adriaen Thomasz. achieved the same high standards as Willem Key, since he became one of the most successful painters of his era in Antwerp.[19] The adoption of the name worked; much to his own benefit Adriaen's Thomasz. managed to associate himself with the reputation of his master. Of course, applying the term *Brand Name* would be very anachronistic in this case. Adriaen Thomasz. Key definitely knew nothing about *Unique Selling Propositions* and other currently fashionable marketing strategies, but he must have been aware of the fact that his master's name offered him better opportunities in the Antwerp art market scene during the turbulent period after 1568, the year in which Willem died and Adriaen Thomasz. took over his workshop.

Another example, of a slightly different nature, was Pieter Brueghel's famous exploits of using Hieronymus Bosch's name for some of his prints. Brueghel apparently used the popularity of Bosch's name and the typical iconography associated with it, to sell his own prints, as Neil De Marchi and Hans Van Miegroet have argued.[20] However, examples of painters who profited from the names of their successful fathers (or brothers), and applied a similar style is much more common.[21] There is, of course, Pieter Brueghel and his son and namesake, but also artist names such as Pourbus, Francken, Teniers, Moreelse, Pynas, Wouwerman, Van Mieris, Van der Werff, etc.[22] In fact, the list is very long. It seems reasonable to conclude that sixteenth- and seventeenth-century painters were well aware of using their family's name as a brand name and that the name of their successful father, brother or former master had economic value, when employed as a brand name.[23]

The young Brueghel understood that it was better to sell paintings using his father's name. Both Albrecht Dürer and Peter Paul Rubens also understood the value of their family names. Dürer found himself involved in several lawsuits against engravers such as Marcantonio Raimondi for 'forging' his monogram.[24] Rubens in turn, discussed the value of several types of workshop products in a discussion with Sir Dudley Carleton. Rubens also investigated using his name on prints.[25] The young Frans Pourbus explicitly referred to his father when signing his first portraits and Frans Floris de Vriendt set up a complex method of signing paintings, differentiating explicitly between *invenit* and *fecit*.[26] However, Floris was not as rigid as he should have been. Certainly by the end of his life, he had signed numerous works as his own, which had presumably been executed in their entirety by his pupils. No wonder that disputes about the authenticity and his signature arose after his death.[27]

If painters deliberately caused confusion about their own names and the quality associated with it, then how did appraisers and auctioneers handle the names and identities of painters? How did appraisers of probate inventories use these names? Should the names they assigned to artworks be read as clear-cut attributions or do they merely refer to production in the studio in general? To investigate that, one can look at Duverger's publication of the Antwerp probate inventories, to see, for instance, whether the names Key, Pourbus, Francken, Brueghel, Floris, etc. appear here.[28] If appraisers were at all concerned with authenticity, both the first and last names of the masters and the suffixes such as 'the Older' or 'the Younger' could help identify the paintings. In other words, did seventeenth-century appraiser-connoisseurs prefer using the initials, the first name or only the surname Brueghel, to leave unclear and open to interpretation whether it was a 'product' of Pieter the Elder, Pieter the Younger, Jan the Elder, Jan the Younger, Ambrosius or from one of their 'studios'? Were they at all interested?

Table 1

	Brueghel	na Brueghel	Pieter Brueghel	Jan Brueghel	Abraham Breughel	Ambrosius Brueghel	Pieter Brueghel de Oude	Pieter Brueghel de Jonge	Helse	Jan Brueghel de Oude	Fluwelen Brueghel	Brueghel Jan de Jonge	Jan Brueghel de Jonge	Brueghel de Oude	Brueghel de Jonge	na Brueghel de Oude	na Pieter Brueghel de Oude	na Jan Brueghel de Oude	na Brueghel de Jonge	na Pieter Brueghel de Jonge	na Jan Brueghel de Jonge
Vol. I	14	6	1	1					10					1		1					
Vol. II	7	1	8	11												2					
Vol. III	9	2	1					1		1											
Vol. IV	20	1	1	2					3					9		2					
Vol. V	19	9		1		1			1					2							
Vol. VI	21	2	1						1		4			8	1	1					
Vol. VII	12	5				1	1		3		3			4							
Vol. VIII	23	0	2	20		2			5		2			2	1			2			
Vol. IX	16	2	1	1		1			8		8			7				1			
Vol. X	26	2									1			1				1			
Del XI	30	1							2		13			8				2		1	
Vol. XII	25				1				2		24			3							
TOTAL	222	31	15	36	1	5	1	1	35	1	55	0	0	45	2	6	0	6	0	1	0

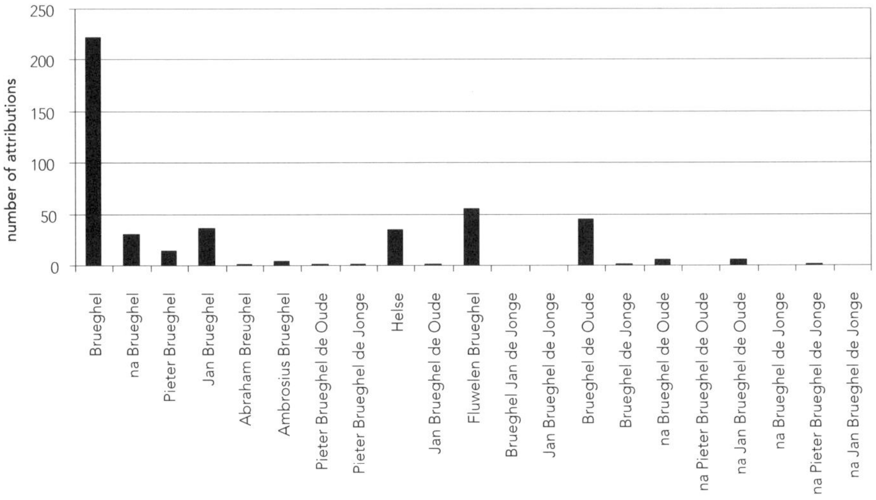

Graph 1

The results of these simple samples in graph 1 and table 1 are astonishing, when we look at the use of the name 'Brueghel'. 'Brueghel' (without first name or other specification), was mentioned 222 times. This means that the appraiser-connoisseur – if they were in fact connoisseurs – rarely differentiated between Pieter the Elder, Pieter the Younger, Jan the Elder, Jan de Younger, Ambrosius, the 'studio' or the copyists. We all know that there is a huge difference between, for instance, the work of Pieter the Younger and Jan the Elder and that Brueghels were pretty much copied en masse. Pieter Brueghel the Younger, one the most productive scions of the family, was mentioned only 36 times while Pieter the Elder was mentioned with his full and precise name only once.[29] As for Jan Brueghel, little differentiation was made between the father and the son.[30] The oeuvres of these two seem to have merged in seventeenth-century Antwerp under the common name of 'Fluwelen (Velvet) Brueghel'. This was perpetrated even while Jan Breughel the Younger was still alive and ultimately produced as much as his father Jan the Elder. Especially interesting in this context is the dispute in 1675 about the Brueghel painting *Deluvion*, published by Duverger. In the document (18 November 1675), Matthijs Musson and Augustijn Tijssens, an art dealer and a painter respectively, testified that a certain painting was not by Brueghel.[31] Curiously enough, the 'connoisseurs' in question did not differentiate between the several scions of the Brueghel family and merely stated that the *Deluvion* was not by '*Brueghel*'.

Jaap van der Veen made this same observation in his recently published essay on connoisseurship. He notes, for instance, that auction catalogues from seventeenth-century Northern Netherlands often feature 'meaningless attributions' to artists like 'Brueghel', among others.[32]

Brueghel	after (or mannor of) Brueghel	Pieter Brueghel	Jan Brueghel	Abraham Breughel	Ambrosius Brueghel	Pieter Brueghel de Oude	Pieter Brueghel de Jonge	Helse Brueghel	Jan Brueghel de Oude	Fluwelen Brueghel	After (or mannor of) Fluwelen Brueghel	Brueghel Jan de Jonge	Jan Brueghel de Jonge	Brueghel de Oude	Boere Brueghel	Brueghel de Jonge	na Brueghel de Oude	na Pieter Brueghel de Oude	na Jan Brueghel de Oude	na Brueghel de Jonge	na Pieter Brueghel de Jonge	na Jan Brueghel de Jonge	Koddige Brueghel ?
30	16	6	1	2	-	2	-	18	-	172	6	-	-	14	1	-	-	-	-	-	-	-	1

Table 2

The data presented in Table 2 (which I based on the database discussed below) confirm Van der Veen's intuition. In the late seventeenth and early eighteenth centuries, auctioneers tended to not differentiate between Jan I Brueghel (the Velvet) and Jan II Brueghel, for example. All of their landscapes be they by one or the other were labelled 'Velvet Brueghel'. Pieter Brueghel the Elder was named only twice. It seems that the Dutch auctioneers followed the lead of the seventeenth-century appraisers in Antwerp.

It is clear that a majority of the paintings were attributed to a broad-spectrum 'brand name', even if the successors or the studio produced many more works than the founding master himself. The appraisers of the estate inventories seldom differentiated between the master, the pupil, or one of the copyists. There are exceptions, but these are rare.[33]

As Van der Veen correctly concludes, this fact does not allow us to conclude, however, that there was no interest at all in authenticity. But it does mean that authenticity was not the primary concern of appraisers and that the value of a painting was not explicitly linked to authenticity, at least not by most of the appraisers or auctioneers. As I will argue further on, art lovers had very different interests and were more concerned about authenticity.

Of course, this sample is very limited, but I believe it is exemplary although it deserves more extensive research. That this kind of research would be fruitful, is something I will try to articulate later on in this article, with the aid of a database of late seventeenth- and early eighteenth-century auction catalogues. Thus far, I hope that I have made it clear that first of all the attitude of painters themselves and appraisers of inventories regarding painter's names in the sixteenth and seventeenth centuries was far more complex than one might have assumed. Secondly, authenticity does not seem to have been the primary issue among appraisers. It seems to me that these practising connoisseurs rarely intended to actually determine precisely who did what painting. At least, not in their descriptions. That they seldom referred to monograms or signatures confirms my point here, as I will discuss below.

Attributions in auction catalogues at the end of the seventeenth century

Did broker-auctioneers in the seventeenth century, contrary to the appraisers, clearly specify the authorship of a painting in their auction catalogues? Auctioneers were there to make money, in contrast to an appraiser. The higher the auction bids, the larger was his take.[34] If an auctioneer had the chance to sell a painting as 'autographed' or 'by his own hand', would he have done so?[35] Would the late seventeenth-century connoisseur-art dealer have been able to tell the difference between Pieter Brueghel the Elder and the Younger, for instance, or would he have – like the appraisers – seen both of them as Brueghels? Did the broker anticipate concern about authenticity on the part of the buyers? To answer these questions, I used a familiar source, namely the Gerard Hoet–Pieter Terwesten publication of auction catalogues printed in the period 1752-1768.[36] I created a database of all the preserved auction catalogues of paintings published between 1676 and 1739. For this article, I selected all of the auction catalogues published by Jan Pietersz. Zomer circa 1700 and then re-published by Hoet.[37]

Jan Pietersz. Zomer was a renowned connoisseur in early eighteenth-century Amsterdam.[38] He was the most successful organiser of auctions and a very busy appraiser. He was thus an obvious choice to study how connoisseurs dealt with painters' names at the end of the seventeenth century in auction catalogues. Did they use a complex system of attributions (e.g., school of, style of, studio of, etc.) or did they always attribute it to one painter or another, or even more generally speaking, to one brand? The possible impact of Zomer's behaviour concerning attributions on the prices fetched at auction, is an issue that I will discuss later on in this article.

Firstly, did Jan Pietersz. Zomer have any knowledge of the implications of sixteenth- and seventeenth-century painters' names and if so, did it have any influence on his attributions? In other words, did Jan Pietersz. Zomer, for instance, use the name Brueghel as a generalising brand name or did he try to find out the actual accurate – i.e., what we consider accurate – authorship on any occasions? Did he recognise that one Brueghel, Rubens or Rembrandt was not the other and that attributions were a complex and nuanced issue? The method I used to investigate the problem is rather simple. I took all the Zomer auction catalogues, annotated with prices and standardised the painter names to be able to rank them alphabetically by last name. In so doing, I could easily determine whether Zomer was at all consistent in his use of names (e.g. spelling.) and I could examine any nuances concerning the attributions he may have made.[39] The results were as clear as they were surprising. In the sample studied, Jan Pietersz. Zomer always attributed the painting to the 'master', without bothering with any fine tuning. This means that all works in the manner of, for instance, Rubens were simply called Rubens.[40] Zomer generally made a distinction between, for instance, fathers and sons if their styles were distinctly different (e.g., Pieter Brueghel and Jan Brueghel), but not between originals, studio copies or inferior copies (e.g., Jan Brueghel the Elder and Jan Brueghel the Younger) if they were of a similar nature. I only found a few exceptions to this rule in all of the lots in the sample. Zomer referred to just two paintings as 'copies after' out of a total of 1226, namely one after Rubens and one after Rembrandt.[41] All of the other paintings were attributed to the masters themselves, without any reservations on the part of Zomer. This indicates that Zomer ranked the paintings in the style of the master under the master's brand name, without questioning their actual nature (copies, style of, etc.). A consequence could have been that Zomer sold many paintings as anonymous, but that was not the case at all.

Only 21 paintings out of the 1226 or 1.7 % were catalogued as 'anonymous'. This seems to indicate that Jan Pietersz. Zomer himself did not raise any questions about the nature of the paintings. On the other hand, these stunning facts illustrate that the practising connoisseurs like Zomer, at the end of the seventeenth century, did not distinguish between an original, a studio copy, or a work by a student. At least, Zomer did not make these distinctions in his auction catalogues.[42] Nonetheless, Zomer was considered one of the best – if not the best – of Amsterdam's connoisseurs.

Even more stunning is the fact that Zomer never mentioned monograms or signatures, even though many of the thousands of paintings he handled during his career must have been signed or marked. Compilers of inventories and auctioneers like Zomer must have made use of the names and the monograms on the paintings for attributions.[43] Nonetheless, he seldom referred to them as such.[44] Zomer chose to keep his information a secret and thus worked against the idea of a transparent market, which is in sharp contrast with some eighteenth-century French art dealers (see Neil De Marchi and Hans Van Miegroet's essay in this volume). He apparently never considered a signature worth mentioning in his auction catalogues. It is therefore impossible to confirm the notion that an art dealer-connoisseur like Jan Pietersz. Zomer was interested in authenticity when attributing paintings, since he deliberately and almost systematically *denied* obvious evidence of authorship.[45] However, Zomer was not unique in this respect. Seventeenth-century appraisers of probate inventories in Antwerp and Amsterdam seldom mentioned signatures or monograms. It is quite easy to check how much attention appraisers paid to signatures. Once again, I refer to Duverger's publication of probate inventories.[46] If one checks Duverger's publication under Frans Floris, for instance, a painter who we know systematically signed his paintings, one sees that signatures were seldom, if ever, mentioned. In the course of the seventeenth century, no appraiser ever referred to Floris's monogram ('FFF' or 'FFF et IV').[47] Issues of authenticity were clearly not their main concern.

One cannot deny that Zomer was like most art dealer-connoisseurs in that he had little interest in the terms 'studio', 'pupil' or 'disciple'. He also paid no special attention to clear-cut evidence of authorship such as signatures. He used painters' names in his catalogues to divide the works of art into certain recognisable categories, rather than to define the precise, correct attributions. He used the names to sort out the vast number of paintings, to in effect 'catalogue' them. He never specifically mentioned whether any particular work was an original or a copy. In doing so, Zomer also dodged any possible legal actions.[48] Zomer never resolved any issues of authorship in his auctions catalogues.[49] He simply suggested or insinuated certain possibilities.[50]

Zomer, like the other auctioneers, was paid a percentage of his turnover. If authorship and authenticity had been a primary concern of auctioneers, art dealers or appraisers, one would have expected them to systematically mention the signatures or monograms and to differentiate between copies and 'originals'. As I will show later on, elite art lovers, who often purchased works at auctions, unlike the brokers, were interested in authenticity and thus a mark of authenticity increased a work's value. So why Zomer and the other appraisers systematically ignored issues of attribution must lie elsewhere. I believe that Zomer simply let the buyers figure it out for themselves. Zomer identified the type, the style, the brand of a particular work, but it was up to the buyers themselves to recognise the quality or lack of quality of a particular painting. Jan Pietersz. Zomer did, however, sometimes help buyers a bit. On some occasions he would add 'quality labels' to the descriptions of paintings, calling them '*extraordinaer, fraei, konstig, kapitael*' (extraordinary, beautiful, artistic, important), etc. Did it help? It certainly did. Whenever Zomer added a 'quality label' to the description of the painting the prices rose to levels above the average prices paid for that particular painter's work. Take, for instance, the example of Gerard Dou. I created a table of the paintings attributed to Dou by Jan Pietersz. Zomer in the sample of auction catalogues and ranked them by the prices they sold for in auctions. I indicated the paintings that Jan Pietersz. Zomer had marked with a quality label, to see if the opinion of the appraiser and auctioneer had any influence on the buyer's judgement. It is not surprising, in lieu of what I noted earlier, that Zomer's quality descriptions almost always helped to escalate the price of a painting.

Graph 3

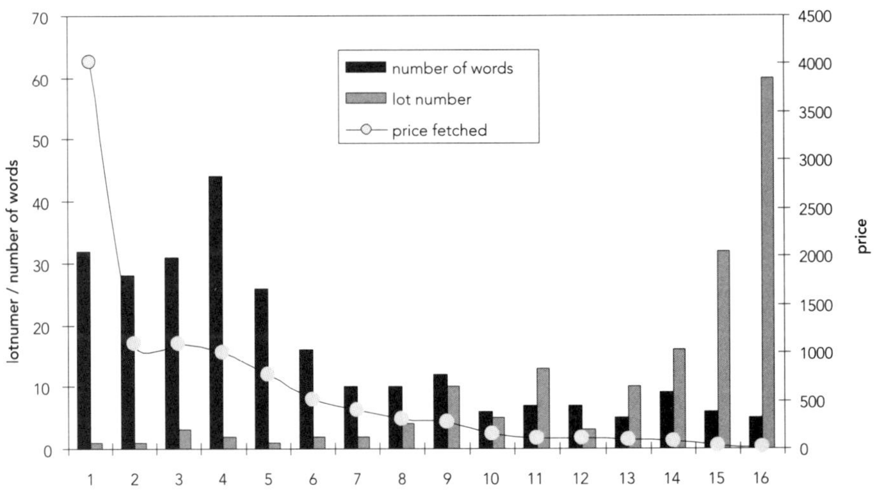

Table 3

Number of words	Lot no.	Description		Price in guilders
32	1	Een Kapitael Stuk met deuren, van Gerard Douw, zynde een Vrouwtje met een Kintje op haer schoot, in een Binnenhuys by een Barbiers Winkel, &c. ongemeen konstig, en 't beste (van hem) bekent	A capital piece with doors, by Gerard Dou, being a woman with a child on her lap, in an interior next to a barbers shop, etc. uncommonly artful and best known (by him)	4025
28	1	Een Vrouwtje in een Keuken, Wortelen schrapende, nevens een Jongetje met een muyssevalletje in de hand, met veel raer bywerk, extraordinaer konstig en natuurlyk geschildert door Gerard Douw	A woman in a kitchen, scraping carrots and a young boy with a mousetrap in his hand, with many unusual details extraordinarily artful and naturally painted by Gerard Dou	1100
31	3	Een Schoon Meysje in een Nisje, rustende met haer een arm op een Koper Emmertje &c. Zoo gracieus en lieflyk als 't door konst te maken is mede van Gerard Douw	A beautiful girl in a niche, leaning with her arm on a copper kettle etc. as gracious and lovely as art can make it by Gerard Dou	1100
44	2	Een Oud Mannetje zittende op een Stoel, daer de Meester by komt, met een Kaers in de hand, hem ziende in de Keel, en een oud Vrouwtje daer by staende met een Lantare in de hand, ongemeen konstig, zagt en heerlyk geschildert, door dezelve	An old man sitting on a chair, the master coming to join him with a candle in his hand, looking in his troth and an old lady adjoining them with a lantern in her hand, uncommonly artful, tenderly en delightfully painted, by the same [Gerard Dou]	1000
26	1	Een Schoon Keukemeysje, met een Visvlootje voor haer, daer by een Jongetje met een Haes en meerder bywerk van Gerard Douw, ongemeen teder en konstig geschildert	A beautiful Kitchen maid, with a fish dish before her, and a young boy with a hare and more details by Gerard Dou, uncommonly tenderly and artfully painted	770
16	2	Een Astronomicus met een Kaers in de hand, ziende in een Boek, zeer natuurlyk door dezelve	An astronomer with a candle in his hand, looking in a book, very natural by the same [Gerard Dou]	505
10	2	Een Maria Magdalena, in een Kas met deuren van dezelve	A Mary Magdalene, in a case with doors by the same [Gerard Dou]	400
10	4	Een Kaersligtend Meysje, kragtig en zeer natuurlyk geschildert, door dezelve	A candle lighting girl, powerful and very naturally painted, by the same [Gerard Dou]	305
12	10	Een biddende Oud-Man, en een Vrouw in een Binnenhuys, van Gerard Douw	A praying old man, and a woman in an interior by Gerard Dou	270
6	5	Een Belleblasertje, heel goet. van dito	A bubble blower, very good, by the same [Gerard Dou]	160
7	13	Een Schilder in zyn Konstkamer, van Douw	A painter in his cabinet, by Dou	112
7	3	Een kas, de deuren geschildert, van dito	A case, the doors painted, by the same [Gerard Dou]	101
5	10	Een Melk-eetstertie van Gerard Douw	A woman eating [sic] milk, by Gerard Dou	100
9	16	Een Advokaet in zyn Studeerkamer, van G. D. ongemeen curieus	A lawyer in his study, by G.D. [Gerard Dou] uncommonly elaborate	75
6	32	Een Vrouwe Tronitje, van Gerard Douw	A woman's head, by Gerard Dou	26
5	60	Een Jongetje van Gerrit Dou	A boy by Gerard Dou	8

A description in an auction catalogue is more interesting than it seems at first sight. The number of words used, for instance, gives a good indication of the probable quality and authenticity of a painting. The numbers of words seem to be proportionate to the prices fetched at auctions. The example of Gerard Dou is fascinating (table 3 and graph 3) in this regard. Dou was a painter with a fairly recognisable and unique style and he was extremely popular in the early eighteenth century.[51] Connoisseurs presumably knew his work well. The various works sold under Dou's name fall into three distinct categories: The first category concerns the very cheap works, compared to the rest. The second category comprises more expensive paintings, while the third category includes Dou's most exclusive works. It is fair to assume that the cheapest paintings were mostly copies or painted in the style of Dou, along with some damaged works perhaps. Material damage, of course lowered the price of a work. Interestingly, the descriptions of these cheaper paintings are always short – between five to ten words – and very little specific. In the second category, one finds more expensive paintings. I assume that these works are mostly 'simple' Dou with one figure and without much '*bijwerk*' (ornamentation). I have come to this conclusion because several of those paintings can be identified. The descriptions in the old auction catalogues were always longer – between ten to 20 words – and more specific. The third category includes the exclusive Dou paintings: complex works with numerous figures and '*bijwerk*'. The descriptions are always long – more than 20 words – and quite specific. Zomer added a lot of praise to the descriptions of these paintings.

At the same time, the place of a painting in an auction catalogue was also very important. As Adriaen Bout, a famous art lover and agent during the period 1710-1730 stated, better-quality paintings were always placed in the early part of the catalogue.[52] He added that this did not necessarily mean that these paintings were the first to be auctioned off, because auctioneers usually only began selling their best paintings after the elite collectors had arrived. That Bout's remark is accurate is confirmed by graph 4, which shows the average prices fetched at auction per lot number.[53]

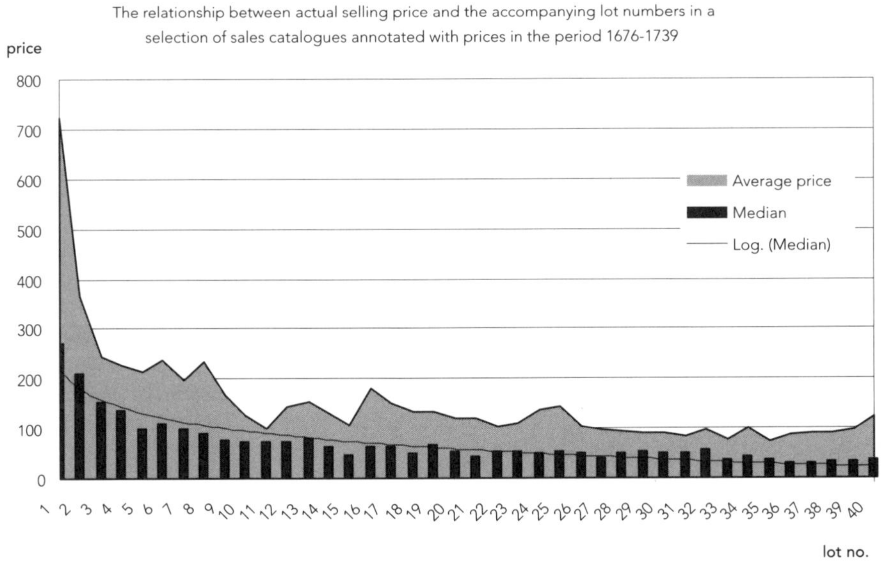

Graph 4

To summarise, then, one can say that the auctioneer used more words and added quality labels to describe better artworks, and that he ranked the works in the auction catalogue according to the alleged quality and monetary value of a particular work. The auctioneer, however, never determined authenticity. The buyers, on the other hand, paid high prices for higher-ranked, and more elaborately described paintings. In other words, I see a direct connection here between the number of words used by the auctioneer to describe a painting, the quality label attached to the description and its place in the catalogue, on the one hand, and the prices paid and the presumed quality of the painting, on the other. If one uses these among other variables, it becomes possible to note, among the vast number of paintings, that we only know from concise catalogue descriptions, these paintings of which the seventeenth-century market believed that they were the best type of pictures produced by well-known masters. In other words, the one 'Dou' or 'Brueghel' has more to do with Dou or Brueghel than the other, and a good analysis of auction catalogues can further help subdivide the distinctions. Observations like these make it possible to attach some value to a description of a painting by, for instance, Dou in auction catalogues of which no price annotations survived. It is, however, important to also analyse each auctioneer's own habits individually, because each had his own idiosyncrasies.

Let me now draw some preliminary conclusions. First of all, an art broker and auctioneer like Zomer did not differentiate between master, studio or school. He used the master's name as a kind of 'brand name', even for works that obviously lacked the necessary quality. If the painting of a certain brand was of an extraordinary quality in his opinion, he might add a 'quality label' in the form of praise, which, in turn, had some 'influence' on the market because buyers were usually prepared to pay more at auction for a work with a quality label, although this label was not a guarantee authenticity at all. It is the way these painters' names were used that makes it difficult for us to understand how connoisseurship in the seventeenth-century art market worked, for it seems that quality and certainly authorship were secondary issues for the art dealer-connoisseurs like Zomer. Zomer arranged paintings by name for the complex and, by the end of the seventeenth century, extensive art market.[54] He began with a preliminary classification and it was up to the buyers to do their own fine tuning. At least, this is the impression one gets from analysing Zomer's auction catalogues. It is possible that Zomer gave more detailed advice face-to-face during viewing days or in private. But his catalogue descriptions do not give any such indication themselves.

Part II. Demand: The connoisseurship of collectors

How '*liefhebbers*' (art lovers) dealt with attributions, quality and authenticity is another issue. I would now like to draw some attention to various aspects of the amateur's connoisseurship in relation to the art market. I will not go into the connoisseurship of the independent experts, but merely look at those amateurs-connoisseurs who risked their money and reputations in the process of purchasing art. I believe that criticism from the sideline has generated a more theoretical kind of connoisseurship, which, of course, does not mean there was no overlap. Someone like Lambert ten Kate, for instance, might have been a well-known connoisseur, but he was not a great collector of paintings, compared to some of his contemporaries.[55] Art buyers had to be, *nolens volens*, pragmatic.

So, how did wealthy art collectors deal with the problem of attributions and connoisseurship? Did they place their recently purchased paintings on an easel, study the works in detail and then decide on the quality and attribution, as we can see on so many collector's cabinet paintings? They certainly did, as Anna Tummers convincingly argued in her essay in this volume (pp. 127-147). But did they base their final decisions completely on their own findings? I doubt it. I believe that connoisseurs at the top end of the art market rarely relied solely on their own good judgement. I will first argue that collector-connoisseurs used their own critical capacities to determine the quality and the monetary value of a piece of art. The mere pictorial quality was often as important as the artist's name as it appeared in the catalogues. Secondly, I will argue that provenance and provenance research were also important in determining the value of an attribution for the elite art collector-connoisseurs in the early eighteenth century. Thirdly, I will argue that collector-connoisseurs were dependent on each other. An implicit, widespread acceptance of an attribution seems to have been a key factor in determining authenticity. Contrary to the art dealer's connoisseurship, the art lover's connoisseurship was, foremost a matter of *falsification*: an attribution was considered correct if it was unchallenged. In other words, elite art collectors formed a closed community in which market transparency was quintessential and from which paintings with challenged attributions were systematically banned.

Some notes on quality and anonymity

It is well known that art lovers, at least in the eighteenth century, did some of their own fine tuning regarding the attributions as they appeared in auctions catalogues. Gentleman dealers such as Willem Lormier often wrote 'more precise' attributions in the margins of auction catalogues, which proves that the names in auctions catalogues were not taken for granted and that art buyers used their own good sense when it came to authorship.[56] However, the importance that amateurs attached to names, although important, must be nuanced somewhat. Buyers at auctions were sometimes clearly more interested in the artistic quality of a painting than in the name attached to it (as Anna Tummers reveals see pp. 31-66 in this volume, this notion can further be confirmed in the art theoretical literature). For example, Eric Jan Sluijter noticed, that, although imported Flemish landscape paintings were all considered anonymous foreign rubbish ('*Brabantse vodden*') by complaining Dutch artists in the early seventeenth century, some art lovers paid abnormally high prices in auction for some of those nameless pieces.[57] As Sluijter points out, the paintings could not have been the junk that the frustrated Dutch painters described it as. I noticed the same differences between cheap and expensive anonymous paintings around 1700.

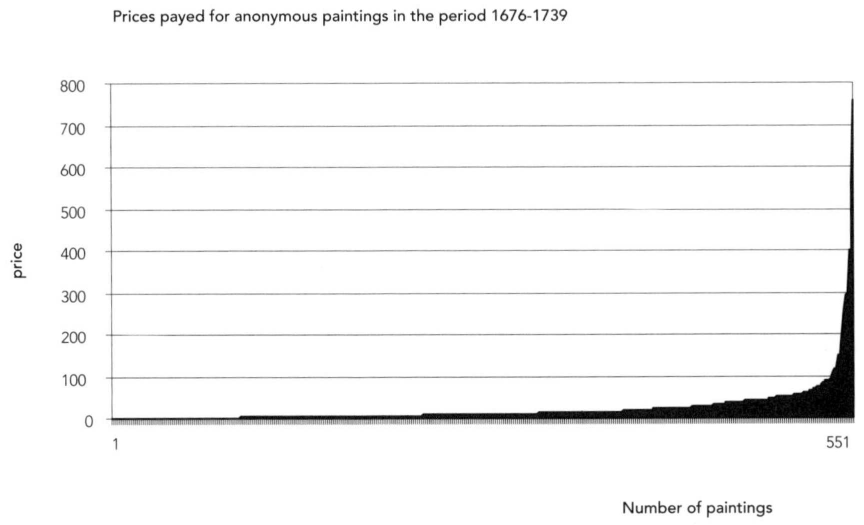

Graph 5

Graph 6

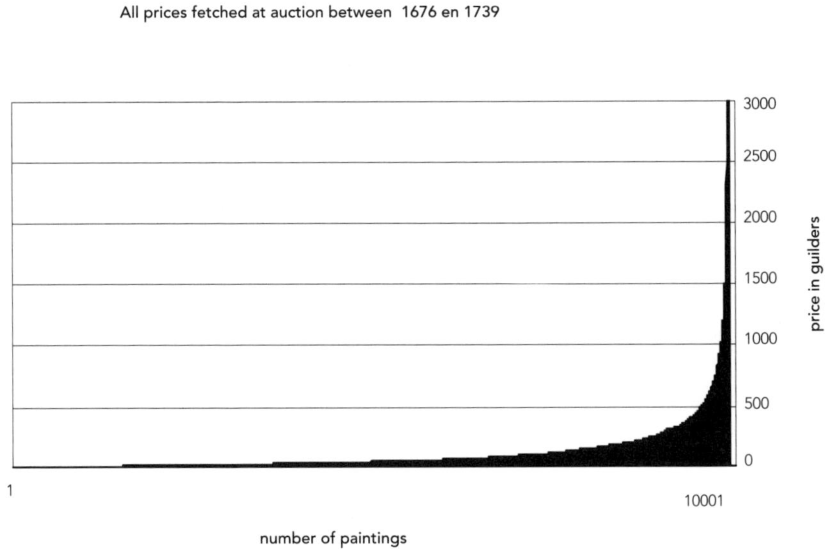

These curves show that the prices paid at auction for anonymous work are a very good reflection of the prices paid for 'attributed' paintings. Both graphs (5 & 6) show a similar exponential curve. In the category of anonymous paintings, the high-priced ones were as rare as the very expensive paintings were rare in the market for attributed paintings. That a painting was a nameless product therefore says little about its quality and an attribution does not automatically guarantee financial gain. Seventeenth-century art lovers were prepared to pay a lot for those nameless products, which subsequently means that the name, however important, was not essential.[58] This confirms, in my opinion, that quality in itself was a significant factor on the art market and that names used by art dealer-connoisseurs (i.e. attributions) did, in the buyer's opinion, not necessarily stand for quality or authenticity - remember the table of Dou paintings mentioned earlier. There was not a strict congruence between attribution and quality (which does not mean of course that issues of authenticity were of no importance at all).

At the same time, these graphs shows that art lovers in Holland circa 1700 were prepared to pay small fortunes for high-quality anonymous paintings. So it seems that they indeed placed the paintings on an easel to judge their quality for themselves, and were prepared to pay for it if the quality met their standards. An attribution was thus not a *conditio sine qua non* for an art collector. However, they seldom paid as much for an anonymous work as for an attributed painting. One gets the impression that an amateur was prepared to pay more for a high quality anonymous painting than for one with a dubious attribution.

Summarising, the graphs showing the prices paid for anonymous paintings compared to paintings in general (during the period 1676-1739 in Amsterdam) indicates that collector-connoisseurs were seriously interested in the quality of a work and were not willing to blindly accept the 'generalising' attributions made by auctioneers.

Provenance – It has hardly been pointed out that provenance was frequently used by art collectors around 1700 as a way of determining the authenticity of a painting.[59] But we can deduce from several sources that the most important European art collectors who were active in the Netherlands circa 1700, paid a great deal of attention to it. De la Court's remarks that were noted earlier are one example of this (see p.70 above). A collection catalogue for Jacques Meyers's collection, printed in 1714, is particularly interesting in this respect.[60] Jacques Meyers was probably the most important private collector ever in the Netherlands. His collection consisted of several dozen paintings by Poussin, Rubens, Van Dyck, Dou, Rembrandt and other superior artists, as well as a few hundred paintings by other renowned artists such as Cornelis van Poelenburch and Adriaen van der Werff. Meyers paid a great deal of attention in his collection catalogue to both the provenance of his paintings and the implicit acceptance of their authenticity and uniqueness (value) by connoisseurs from all over Europe. For example, the catalogue opens with Meyers' crown jewels, the *Seven Sacraments* by Nicolas Poussin.[61] Meyers details the complicated story of their provenance and includes the opinions of various connoisseurs about the seven paintings. Moreover, he did that for every important painting in his collection. About Poussin's *Abduction of the Sabine Women*, for instance, he noted that it came from the collection of 'Monsieur Passart, Maitres des Comptes'.[62] About Rubens' *Jesus playing with three children and a lamb*, currently at Wilton House (fig. 1), Meyers informed his readers that the painting was so familiar to connoisseurs that it was not necessary to discuss its provenance. Roger de Piles, whose books were much read in the Dutch Republic, in one of his writings

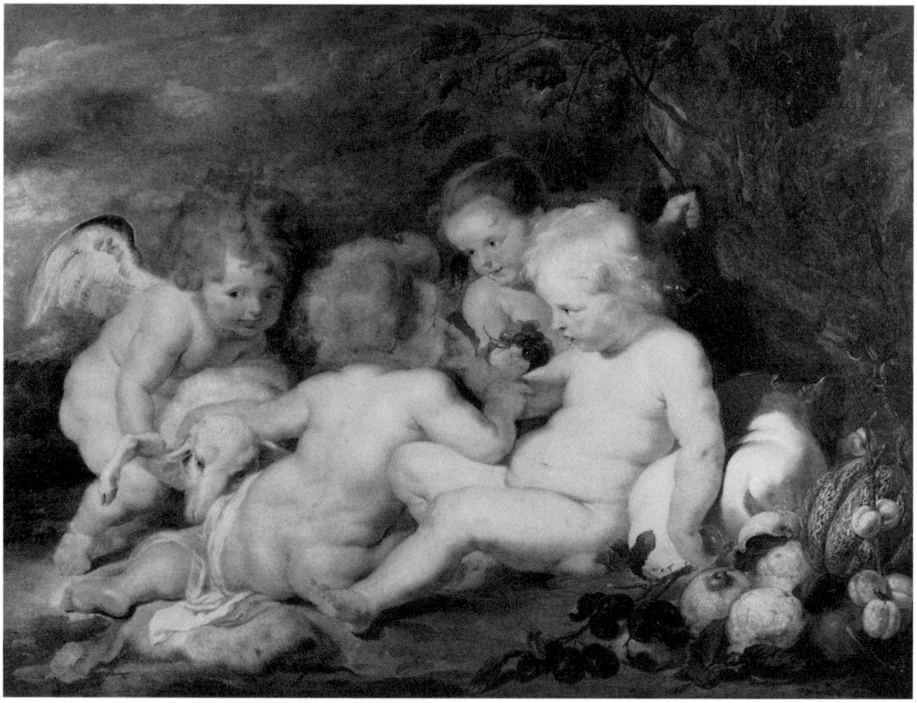

1.

Peter Paul Rubens
Christ, John and two angels, c 1615-1620
Wilton House, Salisbury

pointed out that Rubens himself had given this painting, upon the instigation of the Spanish king, to the Duke de Gramont.[63] Meyers was alluding to this story. According to de Piles, Van Dyck's *Rinaldo and Armida* had long served as 'an ornament in Honselaarsdijck, and later in King William III's collection at Het Loo'.[64]

Jacques Meyers is an exceptional case. Whatever he claims on most of his acquisitions can be double checked among other sources and most of what he said seems true. He did not improvise the provenances to give his collection a certain grandeur, although the pedigree of most of his best pieces had a certain splendour, no doubt. Meyers mentioned the provenance of the paintings to guarantee their authenticity. If there was some doubt about a painting's attribution, even though it had a good provenance, Meyers did not hesitate to mention it. For instance, he owned a *Venus drying her feet* that was attributed to Raphael: 'this painting was perfectly preserved. It was engraved by Marcantonio [Raimondi], the engraver of Raphael's paintings. Several connoisseurs, nonetheless, have doubted that the painting was done by the famous painter and believe they recognise Andrea Sacchi's taste and style. It is from the Duc de Gramont's collection.'[65] In confirming the doubts associated with this painting, Meyers implicitly confirmed the confidence that one could have in the authenticity of the rest of his collection.

What is true for Meyers is true for a number of major collectors in the seventeenth- and early eighteenth-century Netherlands. Jan van Beuningen for instance, in the title of the auction catalogue of stadtholder-King William III's collection of paintings, pointed out that it consisted of 'extraordinary, major pieces by great and prominent painters, gathered through serious efforts and costs from famous cabinets'.[66] The provenance was an important issue here. Whoever drew up this catalogue paid attention to the provenance of the major (i.e. the most expensive) pieces. Valerius Röver, for instance, noted where he bought his paintings and, when known, also noted the provenances.[67] Diego Duarte, another famous collector, did much the same. Duarte urged the person who had sold him an important Raphael, to write him a letter explaining the provenance of the work.[68] The correspondence of the Van den Berghe-Van der Vennen firm in Ghent, published by Eric Duverger, is loaded with remarks about the provenance of artworks.[69] Famous connoisseurs in the seventeenth and early eighteenth century were thus at least as keen as Meyers, Röver and Duarte regarding the pedigree of their acquisitions.

As these examples show, good provenance helped legitimise attributions in the seventeenth and early eighteenth centuries. In circa 1700, most paintings had not moved from collection to collection that often. Therefore, in many cases, it was possible for connoisseurs to trace the pedigree, especially since most of the elite collectors marked the backs of their paintings with wax seals. Most of these seals have disappeared since then, but they were used in the seventeenth and early eighteenth centuries. The provenance was, in other words, often 'sealed' on the back of the painting. A rare example of a painting with interesting information sealed to the back is, for instance, *The Surgeon* by Adriaen Brouwer (fig. 2).[70] A small note, attached with sealing wax onto the back of the panel informs us that a certain 'Cossiau' once had something to do with the painting. Jan Joost van Cossiau was the court painter and art representative of Lothar Franz von Schönborn who bought the painting for his patron at the auction of Adriaen Paets' collection in Rotterdam in 1713 . We know from another source that Van Cossiau was at that auction. This fact makes one wonder if it was a custom to stick buyers' names on the backs of paintings at Dutch auctions in the late seventeenth and early eighteenth centuries.

That collectors actively researched the provenance of paintings can be also be easily demonstrated. One of the best examples I know of are the acquisitions of James Brydges of Chandos, a famous early eighteenth-century English collector. Chandos was very active in the Dutch art market scene.[71] His correspondence with agents across Europe illustrates, in great rare detail, the importance of a good provenance in the elite European art trade. The first time that Chandos performed some provenance research was when an art dealer-agent in Bayonne offered him a painting by Anthony van Dyck.[72] The painting, according to the seller, represented a kitchen scene and contained a (self-) portrait of Van Dyck himself. Chandos did not believe that Van Dyck had ever painted a kitchen scene and asked for a drawing of it, to be able to get an idea of what the painting looked like and come up with a better assessment. Louis du Livrer, the agent in Bayonne, had a better idea of how to convince Chandos to buy the painting. He knew the provenance of the painting. It came from Whitehall and was sold in the Commonwealth Sale.[73] Du Livrer urged Chandos to contact the caretaker of the Queen's paintings to verify that the painting was indeed part of the old inventories of Charles I's first's collection at Whitehall. A second example is Chandos' acquisition

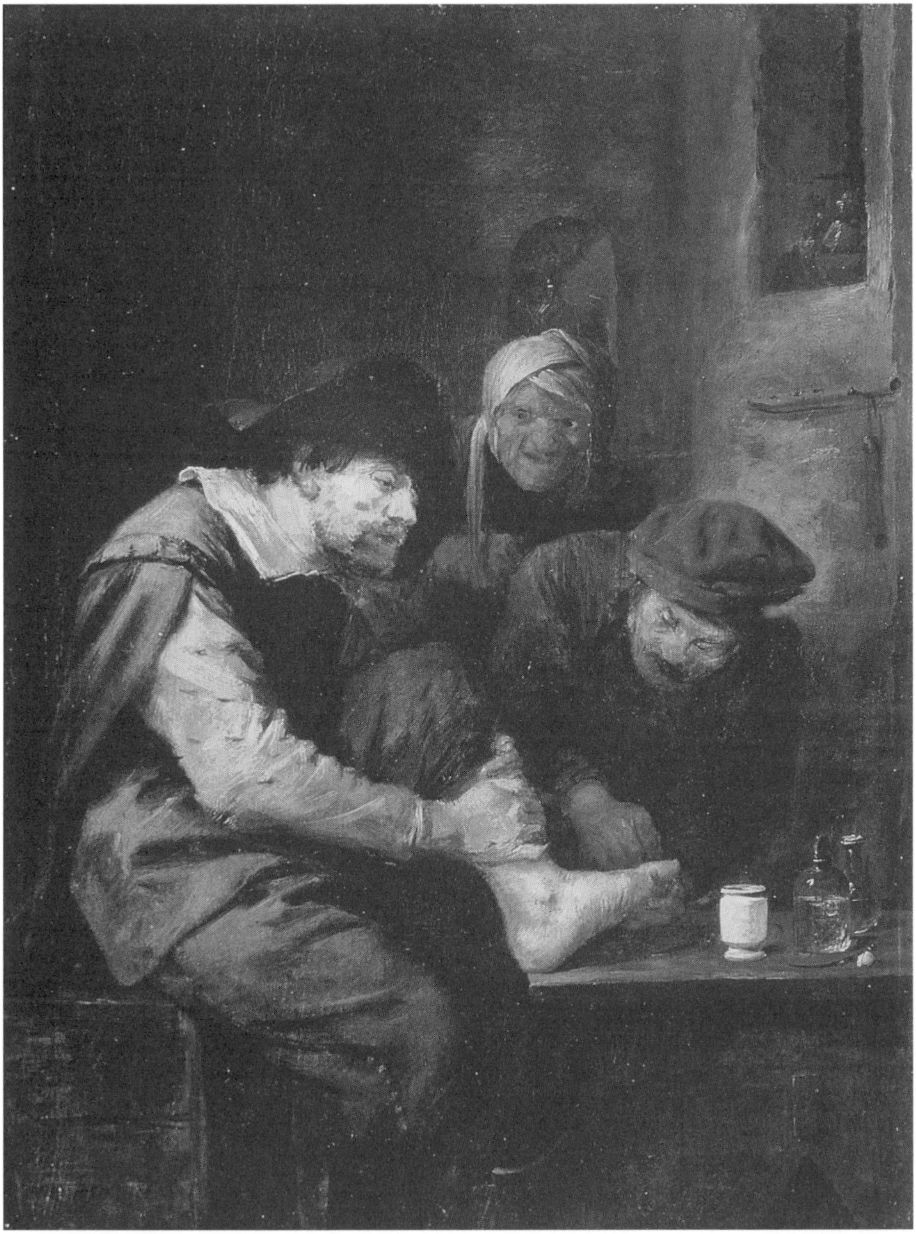

2.

Adriaen Brouwer
The surgeon, c. 1630
Städel-Museum, Frankfurt

of Andrea del Sarto's copy after Raphael's *Portrait of Pope Leo X with two Cardinals*, mentioned by Giorgio Vasari.[74] Chandos describes his concerns about the authenticity and provenance of the famous painting in a striking manner. In a letter dated 22 September 1716, Chandos formulates his concerns as follows: 'The picture ought to be as tenderly handled as a lady and the least question upon them casts a stain upon their reputations, which is hardly ever washed off. Several have seen this picture, all agree it to be a very fine one, but whither it is the same copy which Andrea made, few among us have judgment enough to know. I wish you could inform me whither ever any other copy was made of it, and how the original came to be in the Duke of Parma's gallery, for as I take it, it was paid for and given to the Duke of Florence."[75] Chandos had bought Del Sarto's famous copy after Raphael a few months earlier with the assistance of his agent in Italy, Henry Davenant.[76] The painting had arrived in England and the connoisseurs, as was generally the case when an important new acquisition arrived, assembled to have a look at the painting. All of them agreed about the exceptional quality of the canvas, but to ensure that it was indeed the one and only exquisite copy, someone suggested that Chandos have the provenance checked. After all, they already knew part of the pedigree, but the missing link could dispel all doubt. Everything turned out well. The provenance was proven and the painting was considered to be the one by Del Sarto. There were no further doubts about its authenticity.

One significant phrase used by Chandos was: 'few among us have judgment enough to know'. The duke's words remind us of the problems that connoisseurs in seventeenth- and eighteenth-century Europe had to cope with: they seldom had anything to compare their paintings with. Neither Chandos nor the connoisseurs could compare the Del Sarto with other paintings he had done, since there were practically none in England and they could not readily travel to each location with an expensive work of art. They were dependent on the judgement of their agents and, more importantly perhaps, on the history of its provenance. The more valuable a painting was, the more crucial it was to alleviate any lingering doubts about its provenance, so that 'no stains could be cast upon its reputation', as Chandos so eloquently wrote. Van Gool made a similar remark about Dutch connoisseurship of Italian painting.[77] He also considered it difficult, if not impossible, to verify the attributions of Italian paintings, since there were too few of them to compare it with. Here again, a definitive provenance was essential.

It is often impossible to discover in detail how well-informed the amateurs were when they bought a picture at auction or elsewhere. However, it is important to realise that they did their 'research', for if they did, they were not likely to buy dubious attributions.

Communis opinio – The (implicit) 'acceptance' of the standing attributions by the community of renowned collector-connoisseurs was as important as the provenance itself. In England, the Duke of Chandos invited his friend-connoisseurs over whenever a painting arrived. Lothar Franz von Schönborn invited his court painters to discuss the attributions of newly acquired masterpieces. As Van der Veen and Plomp have convincingly argued, the most important art collectors in the Dutch Republic visited each other often as well and on those occasions discussed the paintings and attributions in detail.[78] In early eighteenth-century Holland '*kunstbeschouwingen*' (art contemplations) were organised, where amateurs discussed their drawings and paintings with each other.[79] Even paintings in transit from France to England were viewed and discussed by connoisseurs.[80] The paintings were discussed by the attending crowds on viewing days and at the auction.[81] All in all, it is difficult to find the details of these discussions, but every now and then, an art collector-connoisseur leaves a clue behind. Jacques Meyers, for instance, informed readers of his collection catalogue that some connoisseurs had other opinions about his Raphael. Some believed that the painting had been done by the Italian Baroque painter Andrea Sacchi. In his inventories of the painting collection of stadtholder-King William III, Jan van Beuningen regularly refered to that the 'community of connoisseur-art lovers', writing down observations such as 'the best known by this painter' or 'rarely seen of this hand'.[82] At the auction of his own collection in 1716, Van Beuningen frequently used the word 'famous', indicating that the community of art lover-connoisseurs knew the mentioned painting well and had no doubts about its attribution. In fact, browsing through the pages of Gerard Hoet's collection of auction catalogues it becomes clear that these kinds of references were made quite regularly.[83]

As a consequence of the provenance research and the importance of a *communis opinio*, the connoisseurship of the elite art lover-connoisseurs seems to have been based largely on *falsification* rather than on inductive or deductive science. An attribution was implicitly accepted as long as no one 'cast a stain upon the painting's reputation'. One could argue that the elite art collector-connoisseurs formed an informal private community in which among themselves transparency was essential (see also the essay by De Marchi and Van Miegroet in this volume).

It must be mentioned, however, that this kind of 'falsifying connoisseurship' was only possible at the highest end of the art market, where connoisseurs were rarely required to make attributions out of the blue, since the paintings they bought usually had good provenances and clear-cut, implicitly-accepted attributions. Many other paintings had to be attributed based on their visual characteristics and it is this kind of inductive type of connoisseurship in which dealers such as Zomer had specialised.

Conclusion: The value of seventeenth and early eighteenth century attributions

In his oft-quoted article on early modern connoisseurship, Jeffrey Muller argued that in the contemporary literature: 'Arguments were provided to give everyone satisfaction with what he or she could afford in an art market where prices were set with increasing regularity on a scale of authenticity'.[84] That 'scale of authenticity' was based on the precarious balance between supply and demand in connoisseurship. An art dealer-auctioneer had different interests than an amateur-collector. To understand the value of an attribution in a seventeenth or early eighteenth century auction catalogue, I believe the buyer's judgement and the art dealer's opinion should both be taken into consideration. The seller's connoisseurship was predominantly an inductive science, intended to guide the amateurs through the vast art market, while the connoisseurship of the elite amateur-collectors in the art market focussed mainly on *falsifying* the attributions proposed by the auctioneers, art dealers and colleague-collectors. In doing so, they assessed quality, did some rudimentary provenance research and discussed the options with other amateurs in order to make sure that the standing attribution would not be challenged. While auctioneers like Jan Pietersz. Zomer in the Netherlands circa 1700 tended to keep the most valuable information to themselves, elite art lovers formed an informal community in which transparency on provenance, quality assessment, etc. were very important.

Let me now turn back to the anecdote I brought up in the introduction to this essay. As a coincidence, a few months after the auction of the anonymous painting attributed to the 'circle of Willem Key' by the auction house, the collector who had bought the lot called me. He believed the painting was by Willem Key, and being ignorant of the discussion between me and the auction house, asked for advice. I repeated my doubts about the attribution. When I asked him later if he had purchased the painting based on the assumption that it was indeed a Willem Key, he replied that he had bought it simply because he liked it and that it came rather cheap.

* I would like to thank Marten Jan Bok, Eric Jan Sluijter, Piet Bakker and of course Anna Tummers for their help and comments.

1 The praiseworthy efforts of the Rembrandt Research Project and the Corpus Rubenianum Ludwig Burchard, for instance, have made it clear how multifaceted attributions sometimes are. Ludwig Burchard et al., *Corpus Rubenianum Ludwig Burchard: an illustrated catalogue raisonné of the work of Peter Paul Rubens based on the material assembled by the late Dr. Ludwig Burchard in twenty-six parts*, edited by Nationaal Centrum voor de Plastische Kunsten van de XVIde en XVIIde Eeuw, 36 vols., Brussels 1968-...; Josua Bruyn et al., *A Corpus of Rembrandt Paintings*, edited by Stichting Foundation Rembrandt Research Project, 4 vols., The Hague, Boston and London 1982-2005.

2 Max J. Friedländer, *On Art and Connoisseurship*, London 1944.

3 The word '*principaal*' was used in the Netherlands as the opposite of copy. Neil De Marchi and Hans Van Miegroet, '"Pricing invention" "Originals", "Copies", and their relative value in seventeenth century Netherlandish art markets', in: Victor A. Ginsburgh (ed.), *Economics of the Arts*, Brussels 1996, pp. 27-70, esp. p. 33; Jaap van der Veen, 'By his own hand. The valuation of authograph paintings in the seventeenth century', in: Ernst Van de Wetering et al. (eds.), *A Corpus of Rembrandt Paintings*, vol. 4, The Hague 2005: pp. 3-44, esp. p. 4. See also above, p.38.

4 In this article, I will limit connoisseurship to attributing. I will thus not discuss the connoisseurship that determines the artistic value of a work of art. I consider this kind of connoisseurship to be art criticism rather than connoisseurship. Roger de Piles, *Abrégé de la vie des peintres avec des reflexions sur leurs ouvrages, et un traité du peintre parfait, de la connoissance des desseins, de l'utilité des estampes*, Paris 1715; Roger de Piles, *Dissertation sur les ouvrages des plus fameux peintres*, Paris 1681; Roger de Piles, *Dialogue sur le coloris*, Paris 1699; Roger de Piles, *Cours de peinture par principes*, Paris 1708; Roger de Piles, *L'idée du peintre parfait, pour servir de régle aux jugemens que l'on doit porter sur les ouvrages des peintres*, London 1707. On Roger de Piles, see also Thomas Puttfarken, *Roger de Piles' theory of art*, New Haven and London 1985. Jonathan Richardson, *An essay on the theory of painting*, London 1715. On Richardson, see Carol Gibson-Wood, *Jonathan Richardson: Art Theorist of the English Enlightment*, New Haven and London 2000.

5 E.g. Karel van Mander, *Het schilder-boeck*, Haarlem 1604; Cornelis de Bie, *Het gulden cabinet vande edel vry schilder const inhovdende den lof vande vermarste schilders, architecte-, beldthowers, ende plaetsnyders van dese eevw*, Antwerp 1661; Arnold Houbraken, *De groote schouburgh der Nederlantsche konstschilders en schilderessen, waar van 'er vele met hunne beeltenissen ten tooneel verschynen, ... zynde een vervolg op het schilderboek van K. van Mander*, 3 vols., Amsterdam 1718-1721. Auction catalogues are found mainly in Gerard Hoet, *Catalogus of naamlyst van schilderyen, met derzelver pryzen zedert een langen reeks van jaaren zoo in Holland als op andere plaatzen in het openbaar verkogt : Benevens een Verzameling van lysten van verscheyden nog in wezen zynde cabinetten*, 2 vols., The Hague 1752. The probate inventories used here are found in: Erik Duverger, *Antwerpse kunstinventarissen uit de zeventiende eeuw*, Fontes Historiae Artis Neerlandicae, 13 vols., Brussels 1984-2005.

6 On these questions, see also: Everhard Korthals Altes, *De verovering van de internationale kunstmarkt door de zeventiende-eeuwse schilderkunst: enkele studies over de verspreiding van Hollandse schilderijen in de eerste helft van de 18e eeuw*, Leiden 2003, pp. 30-44.

7 At another occasion, I argued that there was a discrepancy between regular art dealers and *solliciteurs-culturel* (i.e., elite art lover-agents). See on this: Koenraad Jonckheere, *Kunsthandel en diplomatie. De veiling van de schilderijen-*

verzameling van Willem III (1713) en de rol van het diplomatieke netwerk in de Europese kunsthandel, Dissertation, Universiteit van Amsterdam 2005, pp. 199-206. (See, for the English edition: Koenraad Jonckheere, *The Auction of King William's Paintings (1713). Elite International Art Trade at the End of the Dutch Golden Age*, Oculi: Studies in the Arts of the Low Countries. 11, Amsterdam 2008.)

8 I would like to stress that I will only be discussing the upper segment of the art market, which has distinctive characteristics and only covers a very small percentage of the market. However, this is the segment in which the works of art that have interested art historians over the past few centuries were sold. (cf. graph 4)

9 See also: Korthals Altes, *De verovering van de internationale kunstmarkt* (note 6), pp. 30-44.

10 'Daar ons Heer een Koopman geeft, daar geeft de Duijvel een Makelaer.' Brussels, Royal Library Albert I. Manuscript department, inv. II 1608: *Manuscript Jacob Campo Weyerman*, vol. 1. On this manuscript by Jacob Campo Weyerman, see: Koenraad Jonckheere. 'Een zeedig uijterlijk, en een fijn mans ijthangbordt, is het merk van een modern vroom Konstkoper. Jacob Campo Weyerman over kunsthandel', in: André van de Kerkhove (ed.), *Liber Memorialis Eric Duverger*, Wetteren 2006, pp. 75-90; Ton J. Broos, *Tussen zwart en ultramarijn. De levens van schilders beschreven door Jacob Campo Weyerman (1677-1747)*, Amsterdam 1990, pp. 187-206; Peter Altena, 'Doldriftiger Monster verscheen ons noit aan de Maze. Jacob Campo Weyerman en Rotterdam', *Mededelingen van de Stichting Jacob Campo Weyerman*, 10, 3 (1987), pp. 74-89.

11 Brussels, Royal Library Albert I. Manuscript department, inv. II 1608: *Manuscript Jacob Campo Weyerman*, vol. 1. 'Maer een verstandig Konstkenner moet zich schier half dood lachen, als hij den dommen konstuijl, de namen van eenige konstschilders hoort uijtstameren, want die behandelt hij gelijk als een jongen, die pas begint te leezen, de hebreeusche namen in Genesis behandelt, en echter is hij onbeschaemt genoeg om aen fatsoenlijke wel opgevoede persoonen den baard te willen opzetten door zijne achterstraets onkunde.'

12 Jaap van der Veen, 'De Amsterdamse kunstmarkt en de schilderijaankopen voor Peter de Grote', in: Renée Kistemaker et al. (eds.), *Peter de Grote en Holland. Culturele en wetenschappelijke betrekkingen tussen Rusland en Nederland ten tijde van tsaar Peter de Grote*, Amsterdam (Amsterdams Historisch Museum) 1996 (ex. cat.), p. 137.

13 Jonckheere, *Kunsthandel en diplomatie* (note 7), pp. 32-56 and pp. 72-73.

14 On the satirical poems, see Hanns Floerke, *Der Niederländische Kunst-Handel im 17. und 18. Jahrhundert*, Basel 1901, p. 77; S.A.C. Dudok Van Heel, 'Jan Pieterz. Zomer (1641-1724). Makelaar in Schilderijen', *Jaarboek Amstelodamum* 69 (1977), pp. 89-122. Translation by the author.

15 Jonckheere, *Een zeedig uijterlijk* (note 9), pp. 75-90.

16 Jonckheere, *Kunsthandel en diplomatie* (note 7). (numerous examples)

17 De Marchi and Van Miegroet, *Pricing invention* (note 3), pp. 27-70. See also Anna Tummers' essay of in this volume, pp. 31-66.

18 Koenraad Jonckheere, *Adriaen Thomasz. Key (ca. 1545 - ca. 1589). Portrait of a Calvinist painter*, Pictura Nova. Studies in 16th- and 17th- Century Flemish Painting and Drawing. 14, edited by Hans Vlieghe and Katlijne Van der Stighelen, Turnhout 2007, pp. 19-22.

19 In the sixteenth century, the technical and material quality of a painting was very important due to guild regulations, as is commonly known.

20 On the popularity of work after Brueghel, see Larry Silver, 'Second Bosch. Family Resemblance and the Marketing of Art', *Nederlands Kunsthistorisch Jaarboek* 50 (1999), pp. 31-58. On the Brueghel 'workshop' see: Peter van den Brink, 'De kunst van het kopiëren. Het waarom en hoe van het vervaardigen van kopieën en schilderijen in oplage in de Nederlanden in de zestiende en zeventiende eeuw', in: Peter van den Brink et al. (eds.), *De Firma Breughel*, Brussels (Royal Museums of Fine Art) 2001 (exh. cat.), pp. 12-43.; De Marchi and Van Miegroet, *Pricing invention* (note 3), pp. 27-70.

21 Some attention to this problem is given in: De Marchi and Van Miegroet, *Pricing invention* (note 3), pp. 27-70; J. Michael Montias, 'Artists named in Amsterdam inventories 1607-80', *Simiolus* 31, 4 (2004-2005), pp. 322-347.

22 The index to Duverger's Antwerp inventories (Erik Duverger, *Antwerpse kunstinventarissen uit de zeventiende eeuw*, Fontes Historiae Artis Neerlandicae, vol. 13, Brussels 2005) offers a good indication of the large number of painters' names in early modern Antwerp and the confusion it may cause.

23 This is also suggested by De Marchi and Van Miegroet and by Montias; see note 20.

24 Lisa Pon, *Raphael, Dürer and Marcantonio Raimondi. Copying and the Italian Renaissance Print*, New Haven and London 2004.

25 Nico Van Hout, *Copyright Rubens. Rubens en de grafiek*, Antwerp (Koninklijk Museum voor Schone Kunsten) 2004 (ex.cat.), pp. 40-53.

26 Carl van de Velde, *Frans Floris (1518/1519). Leven en werken*, Verhandelingen van de Koninklijke Academie voor Wetenschappen, Letteren en Schone Kunsten van België. 30, 2 vols., Brussels 1975, vol. 1, pp. 102-104. On the use of the word '*fecit*' see also Anna Tummers' essay in this volume, pp. 31-66.

27 Van de Velde, *Frans Floris* (note 25), vol. 1, pp. 472-473. Also quoted by Van der Veen, *By his own hand* (note 3), p. 14.

The observation that painters were aware of the economic value of a name is verified to some extent by Marten Jan Bok's hypothesis in his article on the Amsterdam artist François Badens. He showed that Badens took over the studio previously owned by first Dirck Barentsz. and later on Pieter Izaacsz. Bok suggested that that studio on the Oude Turfmarkt in Amsterdam was a place where Amsterdam's citizens could buy paintings in the Italian manner. In his view, the building-studio was not merely the place where a specific painter worked and lived, it probably also had some status as a place where paintings in a certain style and of a certain quality were sold. Bok also proposed a similar hypothesis in the case of a studio for portraiture that was founded, so to speak, in 1606 by Cornelis van der Voort and continued by Pickenoy and Rembrandt. In these cases, we cannot speak of brand names but the assumption that a painter worked in a certain manner, while maintaining the reputation of the studio (associated with a place), is similar. See Marten Jan Bok, 'De Ganymedes van François Badens en de werkplaats voor schilderijen in Italiaanse stijl aan de oude Turfmarkt', *Jaarboek Amstelodamum* 92, 4 (2005), pp. 3-14.

28 Erik Duverger, *Antwerpse kunstinventarissen uit de zeventiende eeuw*, Fontes Historiae Artis Neerlandicae, 13 vols., Brussels 1984-2005.

29 I.e., a name or description that cannot cause any confusion about a painting's authenticity.

30 Klaus Ertz, *Jan Brueghel der ältere (1568-1625). Die Gemälde mit kritischen Oeuvrekatalog*, Keulen 1979; Klaus Ertz, *Jan Brueghel the younger. The Paintings with Oeuvre Catalogue*, Flemish Painters in the Circle of the Great Masters. 1, Freren 1984.

31 Duverger, *Antwerpse kunstinventarissen* (note 28), vol. 10, p. 84.

32 Van der Veen, *By his own hand* (note 3), p. 8. Van der Veen calls it 'misunderstandings'. It is hard to believe that they were misunderstandings since precise attributions are the exceptions in most probate inventories. Broad-spectrum attributions were the rule.

33 The same is true for the Dutch Republic. Van der Veen, *By his own hand* (note 3), p. 31. I wonder whether in those cases it was an appraiser / art dealer-connoisseur or a collector-connoisseur who made up the inventory.

34 Jonckheere, *Kunsthandel en diplomatie* (note 7), pp.49-56.

35 See also, on this matter, Anna Tummers' essay 'By his hand...' in this volume.

36 Gerard Hoet (ed.), *Catalogus of naamlyst van schilderyen, met derzelver pryzen zedert een langen reeks van jaaren zoo in Holland als op andere plaatzen in het openbaar verkogt : Benevens een Verzameling van lysten van verscheyden nog in wezen zynde cabinetten / uytgegeven door Gerard Hoet*, 2 vols., The Hague 1752; Pieter Terwesten (ed.), *Catalogus of naamlyst van schilderyen, met derzelver prysen, zedert ... 1752. tot ... 1768. ... openbaar verkogt. Dienende tot een vervolg ... op de ... cataloguen door Gerard Hoet ...*, The Hague 1770.

37 For details on the exact content of the database see: Jonckheere, *Kunsthandel en diplomatie* (note 7), pp. 208-211.

38 On Jan Pieters. Zomer see: Jonckheere, *Kunsthandel en diplomatie* (note 7), pp. 49-56. Dudok Van Heel, *Jan Pieterz. Zomer* (note 14), pp. 89-122.

39 It would be possible to compare the descriptions in these auction catalogues with the descriptions in the probate inventories. Several collections auctioned by Zomer were first appraised by the same. See *Getty Provenance Index* (online: http://www.getty.edu/research/conducting_research/provenance_index/)

40 This is only true for Old Master paintings.

41 As Van der Veen revealed, Zomer was aware of the problems, however.

42 It could be that Zomer informed his clients orally of a more nuanced opinion on viewing days.

43 Van der Veen, *By his own hand* (note 3), pp. 10-17.

44 Van der Veen, *By his own hand* (note 3), p. 20.

45 On the practice of signing in the sixteenth and seventeenth century see: Van der Veen, *By his own hand* (note 3), pp. 10-17.

46 Duverger, *Antwerpse kunstinventarissen* (note 28).

47 Van de Velde, *Frans Floris* (note 26), vol. 1, pp. 12-104.

48 As Van der Veen showed, there were many court cases involving attributions and authenticity in the Northern and Southern Netherlands in the seventeenth century. However, one could only build a case if the seller (e.g., the broker) had taken stand explicitly. Van der Veen, *By his own hand* (note 3), pp. 3-44.

49 Van der Veen gives an example of Zomer's expertise on several Rembrandt drawings and concludes that buyers and dealers had different interests. Van der Veen, *By his own hand* (note 3), pp. 29-30. I agree.

50 To fully explain what Zomer did, one can compare it to today's fashion industry. It may seem far fetched but it is not, since both the fashion industry today and the seventeenth-century painters balanced on a thin line between arts and crafts. Take for instance Versace: you can buy Versace clothes in a department store or unique Versace fashion show pieces. There is hand-made Italian Versace clothing and illegal Chinese mass production Versace clothing. You can buy a Versace piece made by the late Gianni or a dress made by Donatella, his sister. Zomer would have called every item related to the brand a 'Versace', even though there is a huge difference between the Haute Couture and the Chinese mass produced clothing, between Gianni and Donatella. It would take an expert to see whether a piece of clothing by Versace is a unique catwalk piece by Gianni or by Donatella, a confection piece or a complete Chinese fake. Nonetheless, we will call them all Versace. This is, I believe, what Zomer did with paintings. He labelled all paintings 'Rubens', whether it was a unique handmade oil sketch, a studio product or a late seventeenth-century copy by an inferior painter. He called all panels and canvases that were painted in the manner of 'Rubens', Rubens, although he certainly did not ignore the fact that Rubens had a large studio with many assistants.

51 Jonckheere, *Kunsthandel en diplomatie* (note 7), p. 217.

52 On Bouts remark, see Erik Duverger, *Documents concernant le commerce d'art de Francisco-Jacomo van den Berghe et Gillis van der Vennen de Gand avec la Hollande et la France pendant les premières décades du XVIIIe siècle*, Wetteren 2004, p. 268.

53 This graph is based on all price-annotated auction catalogues published between 1676 and 1739. On the database and this graph, see: Jonckheere, *Kunsthandel en diplomatie* (note 7), pp. 208-211 and 65.

54 On the seventeenth-century art market, see: Marten Jan Bok, *Vraag en aanbod op de Nederlandse kunstmarkt, 1580-1700*, Utrecht 1994.

55 Hessel Miedema, *Denkbeeldig schoon. Lambert ten Kates opvattingen over beeldende kunst*, 2 vols., Leiden 2006, vol. 2, p. 21. Lambert ten Kate noticed that connoisseurship was not an inductive science based on empirical observations. He was an 'independent' amateur and mainly discussed quality in art, rather than attributions.

56 Korthals Altes, *De verovering van de internationale kunstmarkt* (note 6), p. 41.

57 Eric Jan Sluijter, 'Over Brabantse vodden, economische concurrentie, artistieke wedijver en de groei van de markt voor schilderijen in de eerste decennia van de zeventiende eeuw', *Nederlands Kunsthistorisch Jaarboek* 50 (1999), pp. 113-144, esp. pp. 119-121.

58 This is in general. It might have been essential for specific art lovers.

59 This paragraph is partially based on a lecture I gave in 2005 at the Symposium *To be or not to be a Connoisseur. A symposium in honour of Hans Vlieghe*, at the Catholic University of Leuven, entitled 'De achterkant van een schilderij. Kennerschap omstreeks 1700'.

60 On this catalogue, see J.G. Van Gelder, 'Het Kabinet van de Heer Jaques Meyers', *Rotterdams Jaarboekje* (1974), pp. 167-183. Jonckheere, *Kunsthandel en diplomatie* (note 6), pp. 95-98. The catalogue is published in Jonckheere, *Kunsthandel en diplomatie* (note 6), pp. 268-280.

61 Nicolas Poussin, *Seven Sacraments* [seven pieces], canvas, all c. 117 x 178 cm, Edinburgh, The National Gallery of Scotland (long term loan from the Duke of Sutherland).

62 'Il a été autrefois entre les mains de Monsieur *Passart*, Maitres des Comptes'; Nicolas Poussin, *The abduction of the Sabine women*, canvas, 154,6 x 209,9 cm, New York, The Metropolitan Museum (Harris Brisbane Dick Fund).

63 Peter Paul Rubens, *Christ, John and two angels*, canvas, 92 x 122 cm, Salisbury, Wilton House.

64 'Ornement à la Maison de Honselaerdyk, en suite dans le Cabinet de Guillaume III, Roi d' Angleterre, à Loo, d' ou il vient présentement'; Anthony van Dyck, *Rinaldo en Armida*, Canvas, 133 x 109 cm, Paris, Musée du Louvre, inv. no. 1235.

65 'Ce Tableau est parfaitement bien conservé. Il a été gravé par Marc Antoine, Graveur ordinaire des Tableaux de Raphaël. Quelques Connoisseurs doutent néanmoins qu'il soit de ce Peintre célebre, & ont cru y reconnoitre la Maniere & le Gout d' Andrea Sacchi. Il vient du Cabinet du Duc de Gramont.'

66 'extraordinaire kapitale stukken van groote en voorname meesters, met extra groote moeiten en kosten, uyt beroemde Kabinetten, byeen [had] vergadert'; Jan van Beuningen was considered one of the best connoisseurs in the early eighteenth century. He was immensely wealthy and he had a famous collection. Foreign princes and noblemen called him their friend. When the collection of Stadholder-King William III came up for sale in 1713, Jan van Beuningen was asked by the inheritors to organise the auction. In preparation for the auction, Jan van Beuningen visited the galleries at Het Loo palace several times. In December 1712, the painting collection was valued and inventoried by Jan Pietersz. Zomer and Jan van Beuningen. In april 1713, another inventory was drawn up. The catalogue was finally printed in June 1713. The comparison between the inventories and preparatory lists of paintings drawn up by Jan van Beuningen and the catalogue, written by the same, illustrate wonderfully how much the interests of the amateur Van Beuningen differed from that of the auctioneer Van Beuningen. While in the inventories, the amateur sets an honest price, in the auction catalogue he tries to sell the same paintings at the highest price. The difference is sometimes striking. The descriptions in the inventories are all very neutral and accentuate the doubts and the deficiencies. The auction catalogue in turn emphasizes the qualities of all the paintings. Although Jan van Beuningen is more open and precise than Jan Pietersz. Zomer in the auction catalogue, he does make efforts to conceal hesitations. For instance, a night piece by Gerard Dou that was ruined by the sun (*Penneschneydertje bij de kaars, seer verschroeyt van de soon, door Douw*), was auctioned as a painting by Dou with some cracks in it (*Een Pennesnydertje by de Kaers,* *wat beborsten*). Cracks could be repaired, faded colours could not. Paintings with an uncertain attribution become paintings with certain attributions. All doubt was erased as it seems.

67 E.W. Moes, 'Het kunstkabinet van Valerius Röver te Delft', *Oud Holland* 31 (1913), pp. 4-24.

68 Korthals Altes, *De verovering van de internationale kunstmarkt* (note 6), p. 33. On Duarte: Frederik Muller, 'Catalogus van schilderijen van Diego Duarte, te Amsterdam in 1682, met de prijzen van aankoop en Taxatie', *De oude tijd* 2 (1870), pp. 397-402; G. Dogaer, 'De inventaris der schilderijen van Diego Duarte', *Jaarboek van het Koninklijk Museum voor Schone Kunsten Antwerpen*, (1971), pp. 195-221; Edgar R. Samuel, 'The Disposal of Diego Duarte's Stock of Paintings 1692-1697', *Jaarboek van het Koninklijk Museum voor Schone Kunsten Antwerpen*, (1976), pp. 305-324.

69 Duverger, *Documents concernant le commerce d'art* (note 52).

70 Adriaen Brouwer, *The surgeon*, panel, 34.9 x 25.9 cm, Frankfurt, Städel-Museum. Some other examples are: Gerard Dou, *The Violin Player*, panel, 31.1 x 23.7 cm, Edinburgh, The National Gallery of Schotland (This painting still has the wax seal of James Brydges of Chandos attached to the back); Joos van Cleve, Portrait of a man, panel, 45 x 43.5 cm, The Hague, The Mauritshuis (this panel has the wax seals of King William III and Mary and of Prince Johan Willem Friso attached to the back); In the probate inventory of Jacques Meyers, the notary noted that several paintings were marked with a wax seal (Rotterdam, Gemeentearcief Rotterdam, Notarieel Archief Rotterdan, inv. no. 1527 deed 15: *Estate inventory of Jacques Meyers*, 25 September 1721.)

71 On the collecting of James Brydges of Chandos, see: Jonckheere, *Kunsthandel en diplomatie* (note 7), pp. 115-148. Susan Jenkins, *Portrait of a Patron. The Patronage and Collecting of James Brydges 1st Duke of Chandos (1674-1744)*, Aldershot 2007, pp. 126-151. C.H. Collins Baker and Muriel I. Baker, *Life and circumstances of James Brydges First Duke of Chandos. Patron of the Liberal Arts*, Oxford 1949.

72 Unpublished letters: San Marino, Huntington Library, Brydges Papers, inv. no. ST 57, Letters from James Brydges to Louis du Livrer, 27th April 1709-21th March 1710, vol. 2, p. 196, 238; vol. 3, p. 23, 47, 97, 118; vol. 4, p. 6, 185. San Marino, Huntington Library, Brydges Papers, inv. no. ST 58, Letters from Louis du Livrer to James Brydges, 18 May 1709-30 May 1713, vol. 4, p. 33, 151, 159, 210, 250; vol. 5, p. 31, 40, 72, 84, 111, 141, 185, 217, 225; vol. 6, 13.

73 On the Commonwealth Sale, see Jerry Brotton, *The sale of the late king's goods. Charles I and his art collection*, Basingstoke 2006; Arthur MacGregor (ed.), *The late King's goods. Collections, possessions and patronage of Charles I in the light of the Commonwealth sale inventories*, London 1989.

74 San Marino, Huntington Library, Brydges Papers, inv. no. ST 57, Letters from James Brydges to Henry Davenant, 21 August 1715-26 December 1719, vol. 12, p. 90, 110, 154, 174, 239, 258; vol. 13, p. 36, 45-46, 83; vol. 14, p. 43, 50, 121, 381; vol. 15, p. 194; vol. 16, p. 261, 422.

75 San Marino, Huntington Library, Brydges Papers, inv. no. ST 57, Letter from James Brydges to Henry Davenant, 22 September 1716, vol. 13, p. 46.

76 Andrea del Sarto (after Raphael), *Portrait of Leo X and two cardinals*, panel, Naples, Museo e Gallerie Nazionali di Capodimonte.

77 Johan van Gool, *De nieuwe schouburg der Nederlantsche kunstschilders en schilderessen: waer in de levens- en kunstbedryven der tans levende en reets overleedene schilders, die van Houbraken, noch eenig ander schryver, zyn aengeteekend, verhaelt worden*, The Hague 1750-1751, vol. 2, p. 110-111.

78 E.g. Jaap van der Veen, 'Met grote moeite en kosten. De totstandkoming van zeventiende-eeuwse verzamelingen', in: Ellinoor Bergvelt and Renee Kistemaker (eds.), *De wereld binnen handbereik. Nederlandse kunst- en rariteitenverzamelingen, 1585-1735*, Amsterdam (Amsterdams Historisch Museum) 1992 (exh. cat.), pp. 51-69; Jaap van der Veen, 'Liefhebbers, handelaren en kunstenaars. Het verzamelen van schilderijen en papierkunst', in: Ellinoor Bergvelt and Renee Kistemaker (eds.), *De wereld binnen handbereik. Nederlandse kunst- en rariteitenverzamelingen, 1585-1735*, Amsterdam (Amsterdams Historisch Museum) 1992 (exh. cat.), pp. 117-134; Plomp, Michiel C., *Hartstochtelijk Verzameld. 18de-eeuwse Hollandse verzamelaars van tekeningen en hun collecties*, Bussem 2001, pp. 104-118.

79 See for instance Miedema, *Denkbeeldig schoon* (note 55), vol. 2, p. 20. Plomp, *Hartstochtelijk Verzameld* (note 78), pp. 104-118.

80 E.g. Koenraad Jonckheere, 'The influence of art trade and art collecting on Dutch art around 1700. The case of Adriaen van der werff', in: Ekkehard Mai (ed.), *Holland nach Rembrandt. Zur niederländischen Kunst zwischen 1670 und 1750*, Cologne 2006, pp. 49-66, p.52.

81 Jonckheere, *Kunsthandel en diplomatie* (note 7).

82 Koenraad Jonckheere, 'When the cabinet from Het Loo was sold. The auction of William III's collection of paintings, 26 july 1713', *Simiolus* 13, 3 (2004-2005), pp. 156-215, esp. pp. 192-215.

83 See on the weight of connoisseurs' judgment in the seventeenth century, Anna Tummers' essay *The Painter vs. the Connoisseur*, pp. 127-147 below.

84 Jeffrey Muller, 'Measures of Authenticity. The Detection of Copies in the Early Literature on Connoisseurship', in: Kathleen Preciado (ed.), *Retaining the original: Multiple Originals, Copies, and Reproductions*, Washington DC 1989.

Chapter 3
Natasja Peeters

'Painters pencells move not without that musicke': Prices of Southern Netherlandish Painted Altarpieces between 1585 and 1650*

Introduction

In an imaginary dialogue from 1538 written by the humanist Johannes Vives, we find Albrecht Dürer in a conversation with two imaginary learned men, Grynius and Velius.[1] They are talking about Dürer's imaginary portrait of Scipio Africanus, which they want to see, either to buy it, or to criticise it, or possibly, to show off their knowledge, to the annoyance of the artist.

Dürer: Go away from here, for you will buy nothing ...
Grynius: Nay, we wish to buy, only we wish you to leave the price to our judgement, and that you should state the limit of time for payment, or, on the other hand, let us settle the time and you the amount of the payment.
Dürer: A fine way of doing business! There is no need for me to have nonsense of this sort! [2]

The price is put at 400 sesterces, whereupon the two connoisseurs become increasingly difficult customers: they want to examine the painting thoroughly to see if it is worth the asking price. Dürer, stubborn, proud and by now probably vexed, is reluctant to accommodate them:

Velius: I should like to be able to see the back of the head.
Dürer: Then turn the panel round.[3]

Although this is an imaginary account which ends on a comic note, it does ring true regarding how artists must have felt when a difficult client examined their work while trying to strike a bargain. As is well-known, the assessment of any work of art is influenced by its material costs, but also by less tangible aspects such as its perceived artistic value.[4] But how exactly prices were determined for specific types of paintings in many instances remains unclear.

In the past decades, a lot of research has been done on different social and economic aspects of the early modern market for luxury objects. Sales inventories, merchants and auction prices concerning paintings have been studied.[5] Moreover, the reception of copies, pastiches and originals on the market has been analysed, as well as merchant's interventions in the establishment of prices.[6] However, not all of the aspects of the early modern market for luxury goods have been analysed. Indeed, we are still unable to trace the exact nature of the interaction between many artists and their royal patrons, the city councils, and the various private citizens who purchased paintings.

This essay focuses on the prices paid for Southern Netherlandish altarpieces made between 1585 and 1650. Not much is known about their prices; only a few scattered case studies exist.[7] This is primarily because of lack of available material evidence. The disasters of 1533 (fire in the Cathedral of Our Lady in Antwerp), 1566 (Iconoclasm), 1581 (silent Iconoclasm), 1585 (Fall of Antwerp), and the large-scale confiscations of Flemish art by Napoleon, all of which destroyed much of the patrimony, its churches, art and archives, caused the dispersal of the material evidence. Although the evidence presented here is largely restricted to Antwerp, some church altarpieces in other towns will also be taken into consideration to broaden our sample, which is limited both by a lack of archival sources and the disappearance of many altarpieces.[8] The evolution of prices will be charted over two periods: before and after 1609, the year when the political, social, economic and religious situation in Antwerp changed for the better, and when Rubens returned to the Southern Netherlands. Moreover, after 1609, there was an evolution in typology, iconography of the altarpiece as well as a shift in patronage (see below).[9]

Altarpieces were among the most valuable types of paintings produced during this period, both in terms of their actual prices and their theoretical status. Religious and other history paintings constituted the greatest artistic challenge according to seventeenth-century Southern Netherlandish art theorists. The artists had often specialised in this genre. Indeed, altarpieces made up a sizeable part of the careers of late sixteenth-century artists such as Marten de Vos, Frans and Ambrosius Francken, Otto van Veen and Michiel Coxcie, as well as Jacob de Backer, Frans Pourbus, Bernard de Rijckere and Chrispijn van den Broeck.[10] In the seventeenth century, Peter Paul Rubens, and the likes of Gaspar de Crayer, Jacob Jordaens, Anthony van Dyck and the little studied Theodoor van Loon, among others, were prolific painters of altarpieces.

When looking at similar paintings produced in many Italian cities during the Renaissance we see that the pricing of these works has been studied in much more depth than the prices of Southern Netherlandish altarpieces. Research that correlates the formats, themes and raw materials used to produce the altarpieces with the pricing mechanisms is based on richly detailed Italian archival sources.[11] What then determines the price of a painted altarpiece? Art historian Michelle O'Malley, in her recent book *The business of Art* on fifteenth and sixteenth-century Italian altarpieces, states that: 'The analysis of the cost of materials and production ... suggests that the elements of a work that were objectively priced and easily quantified could vary widely, and might cost between about 30 and about 80 per cent of the value of the altarpiece. The remainder of the fee was composed, therefore, of the value given to intangible elements. These included skill as well as economic factors related to social needs, such as relationships, honour, piety and reputation. This sum was correspondingly wide. It could have been as much as 70 per cent, which might be represented in commissions in which painter's fees were well above the average, and as little as 20 per cent in commissions for works with fairly low prices. These calculations are very rough indeed, but they offer an initial field for conceptualising the costs of intangibles, and indicate that there was a wide field for decision-making when painters and their clients considered the pricing of a new work of art.'[12]

These large differences, and the fact that there is no one formula for the setting of prices in Renaissance Italy, may come as a surprise. Is the same true for prices of sixteenth and seventeenth century Southern Netherlandish altarpieces?

Prices of painted altarpieces in the years after the Fall of Antwerp: The Francken-brothers, De Vos, Coxcie, and Van Veen[13]

After the Fall of Antwerp, on 9 September 1585, the craft guilds were ordered by the city government (the Monday Council) to repair and reinstall the altars as quickly as possible.[14] In the decades that followed, the restoration and reestablishment of Catholic worship and its symbols were a priority. The most important place of veneration in Antwerp was the Cathedral of Our Lady (fig. 1), which housed as many as 60 or more

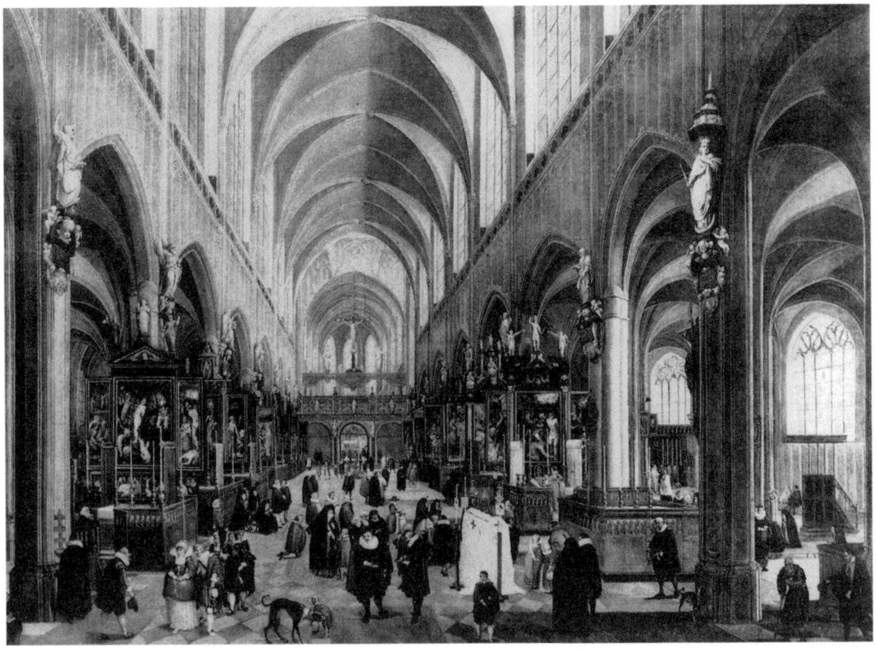

1.

Hendrik Van Steenwijck
Interior view of the *Cathedral of Our Lady in Antwerp,*
before 1585, current location unknown

altars during the 1550s. These had been commissioned by guilds and trades, brotherhoods and private individual donors.[15] In the years after 1600, churches in the small towns around Antwerp, such as Herentals and Lier, were refurbished as well.

The creation or renovation of altarpieces involved a lot of work: preparing, revising with the patrons, reworking certain parts, and lastly, there was a lot of surface to paint. The price was presumably set before the contract was drawn up, and the artist was paid in instalments.[16] In most cases, one-third or one-quarter of the money was advanced upon commencement of the work to allow the artist to buy the necessary materials, another portion was paid as the work progressed, and the final portion was paid upon completion of the work. The panel maker – the sample altarpieces from the period 1585-1609 are all on panel – was usually paid separately by the patron himself. One needs to keep in mind, however, that among all of the chapel or altar's furnishings, the painting itself was often the least expensive, especially when compared to the marble sculptures, bronze ornaments, architectural details, etc. The total cost of the altar was thus much greater than the painted panel, which was part of a much larger and expensive decoration program. Altarpieces were unique creations, made for the occasion; they are also conspicuously public works of art, serving moreover as religious capital within the community of believers.

The sample presented here is of 15 altarpieces painted by the Francken brothers (nine paintings), Michiel Coxcie (one), Marten de Vos (three) and Otto van Veen (two) between 1587 and 1609 (see tables 1/1 and 1/2). The first altarpiece was finished after the fall of Antwerp in 1587 by Frans Francken and represents *Christ among the doctors*. It was painted for the guilds of the schoolmasters and soap boilers in the Cathedral of Our Lady in Antwerp where they shared an altar (fig. 2). The last altarpiece in the sample was painted in 1608-1609 by Ambrosius Francken for the altar of the *Heilige Geestmeesters* (Poor masters) in the Church of Saint Waldetrudis in Herentals, a small town near Antwerp, where the roots of the Francken family lay (fig. 3). What can we deduce from these 15 examples? While the commissions on average were 515.74 Car. (Carolus) guilders, the median was 350 Car. guilders. Before 1594, no altarpiece fetched over 500 Car. guilders (the highest was 360); while after that year, prices readily rose above 500 Car. guilders, and the lowest commission fetched 325. The average for the years 1587-98 was 311 Car. guilders and for the years 1599-1609 rose dramatically to 925 Car. guilders, nearly three times as much. There was a range from 50 to 2,400 Car. Guilders per commission.

What could possibly explain the increase in prices at the end of the sixteenth century? After the difficult Calvinist period of 1581-85, many guilds and other patrons suffered from a lack of funds.[17] They may thus have opted to order altarpieces at discount prices in order to keep within the budget. Could this increase in prices be due to an increase in the artworks' dimensions? The dimensions of thirteen examples range from 5.8 to 23.2 m^2 (see table 1/3). Each commission on average totalled 13.6 m^2. Is there a noticeable increase in the dimensions over the 23-year period in our sample? The average for the years 1587-97 was 12.7 m^2 while that for the years 1598-1609 was 15.4 m^2. This means that there was a tendency towards larger dimensions, but both large and small altarpieces were produced during both periods.

Is there a positive relationship between size and price? 13 of the 15 samples reveal something about the price rates per m^2 (see table 1/4). The average rate was 43 Car. guilders/m^2; the median was 24.3 Car. guilders/m^2 for a total price range of 3.88 Car. guilders/m^2 to 103.4 Car. guilders/m^2, certainly a dramatic difference. Artists like Marten de Vos and Otto van Veen were paid up to 25 times the rate that Frans

Table 1/1 : Altarpieces 1587-1609: chronology#

DATE	FIG.*	NAME	SUBJECT	CAR. GUILDERS	PATRON	RATE/ M^2 (gld.)	DIM (M^2)	PL. PRES	PL. ORIGIN
1587	10f;11h;16H	F. Francken	*Christ among the doctors*[1]	240	Guild of the Schoolmasters & Soap Boilers	15.9	15.2	Antw., Cath	Antw., Cath
1587	/	F. Francken	*Saints Philip and Jacob*[2]	144	City?	-	-	Lost	Antw., Citadel Ch.
1587	9f;5h;HH	M. Coxcie	*Triptych of Saint Sebastian*[3]	150	Guild	11.9	12.5	Mech., St Rom. Ch.	Mech., St. Rom. Ch.
1589	/	F. Francken	*Annunciation*[4]	50	Private don.	3.88	12.8	Lost	Antw., Sodal
1589-90	12f;7h;HH	A. Francken	*Altarpiece of the Holy Sacrament*[5]	360	Broth.	19.7	18.3	Antw., KMSKA	Antw., St. Andr. Church
1594	/	F. Francken	*Altarpiece of Saint Matthew*[6]	220	Guild of the Coopers	-	-	Lost	Antw., Cath
1594	3f;hh;HH[7]	M. de Vos	*Central panel Saint James's altarpiece*[8]	512	Church Fabric	88.3	5.8	Antw., St. Jam. Ch.	Antw., St. Jam. Ch
1594	3f;ff;hh;monsters[9]	M. de Vos	*Saint Anthony*[10]	435.18	Brotherhood	18.9	17.1	Antw., KMSKA	Antw., Cath
1595-98	? [11]	A. Francken	*Wings of Saint George's altarpiece*[12]	500	Church Fabric	35.2	14.2	Antw., KMSKA	Antw., St Georg. Church
1596-97	6f;9h;12H	M. de Vos	*Wedding at Cana*[13]	500	Guild of the Wine tav.	80.6	6.2	Antw., KMSKA	Antw., Cath OLV
1599	3F;4h;*H[14]angels	O. Van Veen	*Martyrdom of Saint Andrew*[15]	1,200	Church Fabric/Philip II	96	12.5	Antw., St. Andr. Church	Antw., St Andr. Church
1604	10f;12h;3H; angels	F. Francken	*Altarpiece for the Brewers' guild*[16]	325	Guild of the Brewers	24.3	13.4	Herentals, Church St. W	Herentals, Church St. W
1607	15f;5h+;14H+ angels[17]	O. Van Veen	*Altarpiece for the Mercers' guild*[18]	2,400	Guild of the Mercers	103.4	23.2	Mainz/KMSKA	Antw., Cath.
1609	6f;7h;4H; angels[19]	A. Francken	*Wings of Saint James's Altarpiece*[20]	350	Church Fabric	36.8	9.5	Antw., St Jam. Ch.	Antw., St Jam. Ch
1609	ff;hh;HH[21]	A. Francken	*Altarpiece for the Poor masters*[22]	350	Poor masters	21.1	16.6	Herentals, Church St. W	Herentals, Church St. W

* 'f' : full figures; h: half length figures; H: heads; ff: number of full figures difficult to count; hh: number of half length figures difficult to count; HH: number of heads difficult to count.
# some rates/m^2 have been rounded.

1 Altarpiece for the guilds of the schoolmasters and soapboilers who shared an altar for their chapel in the Cathedral of Our Lady in Antwerp. Natasja Peeters, *Tussen continuïteit en vernieuwing. De bijdrage van Frans en Ambrosius Francken I, en de jonge generatie Francken, tot de historieschilderkunst te Antwerpen ca 1570-1620*, PhD Dissertation Vrije Universiteit Brussels 2000 (publication forthcoming), cat. No. F 9: oil on panel; dimensions central panel 250 cm x 220 cm; wings 4 x (250 cm x 97 cm).

2 Peeters, *Tussen continuïteit* (note 1), cat. No. F 10. Support unkown, presumably panel. The altarpiece was made for the no longer extant church of the torn-down Antwerp Citadel.

3 Altarpiece for the guild of Saint-Sebastian (militia), for the altar in the church of Saint Romuald (or Rombout) in Mechelen; oil on panel; dimensions central panel 232 cm x 191 cm; wings 4 x (230 cm x 88 cm).

4 Altarpiece for the sodality [Brotherhood] of the Annunication of the Virgin. The painting was a gift from alderman Gillis Gerardi for the brotherhood's chapel in the building of the Sodality on current Conscience place in Antwerp. Peeters, *Tussen continuïteit* (note 1), cat. No. F 12. The author thanks Joost Vander Auwera for help with the conversion of the dimensions: it was 3,4 ft in height and 4,7 ft in width, corresponding to the dimensions 96.5 cm x 133.4 cm, the Antwerp foot being 28.4 cm.

5 Altarpiece for the brotherhood of the Holy Sacrament for their venerable chapel in the parish church of Saint Andrew in Antwerp. Peeters, *Tussen continuïteit* (note 1), cat. No. A 5. Oil on panel. The dimensions of the central panel are 275 cm x 240 cm; the wings 4 x (255 cm x 115 cm).

6 Peeters, *Tussen continuïteit* (note 1), cat. No. F 13. Oil on panel. Altarpiece for the guild of the coopers in the Cathedral of Our Lady in Antwerp.

7 Painting with a multitude of figures.

8 Altarpiece for the high altar for the parish church of Saint James in Antwerp. Martin Zweite, *Marten de Vos als Maler*, Berlin 1980, no. 85, pp. 305-306 and pp. 374-376, doc. 9. Oil on panel. The dimensions of the central panel are 235 cm x 247 cm. Archival documents show that the money was gathered from private donations. Peeters, *Tussen continuïteit* (note 1), cat. No. A 23. The wings were painted by Ambrosius Francken (see further).

9 Number of figures for central panel only. The wings of the altarpiece are not preserved.

10 Altarpiece for the chapel of the brotherhood of Saint Anthony, in the Cathedral of Our Lady in Antwerp. Zweite, *Marten de Vos* (note 8), no. 84, pp. 304-305 and pp. 374, doc. 8; oil on panel. The central panel measures 280 x 212 cm. The wings probably measured 4 x (280 cm x ca 100 cm).

11 The central panel of the altarpiece is not preserved.

12 Altarpiece for the high altar for the parish church of Saint George in Antwerp. Peeters, *Tussen continuïteit* (note 1), cat. No. A 12. Oil on panel. Central panel not preserved, but measuring presumably ca 270 cm x c. 170 cm; wings 4 x (270 cm x 90 cm).

13 Altarpiece for the guild of the Vintners for their chapel in the Cathedral of Our Lady in Antwerp. Zweite, *Marten de Vos* (note 8), no. 86, pp. 306-308, and pp. 376-378, doc. 10; oil on panel; dimensions

central panel 268 cm x 235 cm.
14 Large number of heads.
15 Altarpiece for the high altar of the parish church of Saint Andrew in Antwerp. Pieter Visschers, *Geschiedenis van St. Andrieskerk te Antwerpen sedert hare opkomst tot den huidigen dag*, 3 vols., Antwerpen 1853, vol. 1, pp. 69-73, oil on panel; the panel measures 437 cm x 287 cm. The artist was paid 1,200 Car. guilders and a gratuity/gift of 60 Car. guilders. King Philip II of Spain himself undertook part of the sponsoring of the altarpiece.
16 Peeters, *Tussen continuïteit* (note 1), cat. No. F 27. Oil on panel. The dimensions of the central panel are 231 cm x 208 cm; the wings 4 x (235 cm x 92 cm).
17 Altarpiece with a multitude of figures.
18 Altarpiece for the chapel of the Mercers' guild for their chapel in the Cathedral of Our Lady in Antwerp. David Freedberg, *Iconoclasm and painting in the revolt of the Netherlands: 1566-1609*, New York 1988, pp. 224-227; Stefaan Grieten and Joke Bungeneers (eds.), *Onze-Lieve-Vrouwekathedraal van Antwerpen : kunstpatrimonium van het Ancien Regime*, Turnhout 1996, pp. 367-368 (citing a total of 2700 Car. guilders). Oil on panel. The dimensions of the central panel are 269 cm x 214 cm, the wings 2 x (267 cm x 167 cm) and 2 x (267 cm x 162 cm); according to Freedberg there were also 2 small *predellae*, but nothing further is known about them so we cannot take this into consideration here.
19 Number of figures for wings only.
20 Ambrosius Francken provided the wings for the completion of the previously mentioned altarpiece of Saint James, for the parish church of Saint James in Antwerp, for which Marten de Vos had painted the central panel. Peeters, *Tussen continuïteit* (note 1), cat. no. A 23. Oil on panel. The dimensions of the wings are 4 x (230 cm x 104 cm).
21 Altarpiece with a multitude of figures.
22 Altarpiece for the *H. Geestmeesters* [Poor masters] for their chapel in Church of Saint Waldetrudis at Herentals. Peeters, *Tussen continuïteit* (note 1), cat. No. A 24. Oil on panel. The dimensions of the central panel are 241 cm x 191 cm; the wings are 4 x (246 cm x 85 cm).

Table 1/2 : Altarpieces 1587-1609: prices

NAME	CAR. GLD.	RATE GLD / M^2	DIM (M^2)	YEAR
F. Francken	50	3.88	12.8	1589
F. Francken	144	-	-	1587
M. Coxcie	150	11.9	12.5	1587
F. Francken	220	-	-	1595
F. Francken	240	15.9	15.2	1587
F. Francken	325	24.3	13.4	1604
A. Francken	350	36.8	9.5	1609
A. Francken	350	21.1	16.6	1609
A. Francken	360	19.7	18.3	1589-90
M. de Vos	435.18	18.90	17.1	1594
A. Francken	500	35.2	14.2	1595-98
M. de Vos	500	80.6	6.2	1596-97
M. de Vos	512	88.3	5.8	1594
O.Van Veen	1,200	96	12.5	1599
O. Van Veen	2,400	103.4	23.2	1607

Table 1/3 : Altarpieces 1587-1609: dimensions (m^2)

NAME	CAR. GLD.	PATRON	DIM (M 2)	RATE GLD / M2
M. de Vos	512	Ch. Fabr.	5.8	88.3
M. de Vos	500	Gld. Wine tav	6.2	80.6
A. Francken	350	Ch. Fabr.	9.5	36.8
O.Van Veen	1,200	Ch. Fabr./Ph II	12.5	96
M. Coxcie	150	Gld.	12.5	11.9
F. Francken	50	Private don.	12.8	3.88
F. Francken	325	Gld. Brewers	13.4	24.3
A. Francken	500	Ch. Fabr.	14.2	35.2
F. Francken	240	Gld.	15.2	15.9
A. Francken	350	Poor. mrs.	16.6	21.1
M. de Vos	435.18	Broth.	17.1	18.9
A. Francken	360	Broth.	18.3	19.7
O. Van Veen	2,400	Gld. Mercers	23.2	103.4

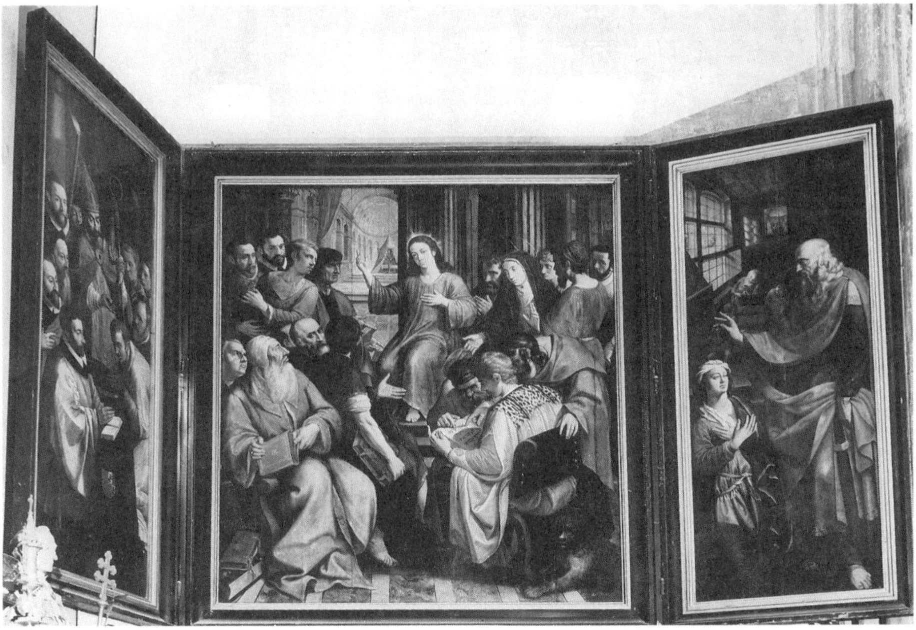

2.

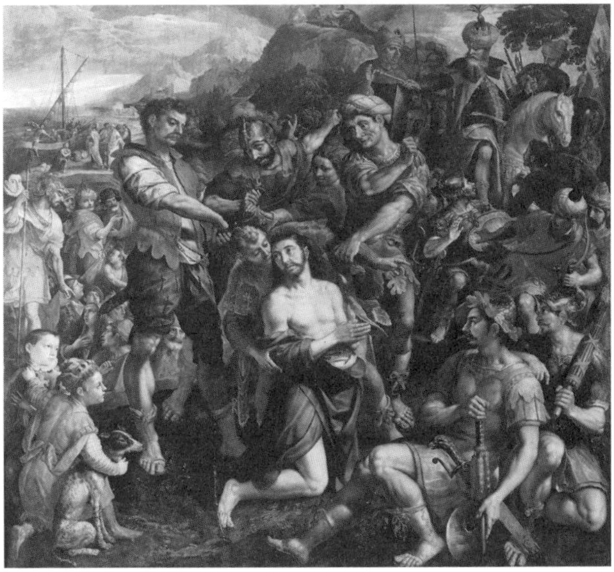

3.

2.
Frans Francken the Elder
Triptych of the schoolmasters and soapboilers, 1587
Cathedral of Our Lady, Antwerp

3.
Marten de Vos
Triptych of Saint James, 1594
Church of Saint James, Antwerp

Table 1/4: Altarpieces 1587 1609: Rates Guilders/M^2

NAME	CAR. GLD.	PATRON	RATE.GLD / M^2	DIM (M^2)
F. Francken	50	Private don.	3.88	12.8
M. Coxcie	150	Gld.	11.9	12.5
F. Francken	240	Gld.	15.9	15.1
M. de Vos	435.18	Broth.	18.9	17.1
A. Francken	360	Broth.	19.7	18.3
A. Francken	350	Poor mrs.	21.1	16.6
F. Francken	325	Gld. Brewers	24.3	13.4
A. Francken	500	Ch. Fabr.	35.2	14.2
A. Francken	350	Ch. Fabr.	36.8	9.5
M. de Vos	500	Gld. Wine taverners	80.6	6.2
M. de Vos	512	Ch. Fabr.	88.3	5.8
O.Van Veen	1,200	Ch. Fabr./Ph II	96	12.5
O. Van Veen	2,400	Gld. Mercers	103.4	23.2

Francken received. Indeed, we note a significant difference between the various painters' prices. However, the chronology fails to show an evolution towards higher rates: both lower and higher rates co-existed in both periods. The average for the period 1587-97 was 34.2 Car. guilders/m^2 and 56.3 Car. guilders/m^2 for the period 1598-1609. We need to keep in mind, however, that the rates for the second period were substantially influenced by the two painted altarpieces of Otto van Veen so that any additional data about other painters who were active in this period would probably decrease this rate. Were the largest altarpieces the most expensive? A comparison between dimensions and rate/m^2 shows that there were significant price differences between the various painters. Van Veen's altarpiece of 1607 was clearly huge and expensive, but this was not the case for Ambrosius Francken's or Marten de Vos's paintings. Thus, size did matter, but not always, because the format did not automatically determine the price.

Could the prices have been influenced by the patron's budget? The interaction between painters and clients, and the context in which prices were set, were important because an altarpiece is part of a representational strategy and stresses the piety, presence, power, and demonstrative consumption, and thus serves as social and religious capital.[18] In fact, the altarpiece served a dual role: it was representative of both the painter and the patron. A high-profile religious commission for the artist could kindle the interest of private patrons, while a patron could use the painting to establish or confirm his own reputation.

Some of the guilds, when comparing all of the patrons between 1587-1609, seem to have been able to pay the highest prices, as shown in table 1/5. But early modern guilds were a far from homogeneous group. The poorer guilds had to make a larger effort than the richer guilds (such as the brewers, mercers, vintners and militias) to secure a commission. The rich and prestigious guilds, such as the militias, clearly wanted to show off their wealth and status, and they were prepared to pay for it. It is not surprising that one of the richest and most prestigious guilds in Antwerp, the mercers, ordered a large and expensive altarpiece for their altar in the Cathedral of Our Lady and were willing to pay Van Veen the highest rates at the time.[19] The financial sway of the churches, on the other hand, varied according to their ability to collect money. In the case of Van Veen's altarpiece for the church of Saint Andrew, King Philip II ensured an exceptionally high rate for the time by generously sponsoring the piece.

Table 1/5 : Altarpieces 1587-1609: patrons

	NAME	CAR. GLD.	PATRON	RATE GLD/ M²	DIM (M²)
city	F. Francken	144	City?	0	0
guild	F. Francken	220	Gld. Coopers	0	0
	M. de Vos	500	Gld. Wine tav	80.6	
	M. Coxcie	150	Gld	11.9	12.5
	F. Francken	325	Gld. Brewers	24.3	13.4
	F. Francken	240	Gld.	15.9	15.2
	O. Van Veen	2,400	Gld. Mercers	103.4	23.2
ch.fabr.	M. de Vos	512	Ch. Fabr.	88.3	5.8
	A. Francken	350	Ch. Fabr.	36.8	9.5
	O.Van Veen	1,200	Ch. Fabr./Ph II	96	12.5
	A. Francken	500	Ch. Fabr.	35.2	14.2
broth.	A. Francken	350	Poor mrs.	21.1	16.6
	M. de Vos	435.18	Broth.	18.9	17.1
	A. Francken	360	Broth.	19.7	18.3
priv.	F. Francken	50	Private don.	3.88	12.8

But the prices quoted in documents do not always cover all: some things were not written down. Friendships, or the promise of extra commissions from the same patron also had an impact on the price. In other cases, gifts such as beer or gloves may have accompanied the payment.[20]

Many a painter seems to have adjusted his price depending on the financial circumstances of his patron. Ambrosius Francken is an interesting case in point: in 1609, the Poor masters of his native town of Herentals paid a rate of 21 Car. guilders/m^2, while that same year the probably somewhat richer church fabric of Saint James Church in Antwerp paid 36.8 Car. guilders/m^2 for the completion of their existing altarpiece with wings. One could argue that the number of figures was perhaps important as an indicator, but based on the sample, there is not enough conclusive evidence to determine this.[21] While the altarpieces of the Francken brothers and De Vos are often overcrowded, and intricately worked out down to the details of clothes and accessories, Van Veen's altarpiece for Antwerp's Church of Saint Andrew is also filled with bystanders, so that neither the number of figures, nor the intricacy of the details can explain the significant price difference (fig. 4). Famous painters could demand higher prices than lesser-known painters and the wealthiest patrons sought out the most famous painters.

As far as one can tell, it seems that there was – certainly in the years before Otto van Veen – an unspoken norm of what was paid for painted altarpieces. When the asking price was too high, noone would pay the price; when the price was too low, there was no advantage or prestige involved for the patron. Based on this set of 15 references from the period 1587-1609, the 'average' price –if one may call it so- for an altarpiece would be less than 500 Car. guilders, a reasonable rate for the client and keeping its balance between the tangible and intangible costs. When one realises that an average altarpiece could take up to three to four months to complete, plus preparation time and meetings, alterations, and keeping in mind that the going wages for a trained journeyman between 1595 and 1600 were 24 *stuivers* per day, the profit margins for these master painters were unexceptional.[22]

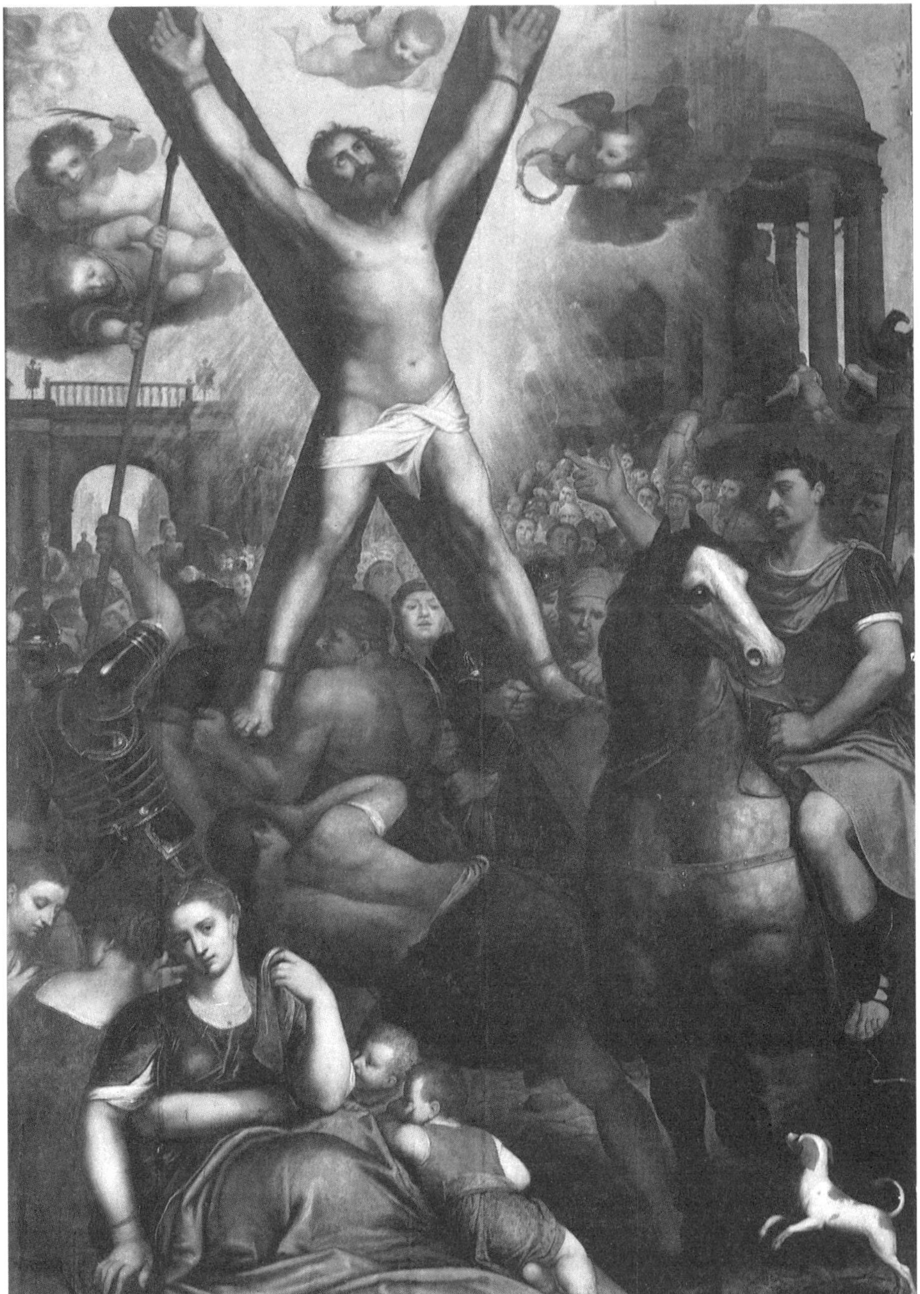

4.

Otto van Veen
Martyrdom of Saint Andrew, 1599
Church of Saint Andrew, Antwerp

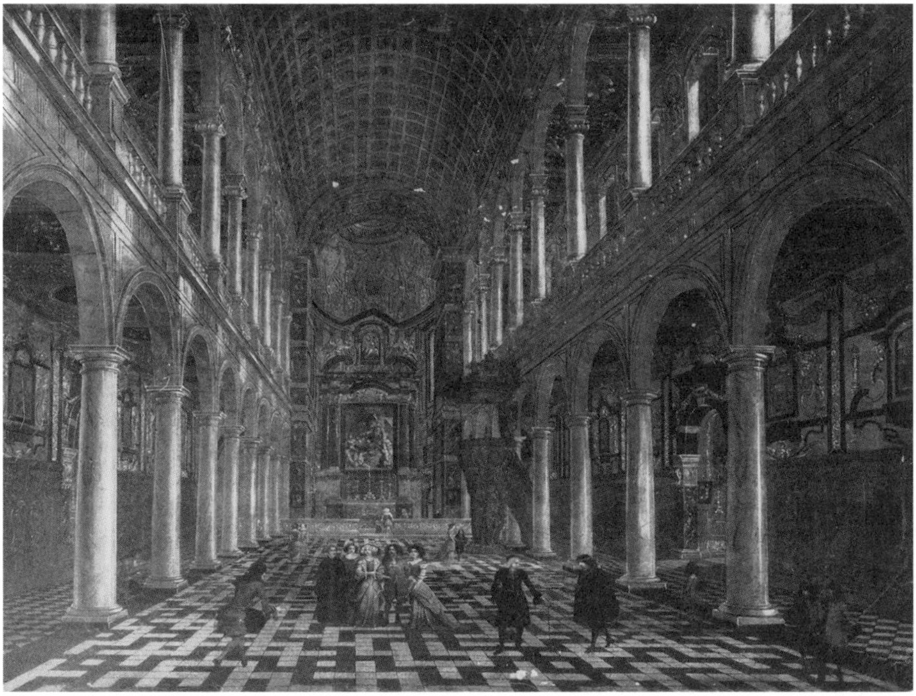

5.

Gheringh
Interior of Saint Walburga church with Rubens's triptych of the Raising of the Cross, after 1613
Saint Paul's Church, Antwerp

Prices of painted altarpieces in the first half of the seventeenth century: The cases of Peter Paul Rubens and Gaspar de Crayer

The political and economic situation in the Southern Netherlands stabilised somewhat in the years after 1609 due to the Twelve-Year Truce.[23] One factor that contributed to the recovery of the luxury market was the reestablishment of a strong Catholic Church. Various religious orders also returned to the city by the century's end and new ones had established themselves there.[24] They all needed various objects and accessories for their religious services and the practice of their faith. Prior to 1600, the secular clergy and the guilds were the most important patrons, while after 1600, many commissions came in from rich regular orders such as the Jesuits, and the Benedictines who commissioned altarpieces for their churches.[25] Rubens secured many commissions from these new orders as well as from the more traditional ones. They commissioned altarpieces in the spirit of a triumphant Catholicism.

Little research has been done on Rubens's prices.[26] Julius Held briefly studied the topic for the *Cardiff Cartoons* in 1983, and compared the prices in correlation with scale.[27]

Rubens's correspondence and related documents give us some idea of how the artist worked and how he thought about price and value. An often quoted letter by Rubens, to Dudley Carleton, dated 1 June 1618 seems especially relevant and enlightening on the issue of price-setting: 'As for the measurements, which proved somewhat less than you had expected, I did my best, taking the dimensions according to the measure current in this country. But you may be sure that this slight difference has no effect upon the price. For one evaluates pictures differently from tapestries. The latter are purchased by measure, while the former are valued according to their excellence, their subject, and number of figures'.[28] A letter from Rubens' good friend Balthasar Moretus to the Flemish merchant Jean van Vucht dated 25 June 1630, reads: 'I have communicated your wish to him [Rubens], but have not found means to make him state a price. Indeed, I have often employed him but I have never been able to make an agreement. [...] However, for 200 or 250 florins, he does not do much, unless you are content with a composition with one or two figures'.[29] On 31 August, Moretus wrote another letter to Van Vucht: 'I openly spoke to Mr. Rubens about the price of 100 pattacons which you want to spend. He answered that none of the three subjects could be done under 200 pattacons as they are too much work. But if you want to have a Diana with two nymphs or some other subject with two or three figures, he would happily furnish this for the aforementioned 100 pattacons'.[30] The matter was resolved slowly, and another letter from Moretus to Van Vucht dated 22 October of the same year states that: 'If you are content with a painting of 3 or 4 figures, he will execute one for you in any format you wish for 100 pattacons'.'[31]

But are Rubens's altarpieces with more figures really more expensive than those with fewer? The triptych *Raising of the Cross* at 2,600 Car. guilders shows ten full figures, 11 half figures and six heads (fig. 5). The *Miraculous Draught of Fishes* at 1,600 Car. guilders includes 11 full figures, four half figures and four heads, while the *Miracles of Francis Xavier*, 100 Car. Guilders cheaper, includes six full figures, one half figure and 13 heads, and is also smaller. These 'inconsistencies' show that one must be careful when extrapolating information from correspondence. In the case of the 1618 Carleton letter, Rubens was probably writing about another category of paintings altogether: mythological pieces for the private market segment of connoisseurs.[32] O' Malley is clear in this respect regarding Italian altarpieces: 'The commonly held idea that the number of figures painted on a work strongly influences its price is largely derived from a few letters and evaluation documents [...]'.[33]

A letter written by Rubens to Gortzius Geldorp in London on 25 July 1637 concerning the *Martyrdom of Saint Peter* (Cologne, Cathedral of Saint Peter) notes that: 'As regards time, I must have a year and a half, in order to be able to serve your friend with care and convenience. As for the subject, it would be best to choose it according to the size of the picture; for there are subjects which are better treated in a large space, and others which call for medium or small proportions. [...] Nevertheless, I leave the choice to the one who will pay the expenses, as soon as we know how large the picture is to be'.[34] Prices were, in some cases, agreed upon before the painter begun his work, as was the case for the paintings for the Salón Nuevo in the Royal Palace in Madrid.[35] But procedures varied. A letter of 12 May 1618 shows how Rubens affably wrote to Carleton: '[I] would always refer the price to the arbitration of any discerning person'.[36]

What can we say about 'excellence', the first thing Rubens listed in the above-mentioned letter of 1618, in terms of determining the price of an artwork? A letter from Toby Matthew to Dudley Carleton on 25 November 1620 states: 'I did with all my discretion, deale with him [Rubens] about the price, but his demands are like the Lawes

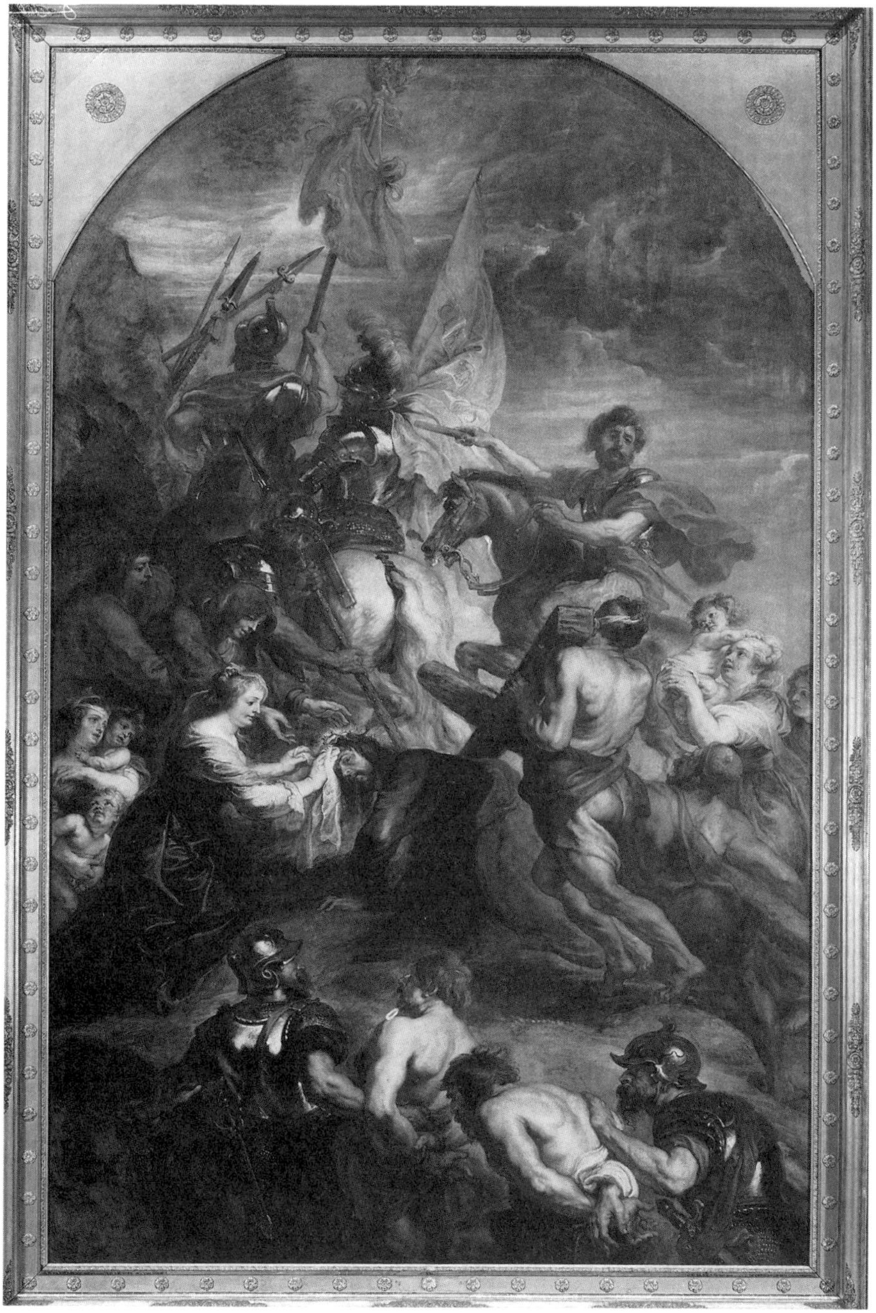

6.

Peter Paul Rubens
Christ carrying the Cross, 1634-37
Royal Museums of Fine Arts of Belgium, Brussels

of Medes and Persians, which cannot be altered. ... I see it helps him to be unreasonable'.[37] Although this passage does not refer specifically to his altarpieces, and shows how royal clients always haggled for a better deal and reacted disapprovingly when their hopes for a good deal were dashed, it also shows how Rubens was aware of his value: excellence needs to be remunerated. The letter further states that Rubens was stubborn, and that his prices were set and not subject to modification, which is perhaps somewhat exaggerated, as we shall see. However, Rubens was a prudent man and a hard bargainer when it came to his fees. For the new Jesuit church in Antwerp, Rubens made the 39 ceiling paintings and two altarpieces, which depicted the *Miracles of Ignatius of Loyola* and the *Miracles of Francis Xavier.* The contract dating 29 March 1620 stated that if the sum of 7,000 and 3,000 Car. guilders respectively were not fully paid on the appointed day, the Jesuit order was to pay the artist an annual rent of 6,25 per cent of the amount, or 625 Car. guilders, until the amount was paid.[38]

The following selection of 22 altarpieces (see table 2/1) by Rubens and his studio, for which archival sources have yielded prices, serves as a first case study and will allow us to make some preliminary conclusions about Rubens's prices. What can we deduce from these 22 examples? The paintings, produced during the period 1610-38, ranged in price from 300 to 2,600 Car. guilders, as can be seen in table 2/2. Added together, we come up with the staggering 27,080 Car. guilders. On average, 1,230.90 Car. guilders was paid per altarpiece. In absolute terms, the highest prices were those paid in the beginning of Rubens's career after his return to Antwerp, more specifically, the 2,600 Car. guilders in 1610-13 and 2,400 Car. guilders paid in 1615. If one divides Rubens's Antwerp career into three decades, the average real (adjusted) prices for the period 1610-19 were 1,650 Car. guilders; in the years 1620-29 they decreased to 816.20 Car. guilders and for the period 1630-38, they increased to 1,140 Car. guilders. On the dimensions, information exists for 21 of the 22 altarpieces: they range from 2.5 to 62.7 m^2 (see table 2/3). The average dimension per altarpiece in our sample for the period 1610-19 is 27.7 m^2; in the period 1620-29 it decreases to 10.2 m^2, and a little more during the period 1630-38, down to 9.8 m^2. These altarpieces – at least as far as for our sample – do not increase in size as we approach the end of Rubens's career, on the contrary: in absolute size, the largest works are the two famous triptychs of the *Raising* and *Descent from the Cross*, which he made in the first decade upon his return to Antwerp.

An important typological change occurred during the second decade of the seventeenth century, as the triptych format with wings, backs of wings, a (winged) *predella* and other elements (such as frontons) painted on panels evolved into the *portico* altarpiece, consisting of one large slab-like canvas.[39] Although these later altarpieces feel and look monumental, one has to keep in mind that they were single canvasses with an actual smaller painted surface. The *Raising of the cross* is three times as large as the largest of the monumental 'single slab' altarpieces, such as *Christ carrying the cross* for the abbey in Affligem (fig. 6).

For 21 of the 22 altarpieces, there is information on the evolution of the rate per square meter (see Table 2/4). The rate ranges from 24.70 to 250 Car. guilders/m^2. Some altarpieces measuring c. 12 m^2 cost 300 Car. guilders, but the price could go up to 1,500 Car. guilders. Larger sizes *in sé* did not automatically imply a higher price. The large difference in rates proves that his prices were not based solely on size. The average rate as a whole is 88.90 Car. guilders/m^2. The average rate for the period 1610-19 is 68.10 Car. guilders/m^2; for the period 1620-29 it rose to 80 Car. guilders/m^2, and towards the end of Rubens's career, during the years 1630-38, it increased to 138 Car. guilders/m^2, or nearly double the rate of the earlier period. Concerning the price trend of Rubens's altarpieces,

Table 2/1: Peter Paul Rubens's altarpieces (1610-1638): chronology[#]

SUBJECT	DATE	CAR. GLD.	PATRON	RATE / M^2 (Gld.)	FIG.*	DIM (M^2)	PL. PRES.	PL. ORIGIN
Raising of the Cross[23]	1610-13	2,600	vd Geest	414	10f;11h;6H;angels	62.7	Antw., Cath	Antw., St. Walburga Ch.
The distress of Job[24]	1612	1,500	Gld.	-	/	-	lost	Bxl, St Nicolas Ch.
Descent from the Cross[25]	1615	2,400	Gld.	62.3	15f;4h;6H	38.5	Antw., Cath	Antw., Cath
Assumption[26]	1616-18	1,200	Ch. Fabr.	101.6	5f;1h;11, angels	11.8	Dusseldorf, KM	Bxl, Chapel church
Adoration Magi[27]	1616-19	1,800	Ch. Fabr.	62.3	5f;7h;11H	28.9	Mech., St John's Ch.	Mech., St John's Ch.
Miracl. Ignatius Loy. [28]	1616-17	1,500	Jesuits	71	8f;2h;17H; angels	21.1	Vienna, KHM	Antw., Car Bor Ch.
Miracl. Franc Xav. [29]	1617-18	1,500	Jesuits	71	6f;11h;13+H; angels	21.1	Vienna, KHM	Antw., Car Bor Ch.
Last communion St Francis [30]	1618	750	Gaspar Charles	79.7	3f;5h;5H; angels	9.4	Antw., RMFA	Antw., Recoll Ch.
Miraculous draught[31]	1618	1,600	Gld.	55.7	11f;4h;4H	28.7	Mech., OL ter Dijle Ch.	Mech., OL ter Dijle Ch.
Descent Holy spirit[32]	1620	1,500	Count duke	117	4f;4h;9H	12.8	Munich, AP	Neuburg, Jesuit Ch.
Adoration Shep. [33]	1620	1,500	Count duke	117	4f;3h;1H; angels	12.8	Munich, AP	Neuburg, Jesuit Ch.
St. Joseph & infant Christ [34]	1621	530	Archdukes	120	?	4.4	Lost?	Marlagne, Ch.
Adoration shep. [35]	1621	300	Archdukes	65.2	?	4.6	Lost	Bxl, oratory archdukes
Adoration Magi[36]	1621	400	Archdukes	63.4	?	6.3	Lost	Bxl, oratory archdukes
Descent Holy Spirit [37]	1621	300	Archdukes	24.7	?	12.1	Lost	Bxl, oratory archdukes
Assumption[38]	1624	1,500	Del Rio	94.3	6f;5h;7H; angels	15.9	Antw., Cath.	Antw., Cath.
St. Roch[39]	1626	500	Broth.	38.7	6f;3;1H	12.9	Alost, St Martin's Ch.	Alost, St. Martin's Ch.
Institution Eucharist[40]	1631-32	1,000	C. Lescuyer	100	3f;3h;8H	10	Milan, Pin. Brera /Dijon MBA	Mech., St Rom Ch.
Christ carrying the cross[41]	1634-37	1,600	Benedictines	79.6	3f;12h;4H	20.1	Bxl, RMFAB	Affligem, Benedictine Abbey
Matryr. St Peter[42]	1637	1,300	church	250	3f;3h;angel	5.2	Cologne, St. Peter	Cologne, St. Peter
Martyr. St Paul[43]	1638	1,500	prior	132.2	?[44]	11.3	lost	Bxl, Rood klooster
Miracl. St Just[45]	1638	300	B. Moretus	120	3f;3h	2.5	Bordeaux, MBA	Antw., Sisters annunciate

* 'f' : full figures; h: half length figures; H: heads.
# some rates/m^2 have been rounded.
23 J. Richard Judson, *Rubens. The Passion of Christ*, Corpus Rubenianum Ludwig Burchard. 6, Turnhout 2000 pp. 88-122; no. 20-28. Oil on panel; the dimensions of the central panel are 460 cm x 340 cm; the wings are 4 x (462 cm x 150 cm), totalling 43.3 m^2. There was also a depiction of *God the Father* (place of preservation unknown), measuring ca 157 x 124 cm.
24 Roger-Adolf d'Hulst and Marc Vandenven, *Rubens. The Old Testament*, Corpus Rubenianum Ludwig Burchard. 3, New York 1989 pp. 170-187, no. 54-56. Support presumably panel. Dimensions unknown.
25 Judson, *Rubens* (note 1), pp. 162-190, no. 43-46; Max Rooses, 'De Afdoening van het Kruis, uit het rekeningboek der Antwerpsche Kolveniersgilde', *Rubens Bulletijn* 5 (1910), pp. 231-233. Oil on panel. The dimensions of the central part are 421 cm x 311 cm, the wings are 4 x (421 cm x 153 cm).
26 Publication of this group forthcoming in the *Corpus Rubenianum*-series. Max Rooses, *L'œuvre de P.P. Rubens, Histoire et description de ses tableaux et dessins*, Antwerp, 1886-1892, 5 vols., vol. 2 [1888], pp. 170-172, no. 358; Thomas L. Glen, *Rubens and the Counter-Reformation, Studies in his religious paintings between 1609 and 1620*, PhD Dissertation Princeton University 1977, pp. 260-261, measuring according to Rooses, 423 cm x 281 cm. Oil on panel.
27 Publication of this group forthcoming in the *Corpus Rubenianum*-series. Oil on panel. The dimensions of the central panel are
320 cm x 278 cm; the wings are 4 x (320 cm x 100 cm) with a *predella* of
3 x (66 cm x 22 cm) and 2 x backs of wings (66 cm x 22 cm). The wings of the *predella* are now in Marseille, Musée des Beaux-Arts; Emmanuel Neeffs, 'L'Oeuvre de P.-P. Rubens à Malines', *Bulletin de l'Académie royale des sciences, des lettres et des beaux-arts de Belgique*, 2e série, 42 (1876),
pp. 214-222; Rooses, *L'Oeuvre* (note 4), vol. 1 [1886], pp. 214-216, no. 162. The dimensions are those referred to in the *Fotorepertorum van het meubilair van de Belgische bedehuizen*.
28 Hans Vlieghe, *Saints*, Corpus Rubenianum Ludwig Burchard. 8, 2 vols., Brussels 1972-1973, vol. 2, 1973, pp. 73-74, no. 115; oil on canvas. The painting's dimensions are 535 cm x 395 cm.
Vlieghe, *Saints* (note 6), vol. 2, pp. 26-29, no. 104; oil on canvas. The painting's dimensions are 535 cm x 395 cm.
29 Vlieghe, *Saints* (note 6), vol. 1, pp. 156-159, no. 102; oil on panel. The painting's dimensions are 420 cm x 225 cm.
30 Publication of this group forthcoming in the *Corpus Rubenianum*-series. Neeffs, *L'Oeuvre de P.-P. Rubens* (note 5), pp. 208-214; Rooses, *L'Oeuvre* (note 4), vol. 2, pp. 19-21, no. 245; oil on panel. The central panel measures 301 cm x 235 cm, the wings 4 x (301 cm x 106 cm), a presumably lost *predella* measures 3 x (75 cm x 40 cm). The *predella* did not return to Mechelen after 1794. The dimensions are those from the *Fotorepertorum van het meubilair van de Belgische bedehuizen*.
31 David Freedberg, *Rubens, The Life of Christ after the Passion*, Corpus Rubenianum Ludwig Burchard. 7, New York 1984, pp. 103-108, no. 27; Glen, *Rubens and the Counter-Reformation* (note 4), p. 290; Rooses, *L'Oeuvre* (note 4), vol. 2, pp. 163-164, no. 353; Konrad Renger, *Peter Paul Rubens, Altäre für Bayern*, München Alte Pinakothek 1990, pp. 39ff; the painting's dimensions according to Freedberg are: 470 cm x 273 cm. Oil on canvas.
32 Publication of this group forthcoming in the *Corpus Rubenianum*-series. Rooses, *L'Oeuvre* (note 4), vol. 1, pp. 190-194, no. 149. Oil on canvas. Renger, *Peter Paul Rubens*, (note 10), p. 39ff; the painting's dimensions are 475 cm x 270 cm.
33 Vlieghe, *Saints* (note 6), vol. 2 (1973), pp. 102-104, no. 124. According to Rooses, the work is identical to a painting formerly in the collection Munro, sold in London in 1878, an identification to which we will stick for the moment. Rooses, *L'Oeuvre* (note 4), vol. 2, pp. 313-314, no. 465; support unknown; the painting's dimensions are 239 cm x 187 cm. Although no image of the work exists, an old description by Mensaert conveys the composition.
34 Publication of this group forthcoming in the *Corpus Rubenianum*-series. See Marcel de Maeyer, *Albrecht en Isabella en de schilderkunst: Bijdrage tot de geschiedenis van de XVIIe-eeuwse schilderkunst in de Zuidelijke Nederlanden*, Brussels 1955, pp. 119-120, 407. Support unknown. The dimensions are known: it was 8,5 ft high and 8,5 ft large, or 234 cm x 234 cm.
35 Publication of this group forthcoming in the *Corpus Rubenianum*-series. See de Maeyer, *Albrecht en Isabella* (note 13), pp. 119-120, 407. Support unknown. The dimensions however, are known: it was 8 ft high and 10,5 ft large, or 220 cm x 288,7 cm.
36 Freedberg, *Rubens, The Life of Christ after the Passion* (note 10), pp. 110, no. 28; de Maeyer, *Albrecht en Isabella* (note 13), p. 119-120, 407. Support unknown. The dimensions are known: it was 10 ft high and 16 ft large, or c. 275,5 cm x c. 441 cm. Oil on canvas. Freedberg remarks upon the fact that there is discussion about the price in the existing literature. We follow de Maeyer here.
37 Freedberg, *Rubens, The Life of Christ after the Passion* (note 10), pp. 172-178, no. 43. Rooses, *L'Oeuvre* (note 4), vol. 2, pp. 173-180, no. 359 ; Max Rooses, ' l'Assomption de la vierge; tableau du maître autel de la Cathédrale d'Anvers', *Rubens Bulletijn* 1 (1882), pp. 70-71. Oil on panel. The dimensions are: 490 cm x 325 cm.
38 Vlieghe, *Saints* (note 6), vol. 2, pp. 142-146, no. 140-143; oil on canvas; the painting measures 412 cm x 258 cm. The *predella* measures 2 x (68 cm x 97 cm). There was also a *Virgin in a tabernacle* measuring c. 150 x ca 70 cm.
39 Judson, *Rubens. The Passion of Christ*, (note 1), pp. 48-52, no. 6; oil on panel; the painting measures 403 cm x 250 cm. The accounts of the commission are well-preserved.
40 Judson, *Rubens. The Passion of Christ*, (note 1), pp. 79-84, no. 19; Ulrich Heinen, '"A Meliori forma". Quellenstudien zum Aufträge für Rubens' Affligemer Kreuztragung', *Jaarboek van het Koninklijk Museum voor Schone Kunsten van Antwerpen* (1993), pp. 135-163; Natasja Peeters, Hélène Dubois and Joost Vander Auwera, 'P.P. Rubens, De marteling van de heilige Livinus', in: Joost Vander Auwera and Sabine Van Sprang (eds.), *Rubens, een genie aan het werk, Rondom de Rubenswerken in de Koninklijke Musea voor Schone Kunsten van België*, Brussels (Royal Museums of Fine Art) 2007 (exh. cat.), pp. 196-200. The painting measures 569 cm x 355 cm. Oil on canvas.
41 Vlieghe, *Saints* (note 6), vol. 2, pp. 137-140, no. 139; oil on canvas; the painting measures 310 cm x 170 cm.
42 Vlieghe, *Saints* (note 6), vol. 2, pp. 131-132, no. 137; oil on canvas; the dimensions are unknown, but according to Vlieghe the painting measures c. 420 cm x c. 270 cm. There is also a preparatory oil sketch (U.S. private collection), which gives an idea of the composition, see Julius Held, *The oil sketches of Peter Paul Rubens. A critical catalogue*, 2 vols., Princeton 1980, vol. 1, no. 423.
43 A description by Mols serves to give us an idea about the composition: 'heilige, beul, achter hem krijgsvolk waarvan men de hoofden en weinig lichaam zag; daarvoor nog vrouwen en kinderen ten halven lijven; verder engelen uit de hemel', in: J. de Wit, *De kerken van Antwerpen [1748], met aantekeningen van P.J.J. Mols [1774], bewerkt door J. de Bosschere*, Antwerpen 1910 [1919].
44 Vlieghe, *Saints* (note 6), vol. 2, pp. 104-105, no. 125; oil on canvas; the painting measures 191 cm x 134 cm.

Table 2/2 : Peter Paul Rubens's altarpieces (1610-1638): prices

TITLE	DATE	CAR. GLD.	PATRON	RATE M2	DIM 2
Adoration shep.	1621	300	Archdukes	65.2	4,6
Descent Holy Spirit	1621	300	Archdukes	24.7	12,1
Miracl. St Just	1638	300	B. Moretus	120	2,5
Adoration Magi	1621	400	Archdukes	63.4	6.3
St. Roch	1626	500	Broth.	38.7	12.9
Sint Joseph and the infant Christ	1621	530	Archdukes	120	4.4
Last communion St Francis	1618	750	Gaspar Charles	79.7	9.4
Institution Eucharist	1631-32	1,000	C. Lescuyer	100	10
Assumption	1616-18	1,200	Ch. Fabr.	101.6	11.8
Matryr. St Peter	1637	1,300	church	250	5.2
Assumption	1624	1,500	Del Rio	94.3	15.9
Martyr. St Paul	1638	1,500	prior	132.2	11.3
Miracl. St Ignatius	1616-17	1,500	Jesuits	71	21.1
Miracl. Franc Xav.	1617-18	1,500	Jesuits	71	21.1
Descent Holy spirit	1620	1,500	count duke	117	12.8
Adoration Shep.	1620	1,500	count duke	117	12.8
The distress of Job	1612	1,500	Gld.	0	0
Christ carrying the cross	1634-37	1,600	order	79.6	20.1
Miraculous draught	1618	1,600	Gld.	55.7	28.7
Adoration Magi	1616-19	1,800	Ch. Fabr.	62.3	28.9
Descent of the Cross	1615	2,400	Gld.	62.3	38.5
Raising of the Cross	1610-13	2,600	vd Geest	41.4	62.7

Table 2/3: Peter Paul Rubens's altarpieces (1610-1638): dimensions (m^2)

TITLE	DATE	CAR. GLD.	PATRON	RATE M^2	DIM 2
The distress of Job	1612	1,500	Gld.	0	0
Miracl. St Just	1638	300	B. Moretus	120	2.5
Sint Joseph and the infant Christ	1621	530	Archdukes	120	4.4
Adoration shep.	1621	300	Archdukes	65.2	4.6
Matryr. St Peter	1637	1,300	church	250	5.2
Adoration Magi	1621	400	Archdukes	63.4	6.3
Last communion St Francis	1618	750	Gaspar Charles	79.7	9.4
Institution Eucharist	1631-32	1,000	C. Lescuyer	100	10
Martyr. St Paul	1638	1,500	prior	132.2	11.3
Assumption	1616-18	1,200	Ch. Fabr.	101.6	11.8
Descent Holy Spirit	1621	300	Archdukes	24.7	12.1
Descent Holy spirit	1620	1,500	count duke	117	12.8
Adoration Shep.	1620	1,500	count duke	117	12.8
St. Roch	1626	500	Broth.	38.7	12.9
Assumption	1624	1,500	Del Rio	94.3	15.9
Christ carrying the cross	1634-37	1,600	order	79.6	20.1
Miracl. St Ignatius	1616-17	1,500	Jesuits	71	21.1
Miracl. Franc Xav.	1617-18	1,500	Jesuits	71	21.1
Adoration Magi	1616-19	1,800	Ch. Fabr.	62.3	28.9
Miraculous draught	1618	1,600	Gld.	55.7	28.7
Descent of the Cross	1615	2,400	Gld.	62.3	38.5
Raising of the Cross	1610-13	2,600	vd Geest	41.4	62.7

Table 2/4: Peter Paul Rubens's altarpieces (1610-1638): rates guilders/m^2

TITLE	DATE	CAR. GLD.	PATRON	RATE M²	DIM 2
The distress of Job	1612	1,500	Gld.	0	0
Descent Holy Spirit	1621	300	Archdukes	24.7	12.1
St. Roch	1626	500	Broth.	38.7	12.9
Raising of the Cross	1610-13	2,600	vd Geest	41.4	62.7
Miraculous draught	1618	1,600	Gld.	55.7	28.7
Adoration Magi	1616-19	1,800	Ch. Fabr.	62.3	28.9
Descent of the Cross	1615	2,400	Gld.	62.3	38.5
Adoration Magi	1621	400	Archdukes	63.4	6.3
Adoration shep.	1621	300	Archdukes	65.2	4.6
Miracl. St Ignatius	1616-17	1,500	Jesuits	71	21.1
Miracl. Franc Xav.	1617-18	1,500	Jesuits	71	21.1
Christ carrying the cross	1634-37	1,600	order	79.6	20.1
Last communion St Francis	1618	750	Gaspar Charles	79.7	9.4
Assumption	1624	1,500	Del Rio	94.3	15.9
Institution Eucharist	1631-32	1,000	C. Lescuyer	100	10
Assumption	1616-18	1,200	Ch. Fabr.	101.6	11.8
Descent Holy spirit	1620	1,500	count duke	117	12.8
Adoration Shep.	1620	1,500	count duke	117	12.8
Miracl. St Just	1638	300	B. Moretus	120	2.5
Sint Joseph and the infant Christ	1621	530	Archdukes	120	4.4
Martyr. St Paul	1638	1,500	prior	132.2	11.3
Matryr. St Peter	1637	1,300	church	250	5.2

it is remarkable that a change occurred around c. 1630. The altarpieces of Rubens's late period (1630-38) have nearly doubled in price per square meter (1.86x) over the rates in his earlier years. Keeping in mind that Rubens's earliest altarpieces were painted on much more expensive oak panels, this increase is even more remarkable. Rubens was clearly demanding higher fees as time went on. The highest rate was indeed paid at the end of his career, for the now lost *Martyrdom of Saint Paul* and the *Martyrdom of Saint Peter* (respectively 132.20 and 250 Car. guilders/m^2), with this last commission being ten times as high as the lowest rate paid for Rubens' altarpieces in this sample, the lost *Descent of the Holy spirit* for the archdukes, at 24.70 Car. guilders/m^2. Although his famous triptychs of the *Raising of the Cross* and *Descent from the Cross* are very expensive in absolute terms, there was a lot of surface to cover as well and the rates charged shows that both were below the average of the first sub-period. This means that Rubens's patrons at that time certainly got their money's worth!

Surprisingly, contrary to Rubens' own statement (see above), that the number of figures in a painting mattered when setting the price, when one actually counts the full figures, half figures and heads per painting, the exercise does not reveal anything conclusive regarding the relation of numbers of figures to the price of an altarpiece. It is certainly not true that paintings with fewer figures cost less than those with more. There is a correlation in the sense that the larger the altarpiece, the more figures could be painted on the picture plane. But it seems that although it is impossible to determine how much Rubens adhered to his own above stated dictum for profane works or paintings for the private market, for altarpieces it is clear that other aspects contributed to the price. Of the 22 altarpieces we are concerned with here, eight (perhaps nine)

Table 2/5: Peter Paul Rubens's altarpieces (1610-1638): patrons

	TITLE	DATE	CAR. GLD.	PATRON	RATE M^2	DIM 2	rate av
guild	The distress of Job	1612	1,500	Gld.	0	0	59
	Miraculous draught	1618	1,600	Gld.	55.7	28.7	
	Descent of the Cross	1615	2,400	Gld.	62.3	38.5	
ch fab	Assumption	1616-18	1,200	Ch. Fabr.	101.6	11.8	206.9
	Matryr. St Peter	1637	1,300	church	250	5.2	
	Adoration Magi	1616-19	1,800	Ch. Fabr.	62.3	28.9	
broth	St. Roch	1626	500	Broth.	38.7	12.9	38.7
priv	Miracl. St Just	1638	300	B. Moretus	120	2.5	94.6
	Last communion St Francis	1618	750	Gaspar Charles	79.7	9.4	
	Institution Eucharist	1631-32	1,000	C. Lescuyer	100	10	
	Assumption	1624	1,500	Del Rio	94.3	15.9	
	Martyr. St Paul	1638	1,500	prior	132.2	11.3	
	Raising of the Cross	1610-13	2,600	vd Geest	41.4	62.,7	
orders	Miracl. St Ignatius	1616-17	1,500	Jesuits	71	21.1	73.8
	Miracl. Franc Xav.	1617-18	1,500	Jesuits	71	21.1	
	Christ carrying the cross	1634-37	1,600	order	79.6	20.1	
royals	Adoration shep.	1621	300	Archdukes	65.2	4.6	84.5
	Descent Holy Spirit	1621	300	Archdukes	24.7	12.1	
	Adoration Magi	1621	400	Archdukes	63.4	6.3	
	Descent Holy spirit	1620	1,500	count duke	117	12.8	
	Adoration Shep.	1620	1,500	count duke	117	12.8	
	Sint Joseph and the infant Christ	1621	530	Archdukes	120	4.4	

were on panel, the remaining were painted on canvas. Panel was still used frequently in the period prior to 1620 but due to the monumental *portico*-altar setting, the lighter canvas began replacing wood in the early 1620s. But Rubens charged both high and lower rates, regardless of whether the altarpiece was on panel or on canvas: the raw material of the support was apparently not important when establishing a price.

The money for the large religious commissions which Rubens and his studio executed came from various sources, as shown in table 2/5: religious institutions, royalty, private donors, church hierarchies and city councils and, to a lesser extent, guilds. Prices were certainly influenced by the patron's wealth: rich orders like the Jesuits and the Benedictines were able to spend more money on their commissions than the more ascetic orders. Rubens's personal relationship with various patrons also influenced pricing, such as was the case for the Count-Duke of Neuburg, who had a well-stocked treasury, and thus paid 1,500 Car. guilders for each altar for the Jesuit Church at Neuburg. The three religious patrons in this sample paid the highest average rate of 206.90 Car. guilders/m^2, followed by the six private patrons (94.60 Car. guilders/m^2), royalty (84.50 Car. guilders/m^2), the various religious orders (73.80 Car. guilders/m^2), the guilds (59 Car. guilders/m^2) and finally the brotherhoods (38.70 Car. guilders/m^2). Interestingly, while some paintings that were made for the archdukes seemed to have been significantly cheaper, one needs to take into consideration the larger context of these royal commissions: one should not forget that Rubens also earned a yearly salary of 500 Flemish pounds or 3,000 Car. guilders from 1610 onwards, when he became a court painter to the archdukes.[40] Apparently, Rubens was also willing to make some concessions for certain patrons. A letter dated 22 October 1630 from Moretus to Van Vucht clarifies some things: 'Concerning Mr. Rubens, he willingly acts out of friendship, provided it does not do him any harm'.[41]

The price could also vary according to the level of studio participation and the amount of work done by studio collaborators, independent masters or journeymen.[42] Kerry Downes wrote a short answer on Held's article in 1983 about the influence of workshop collaboration on prices: 'We may assume that Rubens's prices increased along with his reputation. However, other variations in price may not have depended solely on the degree of studio participation'.[43] A well-known letter from Rubens to Carleton dated 12 May 1618, informs us that the pieces retouched by himself were barely distinguishable from originals (at least according to the master himself) but priced at a somewhat lower rate (see Introduction and p. 41 above).[44] This could also account for some of the 'lower' prices in our sample.[45] The art historian Zirka Z. Filipczak has pointed out that Rubens: '...achieved this unprecedentedly high income without charging inordinately high prices. [...] yet his rates were not exceptionally high: a comparison of payments for large, multi-figured triptychs illustrates that Rubens's prices often matched those that had been paid to the best artists of the previous century'.[46] This was indeed the case up to the end of the 1620s, but after that, Rubens's rates certainly soared and as we remarked earlier, and actually doubled when compared to the earlier years.

Why this great leap? Perhaps the answer can be found in Rubens's artistic life cycle. Perhaps Rubens needed his income from altarpiece-commissions much less than he did at the beginning of his career and he may have considered them less challenging artistically, than he would have c. 1615. At the beginning of his career, the altarpieces probably functioned as a calling card, to entice other patrons, something which he didn't have to bother with in later years. The high demand for his works also pushed his prices up. He was so in demand that even with a studio full of assistants behind him, he could not accept all the commissions that came his way. One also needs to take into consideration that, although Rubens was still a 'craftsman', his collection of noble titles, his castle and his way of life certainly justified higher rates. In his later years, he turned to the freedom of creation in landscapes, and he may have found his designs for projects such as *Torre de la Parada,* the small palatial hunting lodge for Philip IV in Madrid, intellectually more rewarding than churning out altarpieces.

One thing is certain: painting was a profitable business for Rubens. The Antwerp tapestry dealer and humanist Francis Sweerts mentioned rather enviously to John Gruterus on 18 July 1618: 'This Rubens earns 100 guilders every day'.[47] This seems an enormous amount. Indeed, multiplied by 250 work days per year, this amounts to 25,000 Car. guilders per year. Rubens's income from commissions, rent and real estate, sales of gems, prints, royal pensions and gifts and miscellaneous sources could have well resulted in an income of this size. As a comparison, a summer day's wage for a qualified mason's journeyman after 1605 was 24 *stuivers*, and his annual wage was some 300 Car. guilders.[48] But Rubens also had countless expenses: his house, the household staff, pupils, collaborators, assistants, materials, decoration and the art works he purchased himself, his travels, not to mention his growing family. Sweerts wrote to Gruterus on 18 July 1618 that Rubens had spent 24,000 Car. guilders on his house.[49] The money from the great triptychs must certainly have come in handy. Near the end of his life, his beautiful townhouse seemed a 'minor' asset compared to his castle, the Steen, near Mechelen, which, upon his death, was estimated at c. 100,000 Car. guilders.[50] Rubens total assets at the time of his death in May 1640 were difficult to estimate, but were probably around 150,000 Car. Guilders, without even counting his real estate.[51]

Rubens was a gifted, highly professional and well-organised painter with an excellent reputation, who could deliver speedily and produce high quality works. Balthasar Moretus indirectly alludes to this when he wrote somewhat condescendingly to Philip of Peralta that the less refined and discerning would be better served by a less able and cheaper painter than Rubens.[52] The monks at the abbey of Saint Winoksbergen seemed to be proof of Moretus's point. In 1611, they commissioned Rubens to paint a *Last Supper* for them and agreed on a price of 4,000 Car. guilders, an astronomically high sum for this early period. The artist had already made his preparations according to the measures given, when suddenly his patrons decided to back out and offer the commission to the lesser-known painter Lucas Floquet.[53] On 6 September 1611, a dismayed Jan le Grand wrote to Lieven Vuytten Eeckhoutte at Dunkirk: 'They came up with a painter from Ghent who is an impostor, and they are looking for the best deal. I lament that the lords of Berghen shall end up being really cheated'.[54]

Filipczak declared that: 'In general, Rubens's prices were the same as those charged by his most esteemed Flemish contemporaries, though occasionally they increased up to roughly double that amount'.[55] Is this really true? Rubens's rates for the period 1609-29 are lower than the rates charged by his former master Otto van Veen and by Marten de Vos in some cases. To compare, we shall briefly analyse the prices of Gaspar de Grayer, and add a short note on Anthony van Dyck.

For De Crayer, we took a sample of seven altarpieces on canvas commissioned between 1622 and 1665, a period of 43 years (see table 3). In general, De Crayer's patrons were less affluent than those of Rubens: local churches, small town churches, and smaller orders, with less international standing than Rubens's clients. It should thus not come as a surprise that De Crayer's prices were lower than Rubens's. They fluctuate between c. 150 and 500 Car. guilders; with an average price of 339.80 Car. guilders. One needs to keep in mind that, in some cases, only a portion of the actual payment was recorded, so the average was probably somewhat higher. Rubens dips under this average price only three times in our sample, while De Crayer's highest price in our sample (500 Car. Guilders), was equal to one of Rubens's cheaper altarpieces in our sample. De Crayer's altarpiece sizes fluctuate between 4.2 m^2 and 10.4 m^2, and remain well below Rubens's sizes. The rates fluctuate between c. 14.40 Car. guilders/m^2 and 108.60 Car. guilders/m^2; this is an average rate of 62.10 Car. guilders/m^2. Although, by the end of his career, his *Assumption of the Virgin* for the church of Saint Walburga at Oudenaarde fetched more than Rubens's average commission in the early part of his career, De Crayer's prices remained well below Rubens's average rate of 88.90 Car. guilders/m^2, all of which adds some nuances to Filipczak's statement. De Crayer's rates are higher than the general rate received by artists during the period 1585-1607, however. De Crayer – contrary to what historiography wants us to believe – enjoyed a good reputation as a painter, but his somewhat eclectic altarpieces were no match for Rubens's power of invention, and consequently, neither were his prices.[56]

A final and brief note concerns Antony van Dyck, who, according to Vlieghe, received between 500 and 800 Car. guilders for his paintings in the period 1627-32, although more research is necessary to formulate a more complete view. Van Dyck's Ghent *Crucifixion* (Ghent, Church of Saint Michael) was supposedly his most expen-

Table 3 : Gaspar de Crayer's altarpieces (1622-1665): general

SUBJECT	DATE	CAR. GLD.	PATRON	RATE / M^2(Gld.)	FIG.*	DIM (M2)	PL. PRES.	PL. ORIGIN
Martyrdom of Saint Catherine[46]	1622	350	J. Dhont	77.7	3h;3f	4.5	Grenoble, MBA	Courtrai, OL, Chapel St. Catherine
Assumption and crowning of the Virgin[47]	1623	150 +	Church	14.4 +	7h; 6f; 2H	10.4	Dijon, MBA	Courtrai, OL
Virgin and Jesus with Saints[48]	1638	480	Augustines	85.7	5f; 1h; 2H angels	5.6	Vienna, KHM	Bxl, church of the Augustine sisters of St Peter's hospital
Virgin and Jesus with saints[49]	1649	500	Church	57.8	5f; 4h	c. 8.64	Opwijk, St. Paul's ch.	Opwijk, St. Paul's ch.
Carrying of the cross[50]	1650-53	99 +	Church	19.2 +	4f;5h;3H	6.5	Baardegem, St. Margaret's ch.	Baardegem, St. Margaret's ch.
Saint Bernard nourished by the Virgin[51]	1654	300	Church	71.4	3h; angels	c. 4.2	Steenokkerzeel, St. Romuald Ch.	Steenokkerzeel, St. Romuald Ch.
Assumption of the Virgin[52]	1665	500	Broth. Rosary	108.6	1f; 3h; angels	c. 4.6	Oudenaarde, St. Walburga ch.	Oudenaarde, St. Walburga ch.

* 'f' : full figures; h: half length figures; H: heads.

45 Hans Vlieghe, *Gaspar de Crayer, sa vie et ses oeuvres*, 2 vols., Brussels 1972, vol. 1, pp. 86-87, no. A11; oil on canvas. The dimensions are: 242 cm x 188 cm.

46 Vlieghe, *Gaspar de Crayer* (note 1), vol. 1, pp. 91-92, no. A15; oil on canvas. The dimensions are: 382 cm x 273 cm.

47 Vlieghe, *Gaspar de Crayer* (note 1), vol. 1, pp. 135-136, no. A72; oil on canvas. The dimensions are: 279 cm x 201 cm.

48 Vlieghe, *Gaspar de Crayer* (note 1), vol. 1, pp. 185-186, no. A138; oil on canvas. The dimensions are: c. 360 cm x c. 240 cm.

49 Vlieghe, *Gaspar de Crayer* (note 1), vol. 1, pp. 191, no. A145; oil on canvas. The dimensions are: 300 cm x 218 cm. The total sum is higher, as a preliminary payment should be added to the serparate sums.

50 Vlieghe, *Gaspar de Crayer* (note 1), vol. 1, pp. 199, no. A161; oil on canvas. The dimensions are: c. 250 cm x c. 170 cm.

51 Vlieghe, *Gaspar de Crayer* (note 1), vol. 1, pp. 224, no. A199; oil on canvas. The dimensions are: c. 260 cm x c. 180 cm.

sive painting at 800 Car. guilders.[57] For the Sodality of the Jesuits in Antwerp he painted the exceptionally beautiful *Vision of the Blessed Herman Joseph* (Vienna, Kunsthistorisches Museum) for 'a mere' 150 Car. Guilders, but as Van Dyck was himself a member of the sodality, this probably had an influence on the asking price.[58] In any case, Van Dyck's prices could not compete with Rubens's, a fact which Toby Matthew explains in a postscript to a letter of 25 November 1620: 'he [van Dyck] will make a much better piece [...] for half the money he [Rubens] asks'.[59]

Undoubtedly, more research on other seventeenth-century painters of altarpieces, such as Theodoor van Loon, may help put Rubens, an exceptional painter with exceptional prices, into a broader context.

Conclusion

What determined the price of a painted altarpiece? This sample shows that it is not easy to reconstruct the mechanism behind the setting of a price, and that some aspects are difficult to quantify. It has, above all, shown that no single explanation suffices.[60] The pricing of altarpiece paintings does not always have a clear rational or material-based explanation. For the late sixteenth century, it seems that the 'average' price was somewhere below 500 Car. guilders with only a few exceptions. The same can be said for the seventeenth century.[61]

Other than the tangible aspects such as support, pigments and working hours, intangible factors also played a significant role. This essay has shown that various economic, social and religious factors, such as relationships, honour, conspicuous religious consumption, piety, a sponsor's financial means, and the reputation of the artist were important factors that could influence the price. These intangible aspects help explain the price differences between seemingly similar paintings, and the price differences within the career of one painter.

While Van Veen headed the group of painters up to 1609, Rubens was without doubt the most expensive Southern Netherlandish painter of altarpieces in the first half of the seventeenth century. The essay testifies, above all, to Rubens's exceptional status. Intangible aspects in his case contributed much more to the surplus value of the altarpiece than sheer material costs per square meter or the number of figures rendered. Although Rubens indicated in correspondence that the prices of his paintings were based on the number of figures rendered, we proved that there was no correlation for the altarpieces.

The market mechanism of high demand and a supply to match, operated in Rubens' favour and allowed Rubens's to operate a large studio. It seems a sobering thought that Rubens's brand name was indiscriminately applied to the many paintings of lesser quality that left his studio. However, this serves as further testimony to Rubens's entrepreneurial acumen and sound commercial instincts. He certainly gained something by using other hands besides his own, as Julius Held already noted in the case of Rembrandt*:* '...should we not keep in mind that even if they (referring specifically to 'those works now banished to the no-man's land of anonymity' but accepted as by Rembrandt in earlier times) are now recognized as the achievements of some gifted followers, they, too, contribute to and enrich our image of the master's range*?'*.[62] Indeed, the demand for Rubens's paintings was so high that his patrons and clients usually put up with workshop collaboration as long as the Rubens brand prevailed visually and artistically. However, there were exceptions and not everyone put up with this, such as is noted in a letter from Trumbull to Carleton written on 8 December 1620: '... it is not woorth the monney whereat it is prised; because little, or nothing, of it is donne with the said Rubens his owne hande'.[63] Although some worried about the workshop image and the 'authenticity' of his paintings, most of the time, Rubens seems to have gotten away with it. For Rubens, the workshop copy was simply the 'best deal' for a customer: 'well re-touched copies [...] show more for their price', which is how Rubens had explained it in a in a letter to Carleton on 12 May, 1618,[64] and: '... if the picture had been painted entirely by my own hand, it would be well worth twice as much', as Rubens wrote to Trumbull on 26 January 1621.[65] Undoubtedly, this situation was profitable for both painter and patron and obviously, Rubens's paintings, even when excecuted by his studio, apparently still managed to provide the buyer with something extra that most of the other painters could not supply.

Between Rubens and his patrons there was certainly great mutual attraction. As Nils Büttner pointedly remarked, Rubens's correspondence with his patrons read like a *Who's Who* of the times.[66] His altarpieces were calling cards for the richer orders such as the Benedictines, but also, surprisingly, for more ascetic orders such as the Carmelites.[67] Apart from those, there were orders so powerful and rich that they did not even need to permanently expose the altarpiece they commissioned from Rubens. The high altar of the Ghent Jesuit Church was decorated according to a system of rotation in which certain altarpieces were visible during certain periods of the liturgical year. Rubens's *Martyrdom of St. Livinus* was displayed during the saint's octave (the period of eight days with which the celebration of the saint's feast day can be extended), from 12 to 19 November.[68] For the remaining 357 days of the year one of the two alternating altarpieces by De Crayer and Van Loon was on view on the high altar. This arrangement can be taken as a supreme example of 'conspicuous investment'.[69]

Without doubt, Rubens's rates are exceptional in the context of what others were able to charge on average. Intelligence of composition, disposition of figures, storyline and the creative genius of Rubens added to the price. But Rubens's prices were more related to his reputation, and the 'excellence' he held so dear, than to the costs of materials, numbers of figures and canvas sizes. But real excellence had its price. As Balthasar Moretus noted in a letter to Philip of Peralta on 9 April 1615: "We imitate here a distinguished painter such as we have in Antwerp in the person of Rubens. He sends the less competent connoisseurs to a lesser and thus cheaper artist. He himself is not lacking in buyers for his excellent and more expensive paintings.".[70]

* Max Rooses and Charles Ruelens, *Correspondance de Rubens et documents épistolaires concernant sa vie et ses oeuvres* (*Codex Diplomaticus Rubenianus*), 6 vols., Antwerp 1887-1909, vol. 6 [1909], pp. 258-260 (letter DCCCLXXXXIII, letter of Balthasar Gerbier to Inigo Jones, Brussels, 24 March 1640). The author wishes to thank Joost Vander Auwera for the opportunity to study Rubens's work in the Royal Museums of Fine Arts of Belgium in Brussels in the context of the Rubens Research Project (2004-2008). I also wish to thank Johan Dambruyne, Nils Büttner and Hans van Miegroet for their advice.

1 Ernst Gombrich, 'Dürer, Vives and Bruegel', in: Josua Bruyn (ed.), *Album Amicorum J.G. Van Gelder*, The Hague 1973, pp. 132- 134.

2 Juan Luis Vives Valentini, *Opera Omnia*, Valencia 1782, vol. 1, pp. 391-392 : 'Dürer: Facessite hic, nam vos nihil emitis, sat scio; et estis mihi impedimento, quominus accedant emptores proprius./Grynius: Immo vero nos columus emere, modo vel precium relinquas nostro arbitratu, et tempus ipse praescribas, aut contra, nos tempus, tu precium./ Durer: Bella negotiatio, mihi nihil est opus tricis ejusmodi.'

3 Vives Valentini, *Opera Omnia* (note 2), pp. 391-392: 'Velius: Occipitium vellem videre / Durer: Verte tabulam.'

4 On 'cultural economics', a field which has seen much development over the past two decades, see

David Throsby, 'The production and consumption of the Arts: A view of cultural economics', *Journal of Economic Literature* 32 (1994), pp. 1-29; Neil De Marchi and Hans Van Miegroet, 'Art, Value, and Market Practices in the Netherlands in the Seventeenth century', *The Art Bulletin* 76 (1994), pp. 451-461; Toon Van Houdt, 'The economics of Art in Early Modern Times: Some Humanist and Scholastic Approaches', in Neil De Marchi and Craufurd D.W. Goodwin (eds.), *Economic Engagements with Art*, London 1999, pp. 303-331; For the Northern Netherlands, see Marten-Jan Bok, 'Pricing the unpriced: How Dutch Seventeenth-century Painters determined the Selling Price of their Work', in: Michael North and David Ormrod (eds.), *Art markets in Europe, 1400-1800*, Aldershot 1998, pp. 103-111.

5 Studies of merchant's interventions in export sales prices (such as the fascinating Musson-Fourmenois case), and studies of rich patrons such as Van Valckenisse, Van der Geest, Stevens, Rockocx, and Moretus and their influence on the selection of themes and genres, have shed light on their influence on the market. On the Musson-Fourmenois case, see Neil De Marchi, Hans Van Miegroet and Matthew E. Raiff, 'Dealer-dealer Pricing in the 17th-century Antwerp-Paris Art Trade', Duke University, Department of Economics *Working Papers*, number 97-20.

6 Neil De Marchi and Hans Van Miegroet, 'Pricing invention: 'Originals', 'Copies' and their relative value in Seventeenth century Netherlandish art markets', in: Victor A. Ginzburg and Pierre-Michel Menger (eds.), *Economics of the arts, Selected essays*, Amsterdam 1996, pp. 27-70.

7 We refer to, among others: Stefaan Grieten, 'Reconstructie van het altaarstuk van het Antwerpse meerseniersambacht. Nieuwe gegevens over Otto van Veen, Erasmus II Quellinus en Balthazar Beschey', *Jaarboek van het Koninklijk Museum voor Schone Kunsten van Antwerpen* (1995), pp. 137-141; Adolf Monballieu, 'P. Bruegel en het altaar van de Mechelse Handschoenmakers (1551)', *Handelingen van de Koninklijke Kring voor Oudheidkunde, Letteren en Kunstgeschiedenis van Mechelen* 68 (1964), pp. 92-110; Adolf Monballieu, 'De reconstructie van een drieluik van Adriaen Thomasz. Key bestemd voor het hoogaltaar van de Antwerpse Recollettenkerk', *Jaarboek van het Koninklijk Museum voor Schone Kunsten van Antwerpen* (1971), pp. 91-105; David Freedberg, 'The representation of Martyrdom during the early Counter-Reformation in Antwerp', *The Burlington Magazine* 118, 876 (1976), pp. 128-138; Justus Müller Hofstede, 'Zum Werke des Otto van Veen', *Bulletin van de Koninklijke Musea voor Schone Kunsten van België* (1957), pp. 127-174; Jan Vervaet, 'Catalogus van de altaarstukken van gilden en ambachten uit de Onze-Lieve-Vrouwekerk van Antwerpen en bewaard in het Koninklijk Museum', *Jaarboek van het Koninklijk Museum voor Schone Kunsten van Antwerpen* (1976), pp. 197-244; Natasja Peeters, 'Frans I and Ambrosius I Francken, painters of the metropolis Antwerp, and their altarpieces in the years just after the fall of Antwerp (1585-1589)', *Jaarboek van het Koninklijk Museum voor Schone Kunsten van Antwerpen* (2003), pp. 69-91.

8 In this respect, the sample used for this contribution is random and dictated by the availability of material.

9 For the changing appearance of early seventeenth-century altarpieces see: Natasja Peeters, 'Rubens' altaarstukken, in de Koninklijke Musea voor Schone Kunsten van België', in: Joost Vander Auwera and Sabine Van Sprang (eds.), *Rubens, een genie aan het werk, Rondom de Rubenswerken in de Koninklijke Musea voor Schone Kunsten van België*, Brussels (Royal Museums of Fine Arts) 2007 (exh. cat.), pp. 157-159.

10 Armin Zweite, *Marten de Vos als Maler*, Berlin 1980; Natasja Peeters, *Tussen continuïteit en vernieuwing. De bijdrage van Frans en Ambrosius Francken I, en de jonge generatie Francken, tot de historieschilderkunst te Antwerpen ca 1570-1620*, Ph.D. Dissertation Vrije Universiteit Brussels 2000 (publication forthcoming); Bob C. Van den Boogert, 'Michiel Coxcie, hofschilder in dienst van het Habsburgse huis', in: *Acta van het Internationaal colloquium Michiel Coxcie*, Mechelen 1993, pp. 119-140 [*Handelingen van de Koninklijke Kring voor Oudheidkunde, Letteren en Kunst van Mechelen* 96 (1992)]; Müller Hoftede, *Zum Werke des Otto van Veen* (note 7). Anne T. Woollett has written a study on Militia Altarpieces: Anne T. Woollett, *The Altarpiece in Antwerp 1554–1612: Painting and the Militia Guilds*, Ph.D. Dissertation Columbia University New York 2004.

11 Peter Humfrey, *The Altarpiece in Renaissance Italy*, Oxford 1988; Peter Humfrey and Martin Kemp (eds.), *The altarpiece in the Renaissance*, Cambridge 1990; Peter Humfrey, *The Altarpiece in Renaissance Venice*, New Haven 1993; Richard E. Spear, 'Guercino's 'prix-fixe': observations on studio practices and art marketing in Emilia', *The Burlington Magazine* 136 (1994), pp. 592-602; Fiorella Superbi Gioffredi and Eve Borsook, *Italian Altarpieces 1250-1550, Function and design*, Oxford 1994; Michelle O'Malley, *The Business of Art, Contracts and the Commissioning Process in Renaissance Italy*, New Haven 2005.

12 O'Malley, *The Business of Art* (note 11), p. 159.

13 All prices have been converted into Carolus guilders.

14 Antwerp, City Archives [hereafter S.A.A.], Privilegiekamer Collegiale Actenboeken 558 (1585-88), f° 115 v°, 7 October 1585.

15 Carl van de Velde, 'Het Kunstpatrimonium. De 16de eeuw', in: Willem Aerts (ed.), *De Onze-Lieve-Vrouwekathedraal van Antwerpen*, Antwerp 1993, pp. 176-203; Frans Baudouin, 'Het

Kunstpatrimonium. De 17de en 18de eeuw', in: Willem Aerts (ed.), *De Onze-Lieve-Vrouwekathedraal van Antwerpen*, Antwerp 1993, pp. 204-259; David Freedberg, *Iconoclasm and Painting in the Revolt of the Netherlands. 1566-1609*, New York 1988.

16 Natasja Peeters, '"Frivol ende absurd": het altaarstuk voor het Herentalse Brouwersambacht door Frans Francken I (1603)', *Historisch Jaarboek van Herentals* 11 (2001), pp. 5-34.

17 Frederik Verleysen, *Ambachten en Contrareformatie. Godsdienstige aspecten van de corporatieve wereld na de val van Antwerpen (1585-1633)*, MA thesis University Ghent 2000. A case in point is studied in: Natasja Peeters, 'A corporate image? Decoration for the Saint Luke's altarpiece for the Cathedral of Our Lady in Antwerp (1589-1602)', in: Arnout Balis, Paul Huvenne et al. (eds.), *Florissant: Bijdragen tot de kunstgeschiedenis der Nederlanden (15de-17de eeuw), Liber Amicorum Carl van de Velde*, Brussels 2005, pp. 239-252.

18 Johan Dambruyne, 'Rijkdom, materiële cultuur en sociaal aanzien. De bezitspatronen en investeringsstrategiëen van de Gentse ambachten omstreeks 1540', in: Catharina Lis and Hugo Soly, *Werelden van verschil, ambachtsgilden in de Lage Landen*, Brussels 1997, p. 152.

19 Johan Dambruyne, *Corporatieve middengroepen. Aspiraties, relaties en transformaties in de 16de-eeuwse ambachtswereld*, Ghent 2002, *passim*, on the position of the Mercers within the corporate context.

20 Max Rooses, 'De Afdoening van het Kruis, uit het rekeningboek der Antwerpsche Kolveniersgilde', *Rubens Bulletijn* 5 (1910), p. 232, records a present of gloves for Isabella Brandt in 1615, worth 8 Car. guilders and 10 *stuivers*, as part of the payment for Rubens's *Descent from the Cross*.

21 The count is made more difficult by the division between full figures, half figures, and heads: it is impossible to know what the price difference would have been. Moreover, when altarpieces or parts of them are lost, as is the case here, it makes a general count impossible.

22 It is impossible to calculate an average independent guild master's daily and yearly income, as it varied according to the commissions he obtained, which could be irregular. Furthermore, it is difficult to estimate the importance of other sources of income, which any artist's extended family could generate via all kinds of other transactions such as marriage or the buying, renting and selling of real estate. See Natasja Peeters, 'The guild of Saint Luke and the painter's profession in Antwerp between ca. 1560 and 1585: some social and economic insights', *Nederlands Kunsthistorisch Jaarboek* 59 (forthcoming 2008); Dambruyne, *Corporatieve middengroepen* (note 19), p. 690.

23 Hans Vlieghe, *Flemish art and architecture 1585-1700*, New Haven 2004, pp. 1-3 ff.

24 Marie Juliette Hendrickx, *De reconciliatie te Antwerpen (1585-1600)*, MA Thesis University of Louvain 1965, pp. 45-46; Alfons K.L. Thys, 'De contrareformatie en het economisch transformatieproces te Antwerpen na 1585', *Bijdragen tot de Geschiedenis* 70 (1987), p. 110.

25 For overviews of Rubens's altarpieces, see, among others: Frans Baudouin, 'Altars and altarpieces before 1620', in: John Rupert Martin, *Rubens before 1620*, Princeton 1972, pp. 45-91; David Freedberg, 'Painting and the Counter-Reformation in the Age of Rubens', in: Peter C. Sutton (ed.), *The Age of Rubens*, Boston 1993, p. 131-146; David Freedberg, 'Kunst und Gegenreformation in den südlichen Niederländen 1560-1660', in: Ekkehart Mai and Hans Vlieghe (eds.), *Von Bruegel bis Rubens, das goldene Jahrhundert der flämischen Malerei*, Cologne 1992, pp. 55-70; Thomas L. Glen, *Rubens and the Counter-Reformation: Studies in his Religious Painting between 1609 and 1620*, New York 1977; and *Corpus Rubenianum Ludwig Burchard* series.

26 Some research on Rubens's prices and financial situation was published recently: Gerdien Wuestman, 'Prijzen van Rubensgrafiek in de zeventiende eeuw', *Delineavit et Sculpsit* 19 (1998), pp. 1-7; Nils Büttner, 'Aristocracy and Noble business. Some remarks on Rubens' Financial Affairs', in Kathelijne Van der Stighelen (eds.), *Munuscula Amicorum, Contributions on Rubens and his colleagues in honour of Hans Vlieghe*, 2 vols., Turnhout 2006, vol. 1, pp. 67-78.

27 Julius Held, 'The Case Against the Cardiff "Rubens' cartoons"', *The Burlington Magazine* 75, 960 (1983), p. 132.

28 Rooses and Ruelens, *Correspondance* (note 1), vol. 2 [1898], pp. 181-183 (letter CLXXIX); Not in Ruth S. Magurn, *The Letters of Peter Paul Rubens*, Cambridge, MA 1955, pp. 67-68. For tapestry prices, see Rooses and Ruelens, *Correspondance* (note 1), vol. 2 [1898], pp. 161-164 (letter CLXX); Not in Magurn *The Letters of Peter Paul Rubens* (note 28), p. 64. While preparing a commission, Rubens was very scrupulous about format, as is witnessed in a letter to Count Duke Wolfgang Wilhelm of Neuburg, of 24 July 1620: "... I regret to hear that they [the paintings] are too short in proportion to the ornamental frame already set in place. The error however, is not the result of any negligence or fault of mine; nor can it be a misunderstanding of the measurements...". Rooses and Ruelens, *Correspondance* (note 1), vol. 2 [1898], pp. 253-254 (letter CCII); Not in Magurn *The Letters of Peter Paul Rubens* (note 28), p. 75. It was not just the measurements that mattered, but also the horizontal or vertical positioning on the wall, and the position of the windows in relation to the commissioned painting(s). When this was altered, it could put Rubens in an awkward position, as was the case during the preparation of the paintings for the Galerie des Medicis, when things were changed behind his back by Abbot de St. Ambroise, see Rooses and Ruelens, *Correspondance* (note 1), vol. 5 [1907], pp. 339-342 (letter DCXC); Not in Magurn *The Letters of Peter Paul Rubens* (note 28), pp. 368-370.

29 (Trans. author) Rooses and Ruelens, *Correspondance* (note 1), vol. 5 [1907], pp. 300-301 (letter DCLXXIV). Not in Magurn *The Letters of Peter Paul Rubens* (note 28).

30 Ibid. pp. 333-334 (letter DCLXXXV). Not in Magurn *The letters of Peter Paul Rubens* (note 28).

31 Ibid. (note 1), vol. 5 [1907], p. 338 (letter DCLXXXIX). Not in Magurn *The letters of Peter Paul Rubens* (note 28).

32 Thomas Puttfarken, *The Discovery of Pictorial Composition: Theories of Visual Order in Painting 1400-1800*, New Haven 2000, discusses this topic, *passim*.

33 O'Malley, *The Business of Art* (note 11), p. 135

34 Rooses and Ruelens, *Correspondance* (note 1), vol. 6 [1909], pp. 177-178 (letter DCCCXXX); Not in Magurn *The Letters of Peter Paul Rubens* (note 28), p. 406.

35 Roger-Adolf d' Hulst and Marc Vandenven, *Rubens. The Old Testament*, Corpus Rubenianum Ludwig Burchard. 3, London 1989, pp. 96-99, no. 26, refers to a document from 22 December 1629 about the painting *Samson and the Lion* (Madrid, coll. Duke of Hernani in 1977). But different systems applied, as can be read in the letter that Balthasar Moretus sent to the Flemish merchant Jean van Vucht dated 25 June 1630, which states that the price was decided after the designs were delivered. See Rooses and Ruelens, *Correspondance* (note 1), vol. 2 [1898], pp. 149-160 (letter CLXVIII); Not in Magurn *The Letters of Peter Paul Rubens* (note 28), p. 62.

36 Rooses and Ruelens, *Correspondance* (note 1), vol. 2 [1898], pp. 149-160 (letter CLXVIII); Not in Magurn *The letters of Peter Paul Rubens* (note 28), p. 61-63, The original passage, in Italian, is somewhat different from the English translation by Magurn: "mi rimetterei sempre del prezzo al arbitrario di ogni persona intelligente".

37 Ibid. (note 1), vol. 2 [1898], pp. 261-264 (letter CCVII). Not in Magurn *The Letters of Peter Paul Rubens* (note 28). Translation in: W. N. Sainsbury, *Original Unpublished Papers Illustrative of the Life of Sir Peter Paul Rubens, as an Artist and a Diplomatist preserved in H.M. State Paper Office*, London 1859, pp. 52-54.

38 John Rupert Martin, *The Ceiling Paintings for the Jesuit Church in Antwerp*. Corpus Rubenianum Ludwig Burchard. 1, Brussels 1968, pp. 30-32 and appendix I (p. 213ff).

39 Peeters, *Rubens' altaarstukken* (note 9).

40 Rooses and Ruelens, *Correspondance* (note 1), vol. 2 [1898], p. 24 (letter CXXIII).

41 (Translation author). Rooses and Ruelens, *Correspondance* (note 1), vol. 5 [1907], p. 338 (letter DCLXXXIX). Not in Magurn *The Letters of Peter Paul Rubens* (note 28).

42 Arnout Balis ('"Fatto da un mio discepolo", Rubens' studio practices reviewed', in: Toshiharu Nakamura (ed.), *Rubens and his workshop. The Flight of Lot and his family from Sodom*, Tokyo 1994, pp. 97- 127, *passim*) touches briefly upon the pricing in relation to studio execution. Arnout Balis, 'Rubens en zijn atelier: een probleemstelling', in: Joost Vander Auwera and Sabine Van Sprang (eds.), *Rubens, een genie aan het werk, Rondom de Rubenswerken in de Koninklijke Musea voor Schone Kunsten van België*, Brussels (Royal Museums of Fine Arts) 2007 (exh. cat.), pp. 30-51; on journeymen see: Natasja Peeters (ed.), *Invisible hands? The role and status of the Painter's Journeyman in the Low Countries c. 1450-c. 1650*, Louvain 2007.

43 Kerry Downes, 'Rubens' Prices', *The Burlington Magazine* 75 (1983), p. 362.

44 Rooses and Ruelens, *Correspondance* (note 1), vol. 2 [1898], pp. 149-160 (letter CLXVIII); Magurn *The Letters of Peter Paul Rubens* (note 28), pp. 61-63.

45 Nora de Poorter, in her study of the *Eucharist* cartoons, concluded that if Rubens was paid only one-third of what he got for the *Medici Cycle*; this was because of the fact that he had more studio assistants. Nora de Poorter, *The Eucharist Series*, Corpus Rubenianum Ludwig Burchard. 2, 2 vols., Brussels 1978, vol. 1, p. 134; but see remark by Downes, *Rubens' prices* (note 43), p. 362, where the author rightly remarks on the two problems in De Poorter's reasoning, with the exchange rate and the work covered by the price, thus lowering the rate for the Medici gallery.

46 Zirka Z. Filipczak, *Picturing Art in Antwerp, 1550-1700*, Princeton 1987, p. 78.

47 (Trans. author) Jozef Duverger, 'Aantekeningen betreffende de patronen van P.P. Rubens en de tapijten met de Geschiedenis van Decius Mus', *Gentse Bijdragen tot de Kunstgeschiedenis* 24 (1976-78), p. 39, (Bewijsstuk II: 'Desen Rubbens windt dagelijckx 100 guldens').

48 The wages of craftsmen went through many changes in the course of the sixteenth and seventeenth centuries. Those for the building trades are the best known and best studied and quantified. The author wishes to thank Johan Dambruyne for this information.

49 Duverger, *Aantekeningen* (note 47), p. 39 (Bewijsstuk II: "Heeft alreede over 24 duysent guldens versnoept in sijn huys").

50 Max Rooses, 'De plakbrief der heerlijkheid van Steen', *Rubens Bulletijn* 5 (1910), pp. 149-151 and ff.

51 Max Rooses, 'De verdeling van Rubens' nalatenschap', *Rubens Bulletijn* 4 (1896), pp. 236-252. The importance of real estate for painters is

further studied in Natasja Peeters, 'Family Matters: an integrated biography of Pieter Breughel II' (publication forthcoming).
52 Rooses and Ruelens, *Correspondance* (note 1), vol. 2 [1898], pp. 78-82 (letter CXLI).
53 Adolf Monballieu, 'P.P. Rubens en het "Nachtmael" voor St. Winoksbergen (1611)', *Jaarboek van het Koninklijk Museum voor Schone Kunsten van Antwerpen* (1965), pp. 183-205.
54 (Trans. author) Monballieu, *P.P. Rubens en het 'Nachtmael* (note 53), p. 203: with archival references: 'Sy tracteren met eenen schilder van gendt, dat eenen hoetelaer is, ende soecken den goeden coop. Dan het jammert my de heren van Berghen soo sullen bedroghen worden'.
55 Filipczak, *Picturing Art in Antwerp* (note 46), p. 79, also made a brief comparison of the prices of Rubens and De Crayer.
56 Hans Vlieghe, *Gaspar de Crayer, sa vie et ses oeuvres*, 2 vols., Brussels 1972, vol. 1, pp. 29ff and 72-73 for his reputation. The same probably applied for most of the other altarpiece painters of good reputation, such as Theodoor Van Loon, but more research on these painters would help clear up this matter.
57 Hans Vlieghe, 'Beelden van vroomheid en ijdelheid. Van Dycks intermezzi in de Zuidelijke Nederlanden 1627-32, 1634-35 en 1640-41', in: Christopher Brown and Hans Vlieghe (eds.), *Van Dyck 1599-1641*, Ghent 1999, p. 71.
58 Vlieghe, *Beelden* (note 57), p. 71. The author gives more examples.
59 Rooses and Ruelens, *Correspondance* (note 1), vol. 2 [1898], p. 262.
60 O'Malley, *The Business of Art* (note 11), p. 160.
61 It would be interesting to study fifteenth and early sixteenth-century Southern Netherlandish altarpieces in this respect.
62 Julius Held, *Rembrandt studies*, Princeton 1991, p. 13.
63 Rooses and Ruelens, *Correspondance* (note 1), vol. 2 [1898], p. 265 (letter CCIX).
64 Sainsbury, *Original unpublished papers* (note 37), p. 33 (trans.); Rooses and Ruelens, *Correspondance* (note 1), vol. 2 [1898], p. 149 (letter CLXVIII): '... copie en ritocci {...} luçono piu per il lor prezzo'.
65 Sainsbury, *Original unpublished papers* (note 37), p. 56 (translation); Rooses and Ruelens, *Correspondance* (note 1), vol. 2 [1898], p. 273 (letter CCXV): '... si j'eusse fait tout l'ouvrage de ma main propre, elle vaudroit bien le double'.
66 Büttner, *Aristocracy* (note 26), p. 71.
67 It would be interesting to research the studio collaboration involved in the altarpieces made for the richer orders versus the poorer orders and see how this influenced the price.
68 Natasja Peeters, Hélène Dubois and Joost Vander Auwera, 'P.P. Rubens, De marteling van de heilige Livinus', in: Joost Vander Auwera and Sabine Van Sprang (ed.), *Rubens, een genie aan het werk, Rondom de Rubenswerken in de Koninklijke Musea voor Schone Kunsten van België*, Tielt 2007, pp. 196-200. The two other paintings which alternately adorned the main altar were a *Descent from the Cross* by Gaspar de Crayer, on view during the Easter cycle (from the 9th Sunday before Easter to the Saturday before Advent) and the *Birth of Christ* by Theodoor van Loon, which could be seen during the Christmas cycle (from Advent to the 9th Sunday before Easter).
69 James Hall, 'Market forces', *Times Literary Supplement* 28 (2007), p. 10 for a discussion on conspicuous investment.
70 (Trans. author). Rooses and Ruelens, *Correspondance* (note 1), vol. 2 [1898], pp. 78-82 (letter CXLI.) 'Atque ea in re elegantiorem aliquem pictorem imitamur (qualem Antverpiae Rubenium habemus) qui imperitum artis aestimatorem, ad rudem, et proinde minoris pretii artificem, a se ablegat : neque enim ipsi desunt elegantissimae suae picturae, etsi alias carioris, emptores.'

Chapter 4
Anna Tummers

The Painter versus the Connoisseur? The Best Judge of Pictures in Seventeenth-Century Theory and Practice*

Introduction

One of the most intriguing types of pictures that emerged in the Netherlands during the Golden Age shows art lovers contemplating art in a collector's cabinet or in an artist's studio. For example, a painting by Jan Breughel the Elder and Hieronymus Franken depicts Archduke Albert and Archduchess Isabella together with a group of elegantly dressed men and women in a collector's cabinet (fig. 1). Despite the verisimilitude of such scenes, many elements depicted were almost certainly fanciful. In this case, the grandeur of the architectural setting does not match the size of private residences at the time, and the fact that the same setting was used in two other pictures showing different art lovers, also suggests that the scene is imaginary.[1] Rather than records of actual events, such pictures were presumably variations on a popular theme. Art lovers must have liked looking at pictures of other art lovers contemplating art.

A close look at the Breughel and Stalbemt picture presumably encouraged art lovers to discuss positive and negative attitudes towards the liberal arts. A picture within this picture (prominently placed in the foreground) shows a negative counterpart of the main scene: figures smashing paintings and instruments in a collector's cabinet (which recalls the violent iconoclasm of 1566, when many works of art were indeed destroyed). While their clothing may suggest that these figures are human, their heads give them away: the figure standing on the table is a donkey, the one smashing pictures on the ground a monkey – animals associated with ignorance and rudeness.

The positive attitude of the art lovers in the main scene is thus reinforced by the contrast to ignorance and boorishness. Such explicit comparisons are rare in seventeenth century pictures of art lovers. Most of them simply show people respectfully contemplating art without a negative counterpart (fig. 2. Pieter Codde, *Art Lovers in a Painter's*

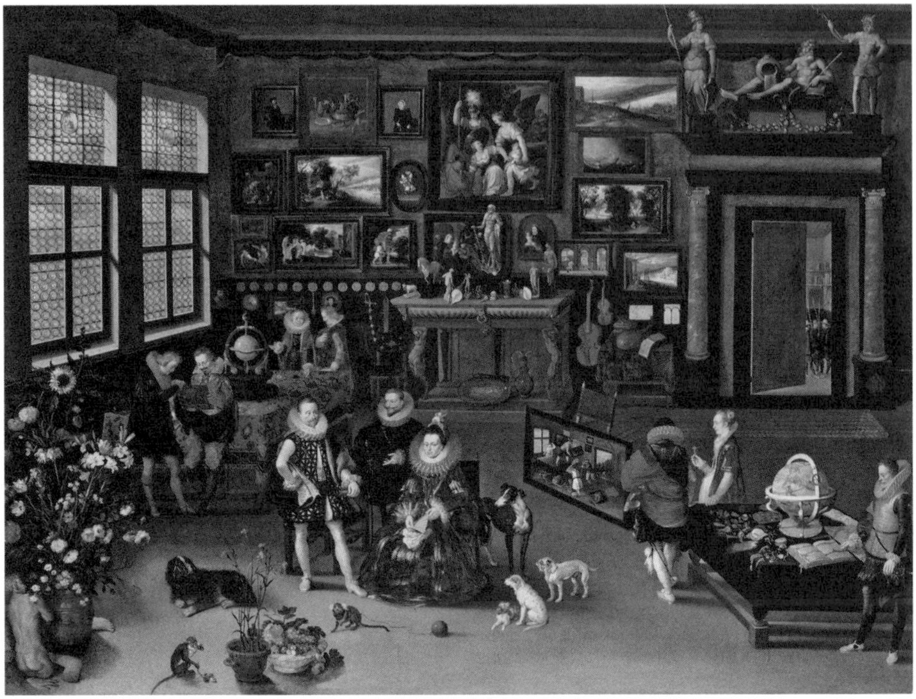

1.

1.
Jan Brueghel the Elder and
Hieronymus Franken II,
see colorplate p. 188
The Archdukes Albert and Isabella Visiting a Collector's Cabinet,
c. 1621-1623
Walters Art Gallery, Baltimore

2.
Pieter Codde
Art Lovers in a Painter's Studio,
c. 1630
Staatsgalerie, Stuttgart

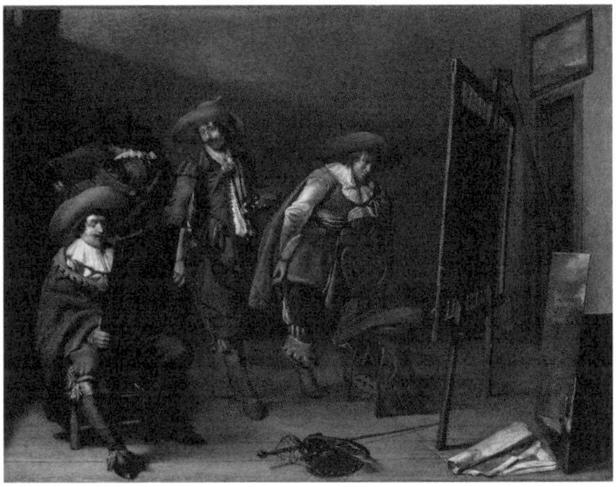

2.

Studio, c. 1630 Staatsgalerie, Stuttgart).[2] The depicted art lovers are as a rule well-dressed and seem to study the works thoroughly, now and again from very close up. Moreover, they often point to the paintings, which suggests that they are talking about the works. Yet, despite these lively references to conversations about art, the paintings remain tantalisingly silent about what exactly such an interested, respectful attitude towards paintings would have entailed.

It would be fascinating to know what elegant art lovers might have said when contemplating pictures in the seventeenth century. Would they have been merely admiring the works? The popular French book on eloquence, Etienne Binet's *Essay des merveilles de nature, et des plus nobles artifices*, which was first published in 1621 and subsequently reprinted several times throughout the seventeenth century, recommended precisely such an attitude.[3] It provided the reader with ready-made compliments celebrating mostly the illusions created by paintings. When contemplating a beautiful painting, one could, for example, say: 'When painting was still in its cradle, and drank its first milk, the brush was so unrefined, and the works so heavy, that one had to write on them, this is a Bull, this is a Donkey, otherwise you might have taken it for a hunk of veal; nowadays one has to write who painted the work underneath, lest one believes that these are dead people glued to the canvas, and they appear like living, but motionless, people, so excellently everything is painted.'[4]

If we are to believe Binet, to be eloquent did not necessarily mean having a balanced opinion. He advises his readers to simply praise admirable elements, while urging them to guard themselves against too much curiosity. Although it was necessary to have a good understanding of the technical aspects of painting, he certainly did not believe that everything was interesting enough to talk about. In fact, he stated quite explicitly that small and insignificant things should not be discussed outside the studio.[5]

Would it have been common for elegant art lovers anywhere in Europe to talk about paintings in such complimentary terms? The remark about the first paintings needing inscriptions in order to be legible, also occurs in Willem Goeree's 1670 treatise on painting, and must thus have circulated widely.[6] Moreover, the practice of writing laudatory poems on high quality pictures and reciting these in polite society seems consistent with Binet's advice.[7] Yet, would it not have been equally common for art lovers to evaluate these paintings in greater depth and to also discuss their qualities and attributions?[8] Would they have singled out stronger and weaker passages? And more specifically, would art lovers, who were not painters themselves, be considered able judges of artworks in the seventeenth century?

This essay focuses on the question of who would have been considered a good judge of paintings in the seventeenth century, both in theory and in practice; that is to say: who was credited with the ability to analyse a painting's qualities, to attribute the work and to appraise it. In secondary sources, it is often assumed that only painters were considered capable of doing so. For example, Peter Sutton states in his 2004 essay *Rembrandt and a Brief History of Connoisseurship*: 'The few art theorists who discussed connoisseurship in the seventeenth century [...] assign the talent exclusively to artists.'[9] Earlier, in 1995, Jonathan Brown stated in his influential book *Kings and Connoisseurs* that it was not until the eighteenth century that art theorists began to prefer the 'amateur (art lover)' over the practitioner as the best judge of art, suggesting that the supremacy of the painter as the best judge of art had not been questioned previously.[10]

The idea that only an artist can ultimately judge art certainly does appear in some seventeenth-century writings. However, not all of the authors agree on the matter.

In order to give a more nuanced idea of seventeenth-century views on the issue, I will discuss a number of art theoretical texts and relate these to market practices. In this area of research, it seems particularly fruitful to study both art theory and the art market, and thus both to see who was credited with the capacity to ably judge art on a theoretical level and to see who actually appraised pictures in practice. While Netherlandish pictures from the Golden Age are my focal point, the theoretical sources I will study are not exclusively Netherlandish. A broader analysis, which transcends national borders is the rule rather than exception in scholarly studies of early modern connoisseurship. In this particular case, a broader analysis seems justified since at the time, like now, experts of Netherlandish art were certainly not all Dutch or Flemish. In fact, experts such as the Italian physician Giulio Mancini or the French art theorist Roger de Piles explicitly applied their insights to Netherlandish pictures in their writings.

'Painters and art experts' (*schilders en konstverstandigen*)

In his widely read treatise on paintings *Het Schilderboeck* of 1604, Karel van Mander makes various remarks about attributing pictures and about judging their quality.[11] The purpose of his book as a whole was to instruct young painters and 'art lovers' (*liefhebbers*) about the art of painting, to give an overview of the most important ancient and modern painters, and – most importantly – to celebrate painting as a liberal art and thus to enhance its status. As Van Mander puts it, painting was still too often seen as a mere craft and he regretted that in cities such as Haarlem and Antwerp fine art painters had to share their professional organisation, the Saint Lucas Guild, with house painters, saddle makers and the like.[12] Considering Van Mander's ambitious premise, it is perhaps not surprising that he did not comment on such pragmatic issues as who appraised paintings on the market.

In Van Mander's view, hands-on experience was certainly very important when judging art. In the introduction to his treatise, he stresses the fact that he himself is a practitioner of the art of painting and he adds somewhat apologetically: 'Someone more eloquent might have written this more beautifully and artfully, however if he was not a Painter, one would have to be concerned that he would miss items and characteristics.'[13] Moreover, when Van Mander discusses a famous anecdote about the ancient painters Apelles and Protogones, he stresses the advantage of having experience as a painter in order to understand the anecdote. Van Mander knew the story via Pliny, who relates that Protogenes was able to recognise the hand of Apelles in one skilfully painted thin line on a prepared canvas: 'since it was impossible (said Protogenes), that anyone but Apelles could have created with paint and a brush such a pleasant, thin line.'[14]

Pliny's story concerns the earliest attribution known in the history of Western art. Yet it is a particularly confusing account, for how could anyone attribute a work simply on the basis of one thin line? The story has baffled many writers on art since Pliny including Van Mander, who explained the story by stating that Pliny did not give sufficient information, and that, in fact, this learned gentleman was not a good judge of painting himself.[15] Pliny told of how, after recognising Apelles' hand in the thin line, Protogenes tried to outdo the master by painting an even thinner line himself. And when Apelles saw Protogenes's line he added a third one that was so well executed that no one could paint one more precisely or pleasantly.

According to Van Mander these three lines painted by Apelles and Protogenes 'were not simple straight lines or brushstrokes, as many who are not Painters believe, but some contour of an arm or a leg, or some profile of a head, or something of the kind, a contour which they had drawn very precisely and in some areas through each other's lines'.[16] Van Mander was all the more convinced of his opinion as Pliny said that many people who were knowledgeable about art greatly admired the picture. According to Van Mander they would not be impressed by a simple, hand-drawn straight line, and he explains that such a line 'is often done better by a School Teacher, a Writer, or another person who is not an artist, than by the best painter in the world.'[17]

Although Van Mander refers on these two occasions to non-painters who are incapable of interpreting art correctly, he does not exclude the possibility that non-painters could sometimes also make sensible comments on art. When discussing attributions of paintings that he had seen himself or the characteristics of an artist's style, Van Mander repeatedly reinforces his own opinion by stating that 'painters and art experts' (*schilders en konstverstandigen*) would agree with him.[18] By differentiating between painters and art experts Van Mander suggests that these art experts were not just painters. Indeed he uses the term 'art expert' (*konstverstandige*) for knowledgeable art lovers throughout his treatise.

An example of such a reference to 'painters and art experts' can also be found in Van Mander's discussion of Holbein's painting *Henry VIII and the Barber Surgeons* of c. 1543 (see also the essay *By His Hand: The Paradox of Seventeenth-Century Connoisseurship*, pp. 53-54 above). Van Mander relates that: 'There are some people who believe that this work was not completed entirely by Holbein himself, but that after Holbein's death, it was completed by someone else. However, if this is the case, this painter has imitated Holbein's manner so sensibly that neither a Painter nor an Art expert would distinguish different hands.'[19] Apparently, in Van Mander's view, knowledgeable non-painters could thus also judge the characteristics of an artist's style and issues of attribution.[20]

Moreover, Van Mander took general quality judgements from knowledgeable non-painters to heart, witness his description of the life of David Vinckboons. By means of an introduction, Van Mander explains how he decided which artists to include in his book. Whenever he visits the house of an art lover, he says, he pays special attention to the works which are regarded as exceptional. And although he trusts his own opinion, he is also happy to follow 'the common feeling of art experts' *('t ghemeen ghevoelen der konst-verstandiger)*.[21] For this reason, he says, he cannot omit David Vinckboons. Although he subsequently continues to praise Vinckboon's works as 'exquisite' (*uitnemend*), his praise sounds rather ambivalent, for his introduction suggests that if it were up to him, he would have preferred to omit Vinckboons from his treatise (fig. 3). Apparently, Van Mander felt he could not ignore the opinions of the collector connoisseurs to whom he refers.

That Van Mander credits the judgement of both painters and non-painters of course does not mean that he thought that every painter and art lover was indeed an able judge of pictures. What skills or talents did he think were needed in order to successfully judge pictures? This very much depended on the type of picture and on what aspect of it one wanted to judge. In Van Mander's view, people with no previous experience of looking at pictures, could make some very sensible comments if they used their own professional expertise, and he used a famous anecdote about the ancient painter Apelles to illustrate this point.[22] Apelles reputedly had the habit of displaying his paintings outside his house while hiding behind them so that he could overhear the comments of passers-by. While doing so, he once heard a cobbler comment on the depiction of a sandal, which did not have enough straps to be worn as a shoe in reality.

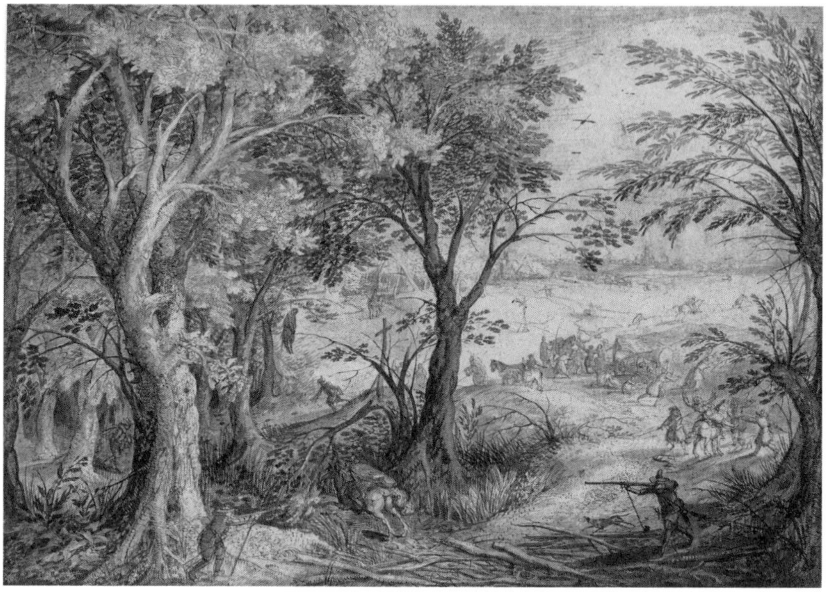

3.

David Vinckboons
Forest Scene with Robbery, c.1612
Private Collection

Apelles gratefully picked up on the suggestion and changed his picture accordingly. However, when the cobbler later began criticising Apelles' depiction of a knee, the painter appeared from behind his work and told the cobbler to 'stick to his last', that is: to stick to his area of expertise.[23] However, Van Mander believed that ordinary people did not have to stick to their areas of expertise, because he believed they were capable of judging the passions, desires and suffering of the figures, their inner lives, if you will.[24] Moreover, when he discussed religious painting, he emphasised that religious images should be relatively easy to understand for onlookers, so in this respect, the opinion of laymen should also be valued.[25]

Other aspects of a painting, the more complicated subject matter and artistic qualities, he considered more difficult to judge without the proper background. Two passages in which he mocks ignorant judgements are telling in this respect. In his biography of Cornelis Ketel, Van Mander relates the story of a farmer, who thought he had understood a painting but who was in fact completely mistaken.[26] When confronted with a painting of the mythological figure of Danae, the farmer boasted that he knew the subject. He identified the scene as the Annunciation, mistaking Cupid for the angel Gabriel and mistaking the nude figure of Danae for the Virgin Mary.

In another instance, Van Mander discusses an altarpiece that Pieter Vlerick painted for a convent. According to Van Mander it had been executed with 'Tintoretto's spirit and invention' in mind, with which he presumably alluded to Tintoretto's Crucifixion in the Scuola Grande de San Rocco (fig. 4). Unfortunately, Vlerick's picture has not survived. According to Van Mander, it showed Christ in the middle ground on the cross with the light coming from the side so that Christ's face was mostly cast in

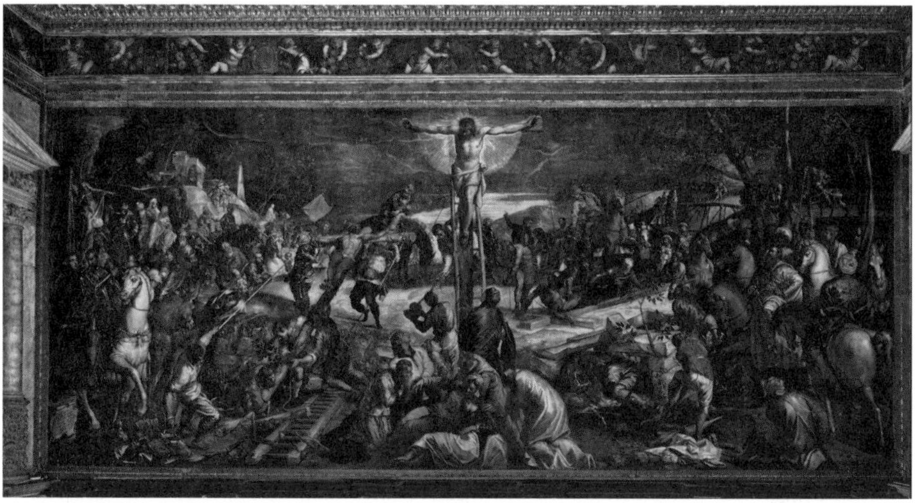

4.

Tintoretto
Crucifixion, 1565
Scuola Grande di San Rocco, Venice

shadow. This was something which 'painters and art lovers' (schilders en konstverstandigen) could appreciate, according to Van Mander, however, the nuns were not pleased with it. Apparently, they were unable to properly appreciate the altarpiece for its artistic merits. In their defence, however, one could argue that for them the picture was not merely a work of art, but first and foremost an object of devotion.

According to Van Mander, a certain amount of erudition was thus necessary to properly interpret certain subjects and appreciate a painting's artistic merits. To understand a scene from ancient history, the Bible or mythology, it was necessary to know the sources from which the story was taken. As to artistic merits, Van Mander mentions that a basic knowledge of the art of drawing would help in the assessment of works of art.[27] Interestingly, Van Mander does not indicate whether hands-on experience in the art of painting was necessary to be able to talk about paintings. He does stress – as we have seen above – the advantage of having the experienced eye of a painter when assessing art on several occasions, but never goes so far as to insist that without this experience one would be unable to properly assess paintings.

Explicit recommendations on learning the art of drawing in order to be able to talk about art intelligently appear in many other seventeenth-century texts.[28] For example, Constantijn Huygens, secretary to the stadholders Frederik Hendrik and Willem II, who was closely involved in major painting commissions for the court, noted in his famous diary that it was very important to learn the basics of the art to be able to talk knowledgeably about paintings. He himself not only learned to draw as part of his education but also how to paint even though his father only considered the art of drawing essential for his education.[29] Recommendations to also get some practical experience in the art of painting are remarkably absent in early modern art theory, presumably because many early art theorists saw drawing as the very core of all visual arts including painting, sculpture and architecture.

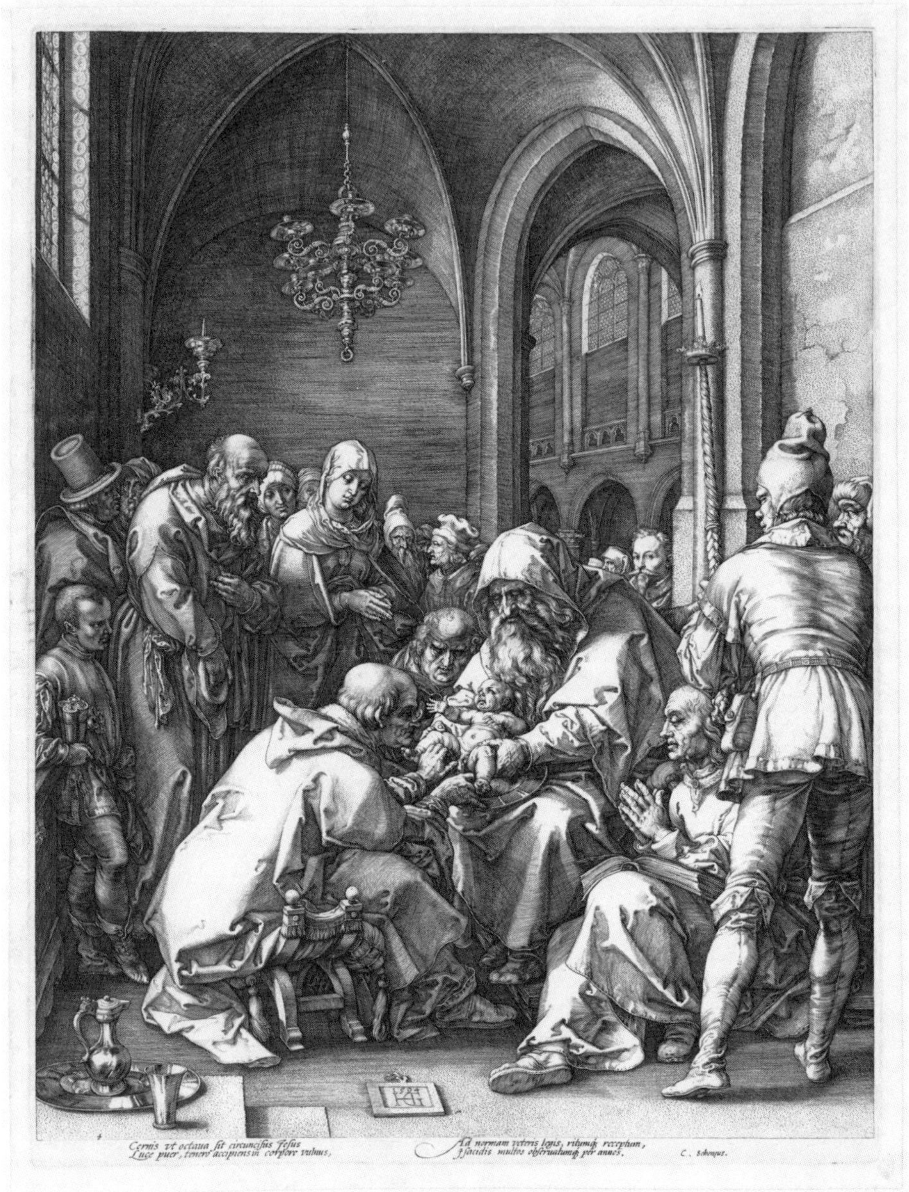

5.

Hendrick Goltzius (in the style of Albrecht Dürer)
The Circumcision, 1594
Rijksmuseum, Amsterdam

A thorough instruction in the art of drawing as well as some training in how to design scenes and depict biblical and mythological figures were a common part of a young painter's curriculum. A well-trained painter thus had the knowledge and experience that Van Mander considered important when judging art. Was a painter therefore an astute judge of paintings? Not necessarily, according to Van Mander, because he believes envy and vanity can easily cloud one's judgement. For example, when he discusses how a series of prints by Goltzius in the styles of old masters had completely fooled painters and art experts and even engravers who thought they knew the manners and incisions of the Masters well, Van Mander concludes that this shows what envy, vanity and prejudices can lead to (fig. 5).[30] Some of these painters and art experts held old masters such as Albrecht Dürer and Lucas van Leyden in such high esteem that they thought that no one could equal their achievements, while others simply disliked Goltzius. In both instances, this seriously clouded the judgement of these otherwise knowledgeable experts.

Ideal judgements and pretentious comments

Many of Van Mander's general comments on assessing works of art hearken back to antiquity and were shared by most other seventeenth-century writers. The idea that some knowledge was necessary to successfully judge art was very common in both ancient and modern texts; laymen were often credited with the ability to judge the depicted passions and/or to judge elements related to their professions. However, judging attributions and the overall quality of a work was very much a specialist affair. As to precisely what kind of knowledge was necessary for a sophisticated assessment, there was no clear consensus in either antiquity or in the seventeenth century. The question what a successful judge of pictures should know, relates to the question of what exactly should be judged, and thus to the question of what elements were considered the most important. This last question had long been the subject of debate.

There was already disagreement on the matter back in antiquity. On the one hand, craftsmanship was considered very important – witness an anecdote about the ancient painter Zeuxis, to which both the art theorists Franciscus Junius and Samuel van Hoogstraten refer. According to the ancient writer Lucian, Zeuxis had painted a picture of a female centaur suckling two baby centaurs, which he thought would be greatly praised for its craftsmanship such as the connection between the human skin of the upper part of the centaurs' bodies and their furry lower bodies and legs. However, when Zeuxis displayed the work to a general audience:

'All of them praised most ... the unusual aspect of the subject, and the novelty of its 'message', which was unknown to earlier artists. Thus when Zeuxis realized that the curiosity of the painting rather than his technique was capturing their attention and was putting the refinement of the work to one side, he said to his pupil: 'Micion, cover it up and take it back home. These people are praising the raw mud of our art, but as for the lighting, how well it looks and how carefully done, they have nothing to say. The novelty of the subject surpasses the discipline of the execution'.[31]

Zeuxis apparently did not agree with the preferences of his audience, and both Junius and Samuel van Hoogstraten use his comment about the audience focussing on the 'mud of the art' (*droesem van de kunst*) to stress the importance of knowing what aspects to praise in a painting.[32]

On the other hand, there was another a story from antiquity in which expertise was needed not so much to properly evaluate the execution, but rather to understand the inventive way of conveying meaning. It is a story by Calistrus, which Junius recounts in *De Pittura Veterum*. Calistratus described how he looked at a statue representing opportunity by the famous ancient sculptor Lysippus. Calistratus discussed the work with his friends and, in doing so, vividly evoked the statue's charm and lifelikeness. However, Junius writes, it took an expert who joined him and his party, to open their eyes to the significance of the wings on Opportunity's feet and the forelock on his head, and to make them see the aptness of this very beauty.[33]

These ancient stories with their different emphases seem to foreshadow the famous *disegno-colorito* debate that erupted in sixteenth-century Italy, which then subsequently spread across Europe and became very heated in France at the end of the seventeenth century. Although the *disegno-colorito* debate focused more on the visual characteristics of pictures than on their possible meaning. The main issue in the debate was which aspect of painting was the most important: the line as the expression of the inventions of the human mind (*disegno*) or the achievement by means of painting from life to create the most natural and lifelike expressiveness through the handling of paint, colour, light and shade (*colorito*).[34] Some advocates of the *disegno*-approach such as the French author Paul Fréart de Cambray valued the invention and arrangement of the subject to such an extent that they dismissed the painter's brushstrokes as just 'mechanical' aspects of painting.[35] The debate was probably quite fierce in the Netherlands as well, as Eric Jan Sluijter has suggested.[36] In 1628, the Dutch painter and amateur mathematician Jacques de Ville published a short treatise in which he sharply attacked painters and art lovers who only looked at the 'manner of painting' (*handelinghe*). Tellingly he gave his Treatise on Architecture and Painting the subtitle: '... warning to all craftsmen and lovers of this art that they should not gape at the manner alone but look further.'[37] In De Ville's view, the drawn design of a picture was essential, which should express a keen knowledge of proportions as well as a thorough understanding of the rules of perspective. However, it is beyond the scope of this essay to closely analyse how pictures were judged and what elements were deemed crucial. In this context, I would merely like to stress that there were different views on how good quality was defined. However, the idea that one needed a certain amount of expertise to properly assess pictures was common.

Similarly, the idea that negative emotions such as jealousy and vanity could cloud one's judgement was widespread. It was especially bad painters who were prone to jealousy and inappropriate expressions of vanity. Van Mander, for example, discusses a mediocre painter who had the audacity to not only criticise a work by a superior master – Peter Vlerick – but to also correct it with his brush, which, of course, greatly irritated Vlerick.[38] Since the sixteenth century, poorly educated painters (*daubers*) were often mocked in the literature – a theme which has been extensively researched by Zilsel, Wittkower, Emmens and more recently by Lyckle de Vries.[39] These bad painters were described as pretentious, badly mannered, having a neglected look, and a great craving for fame. In the seventeenth century, we find this kind of pretentious bad painter, for example, in a witty poem by Jan Vos:

'To Martijn the Painter / Martijn, you always boast about your paintings / The common people neither understand Art nor its worth, in your view, /
You're right; the commoners are slow to understand its characteristic / If they were wise; they would not be so fond of paintings by you'.[40]

Like the bad painter, the inadequate art lover is a figure who often pops up in art theoretical writings. Art theorists described the despicable 'connoisseurs' they had encountered and in so doing warned their readers not to become like them. These charlatans were pretentious, did not know what to look for in a painting, and were often also corrupt and untrustworthy. In the introduction to his treatise *Sentimens sur la Distinction des diverses manières de peinture, dessin et gravure et des orginaux d'avec leurs copies* of 1649, Abraham Bosse stated that he had met many pretentious art lovers who used a great number of art-related terms such as 'of the antique', 'of the great manner', 'expression', 'union', 'well-touched', 'day', 'half-day', 'counter day' – but who had a poor capacity for assessing paintings; they could perhaps distinguish certain aspects of an artist's manner 'that a blind man could recognise when he touching the paintings', but lacked any refinement in their analyses of the works and, even worse – 'out of ignorance or for some other reason, they despise the works by artists who are worth more than the total value of the Paintings they themselves own.'[41] Another example can be found in Junius' book *The Paintings of the Ancients*, in which the author exclaims:

'Away [...] with all of those, who thinke it enough if they can but confidently usurpe the authority belonging onely to them that are well skilled in these arts: it will not serve their turne, that they doe sometimes with a censorious brow reject, and sometimes with an affected gravity commend the workes of great masters: the neat and polished age wherein we live will quickly finde them out'.[42]

However, not all art buyers were dismissed as ignorant and pretentious. The counterpart of the ignorant art lover was the knowledgeable connoisseur. According to Franciscus Junius, there was one connoisseur in particular who inspired seventeenth-century art lovers: a famous ancient art expert by the name of Novius Vindex. According to the ancient writer Statius Papinius, Vindex was an aristocrat who was extraordinary skilful at attributing unsigned works. Moreover, he could see from far away which line had been drawn by the ancient painter Apelles.[45] In the context of this essay it is particularly interesting that this ancient art expert who reputedly had no equal in his day, was probably not a painter, which brings me back to the question of who was considered an able judge of pictures in seventeenth-century art theory: just painters or also knowledgeable connoisseurs?

Fig. 6 - A satirical drawing by Pieter Brueghel the Elder mocks a dauber and his foolish client, much like the art theorists did in their writings. While some scholars in the past interpreted the image as a comment on the ignorance of a non-practitioner when judging art, Lyckle de Vries convincingly argued that in fact both figures in this drawing were being ridiculed.[43] The painter's wild hairdo, inadequate equipment (he's holding the brush of a house painter[44]) and puzzled expression indicate that he is a dauber. His admirer holds a big moneybag, suggesting that he is willing to pay well for the dauber's work, while his glasses only accentuate his lack of discernment.

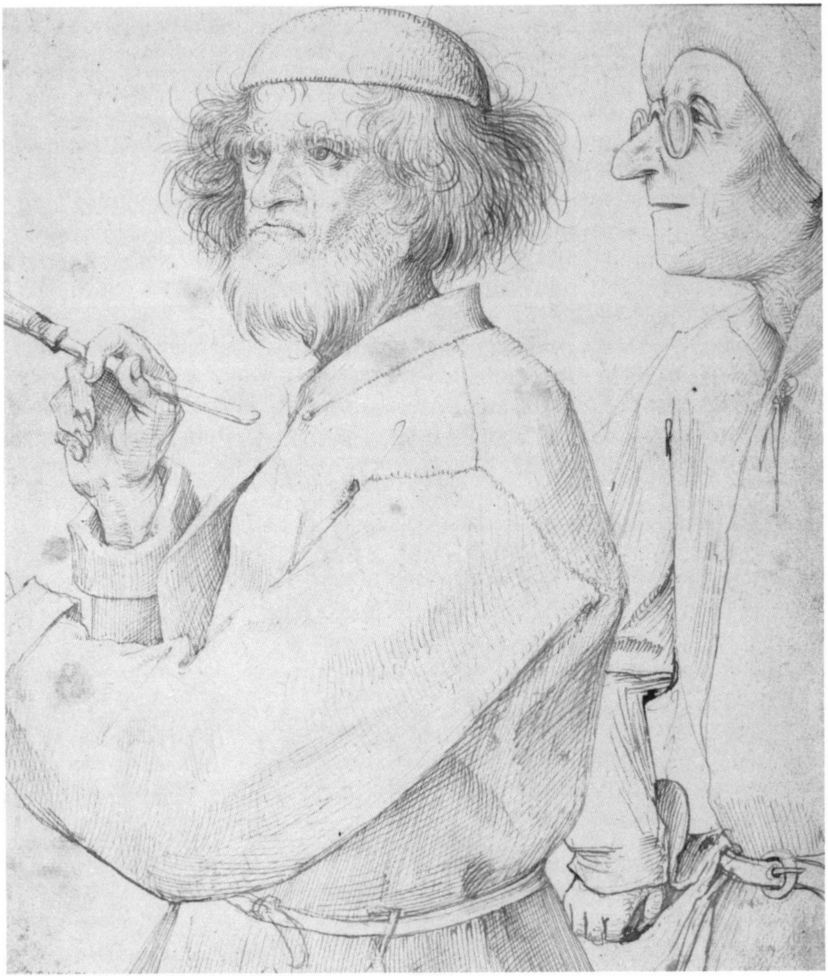

6.

Pieter Brueghel the Elder
The Painter and the Connoisseur, mid-1560s,
Grafische Sammlung Albertina, Vienna

The best judge – the painter?

At least three seventeenth-century art theorists – Etienne Binet, Abraham Bosse and Samuel van Hoogstraten – explicitly declared that only painters were able to adequately assess pictures.[46] Binet, the author of a popular book on eloquence discussed above, wrote somewhat mysteriously: 'Good painters always hide some secret knowledge in their works, which is worth more than the rest, but only the Master Painters recognise it and have a feeling for it.'[47] As discussed above, Binet simply advised his readers to praise admirable characteristics of pictures; a thorough understanding of the works such as master painters could achieve, was beyond their reach, according to him.

The Parisian printmaker Abraham Bosse was somewhat more ambivalent. He wrote a treatise to instruct art lovers on how to recognise various manners of painting, printmaking and drawing, and on how to distinguish between originals and copies (*Sentimens sur la Distinction des diverses manières de peinture, dessin et gravure et des orginaux d'avec leurs copies,* Paris 1649). But despite his premise, he expressed his doubts about how good of a judge he thought his readers might become. He acknowledged that there were good judges of art among both painters and 'art lovers' (*curieux*).

'[O]ne may say that in this art [of judging pictures] as in other Arts, there are natural inclinations for these things, for sometimes even people who have barely any practical experience, have or can have some knowledge in this respect. But to say that they come close to the opinion that Excellent Practitioners who are experienced herein may have, that is impossible in my opinion.'[48]

However, at the end of his treatise, Bosse, nonetheless, notes that distinguishing between various manners of painting, between originals and copies, and between good and bad paintings was in fact 'easy' and that with the help of good artist connoisseurs, non-practising art lovers could learn it.[49] Indeed, Bosse seems to have had difficulties reconciling his premise to teach art lovers how to judge art, with his desire to celebrate the superiority of practitioners in this respect. As Jonathan Brown wittily remarked, Bosse's treatise in fact balances uncomfortably between altruism and self-defence.[50]

Of these three advocates of the hegemony of painters in judging art, the painter Samuel van Hoogstraten was the most outspoken. In the preface to his treatise he declares:

'Thus our Introduction will also be opportune for all art lovers, although they are not experienced [in painting itself], so that they will not be deceived when buying pieces of art, because they will appreciate these to the measure of the virtues that are to be seen in them, and they will not remain name-buyers, of which there are so many, who are being led astray by some boaster, to value poor rags, because they have been led to believe that they were painted by a great Master. It certainly is a ridiculous pastime to esteem something as artful and worthy of high respect, whereas there is nothing artful nor eminent to be seen. I do not pretend that this introduction of mine will open the art lover's eyes to the extent that he will be able to judge art by himself: far from it, but he will more easily come to understand what it is in our work that should be judged, and then will be able, with the help of an experienced painter, to clearly and distinctively detect the virtues and failures in any piece of work.'[51]

In Van Hoogstraten's view, art lovers could thus develop an understanding of the aspects that should be judged in paintings; however, they would never be able to properly evaluate a picture without the assistance of a knowledgeable painter.

The best judge – the connoisseur?

Certainly not all early modern art theorists were as negative as Binet, Bosse and Hoogstraten about the abilities of non-practitioners to sensibly judge pictures. As we have seen, Van Mander, for example, took the judgements of non-practitioners to heart when discussing issues of attribution, the characteristics of an artist's style and the general quality of a painter's work. Nevertheless, he also stressed the advantages of the painter's experienced eye, which suggests that he did not find it self-evident that art lovers could be the equals of good painters when it came to assessing art. Writers on art who were not painters themselves, generally had more confidence in their own judgements, however.

The Italian collector Giulio Mancini, for example, was quite explicit in his comments on the matter. In the introduction to his unpublished treatise on judging pictures, he raises the question of whether he as a non-painter could write a treatise to teach gentlemen how to assess pictures so they could more successfully purchase and collect paintings. The answer is evidently yes. He believed that some practical experience is important, namely knowing how to draw. However, he did not find it necessary to know how to paint; elements such as colour, perspective, and the expression of passions were for Mancini common enough subjects that everyone could recognise and judge them without having to be a painter.[52] He then eloquently turns the question around and asks: why is it that a painter is not necessarily a good judge of painting? Mancini believed it was because the painting and judging of paintings required different talents and qualities. Painting required primarily 'imagination' (*fantasia*). Assessing a painting, however, required prudence, knowledge, intelligence and a certain indifference (to prevent negative passions such as envy from clouding one's judgement). Moreover, to successfully appraise art one needed additional knowledge; because painting was not a necessity like bread and water and thus, its price, Mancini argued, basically depended on the taste and budget of the buyer and the need of the owner to dispose of the work. Mancini believed that creating, judging and appraising pictures were thus three different specialisations, of which the last two did not necessarily require painterly experience.

Franciscus Junius also believed that experience as a painter was not necessary to successfully assess pictures, however, for somewhat different reasons. As we have seen, he repeatedly compared ancient views with those of his contemporaries in his treatise *On the Painting of the Ancients*.

Indeed, his opinion regarding who could best judge art came in a response to Pliny the Younger. The latter had written that: 'none but an Artificer can judge a Painter, Carver, Caster in brasse, or worker in clay', to which Junius immediately adds:

'Observe in the mean time, that in these words of Plinie we must understand by the name Artificer, not such a workman only as doth really paint and carve, but such a Lover [...] of Art as by a rare and well-exercised Imaginative facultie, is able to conferre his conceived Images with the Pictures and Statues that come neerest to Nature, and is likewise able to discerne by a cunning and infallible conjecture the severall hands of divers great Masters out of their manner of working.'[53]

Thus, in Junius's view, painters but also trained art lovers could adequately judge the quality and attribution of works of art. He believed that judging art required a trained imagination. The connoisseur should be able to imagine what a scene should look like and compare this mental image to what he sees in a painting. He thus needs a kind of knowledge that is very similar to an artist's, so that he can also imagine how else the painter could have depicted the same scene. When properly trained, Junius believed that non-painters were often better judges than painters: 'thus provided, they doe often examine the works of great Artificers with better successe then the Artists themselves, the severitie and integretie of whose judgements is often weakend by the love of their owne and the dislike of other mens workes.'[54]

In the 1630s, Junius thus touted the trained art lover over the practitioner as the better judge of art. Interestingly, around the same time, three other writers on art praised painters to the extent that they were popular among art lovers. Jan Orlers and Theodoor Schrevelius, in their descriptions of their respective cities of Leiden and Haarlem, refer extensively to the assessments of art lovers when they celebrated certain painters; the opinions of other painters are not even mentioned.[55] The opinion of art lovers, to them, was a guarantee of quality. Even the painter, Philips Angel, focuses on the opinions of art lovers in his praise of the Leiden painters of 1641.[56] Junius was obviously not the only one who preferred the opinions of non-painters.

Moreover, Junius was also ingenious in how he appreciated the laymen's opinion. Junius opined that even laymen could recognise the quality of an artwork, even though they remained incapable of fully rationalising their opinions. He argued forcefully by comparing it to music, by noting that anyone can recognise a false note, even those unable to explain exactly what caused it or play the passage better themselves.[57]

In the 1660s and 1670s, the French art theorists André Félibien and Roger de Piles expanded on Junius's view that anybody can basically assess a painting's quality, but that it takes greater expertise to fully rationalise one's opinions. Like Junius, they believed that both painters and connoisseurs could potentially assess a painting, emphasising that both needed the same intellectual background in the principles of painting to adequately explain their opinions. Furthermore, they also added a warning to aspiring connoisseurs about the pitfalls. Félibien points out the dangers of solely focussing on one aspect of a painting that one is knowledgeable about such as perspective. Meanwhile, De Piles pointed out that it was important to realise that neither a good painter's nor a reputable connoisseur's opinion is necessarily correct regarding a picture, meaning, in effect that should always also think for oneself.[58] On a more pragmatic level, De Piles warned beginning connoisseurs not to stand too close to the painting when assessing a large or roughly painted work, as he had witnessed many people doing, but to step back to an ideal viewing distance.[59]

In the art theoretical literature, the question of who is the best judge of art was thus an issue that led to some debate. I think that rather than try to see the different views as a linear development based on a general consensus, it is more fruitful to see the various views as part of an evolving debate, and to analyse the individual opinions in relation to the background, training and surroundings of these opinionated writers. While the art theorist-painters tended to emphasise the painter's critical capacities; the art lover--non-practitioners appealed for recognition of their abilities. As we have seen, some of these art lovers believed that non-painters were the equals of painters when it came to assessing art. The question then is to what extent these connoisseurs also actually assessed art in practice. As we have seen, Orlers, Schrevelius and Angel believed that the opinions of knowledgeable art lovers guaranteed the quality of an artwork. But did these connoisseurs also assess and appraise art as a dealer, auctioneer or official arbitrator in attribution issues?

Judging pictures in practice

In the seventeenth-century, the sale of pictures was controlled by the professional organisation of painters, the Guild of Saint Luke, the rules and regulations of which differed per city. The heads of the guild were the traditional arbitrators involving conflicts. Art dealers had to be members of the Guild of St Luke to be eligible to sell art. The guild also granted permission for public sales such as auctions.[60]

Master painters most commonly sold work produced in their studios directly to clients. Sometimes they sold work created elsewhere as Johannes Vermeer did. Some painters gave up painting altogether to devote themselves exclusively to the art trade. They included prominent dealers like Gerrit Uylenburgh, Cornelis Doeck, Abraham de Cooge, Crijn Volmarijn, Matthijs Musson, Albert Meyeringh and Jan Colenbier.[61] Furthermore, it was fairly common for the family members of painters to become involved in art transactions. Did knowledgeable art lovers also sell art?

Interestingly, in the seventeenth century, several membership lists of the various Guilds of Saint Luke mention 'art lovers' (*liefhebbers*), a phenomenon that was researched by Jaap van de Veen and Cindy van Keulen.[62] In the city of Antwerp, 23 art lovers are listed in the guild records during the period 1600-1630. Some of these are described as 'art lover and merchant' (*liefhebber en coopman*), so one can assume that they were also dealers. Two of these have been identified as the well-connected art collectors Cornelis vander Geest and Philips van Valckenisse.

'Art lovers' (*liefhebbers*) are also listed in documents pertaining to the Haarlem Guild of St. Luke. In response to a draft document from the Haarlem headmen proposing a ban on public sales (1642), several guild members protested the decision. One of their objections was that this ban would greatly inconvenience art lovers who encouraged young painters by buying all their work. If they were unable to resell these works freely, they could potentially change their minds about encouraging new talent.[63] Guild records in The Hague also mention art lovers; they paid the Guild 6 stuivers per year in membership fees, the same amount as master painters. According to a 1656 guild regulation, these art lovers were allowed to freely purchase art from out-of-town painters; However, they were not allowed to resell these in public sales without the consent of the burgomasters.[64] The rules and regulations varied quite a bit from city to city. In Bruges and Gent, art lovers were not even mentioned in guild records, which does not necessarily mean that there were no non-practitioner members in the guild of Saint Luke, because they may have been registered as dealers.

The scattered evidence nonetheless leads us to conclude that numerous non-practitioners occasionally sold art and that some were even specialised dealers. For example, one of the most prominent dealers in Amsterdam around the middle of the seventeenth century was a non-practitioner: Johannes de Renialme; other examples include the collectors Marten Kretzer and Herman van Swoll.[65] Similarly, the most well-known auctioneer of the period, Jan Pietersz. Zomer, had not been trained as a painter. Lastly, as Koenraad Jonckheere has shown, at the end of the seventeenth century, collector-connoisseurs like Jan van Beuningen played a crucial role in the sale of high-end masterpieces.[66]

There is also evidence that non-painters acted as official arbitrators in attribution cases in the seventeenth century. As Jaap van de Veen has shown, Marten Kretzer, Isaack van Beest and Herman Stoffelsz. van Swol among others assumed this role; they were all paintings collectors.[67] Interestingly, this practice roughly coincides with the period in which some writers on painting award greater importance to the judgement of non-practitioners than to that of painters when praising artists (see above). Indeed it looks like non-practitioners thus acquired an increasingly important role both in theory and in practice throughout the seventeenth century.

Although most pictures were sold by painters in the seventeenth century either directly or in retail, some non-painters were thus able to establish themselves as art dealer, auctioneer and/or as arbitrator. Of course they did not only judge pictures in these capacities. In as far as these connoisseurs have been identified, they were all collectors themselves. And they would have obviously needed to judge pictures when buying works.

Conclusion

The assumption that only painters were acknowledged as having the capacity to assess art in the seventeenth century does not hold true. It was a topic of debate among art theorists who was ultimately the best judge: the painter or the connoisseur, and most theorists seemed to agree that there were good judges among both master painters and art lovers. In practice, besides painters, some connoisseurs were also considered able judges of art. Successful dealers and auctioneers were not necessarily painters themselves and non-practitioners were sometimes called upon to serve as official arbitrators in attribution issues. Interestingly, the connoisseur's increasingly important role on the art market coincides with the increased importance attached to his opinions in descriptions of cities and in art theory publications. This, in turn, may have provoked stronger expressions of aversion – by Bosse and Van Hoogstraten, for instance – for inept and pretentious connoisseurs.

In hindsight, the conclusion that the opinions of connoisseurs were important both in theory and in practice was perhaps predictable. After all, as De Piles wrote in one of his dialogues on connoisseurship: 'It would have been a strange thing if paintings were made for painters only.'[68]

* I would like to thank Marten Jan Bok, Inge Broekman, Koenraad Jonkcheere and Eric Jan Sluijter for their insightful comments on earlier drafts of this essay.

1 One of these paintings is in the Museo del Prado, Madrid, inv. no. 1405; see Padrón, Matías Díaz, and Mercedes Royo-Villanova, *David Teniers, Jan Brueghel y los gabinetes de pinturas*, Madrid (Museo del Prado) 1992 (exh. cat.), no. 25; another one was on the Brussels art market according to Kristin Belkin, see Guy C. Bauman and Walter A. Liedtke, *Flemish Paintings in America*, Antwerp 1992, p. 167; see also Arthur Wheelock, *A Collector's Cabinet*, Washington D.C. 1998, p. 15 and 60 (note 3 and 4).

2 Examples of gallery paintings can be found in: S. Speth-Holterhoff, *Les peintres flamands de cabinets d'amateurs au XVIIème siècle*, Brussels 1957; Matthias Winner, *Die Quellen der Pictura-Allegorien in gemalten Bildergalerien des 17. Jahrhunderts zu Antwerpen*, Ph.D. Dissertation Universität Köln 1957; Zirka Zaremba Filipczak, *Picturing Art in Antwerp 1550-1700*, Princeton 1987. On depictions of art lovers in painters studios, see

Ernst van de Wetering and Michiel Franken, 'Op bezoek in het atelier', *Kunstschrift/Opembaar Kunstbezit* 27, 1 (1983), pp. 3-12; Arjan de Koomen, "Pictieve bezoekers', in Mariët Haveman (ed.), *Ateliergeheimen: over de werkplaats van de Nederlandse kunstenaar vanaf 1200 tot heden*, Lochem 2006, pp. 234-253; Katja Kleinert, *Atelierdarstellungen in der Niederländischen Genremalerei des 17. Jahrhunderts: realistisches Abbild oder glaubwürdiger Schein?*, Petersburg 2006.

3 This text is often mistakenly referred to as the *Brussels Manuscript* by Pierre le Brun, which credits Le Brun as the author. In fact, Le Brun's manuscript is a hand-written copy of Binet's widely read book on eloquence, which was reprinted several times during the seventeenth century. Etienne Binet, *Essay des merveilles de nature, et des plus nobles artifices*, with an introduction by Marc Fumaroli, Paris 1987 [1621].

4 'Quand la peinture estoit encore au berceau; et à son premier liact; le pinceau estoit si niais, les ouvrages si lourds, qu'il fallait écrire desssus, c'est un Boeuf, c'est un Asne, autrement vous eussiez pris cela pour un quartier de veau; maintenant il faut mettre dessous, qu'un tel peignoit, de peur qu'on ne creut que ce sont des morts qu'on a collé sur la toile, et des personnes vivantes sans vie, tant le tout est bien fait.' Binet, *Essay des Merveilles de nature* (note 3), p. 364.

5 'gardez-vous [...] de la recherche trop curieuse, et des petites chosettes qui sont trop minces et qui ne doivent pas sortir de la boutique.' Binet, *Essay des Merveilles de nature* (note 3), p. 355.

6 Willem Goeree, *Inleydingh tot de practijck der al-gemeene schilder-konst*, Middelbrugh 1697 [1670], pp. 7-8.

7 Although some seventeenth-century poems on paintings have a sharp wit and contain some criticism, the majority are laudatory in general terms, celebrating for example their lifelikeness. Poetry generally enjoyed a higher status than painting, as Jan Emmens has shown, and it seems important to point out that even laudatory poems were often considered superior to the painting they described; these poems were thus not meant simply as evaluations of the painting but rather as a creation in their own right. See J.A. Emmens, 'Apelles en Apollo, Nederlandse gedichten op schilderijen in de 17de eeuw' (article based on Emmens' unpublished M.A. thesis and published in J.A. Emmens, *Kunsthistorische opstellen*, 2 vols., Amsterdam 1981, vol. 1, pp. 5-60 and p. 205). On this topic, see also Karel Porteman. 'Geschreven met de linkerhand? Letteren tegenover schilderkunst in de Gouden Eeuw', in Marijke Spies (ed.), *Historische letterkunde. Facetten van vakbeoefening*, Groningen 1984, pp. 93-113.

8 See also my essay in this volume 'By His Hand. The Paradox of Seventeenth-Century Connoisseurship', above pp. 31-66.

9 Peter Sutton, 'Rembrandt and a Brief History of Connoisseurship', in: Ronald D. Spencer (ed.), *The Expert versus the Object, Judging Fakes and False Attributions in the Visual Arts*, Oxford 2004, pp. 29-38, esp. p. 31.

10 Jonathan Brown, *Kings and Connoisseurs: Collecting Art in Seventeenth -Century Europe*, Princeton 1995, p. 233.

11 Karel van Mander, *Het Schilder-boeck*, Haarlem 1604.

12 Ibid. (note 11), fol. 251v.

13 'Yemandt spraeck-condigher hadde moghen dit veel schoon-taliger en constiger te weghe brenghen: doch waer te besorghen, indien hy self geen Schilder en waer, dat hy in onse dinghen, en eyghenschappen, hem dickwils soude hebben verloopen.' Ibid. (note 11), fol. *4v.

14 'want t'was (seyde hy) onmoghelijck, dat yemandt anders als *Appelles* soude connen maken met verwe en pinceel soo aerdighen dunnen treck als desen was' Ibid. (note 11), fol. 77v.

15 See also Henri van de Waal, 'The Linea sumae tenuitatis', *Zeitschrift für Ästetik und allgemeine Kunstwissenschaft*, 12, 1 (1967), pp. 5-32.

16 Van Mander, *Het Schilder-boeck* (note 11), fol. 78r: 'waren slechte recht uytgetrocken linien oft streken, ghelijck vele meenen, die geen Schilders en zijn: maer eenigen omtreck van een arem oft been, oft immer eenich pourfijl van een tronie, oft soo yet, den welcken omtreck sy seer net hebben ghetrocken, en t'sommiger plaetsen door malcanders treck [...] henen'.

17 'En mijn meyninghe bevest ick hier mede, dat Plinius ghetuyght, datter de ghene die hun aen de Schilder-const verstonden, grootlijcx in waren verwondert en verbaest. Waer door wel te verstaen is, dat het constighe omtrecken, en gheen simpel linien en waren, die dese soo uytnemenste opper Meesters in onser Const tegen malcander om strijdt ghetrocken hadden: want een rechte linie uyt der handt henen te trecken, soude menigh Schoolmeester, Schrijver, oft ander die geen Schilder en is, dickwils veel beter doen, als den besten Schilder van de Weerelt, en sulcx en wordt by den Schilders niet veel gheacht: want daer toe ghebruyckt men de rije oft reghel. maer de Const-verstandige verwonderen en ontsetten sich, wanneer sy sien eenen aerdigen en constigen omtreck, die met een uytnemende verstandt behendich is ghetrocken, waer in de Teycken-const ten hooghsten bestaet: maer de rechte linien souden sy onghemerckt voorby gaen.' Ibid. (note 11), fol. 78r.

18 Only in one instance does Van Mander make a distinction between the opinion of painters and that of art lovers, see Van Mander, *Het Schilder-boeck* (note 11), fol. 256v (biography of Cornelis Molenaer): 'Voorts van d'ordinantien zijner Landtschappen, en achter-uyten, heb ick niet veel te roemen: dan dat alles wat men van hem siet, den Schilders wonder wel bevalt: doch in beelden had hy geen handelinghe. [...] zijn wercken zijn by den Const-liefdighe in grooter weerden.' Although both painters and art lovers thus greatly value Cornelis Molenaer's works, Van Manders wording could imply that he believed that the painters had a better judgement about the execution of Molenaer's works, see also below, p. 140 .

19 'Het zijn eenighe die meenen, dat dit werck by *Holbeen* self niet gheheel voldaen en is: maer dat nae zijn doot, het ghene daer noch aen ghebrack van yemandt anders voleyndight soude wesen: doch indient soo waer, heeft den opmaker den *Holbeens* handelinghe soo verstandigh connen volghen, dat het geen Schilder noch Const-verstandighe van verscheyden handen en souden oordeelen.' Van Mander, *Het Schilder-boeck* (note 11), fol. 222r:

20 This point of view also occurs in Van Mander's descriptions of the lives of Lucas van Leyden, Pieter Vlerick and Hendrick Goltzius.

21 Van Mander, *Het Schilder-boeck* (note 11), fol. 299r. On the art lovers mentioned by Van Mander, see Marten Jan Bok, 'Art Lovers and their Paintings. Van Mander's Schilder-boeck as a Source for the History of the Art Market in the Northern Netherlands', in: Ger Luijten et al. (eds.), *Dawn of the Golden Age: Northern Netherlandish Art, 1580-1620*, Amsterdam (Rijksmuseum) 1993 (exh. cat.), pp. 136-166.

22 Van Mander, *Het Schilder-boeck* (note 11), fol 78v.

23 'Schoenmaker, blijf bij je leest!' is still a proverb in Dutch. On this anecdote, see also Ernst van de Wetering, 'Rembrandt's "Satire on Art Criticism" Reconsidered', in Cynthia P. Schneider, William W. Robinson, Alice I. Davies et al. (eds.), *Shop Talk: Studies in Honor of Seymour Slive*, Cambridge Mass. 1995, pp. 264-270.

24 Ibid. (note 11), fol. 23r ff, esp. 24v.

25 Ibid. (note 11), fol. 18v-19r.

26 Ibid. (note 11), fol. 279v.

27 'Summa, Teycken-const can alderley staten / Behulpich wesen, t'zy jonghen, oft grijsen, / Iae Vorsten, Capiteynen, en Soldaten, / Soo om van der Conste gheschickt te praten, / Als om de gheleghentheden aenwijsen, / Van sterckten en plaetsen, daerom te prijsen'. Ibid. (note 11), fol. 10r

28 See also below, p. 140.

29 Constantijn Huygens, *De Jeugd van Constantijn Huygens, door hemzelf beschreven*, Rotterdam 1971, pp. 65-66.

30 'Aen dese dingen is te mercken, wat onder den Menschen gonst en afgonst vermoghen, oft oock de waensucht: want sommighe die *Goltzium* in zijn Const meenden versmaden oft verachten, hebben onbewist hem boven de oude beste Meesters, en boven hem selven ghestelt. En dit deden oock de gene, die gewent waren te seggen, dat geen beter Plaet-snijders, als *Albert* en *Lucas*, te verwachten waren, en dat *Goltzius* by hun niet te gelijcken was.' Van Mander, *Het Schilder-boeck* (note 11), fol. 284v: See also Huijgen Leeflang and Ger Luijten (eds.), *Hendrick Goltzius (1558-1617): tekeningen, prenten en schilderijen*, Amsterdam, New York and Toledo 2003 (exh. cat.), pp. 210-215, cat no. 75, 1-6.

31 Lucian, quoted in Franciscus Junius, *Catalogus Architectorum, Mechanicatum, sed praecipue Pictorum, Statuariorum, Caelatorum, Tronatorum, aliorumque Artificum*, Rotterdam 1694, p. 423. Samuel van Hoogstraten, Inleyding tot de hooge schoole der schilderkonst, anders de zichtbaere werelt: verdeelt in negen leerwinkels, yder bestiert door eene der zanggodinnen, Rotterdam 1678, p.76. Jan de Bisschop also discusses the anecdote in his *Paradigmata* of 1671, see facsimile in Jan van Gelder and Ingrid Jost, *Jan de Bisschop and his Icones & Paradigmata : classical antiquities and Italian drawings for artistic instruction in seventeenth century Holland*, Doornspijk 1985, 2 vols., II, preface addressed to Jan Six (page not numbered).

32 According to both Junius and Hoogstraten it was particularly important to not focus too much on secondary elements or 'Parerga', see essay above 'By His Hand: The Paradox of Seventeenth-Century Connoisseurship' pp. 31-66, esp. pp. 49-50.

33 Franciscus Junius, *The Literature of Classical Art, Vol. I. The Painting of the Ancients, according to the English translation (1638)*, ed. by Keith Aldrich et.al., Berkeley, Los Angeles and Oxford 1991, Junius, *The Painting of the Ancients*, (note 14), p. 65.

34 This definition is taken from Eric Jan Sluijter. See Eric Jan Sluijter, *Rembrandt and the Female Nude*, Amsterdam 2006, pp. 195-219.

35 Paul Fréart de Chambray, *Idée de la Perfection de la peinture*, Mans 1662 [reprint 1968]. See also Emmanuelle Delapierre and Cécile Krings, *Rubens contre Poussin : la querelle du coloris dans la peinture française à la fin du XVIIe siècle*, Arras (Musée des Beaux-Arts d'Arras) 2005 (exh. cat.).

36 Eric Jan Sluijter, '"Horrible Nature, incomparible art": Rembrandt and the depiction of the female nude' in: *Rembrandt's Women*, Edinburgh and London 2001 (exh. cat.), pp. 37-45, esp. p. 42.

37 Jacques de Ville, *'t Saamenspreekinghe betreffende de architecture ende schilderkonst, dienende tot waerschouwinghe van alle werck-luyden ende liefhebbers der selver konst; Dat zy haer aan de handelinghe alleen niet en moeten vergapen: maer verder moeten zien*, Gouda 1628.

38 Van Mander, *Het Schilder-boeck* (note 11), fol. 252v.

39 Lyckle de Vries, 'With a Coarse Brush: Pieter Bruegel's "Brooding Artist"', *Source, Notes in the History of Art*, 23, 4 (2004), pp. 38-48, p. 42 ff.

40 '*Aan Martijn de schilder* / Martijn, gy snurkt altijdt op uwe schildery. / Het volk verstaat noch kunst, dunkt u, noch haer waardy. / 't Is Waar, 't gemeen is bot om d'eigenschap te vatten. / Was 't volk heel wijs, het zou uw verf zoo dier niet schatten.' Jan Vos, *Alle de gedichten*, Amsterdam 1726, p. 518 no. 583; cited in: Gregor J.M. Weber, *Der Lobtopos des 'lebenden' Bildes, Jan Vos und sein 'Zeege der Schilderkunst' von 1654*, Hildesheim, Zürich and New York 1991, p. 80.
41 Abraham Bosse, *Sentimens sur la Distinction des diverses manières de peinture, dessin et gravure et des orginaux d'avec leurs copies*, Paris 1649, p. 2: 'il y en a divers autres qui apres avoir retenu & proferé quantité de Termes de l'art comme, de l'Antique, du Raphael,du Grand, de la grande ou forte Maniere, du Bon ou mauvais Goust, d'Ordaonnance, de Disposition, de bein Historié, de belle Groupe, du Fier, d'Expression, D'Union, de bien Ensemble, bien Touché ou Heurté, d'Artiste, Croqué, de Vaghezza, Sevelt, Frais, Tendre, Dur, Coupé, Tranché, Noyé, grand Iour, grand Ombre, Teinte, & demye Teinte, & plusieurs autres telles choses, s'imaginent qu'on les doit tenir pour tres entendüs ou connoissans en icelle; & ce qui leur augmente encore davantage cette bonne opinion, c'est qu'ils ont quelque fois rencontré à connoistre quelques manieres de Peindre, ce qui est pourtant tres-peu de chose, dautant qu'il y en a telles, qu'un aveugle les pouroit discerner en les touchant'.
42 Junius, *The Painting of the Ancients* (note 33), p. 296.
43 De Vries, *With a Coarse Brush* (note 39), pp. 38-48.
44 Lyckle de Vries (De Vries, *With a Coarse Brush* (note 39), pp. 38-48.) suspected that the brush was mostly used by house painters. I believe that was certainly the case for a 1635 emblem of the Haarlem 'house painters' (kladschilders) features the exact same type of brush, see Fr. D.O. Obreen, *Archief Nederlandsche kunstgeschiedenis*, Rotterdam 1877-1890, vol. 1, 1877-78, Appendix 'Blazoenen van achttien bedrijven behoorende onder het gild van sint Lucas. anno 1635', plate 7.
45 Junius, *The Painting of the Ancients* (note 33), p. 68-69.
46 The French painter Nicolas Poussin and the Italian painter, sculptor and architect Gianlorenzo Bernini expressed similar opinions, although Bernini reputedly made exceptions. See Nicolas Poussin, *Lettres et propos sur l'art*, with an introduction by Anthony Blunt, Paris 1964, p. 123; Paul Fréart de Chantelou, *Diary of the Cavaliere Bernini's Visit to France (1665)*, with an introduction by Anthony Blunt, Princeton 1985, pp. 226 and 263.
47 '13. Les bons Peintres cachent tousjours quelque secrette intelligence dans leurs ouvrages, qui vaut plus que le reste, mais les Maîtres seuls les recognoissent, et en ont le sentiment.' Binet, *Essay des merveilles* (note 3), p. 358.
48 Bosse, *Sentimens sur la Distinction des diverses manières de peinture* (note 41), p. 5: 'Par ainsi l'on peut dire qu'il y a en cela comme en d'autres Arts, de naturelles inclinations pour ces choses, puis que mesme ceux qui n'ont point de pratique, en ont ou peuvent avoir quelque connoissance; Mais de dire qu'elle soit approchante de celle qu'en peut avoir un Excellent Praticien exercé en icelles, cela est impossible à mon avis'.
49 Bosse, *Sentimens sur la Distinction des diverses manières de peinture* (note 41), p. 71: 'Ainsi l'on peut juger, que tous les bons Praticiens qui se s ont appliquez ou adonnez a esplucher toutes ces particularitez, peuvent estre les plus entendus à discerner toutes ces diverses manieres, & distinctions d'Originaux & Copies, & de plus les bonnes d'avec les mauvaises; & aussi qu'il est facile de juger que c'est par le moyen de tels connoissans, que les curieux non Praticiens, peuvent avoir esté & estre instruits à faire la distinction de toutes ces diverses choses'
50 Jonathan Brown, *Kings and Connoisseurs* (note 10), p. 232.
51 Van Hoogstraten, Inleyding tot de hooge schoole der schilderkonst (note 31), p. **3: 'Soo komt dan deze onze *Inleiding* ook zeer wel te pas voor alle Liefhebbers van de Schilderkonst, schoon zy in de selve onervaere zijn, om in 't koopen van Konststukken niet bedrogen te worden, want zy zullen die waerdeeren nae de maete der deugden, die in de zelve zijn waergenomen, en geen neamkoopers blijven, gelijk'er tans veel zijn, die van d'een of anderen snoeshaen verleyt, kaele vodden in grooten waerden houden, om dat hun is wijs gemaekt, datze van d'een of d'ander groot Meester geschildert zijn. Niet dat ik zeggen wil, dat deeze mijne *Inleiding* allen Liefhebbers de oogen zal openen, dat zy zelfs strax van de kunst zullen kunnen oordeelen: dat zy verre; maer zy zullen uit ons werk gemakkelijk kunnen begrijpen, waer van dat men oordelen moet, en dan zullen zy, met behulp van een ervaren Schilder, de deugden en feilen, die in eenig werk zijn, klaer en onderscheidelijk kunnen naspeuren.'
52 'S'aggiunge che il colore, la prospettiva, l'espression dell'affetto, et altre cose simili rappresentate et espresse dal pittore, son oggetti comuni / che si riconoscono e giudicano senza l'abito della pittura et suo modo d'operare.' Giulio Mancini, *Considerazioni sulla Pittura, publicato per la prima volta da Adriana Maracchi con il commento di Luigi Salerno* (Academia Nazionale dei Lincei), Rome 1956, p. 291 ff.
53 Junius, *The Painting of the Ancients* (note 33), p. 68.
54 Junius, *The Painting of the Ancients* (note 33), pp. 64-65.
55 Jan Orlers, *Beschrijvinge der stad Leyden*, Leiden 1614; Theodoor Schrevelius, *Harlemias, ofte, om beter te seggen, de eerste stichtinghe der stadt*

Haerlem, Haarlem 1648; see also Eric Jan Sluijter, *Verwondering over de schilderijenproductie in de Gouden Eeuw* (inaugural lecture 2002), Amsterdam 2003, pp. 15-17; Eric Jan Sluijter, *Seductress of Sight, Studies in Dutch Art of the Golden Age*, Zwolle 2000, p. 204.

56 Philips Angel, *Lof der schilder-konst*, Leiden 1642.

57 Junius, *The Painting of the Ancients* (note 33), pp. 68-69.

58 André Félibien, *Entretien sur les vies et les ouvrages des plus excellens peintres anciens et modernes*, Paris 1666-1688, p. 86.

59 Roger de Piles, *Conversations sur la Connoissance de la Peinture*, Paris 1677, p. 233 ff. Also in seventeenth-century paintings, art lovers are almost as a rule depicted while studying pictures from very close nearby.

60 On dealers in the seventeenth-century Netherlands, see J. Michael Montias, 'Art Dealers in the Seventeenth-century Netherlands', *Simiolus* 18 (1988), pp. 244-256. On guilds and the expanding market, see Ed Romein and Gerbrand Korevaar, 'Dutch Guilds and the Threat of Public Sales', in: Hans Van Miegroet and Neil De Marchi (eds.), *Mapping Markets for Paintings in Early Modern Europe 1450-1750*, Turnhout 2006, pp. 101-128.

61 Montias, 'Art Dealers in the Seventeenth-century Netherlands' (note 60), p. 245.

62 Jaap van der Veen, 'Galerij en kabinet, vorst en burger, Schilderijencollecties in de Nederlanden', in: Ellinoor Bergvelt, et al. (eds.), *Kabinetten, galerijen en musea: het verzamelen en presenteren van naturalia en kunst van 1500 tot heden*, Heerlen 1993, pp. 145-188; Cindy van Keulen, 'Liefhebbers van de schilderkunst in het Lucasgilde', *Simulacrum* 5, 2 (1996), pp. 21-23.

63 'bij aldien hetzelve volgens de voorschreven articulen werd gepractiseert [het aan banden leggen van de handel] soo sullen voor het eerst verscheijde liefhebbers die (om aencomende konstenaeren in haere konst te animeren) nu meest alle hare stucken afkoopen genootsaekt syn haere handen thuijs te houden also sij anders geene weeg souden weeten haere gekofte stucken te vertieren', quoted in Van Keulen, *Liefhebbers van de schilderkunst* (note 62), p. 22.

64 A 1656 guild regulation stated that: 'Alle liefhebbers Ingezetenen van de Hage ende Jurisdictie van dien sullen sonder becroon en tegeseggen van de Confrerije, vermogen aen uijtheemsche Mrs. eenige stucken en wercken te besteden, deselve haer aff te coopen, In den Hage 't haren huijse te brengen, behoudel.; dat sij daermede niet en sullen vermogen eenige publicque venduen (te houden) ten sij 's selffde bij Burgemeester om redenen wierde toegestaen.', quoted in Van Keulen, *Liefhebbers van de schilderkunst* (note 62), p. 22., see also Montias, 'Art Dealers in the Seventeenth-century Netherlands' (note 60), p. 247.

65 Montias, 'Art Dealers in the Seventeenth-century Netherlands' (note 60), p. 246.

66 Koenraad Jonckheere, *The Auction of King William's Paintings (1713). Elite international Art Trade at the End of the Dutch Golden Age*, Oculi: Studies in the Arts of the Low Countries. 11, Amsterdam 2008.

67 Jaap van der Veen, 'By his Own Hand, The Valuation of Autograph Paintings in the Seventeenth-Century', in: Ernst van de Wetering et al., *A Corpus of Rembrandt Paintings*, Dordrecht 2005, vol. 4, pp. 1-29 and appendix pp. 30-41, esp. p. 18.

68 'Ce seroit une chose bien estrange que les Tableaux ne fussent fait que pour les Peintres.' De Piles, *Conversations* (note 59), p. 21.

Chapter 5

Neil De Marchi and
Hans J. Van Miegroet

The Rise of the Dealer-Auctioneer in Paris: Information and Transparency in a Market for Netherlandish Paintings*

Dealer-auctioneers and connoisseurs

Records indicate that specialist dealers have been operating as intermediaries in markets for paintings since at least the early sixteenth century. Throughout much of that long period, dealers served connoisseurs, who assumed, by virtue of their inherited status and wealth and the leisure and education both afforded, the role of arbiter in determining quality, and taste in the collecting of artworks.[1] During the sixteenth and seventeenth centuries, however, commercial wealth in the Low Countries, began to shift some of that role to specialist dealers; and, during the eighteenth century, in Paris, a new breed of dealer, whom we shall call the dealer-auctioneer, further displaced the connoisseur.

That there was a change can be inferred from the increases in sales held and collections formed. The number of sales in Paris rose from c. 140 in the first half of the seventeenth century to c. 1,600 in the second half. Meanwhile, by Pomian's count, collections grew from 150 in the period 1700-1720, to more than 500 in the four decades immediately prior to the Revolution.[2] These are striking increases. Nevertheless, to read displacement into these changes requires that we specify the change of roles assumed by dealers; or more precisely, successful appropriations of some of the distinctive roles previously associated with connoisseurship. We will try to do just that here.

We can trace this kind of realignment of roles in the moves of two key innovators among dealers: Edmé-François Gersaint, who operated from 1718 to 1750, and Jean-Baptiste Pierre LeBrun, who was active from 1763 to 1813. There were others of note as well. Gersaint stood out in the first half of the century, but LeBrun was merely first among his peers: he competed within a group of dealer-auctioneers who included

Pierre Rémy, Alexandre Paillet and Pierre François Basan.[3] We have not made a group study, so generalizations are inappropriate, but it is probably fair to consider Gersaint and Lebrun as prototypical in key respects. A sketch of contemporary developments in the art market will clarify what we have in mind.

Since the early 1990s, the leading international auction houses have been buying up galleries and dealerships, thus acquiring access to artwork and to additional clients and potential vendors, along with whatever privileged information is linked to both. These secrets complement the in-house expertise in the researching of provenances and authenticity, and in taking the pulse of the market, built up over a much longer period. The leading houses have also branched out into financial services; and, in particular markets, they have blurred the distinction between first sale and resale. Moreover, they have refined the art of courting important collectors through pre-sale viewings that are part social event and, part – like their catalogues – a kind of curated exhibition. And, through their dealerships, they have acquired a connection with the now-ubiquitous art fairs, rendering still more seamless the mix they represent of formerly distinct roles: arbitrageur, dealer, agent, marketer, expert, professional auctioneer and adviser to collectors. All of these roles are now inextricably trade-related, but expertise and the assessment of quality were once the preserve of connoisseurs, while the trade aspects were left to their trusted agents, or dealers. The first to challenge the separation of roles and unite aspects of them all in their own person, were Gersaint and LeBrun. Others preceded or followed them in some respects, but these two broke down distinctions across the board.

They set out at a time when relationships between dealer and connoisseur were fraught. Gersaint maintained good relations with connoisseurs such as the Swedish Ambassador, Count Carl Gustaf Tessin, and the Comte de Caylus, and he even enjoyed close friendships with some, including the chevalier De la Roque. However, his own position was complex. He considered connoisseurs to be the very model of learning and discriminating taste; at the same time, he encouraged would-be collectors in new and radical beliefs. Chief among them were that (a) even without a connoisseur's education, they might become collectors; and (b) even without a connoisseur's wealth, there are affordable paintings that are also acceptable: credible, if more modest, substitutes for work by Italian fifteenth and sixteenth-century masters and such seventeenth-century French emulators as Poussin and Lorrain. As if these general positions were not subversive enough, Gersaint actually laid it down that pleasing affect must be the first consideration of a would-be amateur in choosing a painting. And he both challenged the notion that a high price necessarily signals quality and questioned whether a painting without attribution is necessarily unworthy.

The revolutionary import of Gersaint's views was muted because he also impressed upon aspiring amateurs the necessity of book knowledge and lots of comparative viewing experience. Some of the required knowledge he provided in his catalogue commentaries, along with information to identify family clusters of artists, each of whom could be thought of as substitutable for the others at the level of sensual pleasure. What enabled Gersaint to satisfy both connoisseurs and new collectors was that he considered the two to be non-competing groups. He, and everyone else, knew that aspiring lovers of art could not expect to actually reach connoisseurial status, the necessary conditions for which were partly determined at birth. This meant that the only real challenge in Gersaint's novel advice and inclusive practice was that connoisseurs might lose some of their claim to exclusivity. And even that was not terribly controversial: superficial mixing among classes, for example, could occur at Gersaint's sales without there being any real blurring of social distinctions.[4]

The notion of affordable yet acceptable substitutes helped engender interest in the unfamiliar or lesser-known Netherlandish artists that Gersaint gathered together at sales in the North and took with him back to Paris. There, Nicholas Berchem and Jan Both, for example, were presented as supplying, within the family of Italianate landscapists, comparable pleasing properties to those of the unavailable and unaffordable Claude Lorrain. And for buyers charmed by Jan I Brueghel's peasant festivities, but unable to consider (or find) an original, or who preferred their peasants a little more couth than either Brueghel or Brouwer's kind, there was David II Teniers, whose works were already discreetly appreciated by some collectors in Paris and had been reproduced as colored prints and his peasant festivities at times even appropriated as 'French' farm (*basse cours*) scenes.[5]

Gersaint's success in promoting Netherlandish paintings to the French, in the face of an inherited hierarchy of genres and defining characteristics of the art of paintings that set most of them well below Italian histories, owed something to Roger de Piles' sustained campaign in favor of coloring. Nonetheless, his efforts to reach out to new collectors and modify their attitudes, on the one hand, and the prices Netherlandish paintings fetched in his sales, on the other, cannot have been entirely unrelated.[6]

The dealer-auctioneers of eighteenth-century Paris differed from the dealers who held public sales of paintings in the seventeenth- and early eighteenth-century Netherlands and London, in two important respects. First, they made themselves knowledgeable, and in this respect more like connoisseurs. Gersaint, for example, invented the *catalogue raisonné*; he made a study of prints with advice on how to recognize artist's proofs; and he published a discursive *table alphabétique* of artists. LeBrun must have kept meticulous sales records, for he published both provenances and past prices for individual paintings – details previously known to and closely guarded by connoisseurs and dealers respectively. He also wrote a compendious study of artists comprising the principal national schools. Indeed, this was an element in the important role he played in gaining acceptance for new methods of display, including improved lighting, that stressed classification by school, and chronology, rather than the older connoisseurial mode of juxtaposing the works of a selected artist to reveal superior and inferior achievement, a mode still discernible in Gersaint's advice.[7] Moreover, both men could have claimed to have viewed as many outstanding collections as all but the most widely-traveled connoisseur, certainly to have seen more Netherlandish paintings (and, in the case of LeBrun, possibly also Spanish) than any connoisseur in Paris.

The contrast with dealers who also held sales in Amsterdam and London could not have been greater. Auctioneering in those two cities was professional but did not imply a more than superficial knowledge of the goods being offered. Possibly the leading auctioneer in late-seventeenth century London, for example, openly disclaimed such knowledge, while, as Koenraad Jonckheere has noted in his essay in this volume, the attributions of even the most prominent of Amsterdam dealers were scoffed at by true art lovers in the early decades of the eighteenth century.[8] Similar tension – acknowledged mutual need, but distrust – characterized dealer-connoisseur relations in London until well into the eighteenth century.[9] However, since the knowledge gap that distinguished the connoisseur from the average dealer in London and Amsterdam was virtually obliterated by Gersaint and LeBrun, the relationship between them and the connoisseurs could proceed on a different footing, one of mutual acceptance and something approaching respect.

The second difference is that Gersaint and LeBrun, unlike earlier dealers in London and Amsterdam, developed sophisticated selling strategies that they applied to new collectors. As already noted in the case of Gersaint, this introduced a second, non-competitive, group alongside the connoisseurs. That feature allowed our two dealers to go beyond promoting paintings exclusively by offering an attribution or asserting superior quality, practices that had made their predecessors easy targets for connoisseurs. As Koenraad Jonckheere also shows, earlier dealers made attributions stripped of nuance. They stressed desired and well-known masters, or deployed the family name in cases where there were several artists in a family, appealing to name brand rather than trying to distinguish whether the work was by father or son, an original, a copy, 'circle of', and so on, as is now common. They left it up to connoisseurs to make more accurate distinctions. That connoisseurs were not fixated on attribution – they also valued provenance and, of course, quality – only made the dealers' presentations seem clumsier still, even if, empirically, paintings presented as superior often did reach higher prices in a sale.

Gersaint, however, as noted, distanced himself from mere attribution and inferring quality from price; instead he stressed comparative assessments of quality and the grounds on which these rested. LeBrun published more specific information on provenance, and he added past sales prices. This helped shift the balance of information and power: his citing of past prices was an appeal to a market consensus on value, making it more difficult for connoisseurs to deny its relevance. Even more importantly, he used price increases to encourage new collectors to regard paintings as a reliable investment. Success in this endeavor would have enlarged the market; hence connoisseurs who disdained the market's judgement increasingly risked appearing out of touch. Dealer-auctioneers such as Gersaint and LeBrun thus put connoisseurs on notice that their disputes and their voices perhaps no longer mattered most.

A feature of these dealer-auctioneers' promotional efforts that we will stress is that their sales were more transparent than anything seen in the past. This too put individual connoisseurs at a disadvantage. It is the individual connoisseur who is our focus in this because, while connoisseurs as a group might be willing to share their knowledge and judgements concerning, say authorship,[10] in a sale situation they are competitors.[11] If an auctioneer reveals all that is known about provenance, attribution and condition, this dilutes the private knowledge of any one bidder and correspondingly lessens the chance that the hammer price of a lot will be below the true (informed market consensus) value. On this, see further the section on transparency below. And if individual connoisseurs – those most likely to possess information about attribution, etc. – are weakened as bidders, the market consensus acquires greater credibility, thereby further restricting the ability of connoisseurs as a group to challenge market forces.

From here on we will concentrate on the major innovations made by LeBrun, emphasizing the ways in which his promotional strategies were an advance on those of Gersaint.[12] We do not aim at completeness. In particular, we neglect LeBrun's roles in re-shaping thinking on museum design and the formation and display of collections, which have been admirably treated by others.[13] Our coverage of LeBrun's catalogues, moreover, is partial. The LeBrun record as a whole is enormous: his career spanned five decades and his known auction catalogues alone total at least 172, according to the Getty Provenance Index, while his buying trips abroad numbered 43 by 1802. We are familiar with 85 catalogues, based on their availability. From this group we have studied 21, chosen to include (i) sales with price annotations and buyers' names; (ii) some sales known to have been compiled by Lebrun himself; and (iii) collections of persons linked to finance as well as those of aristocrats. One was included especially because (iv) it survives together with, for each day of the sale, a *feuille de vacation*, giving the actual order of lots. Our selected catalogues cover the period 1763-1784.[14]

Following a short and obviously incomplete biographical sketch, we will proceed through five topics, as follows, emphasizing in each case a contrast with or extension of Gersaint's marketing strategies: the information LeBrun included in his catalogues; his techniques for squeezing more revenue out of a sale; his emphasis on paintings as assets rather than as collectibles exclusively; his exposure of new artists; and his internationalizing of auction sales.

LeBrun, like his father, also Pierre, was trained as a painter. In his own view, however, he 'had not enough talent to become a great painter' and turned instead to the business of art.[15] He supplied and was keeper of the paintings of the king's brother, the Comte d'Artois, later known as Charles X, and of the Duc d'Orléans. In the 1770s, he acquired a house (Hôtel de Lubert) in the Rue de Cléry, where he kept many of his masterpieces, certain of which Louise-Elisabeth Vigée-Lebrun (1755-1842) was allowed to copy.[16] The two were married on 11 January 1776, but he asked her to keep the marriage secret for the moment because he had promised to marry the daughter of a Dutch art dealer with whom he had ongoing business deals.[17] By 1778, the Hôtel de Lubert had become the setting for the most fashionable gatherings in pre-Revolutionary Paris. Vigée-Lebrun became painter to Marie-Antoinette and hosted her own celebrated salon.

Information and transparency

Gersaint, as noted, held the conviction that anyone could become a lover of paintings through exposure and instruction. He therefore prepared catalogues that were long and discursive and in which readers could find a basis for assessing the relative merits of particular artists. Even more practically, he encouraged would-be collectors to trust their senses: to pick out paintings which for them combined similar pleasure-yielding effects, independent of price and whether the artist was known or unknown. He would advise as to whether the paintings in such clusters were acceptable for a credible collection, at which point a prospective buyer might go on to select that subset which provided equal pleasure per unit cost (the likely price at a forthcoming auction). Then, at the actual sale, he or she could bid for the one or ones that were affordable (i.e., within their budget).[18] Gersaint introduced viewing periods prior to sales, when potential buyers could engage others in discussing the paintings that appealed to them or perhaps overhear the judgements of others. And, to further encourage participation by the unpracticed, he eschewed private sales of items in conjunction with an auction, and adopted the 'English' or ascending, open-outcry bidding method, which conveyed important information to bidders, even as a sale progressed.[19]

These innovations simplified choice for the novice, potentially lessened their fears, and gave assurance to participants that they were being treated fairly. Such changes all count as moves toward increasing what in modern parlance would be called transparency. The modern economic theory of auctions treats transparency primarily as an information issue and suggests that sharing all information is the auctioneer's best strategy for maximizing sales receipts. Not to do so runs the following risk. If, in a sale, knowing (and known to be knowing) bidders seem to be holding back on a particular lot, others begin to suspect that there must be something negative about it that has been revealed to some but not to them. They too therefore hold back, in which case the lot is likely to be knocked down at a hammer price below its full market value.[20] There have been counterarguments put forward, specifically for maintaining secret reserves;[21] but this remains a persuasive general line of thinking.

Information may be restricted to information about the condition of a lot, but it can also include its provenance, and realized prices in past auctions. As shown in the page (fig. 1, below) from a 1749 catalogue, Gersaint offered his readers discursive commentaries on selected lots,[22] but it was left to LeBrun to impart provenances and price histories. Thus, LeBrun, in a page from the sales catalogue of the Collection of the Comte de Vaudreuil in 1784 (fig. 2), under the entry for a *Peasant Feast/ fête flamande* by Teniers, mentions both its provenance as well as the prices it fetched at two previous sales.[23] This painting was one of the many paintings by Teniers owned by the Comtesse de Verrue. It passed into the Lempereur collection for 10,001 livres, then sold, in 1773, to Randon de Boisset for 9,999 livres.[24] By mentioning the pedigree of these well-known art collectors and the high and sustained prices fetched in previous sales, LeBrun made it clear that this was both an important painting and one which would hold its value. In 1784, the painting sold for 1,001 livres more than in its last appearance at auction. Whether the work's distinguished provenance and the fact that it had held its value had anything to do with this cannot be determined from the catalogue alone, but the information cannot have hurt. Gersaint, by contrast (fig. 2), gave information about a painting: size, chiefly, but occasionally something more, such as where a painting fell within the career of the artist or one of the collections it had been in. And he added his qualitative assessment of it, but without giving its full provenance or price history.

What possible advantage could there be in disclosing past price history? This is as yet a lightly researched area; however, in stable market conditions such disclosure should assist buyers and sellers to move more quickly towards prices close to the truemarket (i.e., informed consensus) value of the lots on offer. This saves bidders at an auction from making exploratory bids in relative ignorance, just to test the market. Some of those are likely to be inappropriate, which could prove costly; and whether they are too high or too low may result in a winning bid that differs from the true (consensus) market price. Auctioneers themselves also gain from avoiding this: there should be fewer unexpectedly high winning bids but also fewer buy-ins (low bids that fail to reach the reserve). Buy-ins entail costs, both direct and in terms of opportunities lost, to vendor and auctioneer alike.

With transparency, participation is likely to increase, and the bidding to become more honest, generating truer values, which means higher sales revenue and a larger commission for the dealer-auctioneer. But the auctioneer-dealer who discloses all of the known information also gains at the expense of competing auctioneer-dealers who do not disclose, since if bidding is more open buyers (and sellers) would probably gravitate towards the more transparent auctions since they are more efficient: true market prices are reached more quickly *and at lower cost* (because fewer inappropriate exploratory bids are likely).

There is some empirical support for the faster movement of prices towards true market valuations where there is disclosure of price history,[25] while the notion that disclosing dealer-auctioneers can use disclosure as an alternative to price competition with

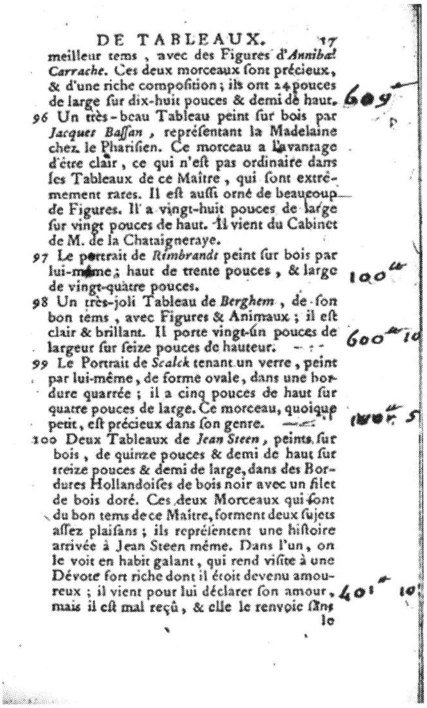

DE TABLEAUX. 17

meilleur tems, avec des Figures d'*Annibal Carrache*. Ces deux morceaux sont précieux, & d'une riche composition; ils ont 24 pouces de large sur dix-huit pouces & demi de haut.

96 Un très-beau Tableau peint sur bois par *Jacques Bassan*, représentant la Madelaine chez le Pharisien. Ce morceau a l'avantage d'être clair, ce qui n'est pas ordinaire dans les Tableaux de ce Maître, qui sont extrêmement rares. Il est aussi orné de beaucoup de Figures. Il a vingt-huit pouces de large sur vingt pouces de haut. Il vient du Cabinet de M. de la Chataigneraye.

97 Le portrait de *Rembrandt* peint sur bois par lui-même; haut de trente pouces, & large de vingt-quatre pouces.

98 Un très-joli Tableau de *Berghem*, de son bon tems, avec Figures & Animaux; il est clair & brillant. Il porte vingt-un pouces de largeur sur seize pouces de hauteur.

99 Le Portrait de *Scalck* tenant un verre, peint par lui-même, de forme ovale, dans une bordure quarrée; il a cinq pouces de haut sur quatre pouces de large. Ce morceau, quoique petit, est précieux dans son genre.

100 Deux Tableaux de *Jean Steen*, peints sur bois, de quinze pouces & demi de haut sur treize pouces & demi de large, dans des Bordures Hollandoises de bois noir avec un filet de bois doré. Ces deux Morceaux qui sont du bon tems de ce Maitre, forment deux sujets assez plaisans; ils représentent une histoire arrivée à Jean Steen même. Dans l'un, on le voit en habit galant, qui rend visite à une Dévote fort riche dont il étoit devenu amoureux; il vient pour lui déclarer son amour, mais il est mal reçû, & elle le renvoie sans

le

1.

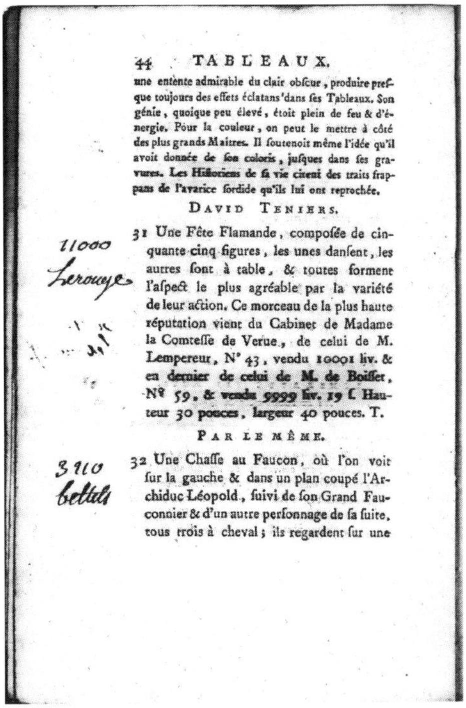

44 TABLEAUX.

une entente admirable du clair obscur, produire presque toujours des effets éclatans dans ses Tableaux. Son génie, quoique peu élevé, étoit plein de feu & d'énergie. Pour la couleur, on peut le mettre à côté des plus grands Maitres. Il soutenoit même l'idée qu'il avoit donnée de son coloris, jusques dans ses gravures. Les Historiens de sa vie citent des traits frappans de l'avarice sordide qu'ils lui ont reprochée.

DAVID TENIERS.

31 Une Fête Flamande, composée de cinquante cinq figures, les unes dansent, les autres sont à table, & toutes forment l'aspect le plus agréable par la variété de leur action. Ce morceau de la plus haute réputation vient du Cabinet de Madame la Comtesse de Verue, de celui de M. Lempereur, N° 43, vendu 10001 liv. & en dernier de celui de M. de Boisset, N° 59, & vendu 9999 liv. 19 f. Hauteur 30 pouces, largeur 40 pouces. T.

PAR LE MÊME.

32 Une Chasse au Faucon, où l'on voit sur la gauche & dans un plan coupé l'Archiduc Léopold, suivi de son Grand Fauconnier & d'un autre personnage de sa suite, tous trois à cheval; ils regardent sur une

2.

Figures 1-2. Page from a sales catalogue (left) of an assortment of paintings brought together by E. F. Gersaint, in 1749, and a page of the LeBrun sales catalogue (right) of the Collection of the Comte de Vaudreuil in 1784, showing both provenances and prices fetched at auction of David Teniers' *Fête Flamande* (lot no. 31).

rivals gains some currency from the impression that LeBrun was regarded as a high price dealer-auctioneer: he could afford to be if his auctions were more attractive because they were more 'efficient'.[26]

LeBrun, like Gersaint, publicized his sales in the *Mercure de France*, as well as the *Journal de Paris* and the *Journal des Arts, des Sciences et de la Litérature*. This was the case, for instance, with the high profile sale in April 1811 of paintings acquired in Switzerland, Flanders, and Holland (collections M.M. Smeth, Clément de Jongh, and Robert de Bale).[27] In contrast to Gersaint, however, LeBrun paid more attention to visualization. In March 1810, for example, the sales catalogue of paintings acquired on a trip to Spain, the south of France and Italy, was accompanied by two volumes with illustrated engravings, a major improvement on the Gersaint catalogue.[28]

LeBrun also appears to have carefully chosen the sequence of clusters (by national school) in which lots were actually offered (see tables 1 and 2 and appendix 1). Sequencing is normally associated with a perceived need to start strong and inject quality paintings at various points when momentum might otherwise be lost. Such moves are deliberate but not manipulative. They do not decrease the amount of information shared and involve no reduction in transparency; they simply represent a more active exploitation of the possibilities for maximizing prices. We shall return to this in the third section, 'Techniques for squeezing revenue out of sales'.

Paintings as asset

LeBrun showed a keen awareness that paintings might be investment assets as well as giving aesthetic satisfaction; but, in an unprecedented move, he also linked these two via the common denominator pleasure. This is expressed in very interesting language in his introduction of the Poullain sale in 1780. In a section on '*la valeur réelle et mercantile des tableaux et sculptures*' – in modern terminology, on the intrinsic and exchange value of paintings and sculpture – LeBrun writes:[29] 'Whether one buys from taste or speculation, it is comforting to know that during one's lifetime the pleasures of ownership will not be troubled by the fear of losing money ... An owner has the advantage, always desired by a responsible man, of enjoying his wealth and seeing it increase ...'[30]

Behind this lays the following extended line of reasoning, based on various remarks by LeBrun.[31] The value of fine paintings rests not solely on their merit but also on their rarity. The number of excellent painters is very small to begin with, and the number of their works is always being reduced, by accident and misuse. Moreover, the rarity of excellent paintings is absolute, in the sense that no two are the same. This unique feature, along with increased wealth and the spread of taste, and a declining supply, makes the market value of fine paintings more secure than that of other collectibles. Moreover, one may take comfort in the fact that fine paintings always increase in price. Hence, even if it is necessary to go into debt to acquire such paintings, one's pleasure in ownership is untrammeled by the fear that one might suffer capital loss.

On the face of it there is an unjustified claim slipped in here: LeBrun could not guarantee that the prices of paintings would always increase. This is clear even from the case of the famous Teniers *fête flamande*, discussed earlier. Prior to its resale for a record price in 1784 it had gone through a period when it merely held its value. Paintings may hold their value when that of other financial assets decline; but, if, as recent research shows, the prices of paintings, broadly speaking, move up and down with perceived financial wealth, then either inflation, which reduces the real value of wealth held in the form of bonds, or a collapse of stock prices, will tend to be followed by a pause or slump in the art market.[32] Political events, moreover, can serve as the catalyst that destroys financial wealth. A knowledge of sixteenth-century inflation, royal disavowals of debt obligations in the past, and the stock price bubble and collapse of 1719-1720, should have warned French investors not to presume that a sustained rise in prices, such as paintings appeared to be undergoing when LeBrun wrote so optimistically, would necessarily continue, LeBrun's argument based on scarcity and uniqueness notwithstanding.

Thus LeBrun's statement is probably better read as saying that the owner of paintings, *at the present time*, has a reasonable expectation of enjoying a price increase. That would take care of the speculative motive he mentions; for the speculator does not buy to hold but to turn a profit by buying and selling again quickly. Even so, however, LeBrun's argument works only if he was assuming that the pleasures of owning fine paintings are real, considerable and assured, even if the guarantee against temporary price declines was not, as it could not be, iron clad. It is interesting that he does, in fact, speak of the pleasures of ownership during one's lifetime.

What are the pleasures of ownership? There is, on the one hand, the enjoyment of viewing. On the other, there is also an accrual of user-value which comes from enhanced knowledge about and understanding of paintings, one's own and those of others. This user-value grows; it thus results in a sort of acquired personal cultural or connoisseurial capital. The first of these pleasures is a flow, the second too, though it accumulates into a stock. Both, in any case, are perks that depend on the ownership of paintings, not on their market value. Hence these pleasures can go on flowing, and in the case of the second, growing, as a form of pleasure accruing to owners of paintings, independently of what market prices do. That could not be said of any other form of investment back then, save perhaps in well-placed land.

Whether we should understand that LeBrun considered knowledge about paintings as a form of subjective wealth (private cultural capital) transferred gradually to an owner, in addition to the flow of viewing pleasure paintings provide, is of course moot. He speaks of a 'natural increment' in the value of fine paintings due to the spread of taste and the growth of wealth. The expression parallels contemporary Physiocratic views on agricultural economy. According to the Physiocrats the annual harvest or value added is partly consumed and in part re-invested as seed-capital. Consuming grain is akin to viewing pleasure and seed capital analogous to cultural capital. This does not settle the issue as to what exactly LeBrun intended. However, he does seem to have adopted a single index – subjective pleasure – to describe both the pleasures of owning fine paintings and the 'comfort' that comes from knowing that their prices will, on the whole, increase. Linking, as this does, both the financial investment aspect of paintings and the direct pleasures from owning them, was a novel move; it took him a step beyond Gersaint, who stressed the availability of the latter to everyone instead. Others prior to LeBrun, of course, knew the intrinsic value-market value distinction; but within the connoisseurial tradition it was generally insisted that the two be kept apart.[33]

Note that LeBrun was hardly the first to acknowledge the role of commercial interests as a force in the art market. Buyers in the Dutch market in the first half of the seventeenth century were predominantly merchants, and they were also central in the early days of the London market, starting in the late 1680s.[34] It was novel, however, for a dealer-auctioneer to actively court merchants and financiers. The list of names involved here is impressive. Financiers to whom LeBrun sold include De Boullongne, de Beaujon, Jombert de Montigny, Legendre and Tronchin (a Swiss). Fellow dealers among his buyers (whether acting on their own behalf or as agent) include Léger, Lange, Basan, Boileau, Desmaretz, Donjeux, Dulac, Dubois, Feuillet, Langlier, Le Rouge, Paillet, Quesne (or Quenet), Rémy, Servat, and Sollier. [35] Some of these no doubt were acting for merchants or financiers.

Techniques for squeezing additional revenue out of sales

Here we look at some of the ways in which LeBrun modified the Gersaint auction not, to repeat, by lessening transparency, but by sustaining bidder interest and enhancing the momentum or mood of expectation (of higher prices) in a sale.

We noted earlier that Gersaint separated private sales from his auctions, probably to create the appearance of fairness. If private sales are allowed to intrude on an open outcry auction, favors can be done. An auctioneer can maintain pretence that a bidding sequence is real, when in fact a pre-determined buyer and price has already been selected; to that buyer at a certain point, the auctioneer peremptorily knocks down a lot for a fictitious price. It might appear that these types of action could harm an auctioneer, but relationships and tradeoffs are involved which make that unlikely in the longer run. The point in any case is that lack of clarity, even a suspicion of favoritism, will deter participation, especially on the part of novices.

LeBrun, like Gersaint, printed catalogues, but he also printed *vacation* sheets (appendix 1), indicating the actual order in which lots would be brought forward, a new sheet for each day of a sale. These sheets superseded the printed catalogue as to the order in which paintings would be presented, though, in many cases, LeBrun also used them to remind participants of the collections a painting had graced – to give abbreviated pedigrees – and to mention the prices fetched by those same paintings at past sales. As such, they maintained and even enhanced transparency, whilst also serving as promotional aids.

LeBrun's *vacation* sheets reveal his close attention to the way lots were grouped and ordered. They also reveal a preferred ordering that may be at odds with what Koenraad Jonckheere has found for Dutch sales in the early eighteenth century, where the most costly paintings always appeared in the beginning of a catalogue, though paintings were not necessarily auctioned according to the catalogue numbers.[36] LeBrun imposed an invariable general order by national school: Italian paintings first, followed by Netherlandish, with French last. Tables 1 and 2 summarize the sequential orders for two sales, one of which is fully transcribed in appendix 1. Note that the order holds not just for the sale as a whole but for each day of the proceedings. Moreover, as charts 1-5, for the first of these sales (the Poullain), confirm, the average price paid for the middle group, the Netherlandish, was distinctly higher than for the opening and closing groups, the Italian and French. There are exceptions for individual lots: two paintings by Lorrain (lot 104) and one by J.B. Santerre (lot 110) from the collection of Augustin Blondel de Gagny (1695-1776), financier and *Intendant des Menus-Plaisirs*, whose collection was perhaps the best known in Paris;[37] and an *Adam and Eve* by Francois F. Le Moyne (lot 114) from the collection of the Prince de Conti (1717-1776). However, the rule is as shown by the charts.

Table 1. Numbers and distribution of paintings offered by national origin over the first five days of a six-day auction, Poullain collection, starting 15 March 1780.

Source: *Lebrun sale (Poullain*, Paris, 1780).

Table 1. Numbers and distribution of paintings offered by national origin over the first five days of a six-day auction, Poullain collection, starting 15 March 1780.

Actual order of lots	Day 1	Day 2	Day 3	Day 4	Day 5
1) Italian	3	4	4	3	3
2) Netherlandish	16	16	18	19	16
3) French	5	5	3	5	5
TOTAL	24	25	25	27	24

Table 2. Numbers and distribution of paintings offered by national origin over the first five days of a six-day auction, Véron Collection, starting 11 December 1784.

Source: *Catalogue d'une belle collection de tableaux des trois Ecoles; Dessins, Estampes, miniatures, Terre cuites, Bronzes, Porcelaines, Laques, Bijoux, Piere gravés et autres objects de Curiosité; par J. B. P. Lebrun* (Paris, 1784)

Table 2. Numbers and distribution of paintings offered by national origin over the first five days of a six-day auction, Véron Collection, starting 11 December 1784.

Actual order of lots	Day 1	Day 2	Day 3	Day 4	Day 5
1) Italian	5	7	4	4	4
2) Netherlandish	24	22	23	23	22
3) French	11	13	12	13	13
TOTAL	40	42	39	40	39

Tables 1 and 2 also show that the Italian and French offerings were very few. They ranged from three to seven and three to 13, combining both sales, whereas the Netherlandish paintings were much more numerous, 16 to 24.[38] In both the Poullain sale and the sale of the Véron collection, LeBrun maintained a roughly constant total of lots for each day: about 25 lots (Poullain) and 40 (Véron), the implied time per lot perhaps reflecting the relative excellence of the paintings in each collection.

Charts 1-5: Poullain sales results over five days: order of lots and groupings (Italian-Netherlandish-French) from each day's feuille de vacation: order (x-axis); prices fetched (y-axis).

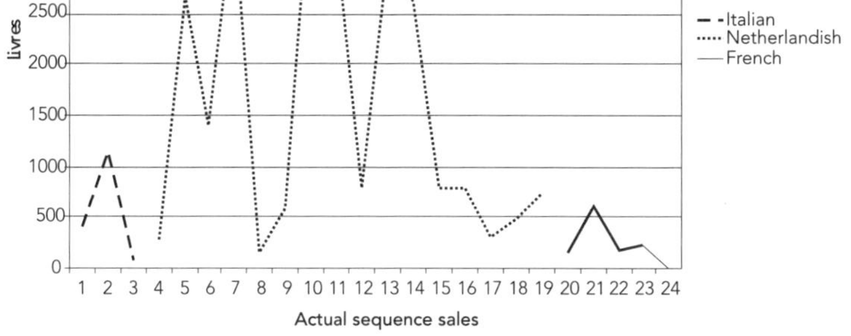

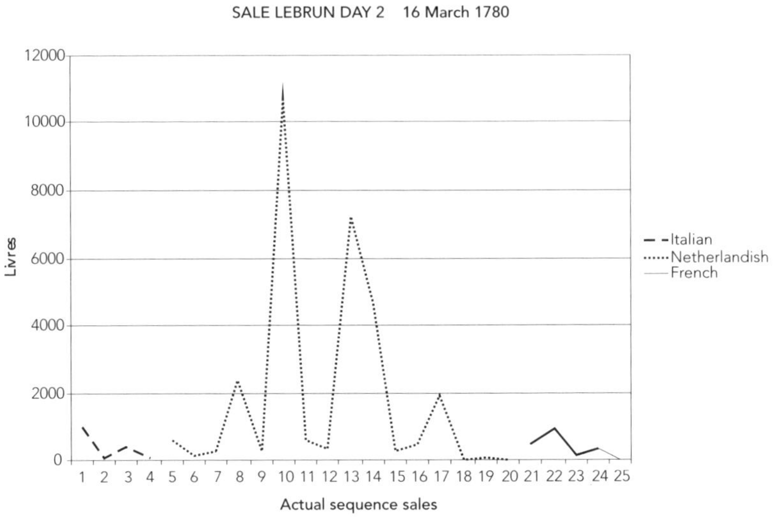

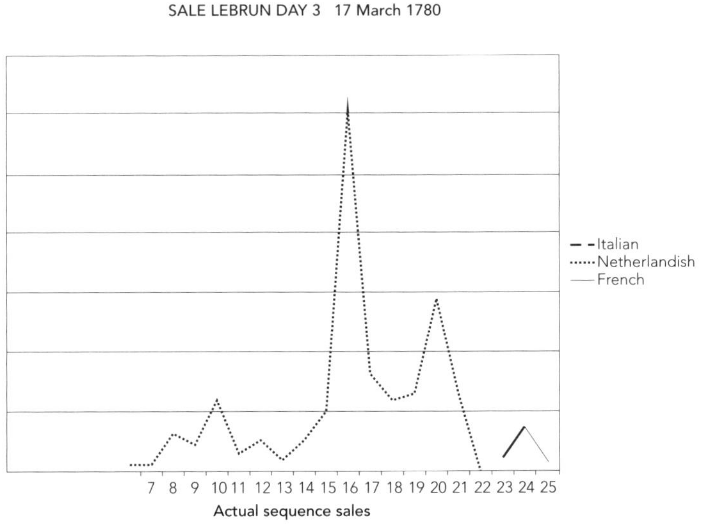

As noted earlier, LeBrun's deliberate grouping and ordering of the lots was not part of a deception. On the contrary, he was quite up-front about what he was doing. Moreover, it is probable that buyers were actually more pleased with his practice; it allowed them to attend and stay only for the lots that interested them.

Did the information LeBrun offered on provenance and sales history, and the attention he paid to the order in which lots were offered actually pay off? An answer might be given if we had a sale actually put together by him, the paintings all having been acquired by him, and we knew the costs of those purchases as well as the sale outcome. If, in such a sale, there was a striking increase in prices compared to what

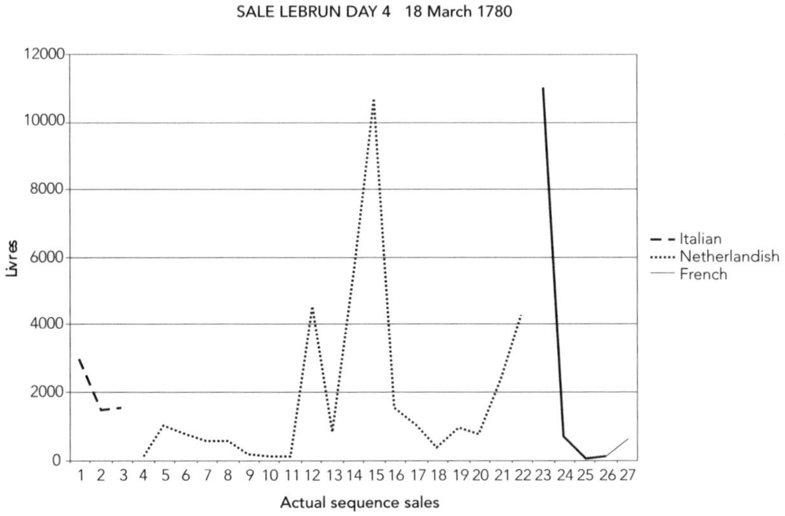

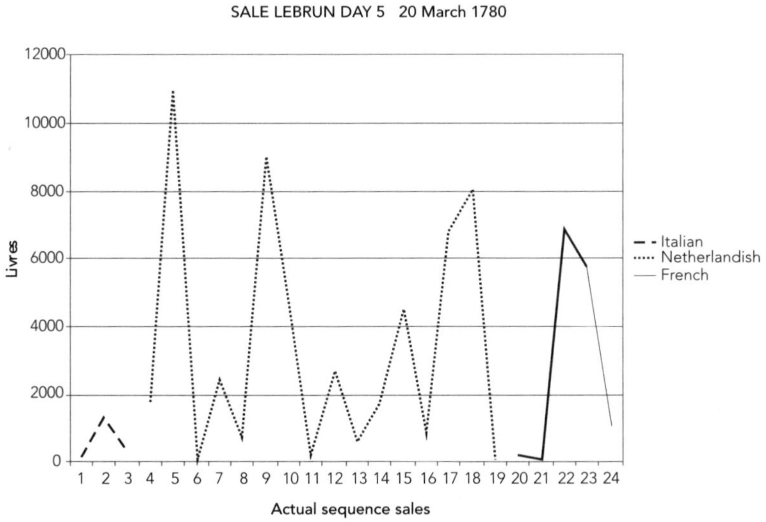

LeBrun had paid, and, more telling, relative to the market as a whole in that period, we might have reason to think his sharing, promotional technique and careful management of the order of the sale, had something to do with this. Unfortunately, there are still too many variables involved – quality and other specificities of the paintings, who attended and actually bid, and so on – to draw any conclusions. Such a 'controlled' test would have to be repeated, over time and across various collections of paintings, before it told us much of anything. And we do not yet have a sales index for the Paris market as a whole at the time. That said, it is nonetheless of some interest to look at an instance that comes close to our conditions.

The Vaudreuil collection, sold in 1784, is one that LeBrun had helped put together.[39] The sale was voluntary, unlike those held after a death. Moreover, since Vaudreuil was in dire straits, having lost his plantations in Saint Domingue, it is likely that LeBrun composed and sequenced it to yield maximum profits for his client (and himself). The sale appears to have been set up to be in line with prevailing buyer preferences, which LeBrun would have known. Once again, Netherlandish paintings dominated, generating 76 percent of the sales revenue.

LeBrun also knew that at this sale his rival Paillet would bid on behalf of d'Angivillers (thus for the crown); and Paillet was in fact the highest bidder on many of the paintings at the sale.[40] Knowing one's bidders' intentions and financial backers helps an auctioneer create positive momentum and good prices. And publishing both provenances and sales histories contributes useful material for the patter. In this sale, there were 31 paintings whose catalogue entries recorded information of both sorts, and where positive gains had been registered at their last appearance at auction. The three collections and sales results most mentioned in the pedigrees were those of Randon de Boisset (Rémy, 1777), Blondel de Gagny (Rémy, 1776) and Louis-Francois de Bourbon, Prince de Conti (Rémy, 1777), at whose sale no less than 760 paintings were offered.[41]

Tables 3 and 4 show that 21 of these 31 paintings increased in price immediately after the sales (on average 1,494 livres). The other 10 registered losses (on average 1,063 livres). That the number of paintings registering gains exceeded the number registering losses by two to one would seem to confirm that LeBrun's overall knowledge and strategizing worked exactly as we would expect. However, the case is not so clear. Some prior sales might have been to an intermediary, possibly even LeBrun himself. It was not at all uncommon for dealers to outnumber collectors at a sale, though the exact mix is impossible to determine since it is never clear whether a dealer was buying for himself or acting as an agent. Since we also do not know LeBrun's or any other dealer's transactions costs , all we can say concerning such instances is that the auction price difference does not necessarily represent net gain. Moreover, it is a problem that we do not possess a Mei and Moses-type all-Paris auction price index for the period, or indexes for sub-markets (Netherlandish paintings, French, etc.).[42] All we can say, therefore, is that LeBrun remained in business for 40 years, so there is a presumption that he made profits; that, and the likelihood that, whatever his gain, it probably would have been less had he been less astute.

Table 3. Price increases of 21 paintings with prior record in the Vaudreuil sale of 1784

% GAIN	LOT	ORIGIN	SUBJECT	AUTHOR	PREVIOUS COLLECTION 1	PREVIOUS COLLECTION 2	PRICE 1	PRICE 2	LEBRUN PRICE	CHANGED MARKET VALUE
88	53	D	Une prairie	Potter	(Julienne) Choiseul (72)	Prince Conty (371)	8,001	9,530	18,000	+8,470
78	66	D	Vue de Schveling	A W Van de Velde	Prince Conty (413)	Trouard (114)	5,072	3,800	6,801	+3,001
75	12	I	Jupiter et Leda	Mola		Menard (55)		799	1,401	+602
61	72	D	Belle prairie	Karel Dujardin		R. de Boisset (149)		5,500	8,901	+3,401
56	58	D	Portrait de Pinaker	Henri de Vos		R. de Boisset (130)		1,150	1,802	+652
42	26	FL	President Richardot	Van Dyck	Gaignat (16)	R.de Boisset (45)	9,200	10,400	14,840	+4,440
39	10	I	Sainte Famille	Schidone	Prince Carignan (43)	Prince Conty (48)		5,001	7,001	+2,000
30	63	D	Maison Hollandoise	Jan Steen	R. de Boisset (128)	Poulain (77)	1,600	2,600	3,401	+801
25	8	I	Femme couchée	Corregio		Julienne (16)		2,400	3,000	+600
23	82	F	Intérieur chambre	Sébastien Bourdon		Trouard		840	1,040	+200
19	28	D	Philosophes (2)	Rembrandt	de Choiseul	R. de Boisset (49)	14,000	10,900	12,999	+2,099
14	54	D	Chambre de paysans	Kalf		Trouard (122)		700	801	+101
13	47	D	Chasse au Cerf	Wouwerman	De Gagny (111)	D'Azincourt (5)	6,620	7,910	9,000	+1,090
10	31	FL	Fete Flamande	Teniers	(Verrue) Lempereur (43)	R. de Boisset (59)	10,001	9,999	11,000	+1,001
10	36	D	Maitre selon costume du pays	Adrien Van Ostade	(Julienne) Boisset (70)	de Pange (19)	6,610	6,000	6,601	+601
9	41	D	Boutique d'un épicier	Gerard Dou		R. de Boisset (76)		15,500	16,901	+1,401
1.9	44	D	Chymiste dans une chamber	Gabriel Metsu	De Choiseul (21)	Prince Conty (329)	3,200	2,501	3,001	+500
0.8	48	D	Paysage montagneus	Wouwerman		Poulain (57)		3500	3,800	+300
0.4	30	D	Paysages (2)	Rembrandt/Rubens	(Julienne) Choiseul (3)	Prince Conty (291)	2,401	1,720	1,801	+81
0.4	46	D	Paysage	Wynants & Vandevelde	De Gagny (76)	D'Azincourt (14)	1,216	1,040	1,091	+51
0	20	FL	Une des femmes de Rubens	Rubens	R. de Boisset	Live de Jully (6)	18,000	20,000	20,001	+1
										+31,393

Table 4. Price decreases of 10 paintings with prior record in the Vaudreuil sale of 1784

% LOSS	LOT	ORIGIN	SUBJECT	AUTHOR	PREVIOUS COLLECTION 1	PREVIOUS COLLECTION 2	PRICE 1	PRICE 2	LEBRUN PRICE	CHANGED MARKET VALUE
-0.02	1	I	Reconoissance de Laban	Beretinni & Cortona		Prince Conty (21)		36,001	35,901	-100
-0.03	34	FL	Interieur chambre de paysans	Teniers		M. Trouard (97)		1,551	1,499	-52
-0.04	65	D	Paysage /grande riviere	Adrien Van de Velde	Lubbeling Amsterdam	R. de Boisset (136)		20,000	19,910	-90
-0.05	49	D	St Jean dans le desert	Breenberg		R. de Boisset (96)		5,019	4,990	-29
-10.6	79	D	Pendans (2) fruits, fleurs, nis	Jean van Huysum	R. de Boisset (159)	de Boeuf (60)	16,019	17,900	16,001	-1,899
-13	62	D	L'entrée d'une foret	Ruisdael	R. de Boisset (127)	Trouard (130)	899	1,200	1,040	-160
-18	13	E	Vierge & Enfant Jesus	Murillo		R. de Boisset (18)		10,999	9,001	-1,998
-33	6	I	Annonciation & Apparition N.S.	Veronese	Prince Carignan (31)	Prince Conty (104)		3,000	2,000	-1,000
-40	15	E	Saint Joseph	Murillo	M. Nogaret (22)	Prince Conty (163)	901	1,592	953	-639
-88	77	D	Loth & ses filles	Adrien van der Werf	De Choiseul (80)	Prince Conty (469)		5,260	600	-4660
										-10,627

Exposing new artists

Gersaint mostly bought and resold seventeenth-century Netherlandish paintings. LeBrun, on the other hand, saw in the exposure of new artists a way to accustom buyers to emerging currents, a sort of investment to position himself well for the future. He did this in spectacular fashion during the Revolution, when, in effect, he took over the *Exposition de la jeunesse*, previously an outdoor exhibition, offering his own gallery space as an indoor alternative.[43] By 1791, no less than 80 young artists were showing their paintings there.[44] These exhibitions also served as one forum, among others, to promote the 'Dutch revival' or the 'Neo-Dutch' movement in French painting.[45]

Here we see LeBrun engaged in demand-eliciting practices as a player in the primary market, adding this market to his more established activities as dealer and auctioneer in the secondary or resale market. There is a parallel to this, as noted, in that auction houses have recently taken to including first-sale paintings in their auctions in certain segments of the contemporary market, blurring the distinction between the primary and secondary markets. One can think of this move on LeBrun's part as one of several in which he sought to proliferate services and products so as to be able to claim a larger share of the market. Gersaint did much the same. This is a pre-emptive strategy, akin to that undertaken by the modern major producers of breakfast cereals. They proliferate new variants, making it more costly for a new entrant, who cannot expect to enjoy the large-scale advantage in the form of reduced fixed costs per unit sold.

The breakfast cereals analogy in the case of the eighteenth-century Paris paintings market is imperfect. LeBrun did not so much add variant brands of paintings as novel selling techniques for the available brands; though both he and Gersaint literally did introduce a variant brand when they brought to the Paris market and promoted unknown Netherlandish (and in LeBrun's case, Spanish) artists. Thus, if the paintings market is imagined to be represented by a Pie diagram, additional segments of which can be claimed by one operator in the form of novel selling techniques which make it more costly for others to compete, in LeBrun's case we would have to list (1) efficiency through transparency; (2) the paintings-as-asset argument to appeal to investors; (3) support for new artists; and, as we will now see, (4) internationalizing both the sources of paintings and the distribution of sales catalogues; and (5) securing agents to act on his behalf at foreign sales. Paillet matched him in getting involved with young artists,[46] but together, they were probably influential enough that we may consider this a particular joint pre-emptive move.

Internationalizing the auction market

Gersaint's tactic of visiting and buying at sales in Flanders, Brabant and the Dutch Republic for resale in Paris was bold for its time; LeBrun, however, travelled much further afield, acquiring paintings for resale in Spain, Switzerland, and Italy as well as the Low Countries. He also secured agents to act on his behalf in selected locations.

As to the number of his buying trips, in 1802 LeBrun, in a letter to Napoleon, claimed that he had made at least 43 trips abroad to buy paintings.[47] In 1807 and 1808, he traveled to Spain to buy Spanish paintings and introduce them onto the Parisian market, well before the Napoleonic confiscation of art in Granada and Seville had taken place.[48] This was travel and arbitrage on a much grander scale than attempted by Gersaint.[49] Moreover, Lebrun not only bought, but also sold in foreign markets. For example, having successfully bid for Hans Holbein's *Ambassadors* at a Rémy auction in 1787, he exported the painting to England.[50]

LeBrun also at least matched Gersaint in successfully introducing lesser-known or forgotten Netherlandish artists to Paris. Gersaint's triumph was Berchem, while LeBrun is credited with having re-discovered Vermeer.[51]

Paris, towards the end of the eighteenth century, had become the center of the international art trade. In addition to exporting paintings, however, dealers also exported their catalogues. LeBrun's were distributed in Paris, Brussels, Amsterdam and London, as were those of some of his rivals, challenging auctioneers in those cities to respond in kind or become backwaters. His (and some of his rivals') catalogues set a new standard for informativeness that similarly challenged foreign norms.

Conclusion

What does our exploration of innovative dealing in Paris contribute towards a better general understanding of how dealers and connoisseurs interacted in the eighteenth-century?An important distinction has emerged that affects the way we may want to think about connoisseurs. Whereas Koenraad Jonckheere identifies a culture of sharing among connoisseurs in discussions of quality and information relating to provenance and attribution, our own focus on the auction has led us to emphasise instead that connoisseurs, setting aside rings, are necessarily competitors when they act as bidders. Both statements may be true as a matter of behavior, with the context deciding which applies. This may be just another way of noticing that participants in an art market may be driven by several motives, of which pleasure in knowing and conversing with equally knowledgeable people about beautiful objects is one, concern with asset value (and, as part of this, purchase price) another. Absolutists may insist that these two are incompatible; but it seems likely that Amsterdam's and London's merchants and Paris's financiers reflected on the possibility of reconciling them in some way. Using pleasure as a common denominator was tried by Gersaint and with more self-awareness by LeBrun. It might prove fruitful to see if there were written reflections on the problem by some collectors who were both lovers of paintings and practitioners in the pursuit of secure investments and returns on them.

An implication of regarding connoisseurs as competitors in the bidding is that it is not necessarily in their interest to wish for or encourage total transparency on the part of a dealer-auctioneer. Indeed, we have argued that an auctioneer stands to gain at the expense of individual connoisseur-bidders by being more transparent. This is an altogether different locus of tension between dealers and connoisseurs than the ones usually mentioned. Interestingly, it is a clash that the auctioneer is bound to win, precisely because he and other bidders are collectively pitted against a single connoisseur (or any other bidder) who seeks personal gain at a cost to all other participants. The recurrence of pools (US) or bidding rings (UK) in auctions suggests that dealers and other regular bidders must believe that they can gain at the expense of an auctioneer and vendors, provided they are willing to organize. At the same time, in principle, the efficiency gains from transparency can benefit the many at the expense of individual self-seeking bidders; it is just a question of isolating those individuals.

At the very least, our argument supplies an historical hypothesis. If it holds, our argument would suggest that we should have observed the history of the art auction from LeBrun's time onwards to have been one of steadily increasing transparency. Has this occurred, in Paris and elsewhere? Sotheby's and Christie's enjoin their own auctioneers from placing further bids once the bid has reached the (nonetheless undisclosed) reserve. It is now understood that normally the reserve, though undisclosed, will not exceed the low pre-sale estimate. The auction houses guarantee the authenticity of the goods they offer, and indicate whether, according to the best of their knowledge, a painting is an original, a workshop effort, a copy or a painting done by the circle or following of the master. Where possible they provide a paper trail for claimed provenance, though full histories of prior ownership and earlier sale prices are not normally published. Serious and regular buyers can even request that a painting be removed to a special room for technical scrutiny. Broadly speaking, this *is* a history of increasing openness, though the trend does not preclude episodes and instances of deliberate deception and improper practice.

May we also infer, then, that, Paris having led the way in transparency, its own art markets should have expanded more rapidly than others in Western Europe? Unfortunately, getting in the way of a clear answer to this question is the history in France of centralized control over auctions, much of it predating LeBrun and his imitators. The controls in question include the exclusive right, held by state-appointed officials, to make required pre-sale valuations. For a long time, these were influenced by perverse incentives to under-value.[52] Controls also extended to restrictions on who may conduct public auctions. And, most significantly, though this occurs at a later date, they involve the right of the state to pre-empt potentially higher bids on paintings deemed part of the national heritage. Until very recently French auctioneers were also protected against foreign competition. This complex of regulations interferes with any simple test of the role that transparency might have played in the relative growth of the French market.

Three more promising fields for further historical inquiry are the following. First, closer study of the buyers at sales by dealer-auctioneers such as LeBrun, to sort out who among the dealers were buying on own behalf and who for others, and in the latter case, for whom. Second, a study of the buyers at Paris auctions who might be deemed connoisseurs, to record what they bought and paid, relative to lots purchased by bidders of known financial background, to see whether traditional and new buyers really did comprise distinct groups. Third, an examination of eighteenth-century auctions in an international context – Paris, London, Amsterdam, Brussels – to see how integrated the international paintings trade was and which mechanisms enabled it to function.

APPENDIX 1

Paris, 15 March 1780.—Transcription of the 'feuille de vacation' in the back of Catalogue Raissoné des Tableaux, Dessins, estampes, Figures de Bronze & de marbre, & morceaux d'Histoire naturelle, qui composoient le Cabinet de feu M. Poullain, Receveur Général des Domaines du Roi; Suivi d'un Abrégé historique de la Vie des Peintres don't les Ouvrages formoient cette Collection par J.B.P.Le Brun. Le Catalogue des Vases, porcelains, Meubles de Boule, & autres effets précieux, est de Ph.F. Julliot fils (Paris, 1780). Paris, Bibliothèque Doucet, V.P.4b.

Feuille de distribution de la vente de M. Poullain (inserted after p. 162), as follows:

p. [1] Première vacation [DAY 1]. Mercredi 15 Mars 1780

Ecole d'Italie
(1) Perugin; (3) Schidon; (15) F.Solineme

Ecole des Pays Bas
(28) Poelemburg; (38) Rembrandt; (50) Jan Asselijn; (57) Ph. Wouwerman; (58) H. Swanevelt; (61) Pynacker; (64) Berchem; (66) P. Potter (printed 'de Boisset 2420'); (72) F. Moucheron; (79) J. Van der Heyden (printed 'de Gagny 3400'); (83) Karel Dujardin; 85 G Schalcken

p. [2] suite de la première vacation du Mercredi 15 Mars
(92) C. Dusart; (94) Ad. Vander Burg; (96) J. Le Duc; 97 E.Dietricy

Ecole françoise
(109) S. Bourdon; (113) A. Watteau; (120) 2.Lantara; (123) 2.Mayer; (124) Favanne

Dessins sous verre
(129) Boete Lavreince; (130) Norblin
Estampes
(42) Le Bas; (143) Idem

p. [3]
(154) Deux vases d'albâtre; (157) deux vases de marbre blanc; (166) Deux Vases Céladon; (174) Deux pots à l'oeil; (181) Quatre plateaux de saxe; (183) Un pot à lait de Chine; (184) Un gobelet de la Chine; (185) Un grand et un moyen Plat bleu et blan; (191) Un bureau satiné; (196) Une table de Poirier noire; (199) Un serre-papier; (205) Deux chandeliers à fut de colonne; (208) Quatre pierres à papier; (217) Deux plinths de granit; (222) Trois plinthes; (224) Trois plinths; (225) Deux plinths; (227) Deux plinths; (246) Sept loupes et lunettes; (248) Quatre rafoirs; (249-250) Quatre pistolets; (250-254) Plusieurs articles qui seront diverses.

p. [4] Deuxième vacation [DAY 2]. Jeudi 16 Mars

Ecole d'Italie
(6) C. Benedette; (7) Louis Carrache; (12) Maria Crespi; (14) F. Solimene

Ecole des Pays Bas
(20) J. Rottenhammer; (27) C. Poelemburg; (30) J. Breughel; (37) Rembrandt; (48)

Adriaen Ostade; (52) G Metsu; (54) B. Breenberg; (55) Ph. Wouwerman (printed 'de Barry 4000'); (62) J.B.Weenix (printed 'de Boisset 6001'); (65) N. Berchem; (73) F.V. Meulen; (80) J. Vander Heiden; (84) K. Dujardin; (87) G. Berkeyden; (99) Dis de Rembrandt; (101) Tableaux de genre

p. [5]

Ecole françoise
(108) S. Bourdon (printed 'P.de Conti 584'); (112) J. Raoux; (116) J.B.Oudry; (121) Lantara; (125) Baptiste

Dessins sous verre
(135) d'après Mayer; (136) Inconnu; (137) 15 de Moitte
Estampes
(141) Moreau; (146) Bolswert

p. [6] suite de la deuxième vacation du Jeudi 16 Mars

(151) Deux coupes de serpentin; (153) Un vase de vert d'Egypte; (165) Deux petits pots d'ancienne; (172) Deux jattes violettes; (178) Deux petits comets blue turc; (182) Une cafetiere de la Chine; (190) Une armoire à glace; (195) Une table de Poirier; (197) Une table à quatre gaînes; (204) Deux petits chandeliers; (207) Deux paires de bras de couleur; (216) Deux plinths; (218) Deux autres plinths; (219) Deux plinths; (229) Deux plinths; (240) Une boite de carton; (242) Un couteau; (245) Une paire de boutons d'or; (247) un Nécessaire; (253) Six ecrans; (254) Plusieurs articles qui seront divisés

p. [7] Troisième vacation [DAY 3]. Vendredi 17 Mars

Ecole d'Italie
(4) Paul Veronese (printed 'P. de Conti 3000'); (8) Guido; (11) Le Pézarese; (16) Paul Matteis (printed 'P. de Conti 701')

Ecoles des Pays-Bas
(24) Peeter Neefs; (26) 2 C. Poelenburg; (32) J. Jordaens (printed 'de Boisset 2050'); (36) Jean Winants; (39) Albert Cuyp; (41) G. Terburg; (42) Both & Poelenburg; (45) D.Teniers; (47) Ad. Ostade; (49) Is. Ostade; (53) Barth Breenberg; (56) Ph.Wouwerman (printed 'de Boisset 10660'); (74) F.Van Mieris; (75) Gasper Netscher (printed 'de Boisset 1598'); (77) J.Steen (printed 'de Boisset 1600')

p. [8] suite de la troisième vacation du Vendredi 17 Mars

(82) G. de Layresse; (91) P. Van der Werf (printed 'de Brunoy 2. 6001'); (98) D Rickaert

Ecole Françoise
(103) Le Nain; (107) S.Bourdon; (122) Lantara

Dessins sous verre
(131) Ph.Caresme; (133) Moreth; (138) 18 Moitte
Estampes
(144) Balechou; (145) Daullé

p. [9] Suite de la troisième vacation du Vendredi 17 Mars

(152) Deux vases de granit rose; (156) Deux vases de prime verte; (161) Un enfant

d'yvoire; (171) Deux coupes violettes; (173) Deux coqs d'ancien blanc; (176) Deux vases de chine; (177) Trois urnes blue Turc; (186) Une casolette de laque; (189) un piedestal de marquetterie; (194) Un Chiffonier; (198) Un Bureau de Poirier noirci; (203) Deux Girandoles; (206) Deux pieds de bronze doré; (211) un table de marbre blance; (223) Deux plinths; (226) Deux autres plinths; (230) Deux Socles; (235) Une bague; (237) Une autre bague; (239) Une Tabatière d'écaille; (254) Plusieurs Articles, qui seront divisé.

p. [10] Quatrième vacation [DAY 4]. Samedi 18 Mars

Ecole Italienne
(5) Alex Veronese (printed 'P. de Conti 3470'); (10) F Albani (printed 'de Boisset 1500'); (13) F. Solimene (printed 'de Boisset 1400')

Ecole des Pays-Bas
(17) Albert Durer; (19) J. Rottenhammer; (23) P.P. Rubens; (25) 2.C. Poelemburg; (29) J. Breugel; (31) H. Stenwich; (31*bis)* Idem; (40) 2. G. Terburg (printed 'de Gagny 3902'); (44) D. Teniers; (46) Ad. Ostade (printed 'P. de Conti 7000'); (52) G. Dow (printed 'de Boisset 8999'); (59) C. Bega; (60) G. Van Eeckout; (63) N. Berchem; (68) L. Backuisen; (71) Fréd. Moucheron

p. [11] suite de la quatrième vacation du Samedi 18 Mars

(78) J.Steen; (86) G. Schalcken (printed on the leaflet 'P. de Conti 2. 2302'); (90) Ad. Vander Werf (printed 'de Brunoy 2.6001')

Ecole françoise
(104) 2.C. Lorrain (printed 'de Gagny 11904'); (105) Blachard; (111) J.B.Santerre; (117) F.Casanova; (119) Casanova frère

Dessins sous verre
(126) J. Breughel; (128) Weirotter; (132) Moreau
Estampes
(139) Porporati; (140) Ryland

p. [12] suite de la quatrième vacation du Samedi 18 Mars

(147) Deux vases de porphire; (149) Deux futs de porphire; (155) Deux vases de prime verte; (160) Une figure de bronze; (162) Deux bouteilles d'ancienne; (164) Deux drageoirs; (170) Deux bouteilles bues; (175) Un vase fond rouge; (187) Un bureau de marquetterie; (193) Une Encoignure; (200) Un luster de Bohème; (202) Une paire de bras; (210) Une table de granit rose; (213) Une plinthe de porphire; (215) Trois Plinthes; (220) Trois autres plinthes; (221) Deux plinthes; (234) Une bague de rubis; (236) Une autre bague; (241) Une canne de jet; (244) Un crayon d'or; (254) Plusieurs articles, qui seront divisés

p. [13] Cinquième vacation [DAY 5]. Lundi 20 Mars

Ecole Italienne
(2) Carlo Maratti; (9) F. Albane (printed 'P. de Conti 3710'); (18) P.Brill

Ecole des Pays-Bas
(21) Ad. Elsheymer; (22) P.P.Rubens; (33) L.C.Van Uden; (34) Ant Van Dyck(printed

'de Brunoy 6000'); (35) Jan Miel; (43) D. Teniers (printed 'de Gagny 11000'); (51) G. Dow; (67) W. Kalf; (69) G. Vanden Velde (printed 'P. de Conti 3151'); (70) Kapel; (76) G. Netscher; (81) Ad. Vanden Velde; (88) C. de Moor; (89) G. Mieris (printed 'de Boisset 6000'); (93) J. Van Huysum (printed 'de Gagny 8000'); (100) Manière de Brauwer

p. [14] suite de la cinquième vacation du Lundi 20 Mars
(102) J. Callot; 106 P. Patel; (110) J.B. Santerre (printed 'de Gagny 3215'); (114) F. Le Moyne (printed 'P. de Conti 6999'); (115) J.B. Pater

Dessins sous verre
(127) P.P. Rubens (printed 'P. de Conti 152'); (134) Six dessins

p. [15] Suite de la cinquième vacation du lundi 20 Mars
(148) Deux futs de porphire; (150) deux vases vert antique; (158) Une coupe de jaspe; (159) Deux figures de bronze; (163) Deux jattes a huit pans; (168) Deux urnes couleur lapis; (169) Deux panniers bleus; (179) Deux bouteilles de Saxe; (188) Deux armoired ed marquetterie; (192) Une table d'acajou; (201) Un luster de bronze doré; (209) Une table de porphire; (212) Une plinthe de porphire; (214) Deux plinths; (231) Deux plinths; (232) Deux socles; (233) Une montre; (238) Une Boetye d'or ronde satinée; (243) Une piognée d'Epée; (251) Un Clavecin de Ruker; (252) Trois violins & un violoncell; (254) Plusieurs articles qui seront divisés

p. [16] Sixième vacation [DAY 6]. Mardi 21 Mars
L'Histoire Naturelle [nothing specified]

FIN

*The authors wish to thank Anna Tummers for her editorial suggestions, and Isabelle Decobecq for sharing her knowledge of Parisian collections, checking our calculations for some sales other than those reported here, and helping to identify amateurs, dealers and buyers with financial backgrounds among the buyers at Lebrun's sales.

1 This historical relationship is reflected in such classic studies as Francis Haskell, *Patrons and Painters: A Study in the Relations Between Italian Art and Society in the Age of the Baroque*, Oxford 1963. Haskell treated dealers as strictly secondary, judging them worthy of notice only to the extent that the artists they were involved with became significant (read: were noticed by connoisseur-collectors).

2 Krysztof Pomian, *Collectors and Curiosities: Paris and Venice, 1500-1800*, Cambridge 1990, pp.159-160.

3 For Paillet, see J. Edwards, *Alexandre-Joseph Paillet, expert et marchand de tableaux à la fin du XVIIIème siècle*, Paris 1996. On Rémy, see Patrick Michel, 'Pierre Rémy: Peintre et négociant en tableaux, et autres curiosités. Bon connoisseur', in: A. Cavina et al. (eds.), *Mélanges en homage à Pierre Rosenberg*, Paris 2001, pp. 328-337; Sévérine Daroussat, *Pierre Remy*, DEA Université Paris IV-Sorbonne 2000; and François Marandet 'Pierre Remy: the Parisian Art Market in the Mid-eighteenth Century', *Apollo* 152 (2003), pp. 32-42. Basan has been treated by Pierre Caselle, 'Pierre François Basan', *Paris et Ile de France: Mémoires* 23 (1982), pp. 99-185. And on Lebrun, there exists a recent study by Fabienne Camus, *Jean-Baptiste-Pierre Le Brun. Peintre et marchand de tableaux*, Ph.D. Dissertation Université Paris IV-Sorbonne 2000. Unfortunately this dissertation is currently classified as restricted access.

4 On all this, see Neil De Marchi and Hans Van Miegroet, 'Transforming the Paris Art Market, 1718-1750', in: Neil De Marchi and Hans Van Miegroet (eds.), *Mapping Markets for Paintings in Europe, 1450-1750*, Turnhout 2006, pp. 383-402. More specific references to sources for our reconstruction of Gersaint's advice to collectors-in-training are contained in note 18 below.

5 We have discussed the cluster of Italianate landscape producers in Marchi and Van Miegroet, *Transforming the Paris Art Market* (note 4). The peasant festivities cluster is discussed in detail in our *Brueghel in Paris*, available in manuscript.

6 Auction prices for Italian and French versus

Netherlandish paintings are analysed in Hans Van Miegroet, 'Recycling Netherlandish Paintings on the Paris Market in the Early Eighteenth Century', in: Sophie Raux (ed.), *Collectionner dans les Flandres et la France du Nord au XVIIIe siècle*, Lille 2005, pp. 251-288. It seems that, not only were individual Netherlandish paintings often among those highest-valued, but collectively they tended to contribute a larger share to sales revenue than their numerical share in an auction. One rationalization of such resuts that retains the primacy of connoisseurial values is to say that the paintings concerned were typified by those acquired by the French bourgoisie in the late sixteenth and early seventeenth century, when there were readily available in Paris 'commercial paintings, of modest quality, produced in large quantity', many of Flemish origin or derivation. We adopt Alain Mérot's convenient statement of this position, which is not, however, to be read as one he holds. See Alain Mérot, *French Painting in the Seventeenth Century*, New Haven and London 1995, p. 159. Extending this rationalization to cover such Netherlandish paintings as entered known collections much later in the seventeenth century would seem to require that that they occupied inferior spaces, perhaps in terms of their actual size but certainly in terms of their display relative the core pieces in a collection. Studies of inventories and valuations, however, as well as the places such paintings were hung, contradict this. The Comtesse de Verrue (1670-1736), for example, not only owned peasant festivities by Teniers but treasured them so much that they were hung in her private chambers. See also the revealing comment of Antoine Schnapper: 'S'il fallut attendre le milieu du XVIIIe siècle pour que la peinture flamande et hollandaise s'impose dans les cabinets des plus grands amateurs français, elle avait toujours eu sur le marché parisien une place énorme mais discrète, trop méconnue jusqu'a présent. Pour schématiser, on peut dire qu'il y avait chez nous marchés apparement bien distinct mais qu'alimentaient les mêmes hommes, comme le confirme l'étude des principaux marchands français ....' Antoine Schnapper, *Curieux du Grand Siècle. Collections et collectioneurs dans la France du XVIIe siècle*, Paris 1994, p. 91.

7 On this, see Andrew McClellan, *Inventing the Louvre: Art, Politics, and the Origins of the Modern Museum in Eighteenth-Century Paris*, Cambridge 1994. De Piles and Jonathan Richardson may be thought of as popularizers of the juxtapose-and-analyse-properties approach.

8 See Neil De Marchi, 'Auctioning Paintings in Late Seventeenth Century London: Rules, Segmentation and Prices in an Emergent Market', in V.A. Ginsburgh (ed.), *Economics of Art and Culture*, Amsterdam 2004, pp. 97-128.

9 Iain Pears, *The Discovery of Painting: The Growth of Interest in the Arts and England, 1680-1768*, New Haven and London 1988, esp. chapter 3.

10 The point is nicely made by Koenraad Jonckheere in his essay (pp. 69-95) in this volume.

11 Unless, of course, they form a ring or pool.

12 Gersaint has been treated in an excellent article by Andrew McClellan, 'Watteau's dealer: Gersaint and the Marketing of Art in Eighteenth-Century Paris', *Art Bulletin* 78 (1996), pp. 439-453. We have offered a complementary interpretation, drawing heavily on newly uncovered archival information in Guillaume Glorieux, *À l'Enseigne de Gersaint. Edmé-François Gersaint. Marchand d'art sur le pont Notre-Dame* (1694-1750), Seyssel 2002. See De Marchi and Van Miegroet, *Transforming the Paris Art Market* (note 4).

13 See McClellan, *Inventing the Louvre* (note 7) and Colin Bailey, 'The Comte de Vaudreuil: Aristocratic Collecting on the even of the Revolution', *Apollo* 130 (1989), pp. 19-26, and Colin Bailey, *Patriotic Taste: Collecting Modern Art in Pre-Revolutionary Paris*, New Haven and London 2002.

14 We have examined the following catalogues of sales, all held in Paris: 21 March 1763 (name not specified); 15 March 1764 (Madame Galloys, widow of the *Receveur Général des Finances de Champagne*); 2 December 1668 (Chez Hallée); 16 November 1771 (paintings of the stock of LeBrun's deceased father, Pierre); 10 January 1772 (not specified); 22 September 1774 (not specified); 21 November 1774 (Comte du Barry); 12 February 1775 (not specified); 17 June 1776 (Duc de Saint Aignan); 10 January 1778 (not specified); 14 April 1778 (M. Gros); 10 August 1778 (M. Le Moyne); 11 November 1778 (Madame de Jullienne); 10 December 1778 (not specified); 12 January 1780 (Tronchin); 15 March 1780 (M. Poullain, *Receveur Général des Domaines du Roi*); 2 June 1780 (Nogaret); 20 November 1780 (Soufflot, *Architecte ordinaire du Roi,*); 27 November 1780 (Prault, *Imprimeur du Roi*); 11 December 1780 (Véron, *Receveur des Finances*, with feuille de vacation); 14 February 1781 (Abbé le Blanc, *Historiographe des Bâtiments du Roi*); 24 November 1784 (Comte de Vaudreuil).

15 Lebrun, quoted by Bette W. Oliver, *Elisabeth Vigée-LeBrun, Jean-Baptiste Pierre LeBrun, and Marguerite Gérard and their Roles in the French Artistic Legacy, 1775-1825*, Ph.D. Dissertation University of Texas 1997, p. 25.

16 'My stepfather having retired from business, we took up residence at the Lubert mansion, in the Rue de Cléry. M. Lebrun had just bought the house and lived there himself, and as soon as we were settled in it and I began to examine the splendid masterpieces of all schools with which his lodgings were filled. I was enchanted at an opportunity of first-hand acquaintance with these works by great masters. M. Lebrun was so obliging as to lend me, for purposes of copying, some of his handsomest and most valuable paintings. Thus I owed him the best lessons I could conceivably have obtained, when, after a lapse of six months, he asked my hand in marriage …' Louise-Elisabeth Vigée-Lebrun, *Memoirs of Madame Vigée-Lebrun*, translated by Lionel Strachey and with an introduction by John Russel, New York 1989 [1903], p. 20.

17 'My marriage was kept secret for some time. M. Lebrun, who was supposed to marry the daughter of a Dutchman with whom he did great business in pictures, asked me not to make an announcement until he had wound up his affairs …' Vigée-Lebrun, *Memoirs of Madame Vigée-Lebrun* (note 16), p. 21.

18 This is not described in so many words, or as a series of steps in Gersaint's catalogues. Rather, we infer groupings of artists by characteristics from the way he lists artists in his first sale catalogue, of 1733, and from his comparative remarks here and there – especially in his *Table Alphabétique*, in *Catalogue Lorangère* (1744) – on selected artists; these, combined, suggest family clusters of characteristics. This element is developed in De Marchi and Van Miegroet, *Transforming the Paris Art Market* (note 4), esp. pp. 395-399. The set of steps an aspiring 'amateur' should follow is an analytical construct inferred from various remarks Gersaint makes on the importance of pleasurable visual and imaginative stimulation in choosing a painting; discussions of the properties that generate these qualities, especially in 'Flemish' paintings; the availability of desirable paintings at various prices, and his de facto promotion of substitute paintings at various prices; and the ultimate independence of visual pleasure from attribution. Relevant remarks are to be found among his Observations sur les Coquillages in his 1736 *Catalogue Raisonné de Coquilles*; his *Catalogue Lorangère* (1744), introduction dealing with paintings (pp. 1-11) plus the appended *Table Alphabétique*; and the discussion of attribution on pp. 25-29 of the *Catalogue de la Roque* (1745). Our test in advancing this analytical construct is not the usual one of whether a direct reference can be found to support each component of it, but whether it makes the most sense, among alternatives, of Gersaint's scattered commentary on paintings, painters and collecting.

19 We do not know whether the ascending bid mode of selling was common in Paris prior to Gersaint, and mention it here simply to emphasize the informational advantage of the technique.

20 Paul R. Milgrom and Robert J. Weber, 'A Theory of Auctions and Competitive Bidding. II', in: P. Klemperer (ed.), *The Economic Theory of Auctions*, Aldershot 2000, pp. 179-194; Robert J. Weber, 'Multiple-Object Auctions', in: P. Klemperer (ed.), *The Economic Theory of Auctions*, Aldershot 2000, pp. 240-266. Both these papers were written in 1980 but remained unpublished. We thank Ilya Voytov for drawing our attention to these papers. The argument given applies to 'dependent value' auctions, where bidders are assumed to form perceptions of value partly based on what others bid. This seems broadly applicable to art auctions.

21 See Orley Ashenfelter and Kathryn Graddy, 'Art Auctions', in: Victor A. Ginsburgh and David Throsby (eds.), *Handbook of the Economics of Art and Culture*, Amsterdam 2006, pp. 909-945, esp. p. 937.

22 E.F. Gersaint, *Catalogue d'une grande collection de tableaux des meilleurs maistres d'Italie, de Flandre & de France*, Paris 26 March 1749.

23 J.B.P. Lebrun, *Catalogue Raissoné d'une Très-belle collection de tableaux des Ecoles d'Italie, de Flandre et de Hollande qui composoient le Cabinet de M. le Comte de Vaudreuil, Grand-Fauconnier de France*, Paris 24 November 1784, p. 44.

24 *Catalogue des tableaux & dessins précieux des maitres célebres des trois Ecoles, Figures de marbres, de bronze & de terre cuite, Estampes en feuilles & autres objects du Cabinet de feu M. Randon de Boisset, Receveur Géneral des finances par Pierre Remy*, 27 February 1777, pp. 31-32, no. 59.

25 See Robert Broomfield and Maureen O'Hara, 'Market Transparency: Who Wins and Who Loses?', *Review of Financial Studies* 12 (1999), pp. 5-35. This experimental study confirms theoretical expectations about more rapid convergence on true values with disclosure of past prices and volumes (in our case just a single painting for each trade). We have drawn on their suggestions concerning who gains and who loses from transparency and as to the possibility that disclosure might be used as a form of non-price competition.

26 D'Angivillers, Directeur-Général des Batiments du Roi, for one, seems to have preferred Paillet to Lebrun, probably on cost grounds, though this is conjecture on our part.

27 Oliver, *Elisabeth Vigée-LeBrun* (note 15), p. 304, quoting G. Emile-Mâle, 'Jean-Baptiste Pierre Le Brun 1748-1813 – Son rôle dans l'histoire de la restauration des tableaux du Louvre', *Mémoire de la Société de Paris et de l'Ile de France*, 9 (1956), p. 377.

28 Paris, Bibliothèque Doucet, 1293 (U11 422), J.-B.P. LeBrun, *Receuil des gravures au trait, à l'eau-forte et ombrées, d'après une choix de tableaux de toutes les écoles receuillis dans une voyage fait en Espagne, au midi de la France et en Italie dans les Années 1807 and 1808 … par M. LeBrun*, 2 vols., Paris 1809. Gersaint probably did – anyway, intended to – produce one illustrated guide that we know of, to shells, for the connoisseur, though it was not for distribution. See Émile Dacier and Albert Vuaflart, *Jean de Jullienne et les Graveurs de Watteau au XVIIIe siècle*, 3 vols., Paris 1929, vol. 1, p. 108 (for sale of 1736).

29 *Catalogue Raissoné des Tableaux, Dessins, Estampes, Figures de Bronze & de marbre, & morceaux d'Histoire naturelle, qui composoient le Cabinet de feu M. Poullain, Receveur Général des Domaines du Roi; Suivi d'un Abrégé historique de la Vie des Peintres don't les Ouvrages formoient cette Collection par J.B.P.Le Brun. Le Catalogue des Vases, porcelains, Meubles de Boule, & autres effets précieux, est de Ph.F. Julliot fils*, Paris 1780, section entitled *Réflexions sur la Peinture et la Sculpure*.
30 Translation by Bailey, *Patriotic Taste* (note 13), p. 17. of Lebrun's remarks on pp. xiv-xv of his Réflexions.
31 See his Réflexions in *Catalogue Poullain* (note 29), esp. pp. x-xv.
32 The most straightforward visual evidence is that comparing the Mei and Moses Fine Art Index for repeat sales of paintings with the Standard and Poor's 500 Index of stock prices over the last 50 years. See Jianping Mei and Michael Moses, 'Art as an Investment and the Underperformance of Masterpieces', *American Economic Review* 92 (2002), pp. 1656-1668. We take stock prices as a rough proxy for financial wealth.
33 The English portraitist and critic Jonathan Richardson may be taken as a representative of this tradition. See Jonathan Richardson, *Two discourses. The connoisseur. A discourse on the dignity, certainty, pleasure and advantage, of the science of a connoisseur*, London 1719. Insisting rather on viewing pleasure, as Gersaint did, offered a common conceptual metric for bringing the two together; Lebrun elaborated on this, in word and practice.
34 On the Amsterdam market, see J. Michael Montias, 'Notes on Economic Development and the Market for Paintings in Amsterdam', in: S. Cavaciocchi (ed.), *Economia e Arte. Secc. XIII-XVIII, Atti della Trentatreesima Settimana di Studi, Istituto Internazionale di Storia Economica 'F. Datini' Prato, 2001*, Florence 2002, pp. 115-130; and, on the London market, Mireille Galinou (ed.), *City Merchants and the Arts, 1670-1720*, Wetherby 2004.
35 We are grateful to Isabelle Decobecq for help in identifying the financiers and dealers, most of whom, nonetheless, have yet to be studied seriously.
36 Koenraad Jonckheere, *The Auction of King William's Paintings (1713). Elite international Art Trade at the End of the Dutch Golden Age*, Oculi: Studies in the Arts of the Low Countries. 11, Amsterdam 2008.
37 Colin B. Bailey, 'Conventions of the Eighteenth-Century Cabinet de tableaux: Blondel d'Azincourt's La première idée de la curiosité', *The Art Bulletin* 69 (1987), p. 434.
38 At the end of each day of these multi-day sales seems to have been reserved for the presentation of a variety of lower-end items: vases, ivory carvings, ancient bottles, musical instruments, items of furniture, lunettes, and so on. See the transcription (Appendix 1) of the Poullain sale of 1780.
39 Bailey, *The Comte de Vaudreuil* (note 13), pp. 19-69, and Bailey, *Patriotic Taste* (note 13), pp. 163-205. Asking prominent dealer-auctioneers to act in this capacity was not uncommon. Gesaint was consulted by Augustin Blondel de Gagny (1695-1776), financier and Intendant des *Menus-Plaisirs*: Bailey, *Conventions* (note 37), p. 434. Boileau realized the collection of the Prince de Conti, while Rémy shaped that of the wealthy banker Nicolas Beaujon in the 1780s: ibid, p. 436. Rémy also sold this collection in 1787 (25 April-4 May). Holbein's *Ambassadors* was lot 15bis at the sale, and was bought by LeBrun.
40 On Paillet's extravagant bidding at the du Barry sale on 17 February 1777, which was widely reported in the Parisian press, see Bailey, *Patriotic Taste* (note 13), p. 115.
41 Bailey, *Patriotic Taste* (note 13), p. 27.
42 Such indexes would greatly assist proper study of the effectiveness of strategies such as those employed by Lebrun.
43 Oliver, *Elisabeth Vigée-LeBrun* (note 15), p. 111.
44 Ibid. (note 15), p. 112.
45 Carol S. Eliel, *1798: French Art during the Revolution*, p. 49; also quoted in Oliver, *Elisabeth Vigée-LeBrun* (note 15), p. 112.
46 Paillet took over the *Société des Amis des Arts* (Oliver, *Elisabeth Vigée-LeBrun* (note 15), p. 111).
47 Francis Haskell, *Rediscoveries in Art*, London 1976, p. 20, also quoted in Oliver, *Elisabeth Vigée-*LeBrun (note 15), p. 302.
48 Ibid.
49 Lebrun was not the only Parisian dealer to travel north to buy paintings. Paillet, for instance, did much of his buying for d'Angivillers in Flanders. Paillet went to public sales in Ghent, Brussels and Antwerp, especially before the dissolution of religious houses in 1777. Between 1783 and 1788 he went at least four times to Holland, twice to London and once to Flanders (Oliver, *Elisabeth Vigée-LeBrun* (note 15), p. 194). Even Paillet's scale of travel, however, pales alongside that of Lebrun.
50 John North, *The Ambassadors' Secret: Holbein and the World of the Renaissance*, London and New York 2002, p. 5.
51 Haskell, *Rediscoveries* (note 47), p. 18.
52 See Alden Gordon, 'The sale of the Marquis de Marigny: valuations and prices', mimeo, Trinity College Hartford Connecticut (forthcoming).

Cover and p. 138, 192:
Grafische Sammlung Albertina, Vienna.

p. 35 and colorsection p. 177:
The Royal Collection, © 2008 Her Majesty Queen Elizabeth II. London.

p. 35 and colorsection p. 178:
Royal Cabinet of Paintings Mauritshuis The Hague.

p. 45 and colorsection p. 180:
Koninklijke Verzamelingen, Paleis Huis ten Bosch, Den Haag.
Fotograaf: Margareta Svensson.

p. 35, p. 47, p. 134 and colorsection p. 178, 179, 181 and 191:
© Rijksmuseum Amsterdam.

p. 48, colorsection p. 183:
Ruisdael: Widener Collection, Hobbema: Andrew W. Mellon Collection,
both images courtesy of the Board of Trustees, National Gallery of Art, Washington

p. 48 and colorsection p. 182:
© Museo Thyssen-Bornemisza. Madrid.

p. 54 and colorsection p. 184:
with permission of The Worshipful Company of Barbers, London.

p. 128 and colorsection p. 188:
Photo ©The Walters Art Museum, Baltimore.

p.128: Staatsgalerie Stuttgart.

Plates

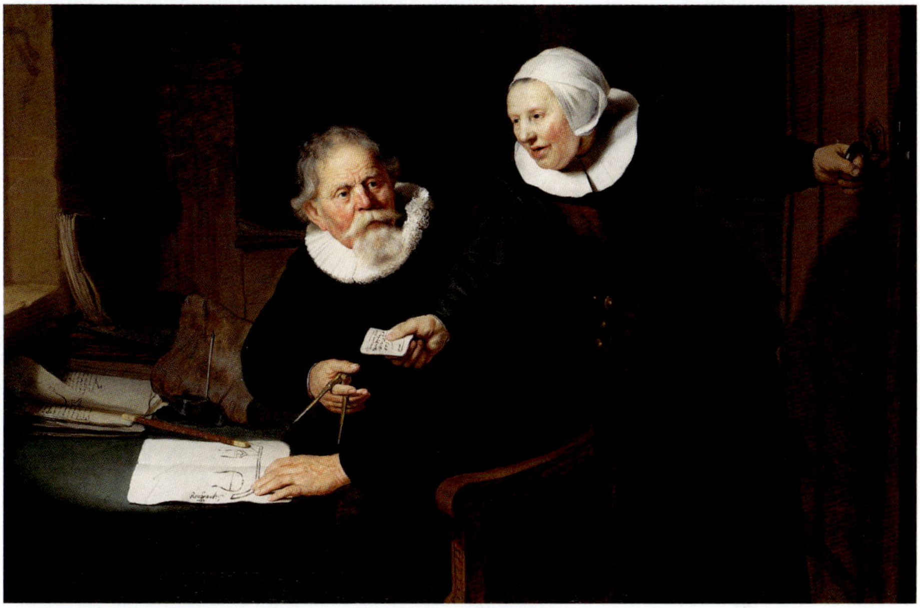

Rembrandt
The Shipbuilder and his Wife, 1633
The Royal Collection, Her Majesty Queen Elisabeth II, London

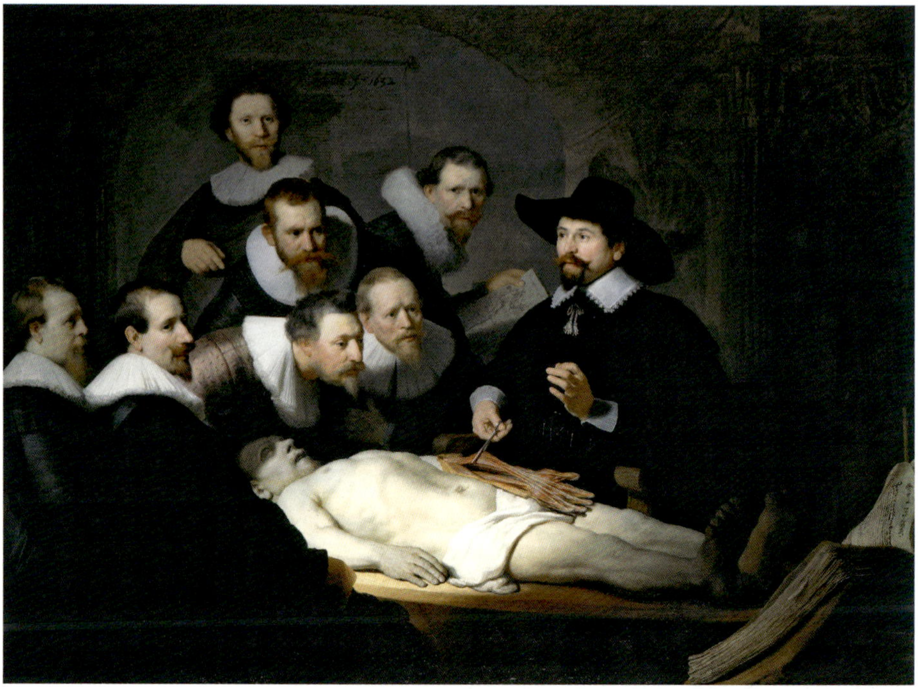

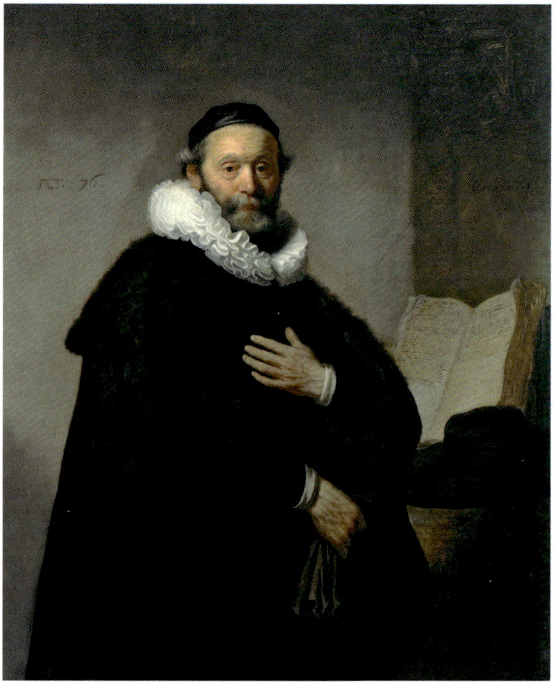

Rembrandt
The Anatomy Lesson of Doctor Tulp, 1633
Royal Cabinet of Paintings
The Mauritshuis, The Hague

Rembrandt
Portrait of the Preacher Johannes Uyttenbogaert, 1633
Rijksmuseum, Amsterdam

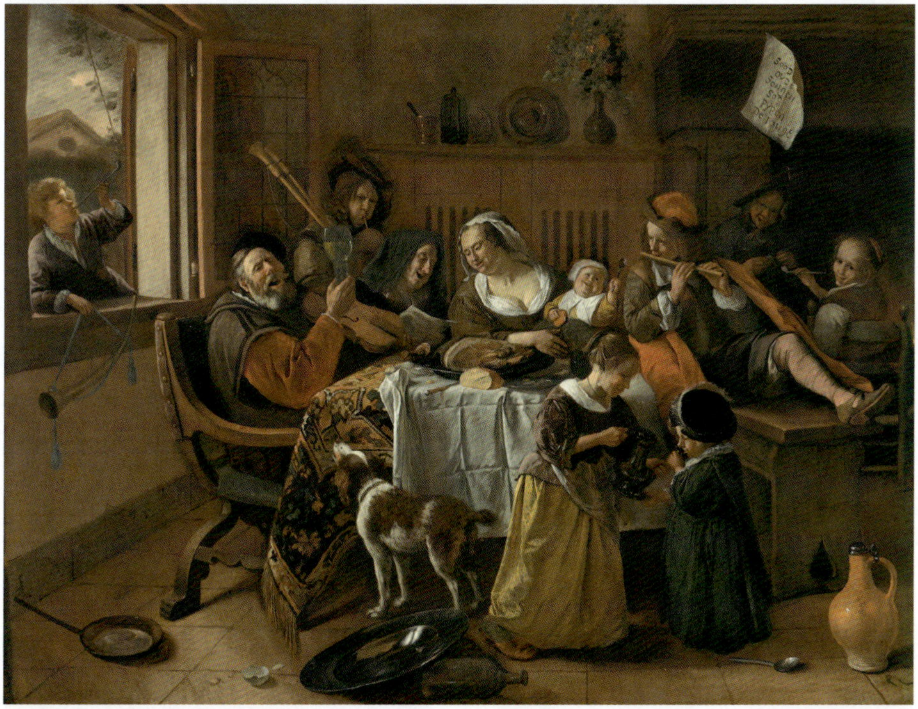

Jan Steen
Merry Family, 1668
Rijksmuseum, Amsterdam

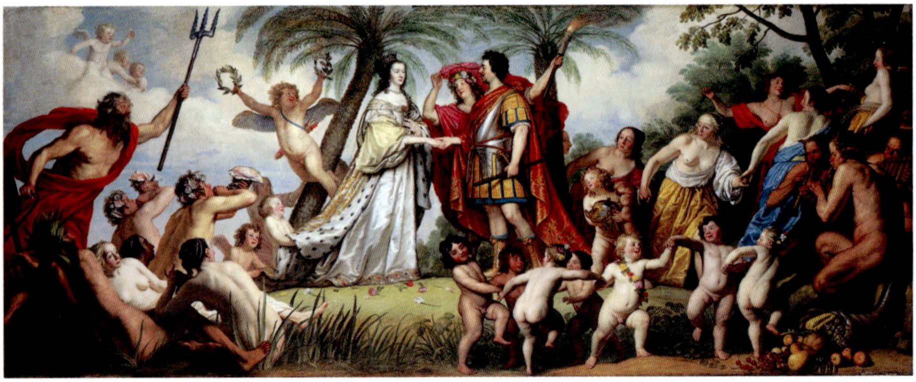

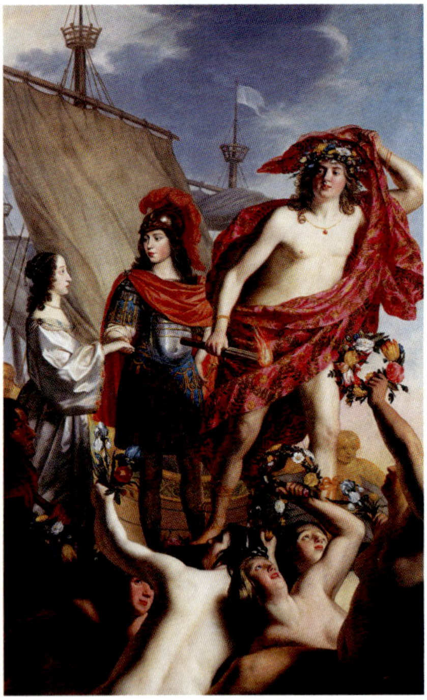

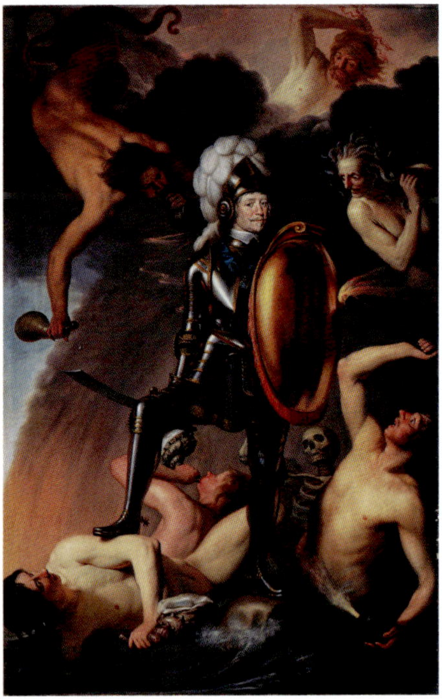

Gerrit van Honthorst
Allegory on the Marriage of Frederik Hendrik and Amalia van Solms,1651
Oranjezaal, Huis ten Bosch

Gerrit van Honthorst
Wiliam II's Reception of Mary Stuart upon her Arrival in the Netherlands, 1649
Oranjezaal, Huis ten Bosch

Gerrit van Honthorst
The Constancy of Frederik Hendrik, after 1649
Oranjezaal, Huis ten Bosch

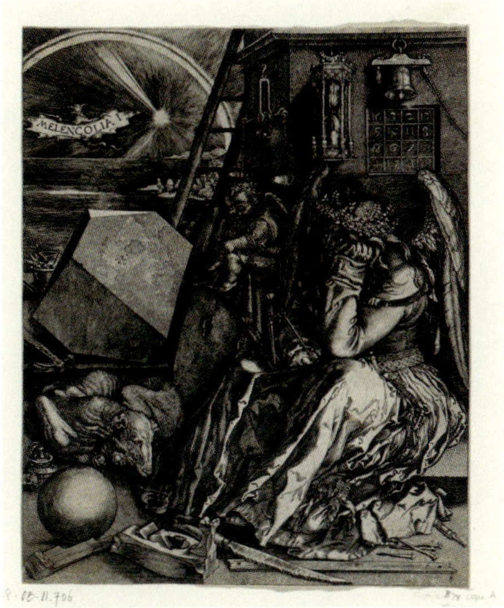

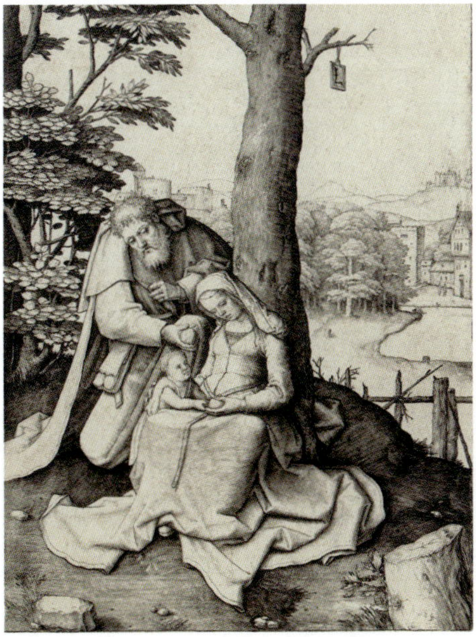

Albrecht Dürer
Melancholia, 1514
Rijksmuseum, Amsterdam

Lucas van Leyden
The Holy Family, c. 1506-1510
Rijksmuseum, Amsterdam

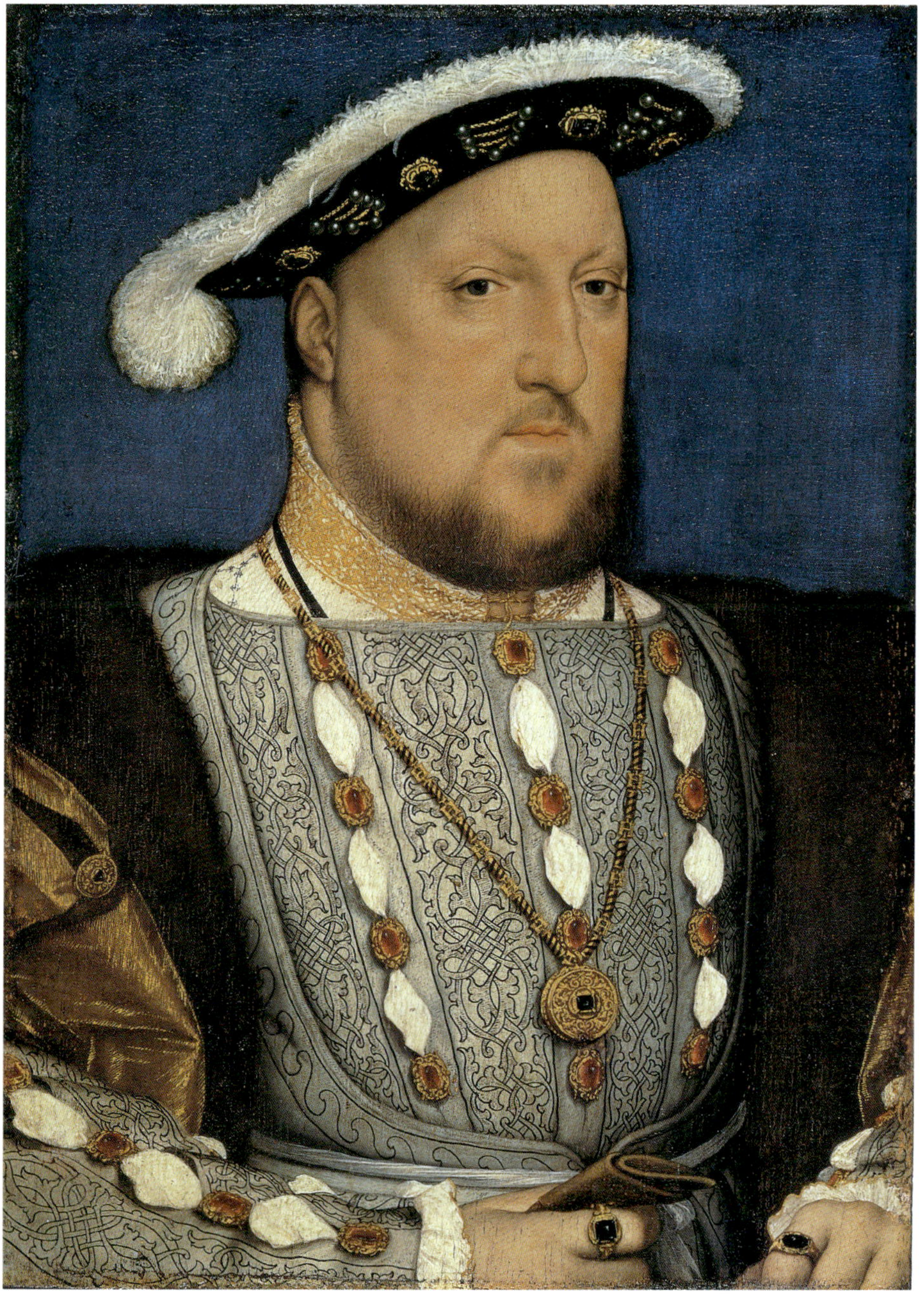

Hans Holbein
Henry VIII, c. 1536
Thyssen-Bornemisza Collection, Madrid

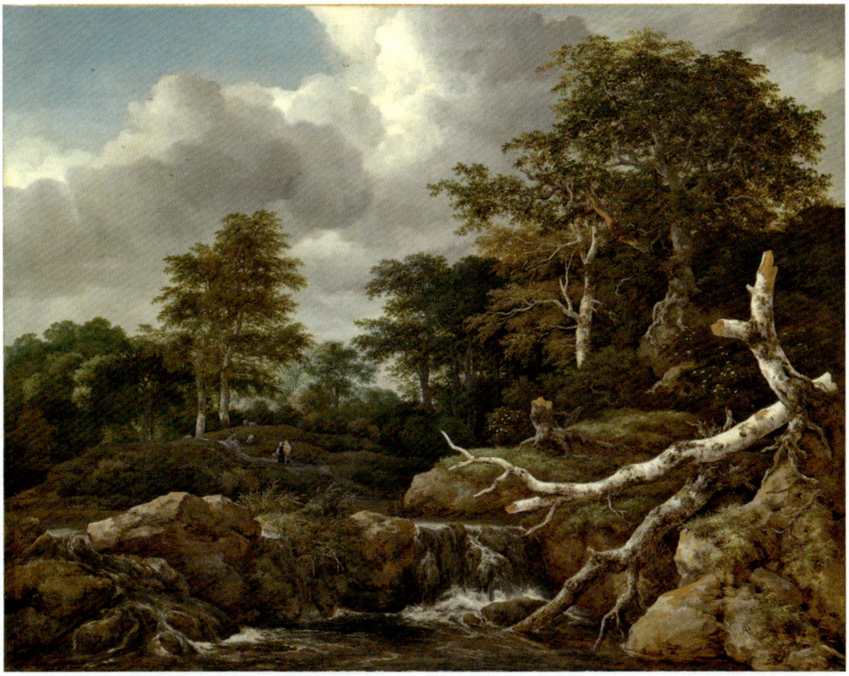

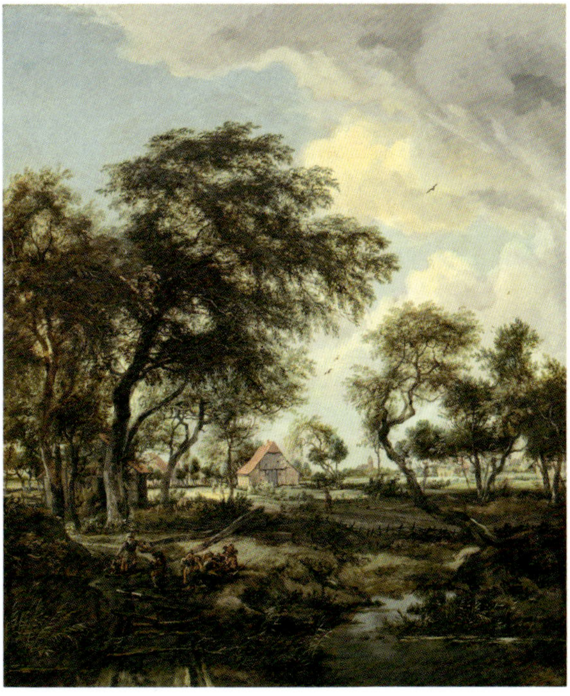

Jacob van Ruisdael
Forest Scene, c. 1655
Widener Collection,
National Gallery of Art,
Washington, D.C.

Meindert Hobbema
Farm in the Sunlight, c. 1668
Andrew W. Mellon Collection,
National Gallery of Art,
Washington, D.C.

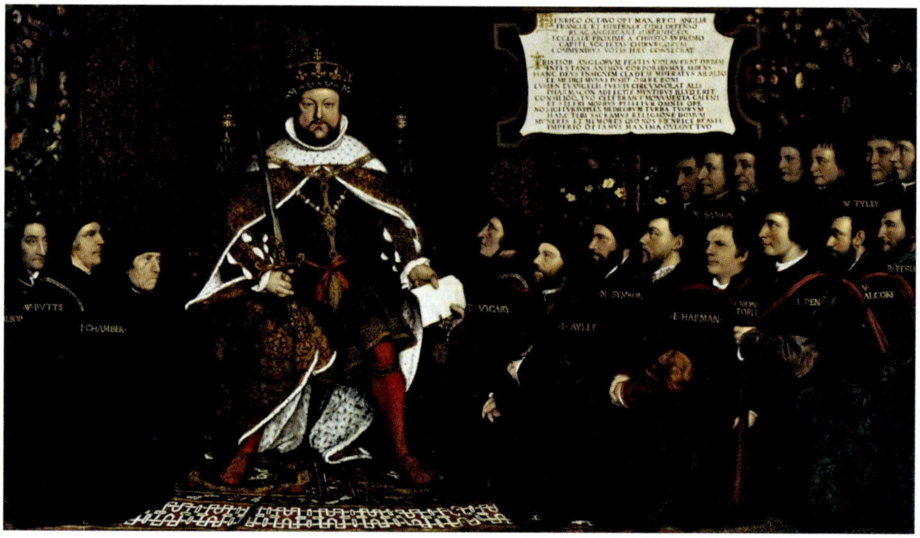

Hans Holbein
Henry VIII and the Barber Surgeons, begun 1541-43
Hall of the Barber-Surgeons Guild, London

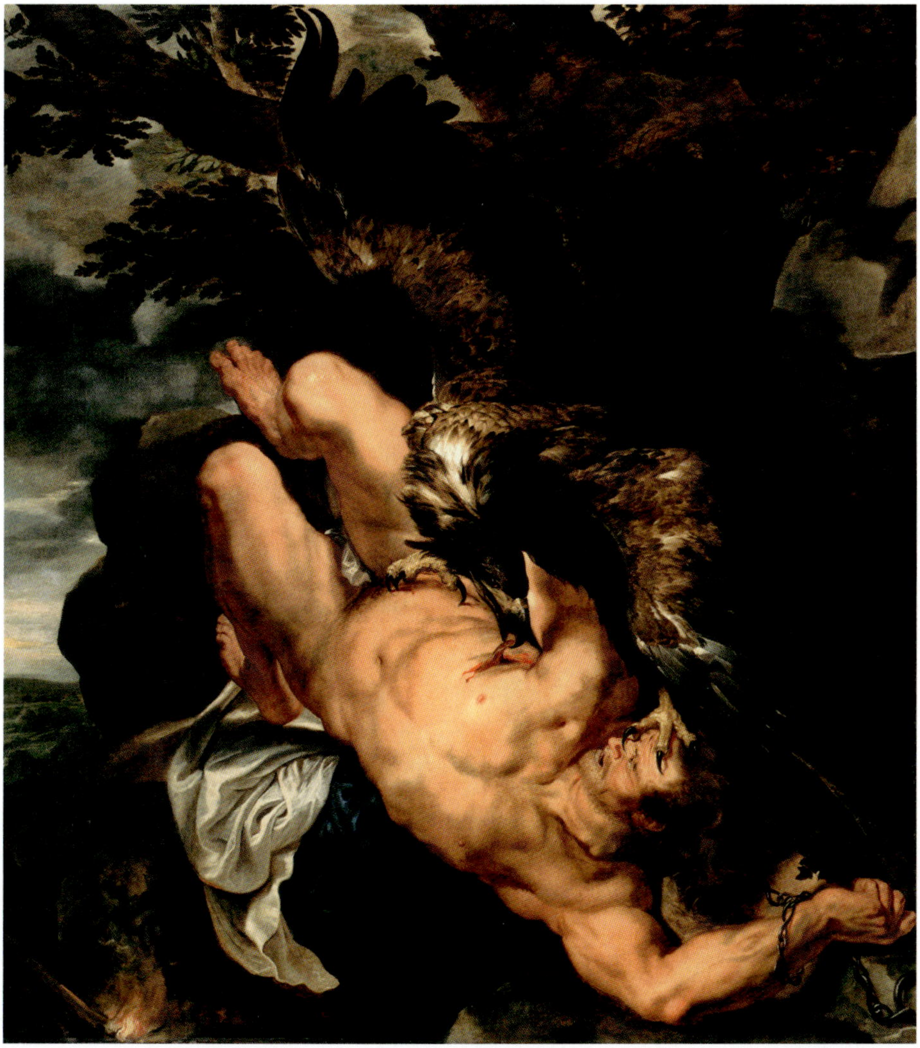

Peter Paul Rubens and Frans Snyders
Prometheus, c. 1611-1612
Philadelphia Museum of Art, Philadelphia

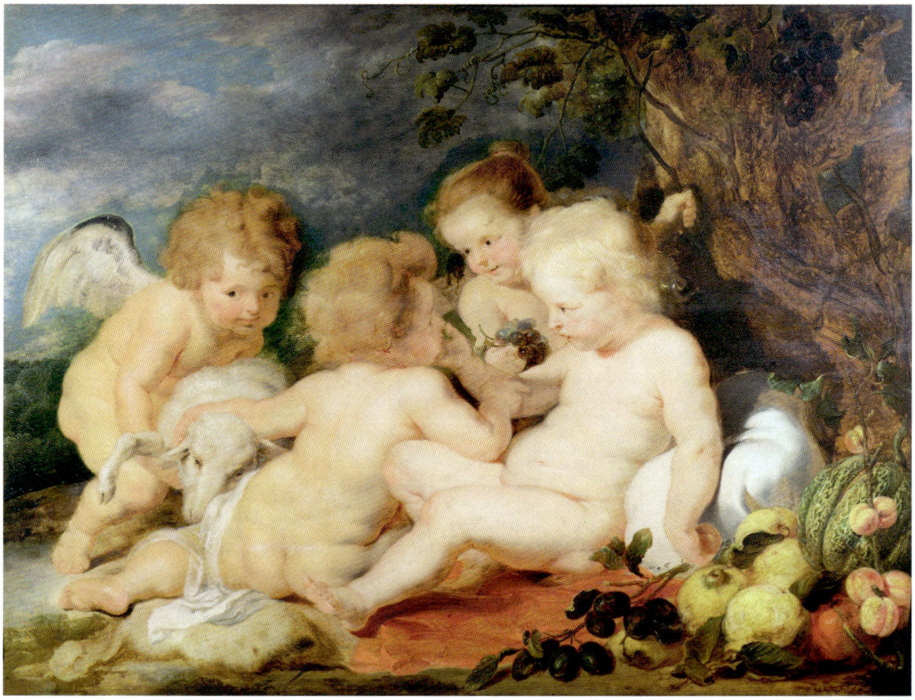

Peter Paul Rubens
Christ, John and two angels, c. 1615-1620
Wilton House, Salisbury

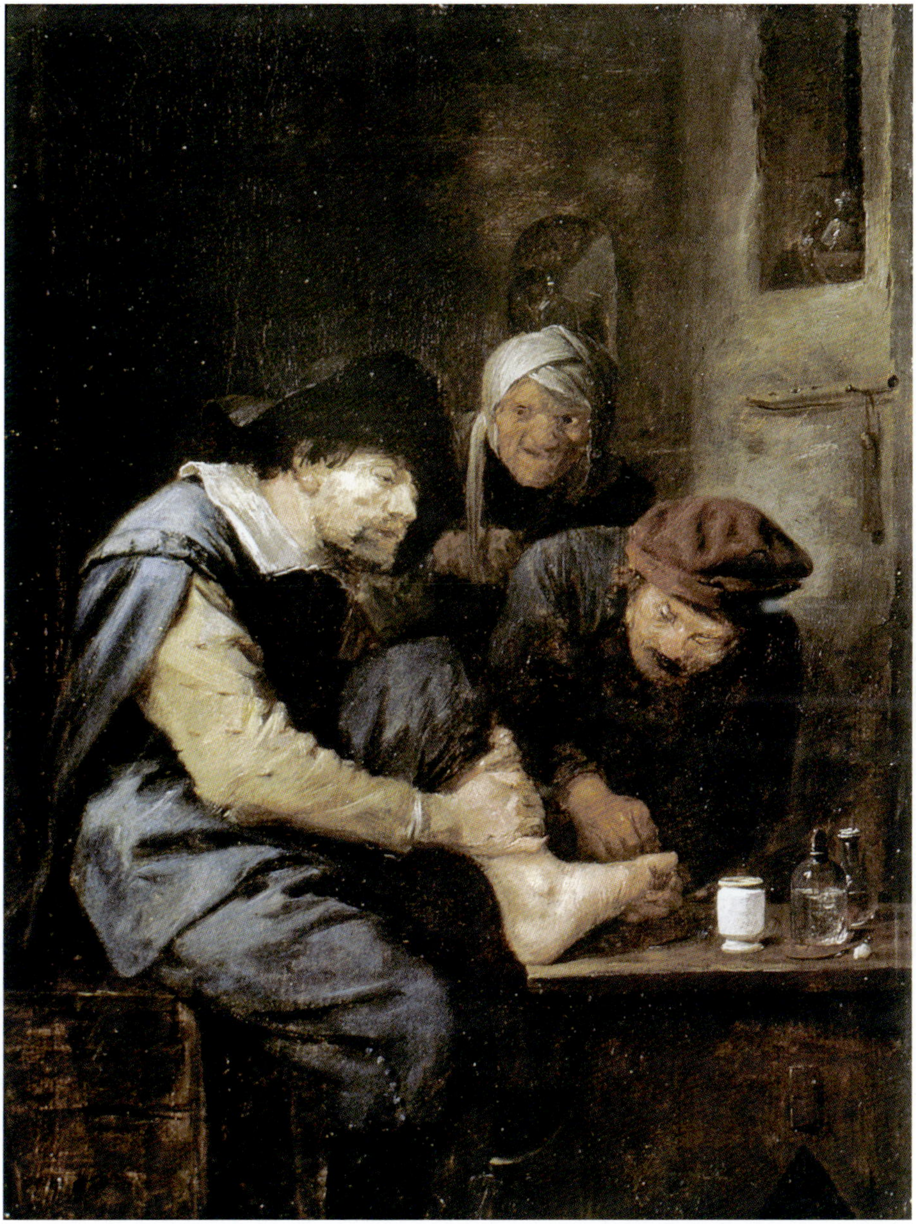

Adriaen Brouwer
The surgeon, c. 1630
Städel-Museum, Frankfurt

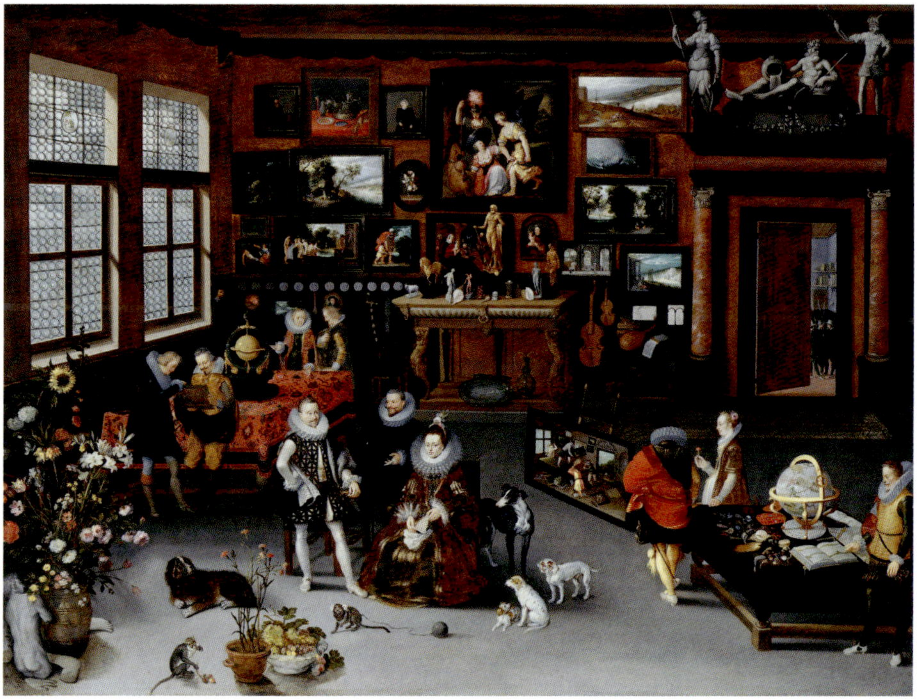

Jan Brueghel the Elder and Hieronymus Franken II
The Archduke Albert and the Archduchess Isabella in a Collector's Cabinet, , c. 1621-1623
Walters Art Gallery, Baltimore

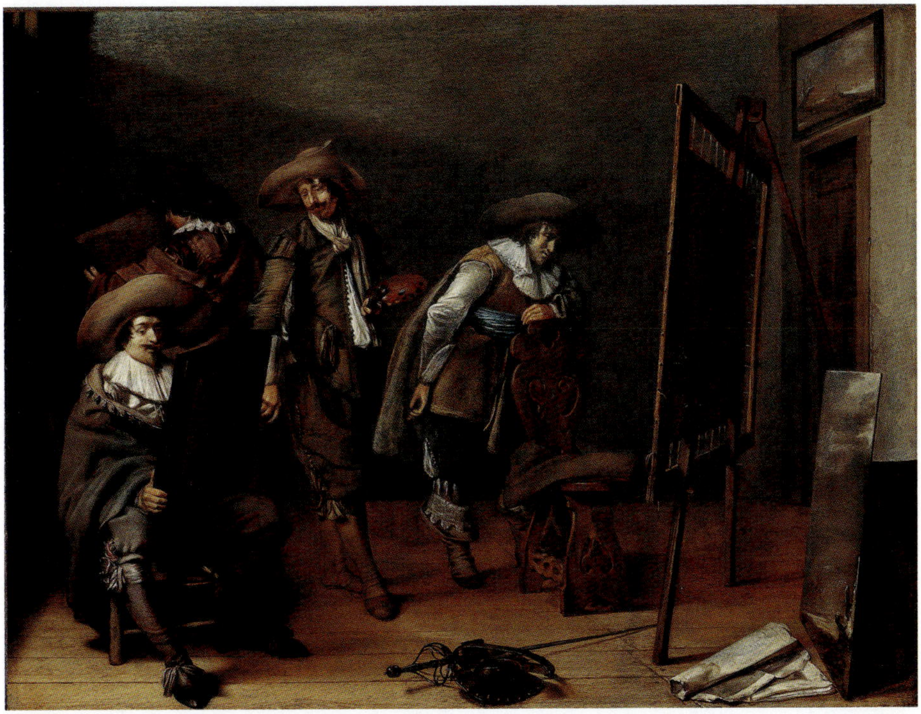

Pieter Codde
Art Lovers in a Painter's Studio, c. 1630
Staatsgalerie, Stuttgart

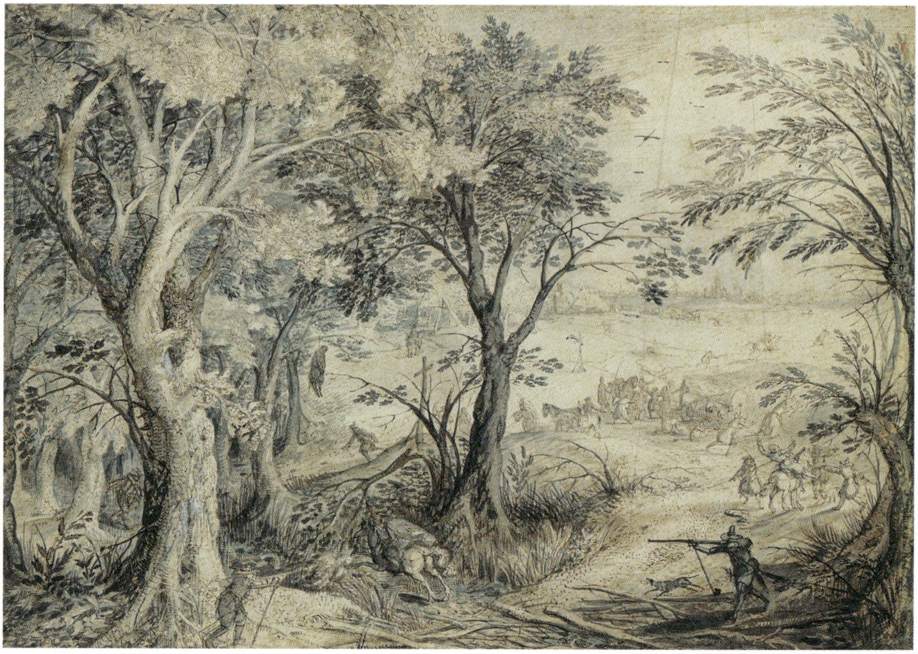

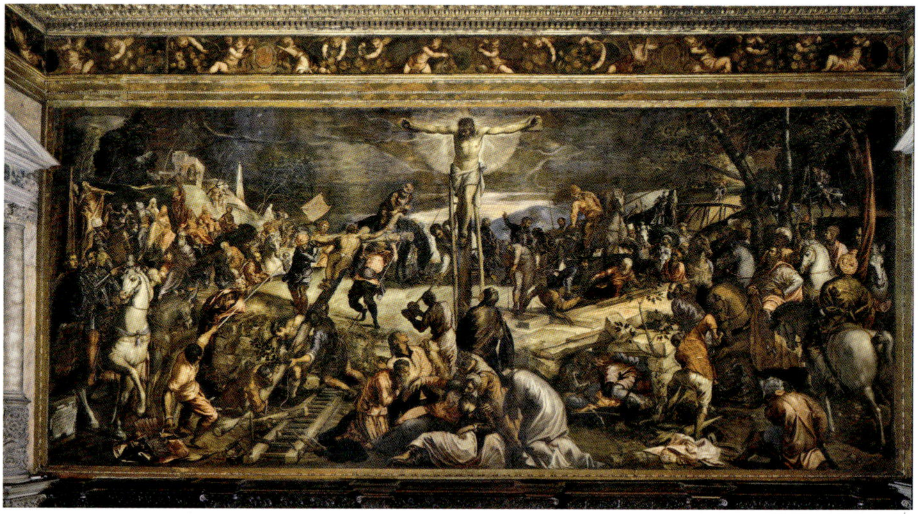

David Vinckboons
Forest Scene with Robbery, c. 1612
Private Collection

Tintoretto
Crucifixion, 1565
Scuola Grande di San Rocco, Venice

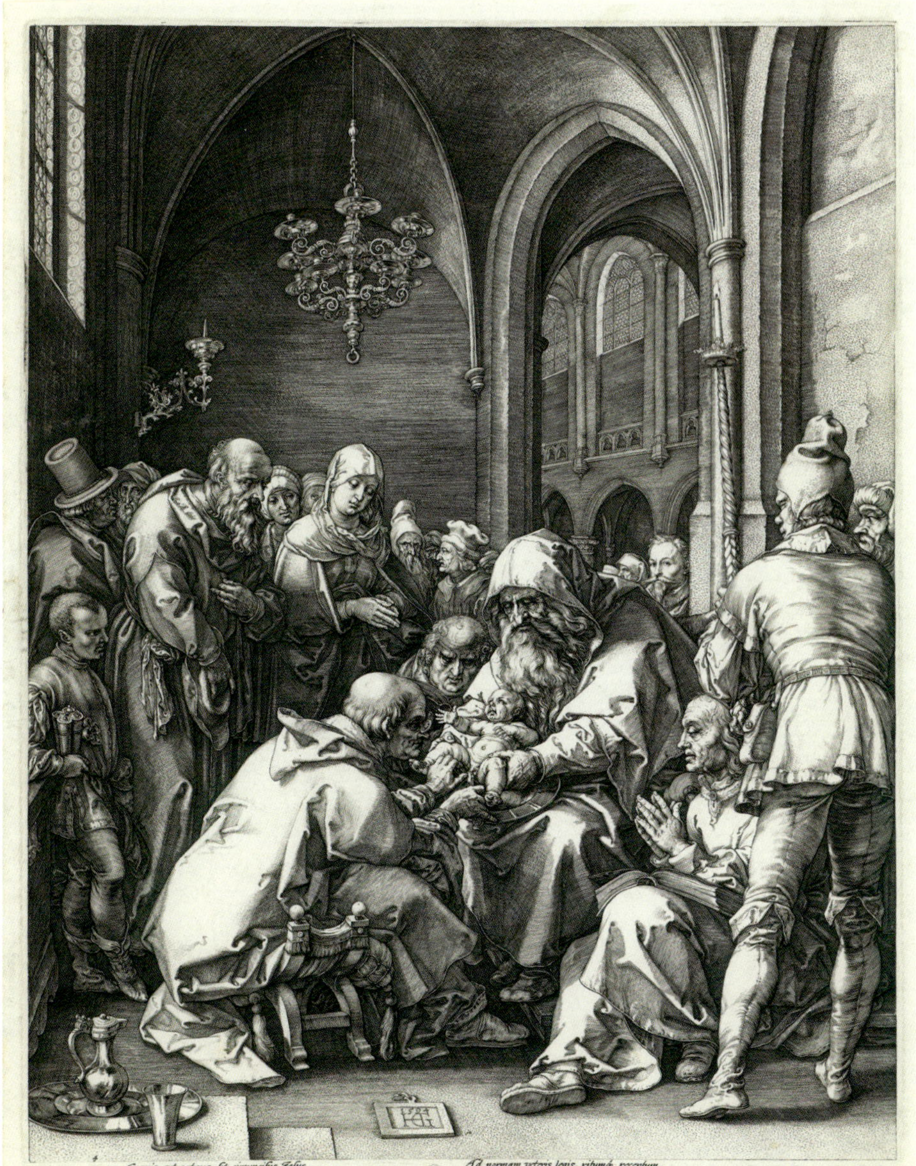

Hendrick Goltzius (in the style of Albrecht Dürer)
The Circumcision, 1594
Rijksmuseum, Amsterdam

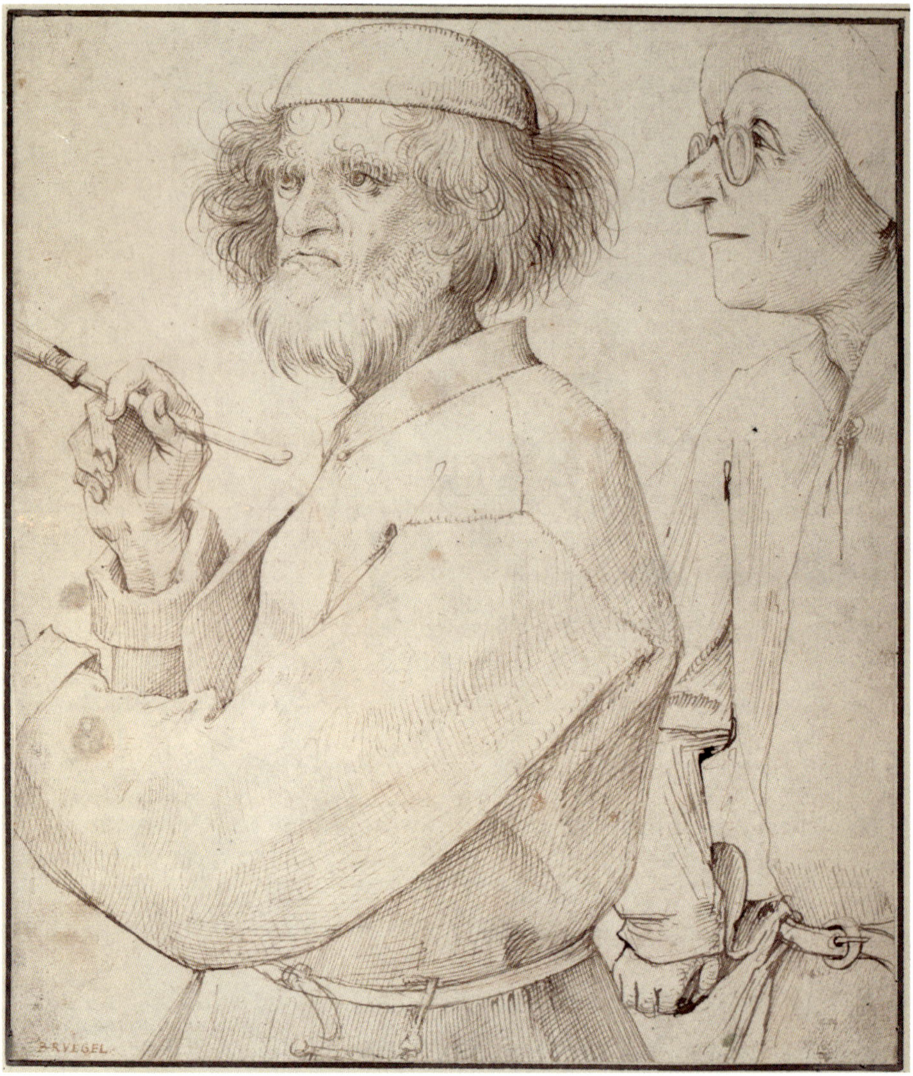

Pieter Brueghel the Elder
The Painter and the Connoisseur, mid-1560s
Grafische Sammlung Albertina, Vienna